The Way of Words

*To question all things—never to turn away
from any difficulty; to accept no doctrine
either from ourselves or from other people
without a rigid scrutiny by negative criticism;
letting no fallacy, or incoherence, or
confusion of thought, step by unperceived;
above all, to insist upon having the meaning of
a word clearly understood before using it, and
the meaning of a proposition before assenting
to it;—these are the lessons we learn from
ancient dialecticians.*

JOHN STUART MILL

The
Way
of
Words

An Informal Logic

RONALD MUNSON
University of Missouri—St. Louis

HOUGHTON MIFFLIN COMPANY · BOSTON
Atlanta   Dallas   Geneva, Ill.
Hopewell, N.J.   Palo Alto   London

To my parents and to Lance and Carol

Printed in the U.S.A.

Library of Congress Catalog Card Number: 75-31028

ISBN: 0-395-20625-1

Contents

Preface

WHILE I was working on part of this book, one of my colleagues asked me what I was doing. I told him I was writing about informal logic. "There's no such thing," he informed me. It's disappointing to be told you're writing about the null class under a misleading description, but I kept on anyway.

In the opinion of some hard-eyed logicians like my colleague, informal logic is to logic as military music is to music. Namely, any resemblance is purely coincidental, and if you can't play the real thing you should stop beating the drum.

I obviously don't share that view, and I hope and trust that most others don't either. I don't want to preach a sermon on moral rearmament or enter a plea for relevance, but I would like to say a couple of things that verge on both.

First, it seems to me that our society can only profit from raising the standard of rational discourse. I'm not convinced that "reason alone" can solve all our problems, that social injustices can be wiped out merely by learning to argue better. To believe this would be as crazy as believing with Moliére's dancing master that all the troubles between nations arise because diplomats don't know where to put their feet.

Yet rational discussion, rational persuasion, is an ingredient in the life of our society. It plays a role in making decisions, determining policies, and passing laws. Furthermore, it plays a role in our private lives as well as in our institutions. The development of a greater awareness of what constitutes a persuasive argument, of what counts as a relevant consideration, of how words can deceive and arguments mislead—this is something important to us all. And it's something important enough to be worth working for.

The accomplishments of formal logic are many and impressive, and we won't completely ignore them in this book. Yet even the most ardent advocate must admit that formal logic has not yet developed tools that can be adequately and easily applied in everyday situations. The world is a briar patch, and the machetes of formal logic simply can't hack through it.

Nearly every logician since the Great Aristotle (capital letters) has been willing to admit that there is a need to supplement the formal approach to argument with a looser one, one suitable to understanding the processes of convincing and communicating as they take place in the free-for-all of ordinary life.

In any event, these are some of the considerations that, it seems to me, favor taking informal logic seriously. If philosophy is going to continue to play its traditional role of encouraging the development of critical thinking, it can't afford to ignore the tools machined over time and stored in the very unimpressive shed of informal logic.

But enough philosophizing. Prefaces are supposed to give practical advice about using a book. So here goes.

If you are reading this book just because you want to, start anyplace you like. Pick a topic that interests you and read about it. The chapters are sufficiently independent that you won't feel wholly lost about what's gone before.

If you're using the book to teach a course, I suggest either of two general approaches. First, start at the beginning and go through the chapters dealing with various aspects of language (2-5), then take up the chapters that deal with matters connected with argument (6-11). The other general approach is to reverse this one and start with the chapters concerned with argument, then go through those on language.

Starting with "Disagreement" in Chapter 6 gets things off to a running start and gets students quickly involved. In this respect, the second approach is superior. The first approach is superior in the respect that it's useful to have a clear understanding of meaning, definition, ambiguity, and so on before dealing with argument. My colleagues and I have used both approaches, and either one will work.

So far as the chapter on writing (10) is concerned, it's possible to leave it out. But I've found that students often think it's the most important chapter in the book. Apparently, most of them have never been told how to structure essays to bring arguments and evidence to bear on some major claim or thesis. Students probably ought to be asked to read Chapter 10, even if it isn't discussed in class.

The chapter on logical puzzles (11) can also be left out. It's fun, but it's not essential by any means. It provides a nice end to a course. Also, it can provide quite an effective beginning. The puzzles represent some very structured cases in which it's easy to see how inferences can be drawn from the information given. This is a pleasant lead-in to a discussion of argument.

Of course, most people will probably avoid all this advice and do what seems best to them in their circumstances. My own opinion is that that's an excellent idea. I've yet to see a preface that dealt with my specific problems.

If I made an alphabetical list of all the people who have helped me with this book, this page would look like part of a telephone directory. My largest intellectual debt is to the advice given over the course of about four years by my colleague John Clifford. In a real sense, he has been a coworker on this project.

John Clifford, Judith Tormey (Temple University), James Roper (Michigan State University), George Berry (Boston University), and John Hodge provided me with detailed and systematic evaluations of the work as a whole. Their criticisms and suggestions not only saved me from several stupid blunders but also were of much help in rewriting and revising.

Clifford, Marlene Fried (Dartmouth College), Tormey, Roper, Stephen Norris, Douglas Soccio, and Richard Friedman used copies of parts of the manuscript in their classes. I'm grateful both for their willingness to take a chance and for their kindly phrased advice. I am grateful, of course, to the several hundred students who had the material tried out on them. (Fortunately, they liked it well enough that I don't have to feel guilty about it.)

My friend Peter Kivy read some of the earlier chapters, and I'm indebted to him for that and for his continued encouragement. I thank David Conway for being daring enough to test out all the puzzles in Chapter 11 before I could guarantee that there were solutions. Richard Lowry hasn't read a word of this book, but I learned so much about rational discussion from him that his name belongs here.

Over the course of years, Miriam Grove Munson read and reread endless drafts and versions. It's due to her intelligence and sense of style that many opaque passages became lucid and many lame explanations were made to walk. It's also due to her willingness to stay home at night that the book was written at all.

Janiece Fister typed a lot of pages, many of them more than once. The job was so boring that I'm grateful to her for doing it at all. But what I most appreciate is the care she showed in not just typing up my mistakes and misspellings. Part of the typing expense was paid for by a grant from the University of Missouri—St. Louis Graduate School.

Gloria McCarthy helped in reading proofs and in making the index. Her sharp eyes were useful, but her sharp intelligence helped even more.

I got a lot of good advice, but I didn't take it all. The people I've named did their best and can't be held to account for the dark sins I insisted on committing.

The English chemist Sir Humphry Davy threw away a book after he had finished reading it—on the principle that nobody has time to read a book twice. I can't really dispute that principle, but before you throw this book away, I would appreciate it if you would take the trouble to send me any comments or criticisms you might have. I've tried to be clear and accurate, but if trying were succeeding, every five-year old would be able to fly. In the next edition, I would like to come a little closer to success.

1/Preview of Coming Attractions

Let's go out to the lobby and get some 7-Up.

THE purple shadows of twilight had changed to the dark shadows of evening as Sheriff Kit Cranshaw reined up in front of the dynamite shack on Hank Faraday's claim.

Cranshaw was just raising his right leg off the saddle when a bullet cut through the darkness and slammed into his chest!

Molten lead poured through his veins, and fingers of fire ripped at the wound. The pain seemed unendurable, but it lasted only for a split second.

The sheriff was no longer conscious when his limp body crashed to the sandy ground.

The advice given to an entire generation of pulp adventure-story writers was this: *Shoot the sheriff on the first page.*

The point to the advice, of course, was to grab the reader's attention, get him hooked on the story, before he had the chance to throw down the book.

I've always thought this advice was excellent, because I always liked writers who got right into the action and didn't spend time providing historical background, describing the scenery, and so on.

It's for this reason that I feel somewhat apologetic and disappointed here on the first page. My inclination is to start right in doing some informal logic and hope that you, the reader, will eventually catch on to what it's all about.

But I also have another (and stronger) inclination to resist this one. There is a mountain of pages stretching up from this point that will have to be climbed step by step. It seems to me, then, particularly important to spend a moment helping the reader get a toehold to hoist himself up to the first ledge. Once he has a start and knows where he's going, a major stumbling block to learning informal logic has been hurdled.

This means not shooting the sheriff on the first page. It means taking the time before the real action starts to do three very important things.

First, we need to set the stage for everything that follows by discussing the nature, aims, and limitations of informal logic. We need to say a few things about what it's concerned with and why we should be concerned with it. (This won't be as dull as it sounds, by the way.) This we'll do in the first section.

Next, in the second section, we'll lay out the game plan that we'll be following for the rest of the book. Here we'll try to indicate the organization of topics that we'll be concerned with and why we'll be following that order. This section will be a program that will allow you to identify the players in the game.

The last section of this chapter introduces a tool that will make it easier to break into the remaining chapters. More prosaically, it introduces a distinction that will make it easier to avoid confusions in future discussions about words, their meanings, uses, and so on.

By the way, Sheriff Cranshaw was not seriously wounded.

What Is This Thing Called Informal Logic?

The story goes that a newspaper reporter assigned to do an article on Chinese metaphysics did his research by going to the dictionary and looking up "Chinese" and "metaphysics." He then sat down and wrote a half-page feature article.

The truth is that not a whole heck of a lot about a complicated subject can be learned from a definition of it. Suppose you knew no arithmetic and someone trying to be helpful told you that arithmetic is "the mathematics of integers under the operations of the four basic functions." Chances are you would be more resentful than grateful.

Definitions have their uses, but they also have their limitations. They are like flashes of lightning that illuminate a landscape with intense brilliance for a brief moment. If the landscape is already familiar to you, you can locate yourself in it. If it isn't, then there is a possibility that you'll become even more confused and disoriented.

In the same way that a whole book on arithmetic might be said to be an explanation of the definition given above, this book might be said to be the working out of a definition of informal logic. That is, it involves discussing and doing informal logic.

Of course, the choice is not between giving a very terse definition and offering a whole book. The third way is to present a definition and provide a brief explanation of it. No one would expect a brief explanation to capture the whole subject. He would only be looking for a few stars to guide by, some simple navigational aids to help him keep his bearings while crossing the stormy seas ahead. This is neither too much to ask nor too much to carry out, and the aim of this first section is to supply a crude sketch map of the constellations, which will be filled out in fuller detail in coming chapters.

Let's be straitlaced and no-nonsense for a moment, and consider the following rough-and-ready definition:

> Informal logic is the attempt to make explicit the principles or standards that are involved in the ordinary everyday activities of establishing and evaluating claims and of using language effectively in the processes of communication and rational persuasion.

If the truth is told, this definition captures the nature of informal logic only to about the same extent that "Love is never having to say you're sorry" captures the nature of love. There's a lot more to it than that, we want to say in each case. Still, our definition is only a temporary bridge to allow us to cross over into our subject, and we shouldn't complain if it's a little rickety. Once it's done its job, it can collapse without any great loss, for we won't need it any longer.

We could take this definition and give it the "Chinese metaphysics" treatment. That is, we could pick out crucial expressions like "establishing and evaluating claims" and "rational persuasion" and subject them to careful scrutiny and extensive explanation.

A more useful approach at this point, however, is to remain at the level of high generality and try, instead, to convey something of the basic character of informal logic.

Perhaps the most important thing to stress is that informal logic is a supremely practical enterprise. It's willing to go out onto the street and into offices, to attend political meetings, and to show up at parties. It's willing to climb down out of the ivied tower, because it's directly concerned with such ordinary human activities as defending positions, attacking unsupported claims, and detecting misleading examples and bad analogies.

The phrase is regarded as rather corny now, but if you wanted a short expression that would sum up what informal logic is basically interested in, here it is: straight thinking. Not "thinking" in the sense of psychological processes, of course, but in the sense of reasoning well. This doesn't mean reasoning perfectly or never making a mistake, but it does mean avoiding fallacies and ambiguities, sidestepping the snares of language, and communicating effectively.

The standards or principles by which we judge what is "straight thinking" aren't ones that we simply sit down and make up in an arbitrary way. They are, rather, ones that we already recognize in practice when we characterize an argument as a bad one or say that an analogy is misleading. The standards are ones that are implicit in (lie within) our ordinary everyday practices. It's the job of informal logic to make explicit what we ordinarily assume or take for granted in our praises or criticisms.

This is a theme that we will return to again and again in discussing particular topics. Informal logic is not some sort of god or lawgiver who imposes on us a set of standards that we have to follow. Rather, the standards are ours, we make them ourselves, and all that informal logic attempts to do is to bring them to light and to state them in a clear and consistent manner.

Another way of explaining something of the basic character of informal logic is to focus on what it can do for people. It aims at expanding, improving, and honing to a finer edge the skills that most of us already possess to some degree.

If somebody tells you that the wheat crop in China is not likely to be very good next year, because the Beagle Boys escaped the cops in the last issue of *Uncle Scrooge,* you don't need a logic textbook to point out to you that this claim is not well supported and shouldn't be accepted on the grounds offered.

Similarly, if you read in the newspaper that surgeons use the word "scalpel" to refer to what we commonly call "butcher knives," you don't have to be told that the writer probably made a mistake of some kind. There is clearly something dead wrong with his definition.

All of us are already rather good at spotting definitions that are obviously haywire, recognizing words that are vague or ambiguous, detecting claims that aren't well supported, and so on. We start learning these skills from the time that we learn to talk and read, and over time and through experience we improve them.

Most of the improvements that come about ordinarily, though, take place in a rather accidental fashion. What informal logic does is to attempt to turn the process of accidental recognition into a systematic and critical discussion of the kinds of activities that we engage in when we judge claims, present and support claims of our own, frame definitions, and so on.

Let's make this point clearer by taking an analogy that points up just the sort of relationship that informal logic has to people and their activities.

Suppose you learned to swim by your own efforts when you were five or six years old. As time passed you grew a little better, and despite the fact that you were self-taught, you noticed that you could swim a lot better than most of your friends. It turned out that you were a natural.

You enroll in college and, like every freshman, you have to take a swimming test. Showing off a little, you streak across the pool, following your own style and using your own strokes.

The swimming coach, who always watches the freshman tests, notices your performance, and afterwards calls you over. "You know," she says, "you show some real talent there. I'd like for you to try out for the freshman team."

You try out, get accepted, and spend the next months being coached in swimming. Now, of course you already know how to swim and manage to do it quite well. But the coaching concentrates on *improving* your swimming. You are taught some new strokes, and you are helped to polish up the ones you already know.

Most importantly, though, you are made a lot more self-conscious and self-critical of your swimming performance. You grow to appreciate how you can do better—how to control your breathing better, how to pace yourself, how to make turns without losing your momentum.

The new techniques that you are taught, the exercises you are forced to go through, and the coaching you receive unquestionably turn you into a better swimmer than you were before. They also turn you into a better *judge* of swimming. You learn to recognize sloppy style, self-defeating techniques, and bad habits. Because you are now more self-conscious about what is involved in swimming well, you can identify some of the marks of poor swimming.

Not everybody knows how to swim, of course, but everybody does know a lot about informal logic already. He knows it in the sense that he is able to engage in all of the processes or procedures that it is concerned with. He does not know it, usually, in the sense that he has become self-critical and can mention rules or standards for judging arguments or definitions, can say exactly why an argument is a fallacy, and so on.

To become self-conscious and self-critical is our aim in the following pages. This means that, in a sense, we won't be talking about anything that is wholly unfamiliar to anyone. What follows is an extended bit of coaching that aims at improving individual performance and judgment.

Informal logic has a long history. To the extent that it can be identified with the process of criticizing arguments and detecting the misleading uses of language, it could be said to be as old as rational discourse itself. But in the way that we are concerned with it, as the attempt to make explicit the standards of rational discourse, it goes back to at least the time of Aristotle in the fourth century B.C.—almost twenty-three centuries ago.

Aristotle wrote down definite rules for judging arguments and for avoiding errors in reasoning. In part he codified an older tradition and in part he performed his own analyses of the standards that underlie persuasion and communication. (He was also careful to devote attention to illegitimate techniques that might trap those who were careless or hasty in thought.)

In the time after Aristotle, innumerable others in the Western tradition devoted themselves to trying to formulate what was, in effect, good advice to follow when you want to avoid reaching conclusions that are not justified and want to communicate clearly and exactly with others.

We are now the inheritors of that tradition. Many of the standards that we will be discussing, many of the warnings that we will be issuing, are as ancient as the stone temples of Greece. They are ones that were refined and restated in times when the great cathedrals were still under construction and, still later, when the industrial revolution changed the character of the world.

It is much too grand to say that they express the "wisdom of the ages." But what they do represent are practical rules and advice that people have found it important to pay heed to, for when the advice is followed it minimizes (but does not eliminate) mistakes and difficulties.

Theme and Plot: What Happens Next and Why

Any book that shoots the sheriff on the first page ought to have both a theme and a plot.

A common theme in Westerns is "Even a good man can be pushed too far," and another is "Even a bad man can turn good." The theme of this book isn't as moralistic as either of these, but it's just as important. We discussed it already in the last section, but now we can state it in a short and succinct way.

The theme is this: Anyone can improve his skills in reasoning and communicating by becoming aware of the distinctions and standards implicit in ordinary practice.

This theme is the golden thread that runs through the labyrinth of topics that make up this book. We'll return to it time and again to make certain that we don't lose the way. Even when we aren't talking about it openly, it's there to supply us with direction and reassurance.

The theme of the book is easy to state in a brief way, but a plot outline takes a little longer. We need to mention the matters we'll be talking about in the coming chapters, but we need to do more than this. As with any good story, our plot should be plausible and it should be unified. It should all hang together. This means that we need an explanation of why we'll be dealing with certain topics and why we'll be taking them up in the order in which they appear.

Anyone who doesn't want the delights of anticipation and suspense spoiled by having the future revealed to him can safely skip the next few pages. However, there is a good reason not to do this. (What one hand gives, the other takes away.) If you were about to sit down to do a jigsaw puzzle, it would be a good idea to take a look at the picture on the box before trying to assemble the pieces. This book isn't as bad as a jigsaw puzzle, but it's still a good idea to get some idea of its plan and organization before setting out to read it. It will help you keep your bearings and avoid getting lost in the fog of words.

Even though the seam is invisible, this book is divided into two parts. The first part is made up of Chapters 2, 3, 4, 5, and the last section of this one. This part is dedicated to the great god Language, which influences so much in our lives. Our prime interest in the chapters that make up the first part will be in understanding the features of language that are relevant to using it clearly and effectively.

Our first major job, in Chapter 2, will be to develop an adequate theory of linguistic meaning. Now this sounds as exciting as an invitation to acquire a terminal case of lung cancer, but what the job involves is merely stating in an exact way what we are committing ourselves to when we say that a word has a meaning. Or to put the point another way, just what sort of thing do we know when we know the meaning of a word?

Most people, when they think about the question at all, will say that the meaning of a word is what the word stands for or is the idea it expresses. We'll show that these popular views will hold no more water than a tea strainer. The view we'll end up with will be that the meaning of an expression is the way it's used in actual situations by people who speak the language (that is, by us).

This topic might seem as remote from our concern with informal logic as Des Moines is from the Sargasso Sea. But it's no news that appearances can be deceiving, and it will quickly become obvious that that's the case here.

Once we've got a firm grasp on the slippery eel of linguistic meaning, we're in fine shape to deal with cases in which what a word means is a source of confusion or puzzlement. This will become obvious in Chapter 3, for there we'll talk about identifying and eliminating vagueness and ambiguity. Our theory of meaning will give us a genuine understanding of what it means to say that an expression is vague or ambiguous. With such an understanding, eliminating vagueness and ambiguity becomes a clear and straightforward matter. We'll also be in a position to understand the difference between a word's connotation and its denotation.

One of the more important ways to avoid trouble with words is to define them. In Chapter 4 we'll face up to the matter of definitions. Since giving a definition involves no more than explaining what a word means, in ordinary life or in some special situation, there's nothing particularly difficult about the topic. (Having a clear understanding of meaning in hand will make it much easier to grasp the whole idea behind giving definitions.) There are particular ways of explaining the meanings of words and certain standards that ought to be met in giving such explanations, and in the chapter we'll run through some of the more important ones.

Chapter 5 is called "Climbing Jacob's Ladder," and it supplies the transition from the first part of the book to the second. The skills and understanding of language acquired in the first part serve as groundwork for the discussion of effective rational persuasion that forms the sum and substance of the second part of the book.

In Chapter 5, we'll identify some of the major uses to which language is put, then we'll zero in on two of them. The uses that we'll be interested in are those in which by saying something we make claims or assertions. It's in these cases that it's proper to ask for reasons or evidence to back up claims, and this process is the very blood and bones of rational persuasion. So it is the use of language to make claims that marks the spot where our focus shifts from concern with language to concern with arguments. Chapters 6-11 reflect this shift of focus, though we'll often have reason to refer to what we've learned about language.

Chapter 6 will plunge us headlong into the pool of disagreement and argument. Since we aren't obliged to agree to the claims that other people make, we often find ourselves in sharp disagreement with them. It's useful, then, to talk about some of the major types of disagreements that set people at each other's throats. We'll particularly stress identifying the sort of matter that is at issue in disputes and the ways in which it makes sense to go about resolving the disputes.

Since one of the major ways of getting people to agree with claims is to present them with arguments (claim + reasons or evidence), we'll also spend some time in Chapter 6 talking about the nature of arguments and how to go about finding out when one has been given. Not everybody carefully labels his formulations "arguments," even when they are, so it's useful to learn how to identify arguments even when they are wearing disguises.

Once faced with an argument, it's only sensible to want to know whether to accept it and be convinced by it. To make this decision, we usually want to question and test the argument to see whether it's adequate and how it stands up to pressure. In the last part of Chapter 6, we'll walk over some of the grounds on which arguments can be challenged and point out a few of the more interesting landmarks.

Like a country boy going to the city and exchanging his overalls for a dinner jacket, when we move from Chapter 6 to Chapter 7 we'll become more sophisticated about arguments. In Chapter 7 we'll make the acquaintance of those stars of rational persuasion, deductive and inductive arguments. After carefully drawing a distinction between them, we'll discuss them individually.

We'll see that if you are willing to accept the premises of a good deductive argument, then you have to accept the conclusion as well. Certainly there is no more decisive way of resolving a dispute than by showing that the claim at issue follows from premises that both parties to the dispute accept.

We'll examine what it means to say that an argument is valid and talk about the relations between the truth of the sentences that make up an argument and the validity of the argument. To the delight of many (and maybe the disgust of a few), we'll also spend a few pages talking about *formal* logic and try to make clear what is involved in deducing or deriving a conclusion from a set of premises by means of a set of rules. This won't give anybody a full grasp of formal logic, but it should do a great deal to take the mystery out of it. (It's like having been to Europe: you might not have learned much, but you're in a better position to judge what others have to say about it.)

In the second part of Chapter 7, we'll see that inductive arguments don't supply the same kind of guarantee for their conclusions that deductive arguments do. It's possible, in their case, to accept the premises and yet not accept the conclusion—and still be rational.

This is not some kind of flaw that inductive arguments have. Rather, it's just in the nature of inductive arguments that this should be so. And it certainly doesn't detract from their importance in ordinary life. The majority of the arguments we offer in order to get others to accept our claims are undoubtedly nondeductive (inductive) arguments.

For this reason, it's particularly important to devote some attention to the kinds of things that ought to be looked for in judging whether an inductive argument should be accepted. There are some traditional "rules" for guiding evaluation. Unfortunately, the rules are no more than helpful hints about the sorts of questions that you ought to ask when faced with an inductive argument. But since the rules offer the only lifeboat in the running sea, they are important enough to be worth our close attention.

Good money can be counterfeited in copies that can fool almost anyone who isn't careful. The same is true of arguments. There are arguments that look quite good and worthy of acceptance at first sight but on a closer examination turn out to be as phony as an eleven-dollar bill. In Chapter 8 we'll spend some time examining various kinds of arguments that crackle like real money but are really counterfeit. These counterfeit arguments we call "fallacies," and our discussion of them is simply a natural outgrowth of our general aim of developing standards and skills that are relevant to evaluating claims and the grounds put forward to support them.

In the last part of Chapter 8, we'll keep on this same road and consider some of the tricks that are often used to escape from objections to a position or to attack a position in an unfair way. These tricks are known in the logic trade as "sophistries," and we'll develop a brief handbook of what they are and how to detect them.

Rational persuasion and rational discussion involve more than giving arguments, of course. They also involve illustrating a point or position to make it clear or easier to understand. Our topic in Chapter 9, then, will be the use of the double-edged weapons of analogies, examples, and other such devices. They are double-edged because there are ways in which they can be used to good advantage, but there are also ways in which they can be used in an unfair or misleading fashion. Like a sharp sword, they can turn in the hand and do damage to friend and foe alike. We'll talk about some of the more significant standards that in ordinary practice we demand such devices satisfy.

We'll cap off the chapter by returning to the topic of argument and talking about the ways in which analogies (which are only comparisons) can be used to support a claim. Knowing how to judge the worth of arguments from analogy is not as important as knowing how to live happily forever after, but it's important enough for us to devote careful attention to it.

Putting words on paper is a task almost as agonizing as inserting splinters under the fingernails. There is no way to make it fun. But since most of us have to do it from time to time, it's worthwhile to spend a little time talking about a few of the strategies and techniques that are involved in writing expository prose. We'll do this in Chapter 10.

Despite appearances, by talking about writing we aren't really departing from our general topic of rational persuasion. Essays or papers can be regarded as long arguments with many subarguments and illustrations as parts. In a sense, it is altogether fitting and proper that we should talk about essay writing at this point, for it is in the essay that practically everything else that we will have discussed throughout the book will come together in a focal point. It is there that a knowledge of language and meaning, of definition, of ambiguity and vagueness, of deductive and inductive arguments, of the avoidance of fallacies, of the use of examples and analogies—of everything in the whole ball game—can be put to use.

What's left for the last chapter, Chapter 11? Well, it's mostly pure fun. It deals with logical puzzles of various kinds. But before someone gets the idea that this isn't a serious book, I want to point out quickly that this is fun with a serious purpose.

The logical puzzles will give you an opportunity to get some practice in making use of apparently irrelevant information to establish a clear and definite conclusion. In that sense, they are good exercises in imagination and thinking. But they are also good exercises in using arguments to reach conclusions that, at first glance, were not apparent.

Because of these features, the puzzles are either a good introduction to the processes that are involved in arguments, or they are a good end to a discussion of arguments. But on top of that, they are simply fun—frustrating fun, but fun nonetheless.

That, you might say, is that. It's the whole shooting match, the whole plot to our story. It's at this time that Sheriff Cranshaw, having suffered through numerous troubles and bearing the wounds from a dozen battles, rides off into the sunset.

"Come to me every day, and I'll make you a better person," the Sophist Protagoras is supposed to have told his students. No such promise can be made here. But at least one very important prediction can be made.

It's this: if you read the following chapters carefully and thoughtfully, if you do the exercises and pay attention to what's going on in them, then you will surely end up a more critical thinker. You will be in the same position as the swimmer who has the advantage of several months of intensive coaching. He swims better and more confidently, he knows new strokes, and he has a better style. Just as importantly, he has become a better judge of the performance of other swimmers.

A Small Kit of Tools: Use and Mention, Scare Quotes

If you were about to step into your special Z-Ray-powered stratocruiser to take your yearly trip around the world, you would probably want to check to see that you had the proper tools with you to make repairs on the way. It's very difficult, after all, to come by Z-Ray engine wrenches on the island of Madagascar.

The journey that begins in the following pages is not such an exotic one, but the need for special tools is equally pressing. Throughout the book we will need to be able to talk about words, and because of this we need some special technique to indicate just when it is that we are doing this—when a word is the subject of the sentence and not just part of the sentence. That's why we'll spend a moment making the use-mention distinction.

Talking about the use-mention distinction will involve us in talking about—of all things—quotation marks. After finishing with the distinction, we will go on to say a few things about the special uses of quotation marks. Since knowing how they are used will help us avoid certain kinds of confusions, this is a game worth at least a small candle.

You may think it strange just to tack this discussion on at the end of Chapter 1. It is a little strange. But the truth is that we need to make use of the information presented here as soon as possible, and it would be a nuisance to interrupt a discussion to give it. So it's better to stick it here as part of the windup before the pitch.

How to Use and How to Mention

Anybody who has ever been in the third grade has probably heard a riddle that goes like this:

> Railroad crossing without any cars,
> How do you spell it without any R's?

Try hard as you will, it soon becomes obvious that there is no way to spell the first two words in the riddle without making use of the eighteenth letter of the alphabet.

The trick, of course, is that those aren't what you are supposed to spell. You're supposed to spell the word "it," and even a third-grader can do that without any R's.

The point to presenting this little puzzle is to emphasize that it's often convenient to have a way to make it certain when we are using a word and when we are talking about the word itself. Sometimes we want to say how many letters a word has, how a word is spelled, what words the senator whispered to the chorus girl, what God said on the first day, and so on. Also, we sometimes want to warn people to be careful of certain words because they can be used in a vague or ambiguous way or can cause confusion and puzzlement.

In short, we want to be able to talk about words in the same easy way that we talk about the millions of other things in this crowded world. We have to be especially careful with words, though. Otherwise, we will, as in the riddle, confuse talking about the word and using the word to talk about something else.

In talking about things in the world we generally use words to refer to them. For example, when we talk about a dog, a small furry animal doesn't pop out of our mouths. Rather, the word referring to such an animal does. We use the word "dog" to talk about, refer to, or *mention* some canine creature.

Now if we want to talk about a word, we obviously can't use the word itself. If we did this, we would be talking about whatever it is the word refers to. This would produce a lot of nonsense. Suppose, for example, we said, "Sin has three letters." We seem to be saying that some sort of religious or moral failing has three letters.

But whatever sin is, it's certainly not the sort of thing that can have three letters. Or any letters at all. What we really want to say, of course, is that the *word* has three letters. How can we make it clear that this is what we mean?

We have to have a name for the word. Once we have names for words, then we can talk about them freely and avoid confusion and nonsense.

The easiest way to form names for words is to make use of a procedure widely followed by logicians, philosophers, and others. According to this convention, *the name of a word is formed by putting quotation marks around the word itself.*

A word in quotation marks is the name of a word that is *mentioned* (i.e., talked about), and the same word without quotation marks is a word we are *using* to talk about something else—a dog, for example.

If we take our sentence above and rewrite it in accordance with this convention, it stops being nonsense:

"Sin" has three letters.

Also we can now see a very neat philosophical point to the riddle. The trick lies, we might say, in leading people to believe that the word "it" is being used when, as a matter of fact, it is only being mentioned.

Words that have quotation marks put around them are generally called "quotation-mark names." They are called "names" because they name or refer to words. They are words too, of course. They are words that are used to talk about other words.

Maybe it's not a bad idea to go over this again in a slightly different way. The distinction between using a word and mentioning a word is not a terribly difficult one to understand, but it's still rather easy to get confused about it.

Let's take another example, then. Suppose you pick up a book on J. R. R. Tolkien and *The Lord of the Rings.* Let's suppose it's Lin Carter's *Understanding Tolkien.*

Carter's book refers to Tolkien many times. That is, the man Tolkien is frequently *mentioned* in the book. Most often and quite naturally, Carter mentions Tolkien by *using* Tolkien's name.

Carter doesn't always mention Tolkien by using his name, though. Sometimes he mentions him by using phrases like "the author of *The Lord of the Rings*" and "the finest fantasy writer of our time."

It's very unlikely that anyone will be at all inclined to confuse Tolkien with his name. Names don't write novels or deliver lectures. Names don't do scholarly studies of *Beowulf* or prepare editions of *Sir Gawain*.

Suppose, though, we now want to talk about Tolkien's *name*, rather than Tolkien the man. To do so would be to *mention* his name, as opposed to using it. In order to do this, it is convenient to have a word to *use* that refers to Tolkien's name and not to the man himself.

Quotation marks will again do the trick, and when we put Tolkien's name between them, then we will have a word we can use to mention his name.

We can now say such things as

"Tolkien" is a rather uncommon name in England.

and

The name "Tolkien" is probably Welsh.

Quotation marks, then, allow us to form the name of a name. The name refers to the man, and the quotation-mark name refers to the man's name. Tolkien's name is *used* to refer to the man Tolkien, and the quotation-mark name is *used* to refer to his name. The man Tolkien is *mentioned* by his name, and his name is *mentioned* by the quotation-mark name.

We now have a way of giving a name to Tolkien's name. But, mind-boggling as it may seem, we don't really have to stop here. If we want to talk about the name we have for Tolkien's name, then we have to have a name for it also. (That's why there is some circumlocution in the last paragraph.) Consider how we can do this by making use of another pair of quotation marks:

The word " "Tolkien" " is the word we shall use to refer to the word "Tolkien," which refers to the man Tolkien.

We could, if we had any earthly reason to do so, go on forming names of names of names . . . until we got to the place at which we could talk about what we wanted to talk about. In each case, we would simply put another set of quotation marks around the word we wanted to mention. If it had six sets of quotation marks around it, to talk about it we would simply add a seventh. We could then use the seven-quotation-mark name to refer to the six-quotation-mark name. (Chances are we wouldn't have anything very interesting to say, though. Six-quotation-mark names aren't terribly exciting.)

This is a good place for a summary of the main points so far. First, the distinction between a word used to mention a thing (including another word) and the thing mentioned is called "the use-mention distinction." Second, when something is being talked about (mentioned), its *name* must be used. Third, when a *word* is being talked about, the *name* of the word must be used. Fourth, the name of a word is formed by putting quotation marks around the word; this is called a "quotation-mark name."

Though we have so far talked only of forming the names of words, it should be clear that the quotation-mark convention can be used to give names to all linguistic items. Should we want to talk about expressions, sentences, phrases, or even letters of the alphabet, we can give them names merely by putting quotation marks around them. If we say, then, that "Batman has a new job" is made up of five words, it's clear that we're talking about the sentence and not the Caped Crusader.

There are plenty of other ways of making it clear when we are using a linguistic item and when we are mentioning it. It would be excruciatingly boring to discuss them all, but since we'll have occasion to make use of three of them, we ought at least to mention them. Words being mentioned

1. can be written after a colon;
2. can be displayed on a line to themselves;
3. can be written in italics.

In the ordinary course of events, we will most often make use of quotation-mark names. But sometimes it will be convenient to list after a colon words being talked about. This keeps us from having to write a whole string of words with quotation marks around each of them and making the sentence look like someone spilled a bag of confetti on it. Also, to avoid a double dose of quotation marks, when a word is mentioned in a sentence that is being quoted, we'll put the word in italics. Finally, when dealing with sentences, it will be most convenient to display the expression being talked about on a line all its own.

The use-mention distinction and the ways of showing that you are making it have been presented here merely as part of the nuts and bolts of logic. That is, we've discussed the distinction as a technical device for avoiding confusion and getting on with the job of saying what we want to say. But there is really more to the distinction than this. It involves and is involved in various philosophical and practical problems and uncertainties.

We can't get into them here but we can at least indicate what some of them are. For example, the use-mention distinction is implicated in what has turned out to be a very serious paradox in modern logic—the Liar Paradox. Also, just how well does the use-mention distinction illuminate our actual practice? When someone says "I christen you Adeodatus," is he using or mentioning "Adeodatus"? What are we to say about words following other words like "called," as in "We called him king"? Is "king" being used or mentioned?

These are all questions that we'll just shrug aside. Nonetheless, it's important to know they're there just as it's important to know the strengths and weaknesses of any tool. We know then that we can use them within limits, but beyond those limits they become unreliable.

Scare Quotes: AAAAGHHHhhhh

You have nothing to fear from me, my sweet.
Just a small puncture in the neck.

A bullet is so small that it is measured in grains, but placed in certain spots in the human body, it can become immensely important. Quotation marks are no more than small marks on paper, but they can play a role in communication greatly disproportionate to their diminutive size.

We have already seen how they can be used to form the names of words and other linguistic expressions. And, most familiarly, they are used as frames for displaying what someone, real or imaginary, said or wrote. Thus Shakespeare has Hamlet say, "The time is out of joint;—O cursed spite, That ever I was born to set it right!" We now know the exact words Hamlet said.

But quotation marks play more roles than these. Though it seems to border on the absurd to be talking about them, knowing what they are typically used to do allows us to sidestep pitfalls and avoid confusions. Anything that holds out a promise as bright as this is worth talking about, no matter how foolish it may make us feel.

1. A frequent use of quotation marks is to call attention to the fact that an author is employing an ordinary word in a technical or restricted way. A writer on economics, for example, might tell us:

> To Ricardo and his followers, "savings" are the money that is reinvested in the business. It is not money held back from investment.

From the fact that "savings" is put in quotation marks, we know that the word is not to be taken to have its ordinary meaning in the context of the discussion. It is to be understood as a special term that is given its meaning by the economic theory that uses it. We know, for example, that money put under the mattress doesn't count as savings, though that's what we would ordinarily consider it to be.

2. Furthermore, quotation marks are used around a word when an author wants us to realize that he is speaking in terms of an analogy. If in a book on brain physiology you read that

> The brain is the best "computer" we have access to.

you would know from the marks that we are not to take what the author says literally. He is not in fact saying that the brain is a computer in the way he might say that the IBM-5000 is a computer. He presumably wants only to stress that, compared with computers in certain respects, the brain comes off well.

3. Another use, similar to the last one, involves relying on quotation marks to indicate that a word is meant only loosely. A writer who tells us that

> The "philosophers" of the Bloomsbury group of writers and critics knew very little about philosophy.

is not really propounding a paradox. He isn't saying, literally, that some philosophers were not philosophers. He is indicating to us that the people in the Bloomsbury group were philosophers only in a very loose or general sense of the word.

4. Sometimes quotation marks are put around a word for ironic effect. The author wants us to realize that, so far as he is concerned, the word doesn't properly apply to the case he is discussing. Someone who writes that

> Today's "patriots" seem to believe that an uncritical acceptance of every government policy is required.

is telling us that people who believe such a fool thing are not really patriots at all.

There are other uses of quotation marks, but these are enough to show that they can be used to do more than indicate direct quotation or provide the names of words. In none of these cases, in fact, is the word in quotation marks being mentioned.

The quotation marks around words used in these and similar ways are called "scare quotes" or "warning quotes." The quotation marks perform the obvious and important service of calling attention to the words they enclose. They alert the reader to the fact that he has to pay strict attention to the words in the quotation marks because something out of the ordinary is being done with them.

We won't have much occasion to make use of scare quotes, but we will have some. How, then, do you tell when quotation marks are being used as a warning of the need for special attention and when they are being used to form the names of expressions? There aren't any rules for knowing something like this. You must simply depend on the context to settle the question. The very presence of quotation marks is enough to put the careful reader on his guard that something unusual is going on. It's up to him to figure out what it is.

Exercises

Well Employed

The bronze plaque on the red-brick Victorian building is lettered in a modern style: LOGIC, INC.

You already feel a touch of pride, a feeling of belonging, and you haven't even been hired yet.

But you're certain you will be. Despite the fact that so many people want to work for Logic, Inc. Despite the competition for a very few jobs.

The competition is understandable. Who wouldn't want to work for a company that let you set your own hours, decide what you want to work on and when you want to do it? Who wouldn't want to work for a company that encouraged you to use your intelligence and never put you to doing some dull routine task?

All you have to do is to do well on the entrance exam.

"This is not an examination," the supervisor explains. "All we want to do is to get some idea of the ways in which you approach certain kinds of situations. We want to see what you regard as a problem and what you have to say about resolving it. In short, we want to get some idea about how your mind works.

"I confess that we also want to get some idea of what kind of training program would be best suited for you, assuming that we both agree that you would be happy at Logic, Inc.

"Simply follow the directions you are given. You may set your own time limit."

Is One Person's Opinion as Good as Another's?

Below are five scenarios. Read them carefully and decide whether or not you agree with the last speaker in each case. Be prepared to explain the reasons for your agreement or disagreement. (Notice, by the way, that the matter of being free to *express* an opinion as a part of the right to free speech is not to be considered an issue.)

Scenario 1   Farber and Smith, neurosurgeons, and Lolton, a janitor, at Franklin General Hospital are standing around an operating table. On the table is a patient who has been prepared for brain surgery.

FARBER: Well, should we perform a lobotomy?

SMITH: I'm not really sure. What do you think, Lolton?

LOLTON: I say go ahead.

FARBER: Why not? One person's opinion is as good as another's.

Scenario 2   Coulton and Roth are standing in front of Claes Olden-burg's sculpture "Giant Soft Icebag" at the Museum of Modern Art.

COULTON: That is really a marvelous work.

ROTH: You're crazy. It's just an ugly piece of junk.

COULTON: Who knows? One person's opinion is as good as another's.

Scenario 3   Skyler and Tippinetti are seated comfortably in their neighborhood bar discussing the state of the nation.

SKYLER: Most of the people who are on welfare are Blacks.

TIPPINETTI: Wrong! Most people on welfare are white.

SKYLER: I still say I'm right, but I won't argue with you. One person's opinion is as good as another's.

Scenario 4   In a small cabin high in the Himalayas, Williams and Vann are discussing mountain climbing.

WILLIAMS: Rappelling is quite dangerous when the ice is rotten.

VANN: Nonsense! It's as safe as eating custard.

WILLIAMS: Well, I suppose one peson's opinion is as good as another's on the topic.

Scenario 5   Friedman and Lewis have been invited to a Gay Liberation meeting to present their opposing views.

FRIEDMAN: The laws against homosexual practices prohibit the free exercise of sexuality and are morally wrong.

LEWIS: On the contrary, the laws help protect people from themselves and are the very expression of right conduct.

FRIEDMAN: Oh well, perhaps you're right. One person's opinion is as good as another's.

Scenario 6   Golonza and Musette are on their way to a party, and each is carrying a bottle of wine he has just bought.

GOLONZA: I always buy muscatel because of its rich sweet taste.

MUSETTE: I go for the fortified wines because they're sweet but not so heavy.

GOLONZA: Well, I guess one person's opinion is as good as another's so far as wine goes.

The Quotation-Mark Magnet

It wasn't that Mario Foyle's inventions didn't work. In fact, they always worked very well. It was just that Mario was often very careless about what he did with them. After all, if you unleash new inventions on the unsuspecting world, you have to be careful to see to it that they don't do more harm than good.

That was the way it was with the quotation-mark magnet. Mario really stumbled on the device by accident. He was working on an invention that would allow the user to remove unnecessary commas from books and other printed materials. That's not what he got. He got a contraption that would remove all *quotation marks*.

And as bad luck would have it, after he finished work on the night of the invention, he carelessly tossed the magnet on a pile of papers on his desk. The papers were typescripts of articles that Mario had written and was about to send to the printer.

The next day, to his dismay, he discovered that all the quotation marks were missing. He wouldn't be able to send off the articles until they were restored. But he was too busy to spend the time on the job himself.

Instead, he decided to have it done. But he took the first step himself. He made copies of all sentences that might have to have one or more sets of quotation marks restored in order to make the use-mention distinction.

That's where you come in.

Mario calls up Logic, Inc., and asks for an expert in quotation marks to be sent over to his house.

You're a little uncertain about being called an "expert," but you're the closest thing to it the organization has around so you're the one who gets the job.

"Now," Mario says, "I know that some of these sentences are going to be ambiguous without quotation marks. So what I want you to do is to supply the quotation marks where you can, and in cases in which it is possible to interpret the sentence in two ways, give me both interpretations. A few sentences probably won't need any quotation marks at all."

These instructions seem clear enough. Mario gives you a box filled with the quotation marks that the magnet snatched off his papers, and you start to work.

1. Whenever I say now, it is always then.

2. Western civilization begins in the fertile crescent.

3. Western civilization begins with a W.

4. Bertrand Russell died on February 2, 1970, is a sentence that we accept as true.

5. Anyone who can spell well can certainly spell Wellington.

6. Awkward is awkward to write, but sex is pleasurable.

7. The phrase use-mention distinction is often used to refer to the difference between using a word to talk about something and talking about the word itself.

8. Christianity begins with Christ, according to Christians and many others.

9. Darwin's birthday picks out the same day as the expression Lincoln's birthday, namely February 12.

10. The cow was scrawled at the bottom of the page.

11. The Joker danced in lights across the top of the building.

12. The very sounds of San Francisco are music to my ears.

13. To use to refer to to refer to to refer to is little more than an academic exercise apparently designed to use up quotation marks.

14. Flashing across the midnight sky, bright enough for all to see, was The Eagle.

15. Boring is not particularly boring, but short is rather short, even though long is not particularly long. The question is, is English English? We know that Dutch is not Dutch, nor is French French or German German.

16. The people called her by the words laona l'loc, which means the woman without pity. But to me she was always just plain Mona.

17. Big Bear was right behind Little Bear, at least it was until I rearranged the cards.

18. Six men sitting in a car
    If they can't spell it, they won't go far.

19. Aldebaran is the name of the word Aldebaran.

20. New York is full of people, and Boston full of lies.
    Houston is full of money, and Cincinnati is full of I's.

21. Darwin's birthday is February 12.

22. The Museum of Alien Antiquity lay in fragments on the green lawn, the heavy granite smashed to rubble.

23. The Last Man on Earth was cast in bronze and placed atop the tallest of the green-glass buildings.

24. I saw a saw and you saw a see,
    I saw it, and you saw me.

What Are They Trying to Tell Us?

Mario is so impressed with the high quality of your work that he asks you to stay on awhile and help him with a special project.

"I want you to do something for me," Mario says. "For pay, of course. I want you to go over this small collection of pieces that I've gathered up and explain to me just why it is that the writers use the quotation marks that they do."

"You mean," you say, "that you want me to tell you what they are trying to tell us by using quotation marks?"

"Yeah, that's it. What are they trying to tell us? Just tell me that."

1. The body is a "machine," and like all machines it has to have fuel to keep it running. After three or four hours, food in the stomach has been digested, and the body then begins to feel the need of taking in more fuel. That's one of the reasons that a good breakfast is so important. Without it, the body must try to keep operating on its reserve supply, and this does not supply such direct and immediate energy.

   HERSHEL LONGER

2. Was [Christian Gauss] a "power" in American education? I do not believe that he was. That kind of role is possible only for a theorist like John Dewey or an administrator like Charles W. Eliot.

   EDMUND WILSON,
   A Literary Chronicle

3. At no stage are we able to prove that what we now "know" is true, and it is always possible that it will turn out to be false.

   BRYAN MAGEE,
   Karl Popper

4. In order to understand the definition of poetry as language that says more and says it more intensely than other forms of language, we must first of all understand just what it is that poetry "says."

   Based on LAURENCE PERRINE,
   Sound and Sense

5. One day after the drug bill was passed, a House Subcommittee approved a proposal that would permit Washington judges to jail "dangerous" criminal suspects for up to sixty days before trial.

   TOM WICKER

6. Qualified people were at a great premium during World War Two. When the secret Manhattan Project started, it needed a considerable number of technical people and it needed them fast. About the only way that the head of the Project could get the personnel he needed was to "shanghai" them from their current jobs.

   LAURI CORVEZI

7. The "liberal" press in this country is often against any program sponsored by the government that seeks to provide any help at all to any group that is not a "minority" or "disadvantaged" one.

8. There is considerable reason to regard the moon landing as "the last great triumph of mankind." It seems clear now that our industrial capacities have been strained beyond the breaking point and that, coupled with continuing increases in the world's population, is very likely to spell the end to any future technological accomplishments that are in any way comparable.

9. The "good student" is all too often the student who discovers early just what is required of him and shows a remarkable adeptness in adjusting himself to the mold manufactured by others. The "bad student" is just as often the student who refuses to allow himself to be forced into the established pattern.

10. This is fast becoming as bad a world for a dog as it is for people. He receives the blame for attacking people, even though it's his frightened owner who has sent him through a course to train him to attack. His very breed is deteriorating, because unscrupulous breeders out to make a fast buck run "puppy mills" that churn out puppies of the breed that is currently in favor. That this kind of breeding generally results in "overbreeding" and produces dogs in which deafness, blindness, and numerous physical defects occur with increasing frequency doesn't seem to bother the fast-buck folks at all.

2/Words and Their Ways: What Meaning Is

Words are wise men's counters—they do
but reckon by them. But they are the
money of fools.

THOMAS HOBBES

IN 1832 Charles Darwin and the crew of the sailing ship *Beagle* paid a visit to the inhospitable island of Tierra del Fuego. The inhabitants of the island were definitely "savages," to use the term popular in the nineteenth century. They wore animal skins thrown over their shoulders, painted their faces, grew no crops, and slept in the open. "I could not have believed how wide was the difference between savage and civilized man," Darwin remarked in amazement. Compared with England and the European countries, Tierra del Fuego was in almost every respect a barbarous and primitive land.

Though Darwin did not recognize it, the Fuegians were in one way as sophisticated and advanced as any people he could have met—they had a language. To Darwin's ear it was just so many "hoarse, guttural, and clicking sounds," and he made no attempt to learn it. Had he, he would soon have found out that it involved an extensive vocabulary and an elaborate grammar. He might have discovered what linguists and anthropologists have since learned: *there are no primitive languages.*

One of the more intriguing puzzles about language lies in the curious fact that all natural human languages ever studied seem to be exceedingly complex. However primitive or undeveloped in technology or social organization, no group of people has anything but an elaborate and highly developed language. What's more, though languages do change over time, no one has ever been able to show that any language changes from simple to complex, from primitive to sophisticated. Languages of the past, unlike modes of transportation and ways of executing criminals, are as complicated and developed as the ones of today.

Whether human languages evolved from the simpler communication behavior of animals is another puzzle which hasn't been solved. It used to be assumed as a matter of course that this is what happened, but today no one is quite sure whether this is correct. A beaver slapping the water with his tail and a man complaining about his salad at Howard Johnson's don't seem that much alike. Many scholars think that language is different in a basic way from animal communication, and an adequate biological explanation of the origin of language still doesn't exist.

The Greeks sometimes spoke of language as a gift of the gods, as if it had been handed over to man ready-made and highly developed. This way of talking solves no puzzles about the origin and development of language, but it does provide an image which captures the way things appear to us now.

Imagine that a visitor from another planet has come to earth to investigate whether or not we are eligible for membership in the Galactic Federation of Peace. While making inquiries, he is attacked by muggers, and you arrive just in time to keep him from being knifed. Before returning home with his negative recommendation, he rewards you for your help by giving you a set of instruments that will do marvelous things. One, which looks like a pocket flashlight, will disintegrate matter. When its beam is directed toward an object, it will reduce the object to a whitish powder. Another is a silvery band, which, when placed around the head, will give the wearer total recall of everything he has ever read. The final gift is a small packet, about the size of a transistor radio, that keeps a person carrying it at a comfortable temperature no matter what he is wearing or what the weather is like.

These devices are easy to use, and what they do is clear enough for the most part. But *how* they perform their functions is unknown. In engineering terms, each is a black box, and the sort of things you would want to know has to do with the content of the boxes. What kinds of mechanisms, circuitry, and the like are inside the devices? What are the principles in accordance with which they operate? Such questions as these don't imply that you don't see the results of the instruments' operations or that you don't know how to use them to produce those results. The questions start here and push past the surface of the obvious. Clearly, a better understanding of the instruments would allow you to produce more like them or to apply the same principles to make somewhat different ones. Moreover, you might be able to improve on the ways you have been using the devices. Finally, you would probably get some pleasure from satisfying your curiosity and learning how the devices perform their functions.

Language—whether English, German, Spanish, Fuegian, or any other—is as marvelous a device as any of the three instruments we've mentioned. And, to use the image of the Greeks, it also has simply been handed to each of us. We all acquired it, in a process not now fully understood, and yet none of us invented it. We know how to use it to do a vast variety of things, yet none of us completely understands the principles that underlie what we do so often and so well. In short, we have at our command a powerful and subtle instrument, which by practice and experience we employ with an easy skill. But in many ways it too is a black box. Seldom in ordinary life do we turn our attention toward the instrument that makes it possible to convince, argue, tell jokes, give directions, warn, greet, and perform the rest of the myriad tasks in the ways we typically do.

In this chapter we will begin looking inside the black box of language. Our looking will be done from a particular point of view, though, and the range of our interest will be correspondingly narrow.

Our prime concern is with informal logic, and it is the microscope that will limit our field of focus. It restricts our consideration to just those matters that have to do with clear and effective communication and with rational persuasion and deliberation.

Language is *used* in formulating and evaluating arguments, explaining the meanings of words, presenting analogies, and giving and criticizing illustrations and examples. Furthermore, it is also a *source* of ambiguity, vagueness, and various sorts of confusions and uncertainties. We need an understanding of certain features of language to understand better some of the uses to which it is put and some of the ways in which it can be misleading or puzzling.

We can skip questions about the origin of language, the way in which children acquire language, the development of and historical changes in particular languages, and the laws that have been offered to describe the character and structure of language. These matters fall outside our scope and are the concerns of such disciplines as biology, psychology, philology, and scientific linguistics. What is there about language that we will take an interest in?

This chapter will be given over to providing a correct answer to just one question: What is the meaning of a word?

It may seem as strange to devote an entire chapter to a single question as to devote a whole day to toothbrushing. As you will see, though, the question has a number of aspects, and we will be talking about a variety of matters under one heading. Furthermore, it's important to see why the answer we'll come up with is a *good* answer and some of its more seductive alternatives are not good answers.

The time we spend here will be a good investment that will pay handsome dividends later on. In the following chapter we'll be discussing ambiguity, vagueness, connotation, and chameleon words, and in the chapter after that we'll be talking about definitions. An adequate theory of meaning will make it possible to get a genuine understanding of these topics—one far deeper and more sophisticated than can be gotten without an account of meaning. This means that we won't have to be satisfied with the sort of half-right, half-wrong, secondhand opinion on these matters that often gets palmed off as knowledge.

And now to the question before the house.

What Is the Meaning of a Word?

If jesting Pilate had asked, "What is the meaning of a word?" instead of "What is truth?" chances are he still wouldn't have stayed for an answer. Our question is just about as hard to answer satisfactorily as his, and wise Pilate wouldn't have expected a solution from the crowd. The Cambridge philosopher Ludwig Wittgenstein pointed out that the question is one that gives us a mental cramp when we try to think about it. We feel sure that we know the answer to the question, yet when pressed we don't know exactly what to say. We feel we should be able to point to something and simply say, "Why, this is meaning," but we really don't know what to point to. We are as puzzled about meaning as Pilate was about truth.

The English language consists of about half a million words, and no one person knows them all. Yet each of us knows at least a few thousand of them. Some are plain words, and some are fancy; some are old friends, and others are merely distant acquaintances. We all know a large number of words, and in some sense or other we must know the meanings of these words. Granted that this is so, what is meaning?

Even a fool might hesitate before rushing in to try to answer this question, and an angel wouldn't budge an inch. On the theory that it's better to be on the side of the angels, we too would be wise to pause before answering. Our question is one subject to various interpretations, because the word "meaning" is ambiguous. We aren't concerned with an answer to the question in just *any* way it might be taken, and to make it clear exactly what we are asking it's worthwhile to spend a little time talking about the word "meaning" itself.

Let's start in a relatively painless manner by considering the word "meaning" (and its various related forms) as it appears in the following episode.

It was almost dark when Walker reached the outskirts of the devastated city. The ruined buildings were jagged silhouettes against the sky, and the debris-clogged streets were already hidden in the shadows. She had *meant* (1) to cross through the city in full daylight, when the dangers would be less, but she had spent too much time searching for fresh water. The Scavengers—those who lived by plundering the few remaining stocks of food and water in the city—would be out. With her water bags Walker knew she would make an inviting target.

She hesitated and toyed with the idea of sleeping outside the city and crossing in the morning. But that would *mean* (2) that she would lose her chance to fly to the Arkansas commune with Burton, who had stressed that he would not wait. The commune would be a better place to be than the area around the destroyed and contaminated city, and Walker decided to go on.

She moved fast and stayed alert. Once she heard voices coming from an undamaged grocery store, but no one came out. She passed by as quietly as she could manage to.

The bridge leading out of the city was at last in sight when Walker was stopped. The Scavenger must have heard her coming and waited for her to pass. He had then simply stepped out of a doorway and told Walker to halt. Walker had halted.

"What's the *meaning* (3) of this?" Walker asked, pretending innocence and anger but feeling nothing but fear. "I'm not bothering you, and I'm just trying to leave town."

The Scavenger's voice was surprisingly gentle. "Just don't turn around," he said. "I don't want to risk putting a hole in one of those water bags."

Walker didn't move. "Killing me would be a *meaningless* (4) act," she said. "You can have the water. It's not worth getting killed for."

"I'm glad you feel that way, because that water *means* (5) more to me than your life does. I haven't had a drink since yesterday. There's almost no bottled water left in the city, and everything else is contaminated. Just drop the bags slowly."

Walker hesitated. The Scavenger seemed to have trouble talking. Perhaps that *meant* (6) that he was physically weakened by doing without water. Still, he had a gun—he must have a gun—and trying to fight him was too risky. Walker *meant* (7) every word she had said about the water not being worth her life. She dropped the water bags.

"Thanks," said the Scavenger. "Now, do you see that bridge?"

"You *mean* (8) the one right in front?"

"Yes, that's the one. Without turning around, you just start running for that bridge."

"That *means* (9) you intend to shoot me, doesn't it?"

The Scavenger grunted. "I live a *mean* (10) existence, but I haven't yet got to the point that I enjoy killing people. I have tried to strike a *mean* (11) between wanton murder and an absolute refusal to kill. Besides, I don't want to waste any ammunition. But I will if you don't start running."

Walker ran. She was tired, the muscle in her right leg ached, and breathing was painful. Running across the brdige was no *mean* (12) feat, but she did it. Arkansas would be better, she hoped. At least there would be plenty of water.

The word "meaning" and related words like "mean" and "meant" occur a dozen times in the above passage, and each case differs in a slight or significant degree from every other case. By no means does this exhaust the possibilities, but these twelve cases are enough to illustrate the vagaries of the forms of "meaning." To help make clear the differences among the cases, consider how the sentence involved in each instance might be paraphrased into one roughly equivalent that doesn't employ "meaning" in any form. The following words and phrases can be used as appropriate substitutes in the respective cases:

1. intended
2. have the effect that
3. justification *or* explanation
4. serve no purpose
5. has more value
6. sign *or* indication
7. was sincere about
8. referring to
9. suggests that *or* implies that
10. degraded *or* ignoble
11. an intermediate point
12. simple *or* inconsequential

It's interesting that "meaning" (and its forms) is used in so many different ways—that "meaning" has multiple meanings. But the basic reason for pointing this out isn't merely to wonder at the oddity of the word. Rather, the fundamental purpose is to make it clear that we will not be concerned with "meaning" in any of these senses. Our concern will be with *linguistic meaning*—with the meaning of words, phrases, expressions, and other linguistic forms.

Our interest in meaning isn't at all recondite or obscure, for it's closely tied to the ordinary fact that we started with: that we all know what many words mean. The question we want answered can be put this way: "What is it that we can be said to know when we know the meaning of a word?" Or this way: "When we tell someone the meaning of a word, what is it that we are telling that person?" Or, as we started out, "What is the meaning of a word?" These questions may not be equivalent ones, but they are quite closely related. If we can get ourselves in the position to answer one of them, we ought to be able to answer the others.

Let's grant that we already know in some sense or other what linguistic meaning is, because we do know the meanings of a number of words. What we want is an *analysis* of what we know, of what it is we're claiming when we say something like "I know what *adamantine* means." Attempts to provide an adequate and consistent analysis of this sort—and to answer the questions we raised above—are traditionally called *theories of meaning.*

We'll now take a fairly careful look at the strengths and weaknesses of three standard theories of meaning. All of them are attempts to make sense out of what it is that we mean when we talk about knowing or not knowing the meaning of a word, about explaining the meaning of a word to someone, and so on. They are *theories,* not in the sense that they are airy speculations, but in the sense that they are attempts to formulate systematic principles adequate for an understanding of linguistic meaning.

The standards that we have for judging such theories are drawn from our own knowledge and experience. We, after all, are masters of our own language. Consequently, no theory of meaning can be acceptable or correct if it misrepresents or distorts what we know to be so about language. No theory of meaning can be allowed to get by if it alters or ignores basic facts about the words we know.

The three theories we are going to examine exist in many versions, and some versions are more subtle and detailed than others. We shall be considering only the general tenets of each theory, so no one should believe that a theory can't perhaps be patched up to meet our objections. Still, we will be examining fundamentals, and if a theory seems weak there, this is a good reason to doubt whether it's worth trying to patch up. Two of the theories we'll criticize and give reasons for rejecting. The third theory we'll examine in greater detail and try to show how it can solve some of the problems that the other two can't handle. Hopefully, it will emerge as a correct and adequate theory of meaning.

The Hard Truth: Two Theories That Don't Work

We'll start by letting ourselves be lured by the seductive song of the Sirens and consider the two wrong, but very appealing theories of meaning. These theories seem so obvious and so natural that at first it's hard to believe that they can't be right. But, in each case, before we founder on the rocks of intellectual destruction, we'll present some unanswerable objections to the theory and show that it simply will not work as a correct and adequate account of meaning. We'll start with the Reference theory, then turn to the Idea theory.

Meaning as Reference

The second chapter of Genesis tells us that God created all the birds and animals, and when he had done this, he brought them all to Adam "to see what he would call them." Adam was obedient to God's command at the time and supplied them with names. As a result, "Whatsoever Adam called every living creature, that was its name."

The story of Adam's naming of the animals is a pleasant one, and it's possible to see in it an early attempt to come to grips with the problem of how language developed, of how things acquired names. But for our possible to see in it an early attempt to come to grips with the problem of meaning of words.

Adam presumably said something like "I shall call this animal *cow*," "That bird I'll name *robin*," and "I'll call this creature *dog*." His procedure suggests that perhaps words and other meaningful expressions can best be regarded as fundamentally the same as proper names. The name "Chicago" refers to the city of Chicago. "Malcolm X" refers to the man previously called Malcolm Little. "Eiffel Tower" refers to—what else—the Eiffel Tower. The relationship between "Chicago" and the city is simply that the name designates the city, and the same sort of relationship holds in the other cases. If proper names can be said to have a meaning, then their meaning is what they refer to.

Using proper names as a guide, the Reference theory of meaning can be stated this way: *The meaning of a word is that to which the word refers.* When Adam said "I'll call this creature *dog*," he gave the word "dog" a meaning. Its meaning was simply the animal God presented to him for naming.

The Reference theory has the twin advantages of simplicity and clarity. It cuts through the vague and woolly thoughts which fill our heads when we think about meaning and replaces them with a hard-edged idea that is bright as a new penny. We all know quite well what it is to give a name to a city or a sewage plant, to a boat or a baby. We label a thing with a name, and we use the name to designate the thing. We clearly understand naming, so can we solve the puzzle of meaning by saying that meaning is no different from designating?

Even a moment's thought shows that we have to make at least a slight adjustment. We can't treat all words *exactly* like proper names, because proper names are applied to just one thing. Even if we both decided to call our dogs "Phideaux," the dogs have the same name only because we each decided to use it. When you call "Phideaux!" you will be calling your dog, and when I do I'll be calling mine. For each of us, "Phideaux" will refer to only one dog. But the case is quite different for words like "dog," because there isn't just one object designated by them. Words aren't generally like proper names in every respect, then.

Perhaps, though, we can modify our view and say that words are *common* names. Thus "dog" doesn't apply to just one dog but to *any and every dog*—to the class of dogs. The meaning of a word, then, we can say is the class of items that the word refers to. Meaning is still reference, but what is referred to is a class of objects and not just a single object.

Also, what is referred to doesn't have to be an object like a dog or a lump of lead. It might be a trait or characteristic (redness, laziness, brilliance). Or a situation (confusion, democracy). Or a relationship (on top of, is guilty of, is responsible for). The meaning of a word like "lazy" would be the class of actions, or people, or events to which the word applies—all those things designated by the word.

Having made these minor adjustments, the Reference theory looks rather persuasive. It permits us to answer our original question in a clear, no-nonsense fashion: we know the meaning of a word when we know what it refers to. Meaning is reference. Unfortunately, in spite of its polished and shining surface, the Reference theory shatters when hit by a few solid objections.

Objection 1: Some Words Don't Seem to Refer to Anything

Consider the words that are used as glue to stick together words, phrases, and sentences: and, but, yet, so, for, also. And consider words that express conditions: if, unless, nevertheless. And transition words: however, likewise, moreover. Now just exactly what is it that these words refer to? Unlike words like "dog" and "lazy," they don't seem to designate or apply to anything at all. Though they obviously are meaningful—they aren't nonsense—the Reference theory can't account for that fact.

Consider also words like "werewolf," "goblin," and "unicorn," and phrases like "the first man to travel faster than light," "the discoverer of a cure for cancer," and "inhabitant of the moon." These expressions don't refer to anything, because there are no appropriate objects for them to apply to. They, too, clearly have meanings, but according to the Reference theory, they shouldn't have. This, of course, is just a sign that the theory is flawed.

Objection 2: Two Expressions Can Have the Same Reference but Different Meanings

In the early part of the nineteenth century, Sir Walter Scott became quite famous in the British Isles for long narrative poems like *The Lay of the Last Minstrel*. In 1814 Scott decided to test his talents as a novelist, and he published a historical novel called *Waverley*. Because he was unsure of the reception his novel would get and didn't want to risk his reputation as a poet, *Waverley* appeared anonymously. As a matter of fact, the novel was a resounding success, and there was much speculation about its authorship. Scott finally admitted that he was the author and went on to write many more highly popular novels.

This bit of literary history contains a seed of destruction for the Reference theory of meaning. Notice that the two expressions "the author of *The Lay of the Last Minstrel*" and "the author of *Waverley*" both refer to the same man: Sir Walter Scott. According to the Reference theory, the two ought to have the same meaning. Since meaning *is* reference, two expressions which refer to the same thing should be identical in meaning.

Obviously, though, the two expressions don't have the same meaning. If they did, then if you knew the meaning of one you would also know the meaning of the other. The sentence "The author of *Waverley* is the author of *The Lay of the Last Minstrel*" would be like the sentence "My father is my male parent." You could know that both sentences are true just by knowing the meanings of the words involved. Anyone who knew that Scott wrote *The Lay* would also know that Scott wrote *Waverley*—in the same way that someone who has met Gray's father knows he has met Gray's male parent.

But this of course is just what people *didn't* know about Scott. They had no idea whether the sentence "The author of *The Lay* is also the author of *Waverley*" was true or not. It was necessary for them to *discover* that the two expressions both refer to Scott. Knowing that the first did was not enough to guarantee that the second did. If two expressions which refer to the same thing can differ in meaning—and they can—then the Reference theory is sunk.

Anyone who is inclined to hold the Reference theory apparently never took a matching exam. If he had, he might have been forced to recognize that it's quite possible to understand the meaning of two expressions without having the slightest idea whether they refer to the same thing. How many people know that "commissioned to convey General Gordon to the Sudan" and "founder of a British travel agency" both refer to the same man: Thomas Cook. Very few. Yet everyone understands the expressions well enough.

Similarly, no one in Scott's time had any difficulty understanding "the author of *Waverley*." They knew quite well what it meant, but its reference was a mystery to them. But if we admit that it's possible to know the meaning of an expression without knowing its reference, the Reference theory is doomed. If meaning *is* reference, this should not at all be possible. But it is.

In the final analysis, the bright glow of the Reference theory disappears beneath the dust of objections. It seems to promise a clear and simple way of understanding what meaning is. But it promises more than it can deliver. With its collapse we are left where we began, with our question "What is the meaning of a word?" Perhaps the Idea theory can give us a more satisfactory answer than we've got so far.

Meaning as Idea

John Locke was a dour man with a long face, who once went to pay his condolences to the widow of a friend who rented a house from him and ended up by asking her for the rent money. More importantly, though, he was a seventeenth-century English philosopher whose writings have had a vast influence on our culture. Many of Locke's ideas have become so ingrained that they often seem to be no more than common sense. This is certainly the case with what we'll call his Idea theory of meaning. Anyone who hasn't given much thought to meaning and who doesn't hold the Reference theory is almost sure to lean toward the Idea theory when pushed to take a position.

The Idea theory can be put simply in this way: *The meaning of a word is the idea that it produces in us.* Thus, the word "dog" refers to dogs (the members of the class), but its *meaning* is the idea it evokes.

This view of meaning is clearly a bit more sophisticated than the Reference theory. It assumes that words are used to refer to things, but it doesn't identify the reference with the meaning. It adds an extra element—the idea—and it is this added element that constitutes the meaning of a word.

The theory of meaning as *idea* is closely connected with a certain view of how communication takes place. The view very much resembles what's involved in piano playing. When Van Cliburn sits down to play, he looks at the score in front of him, then strikes the appropriate keys on the piano. The notes that are produced are then grasped by his listeners as a musical form. Similarly, on the Idea theory view, before we begin to talk, we have some ideas in mind. Depending upon what they are, we speak an appropriate word or words . Our listeners hear the words, and appropriate ideas come into their minds.

The strength and appeal of the Idea theory, as this image suggests, lies in the simple fact that when we talk to other people we are trying *to communicate our ideas.* We use language to convey our thoughts, and by talking we hope to get others to have the same ideas that we do. Since we can't literally put our ideas in someone else's head, it seems that by using words to stand for ideas we can do the next best thing. We can get them to have the ideas we want them to have—ideas that correspond to our ideas—by supplying them with the proper words.

This is surely only common sense. But then it was only common sense in the sixteenth century to believe that the world couldn't be turning—otherwise we would all be thrown off. The Idea theory is really not very satisfactory, in spite of its common sense appeal.

Objection 1: The Concept of an Idea Isn't Clear

If words are said to have meanings because they stand for ideas, we need to know what ideas are. Well, just exactly what are they? Is an idea the same as a sensation or feeling? This definition doesn't seem sensible. You can have the *idea* of getting your head cut off without (fortunately) the actual *feeling* or sensation of getting your head cut off. You can have the idea of sadness without feeling sad, the idea of happiness without feeling happy, and so on.

Perhaps ideas are mental images? My idea of a dog is an image of a dog in my mind, and the word "dog" stands for this image. This seems persuasive enough. But what about words like "whoever," "an," and "also"? What sort of mental image do we have to accompany such words? The right answer seems to be: none at all. If someone tells us to imagine a dog—to picture it to ourselves—we don't have any trouble doing so. But if someone tells us to imagine "however," we don't know what to picture to ourselves. If there are any ideas which accompany such words, they don't seem to be the same as mental images.

We simply have no clear understanding of what an idea is. Since we don't, it's hard to make sense of a theory of meaning which says that words stand for ideas. (It's almost as hard as it would be if someone said, "The meaning of a word is bltzksp.") The concept of idea is at least as obscure to us as the concept of meaning, and we aren't likely to understand meaning better by appealing to idea.

Objection 2: Different Ideas May Accompany the Same Word

Let's forget about words like "however" and just deal with words like "dog." With such words, it's plausible to assume that the ideas they stand for are mental images.

Suppose, then, Levinson says to Johnson, "I just bought a dog." The image Levinson has in mind is that of a seventy-five-pound fully grown German shepherd he just got to guard his apartment. But the image Johnson has in mind is of a two-pound, six-week-old beagle puppy. If the meaning of a word is the idea it refers to, then for Levinson and Johnson, "dog" doesn't have the same meaning.

But it's false to our experiences of using language to say that "dog" doesn't mean the same to two people when they have different mental images. A difference in *meaning* does make a difference in what we communicate to people, but a difference in mental image oridinarily doesn't. When we say, "I'm going to buy a dog," we may not have any images in mind at all. Or we may have the unrelated image of the Lone Ranger riding into the sunset. It makes no difference at all in the *meaning* of what we say.

Objection 3: The Same Idea May Accompany Several Words

Consider the words "pet," "animal," "mammal," "organism," "man's best friend," "good with children," "nuisance," and "the oldest domesticated animal." It's easy to imagine that the same mental image of a dog might accompany each one of these expressions. That is, *dog* is the idea which each of the expressions stands for. According to the Idea theory, the expressions ought to be equivalent in meaning. They refer to or stand for the same idea, after all. But the expressions obviously don't have the same meaning. The Idea theory is false to the facts.

Ideas flashing onto the screen of the mind as each word we speak makes its impact on a listener is a powerful image, but the image is misleading and its bright colors fade in the light of our objections. But we really don't have to give up the satisfying notion that when we talk we're communicating our ideas. All we must do is not take this literally and not believe that our words *stand for* our ideas. What we mean by such expressions as "getting our ideas across" is better interpreted as people *understanding* what we say than by the notion of people having ideas pop into their heads in concert with what we say.

The Simple Truth: Meaning as Conditions for Use

The theory that the meaning of a word is the conditions for its proper use isn't as transparently obvious as the two other theories we have discussed. Basically, it's quite as simple as they are, but it has as many nooks and crannies as a Venetian palace. To make the theory clear and plausible, some of these have to be explored. We'll start our exploration in this section and finish it up in the next.

Rather than jump into the Use theory with both feet, as we've done with the others, a better strategy is to creep up on it gradually. We'll start by restricting our discussion to words like "dog," "polluted," "unjust," and the like that are used to refer to things, people, actions, and so on. This first note will eventually develop into a theme encompassing other words that don't refer and don't even seem to.

Let's start by considering the simple, common, everyday word "aunt."

We know very well how to apply this word to people who have a certain family relationship to us or to others. We can correctly label Aunt Tilly, Aunt Fanny, Aunt Minerva, and Charley's aunt. That we know the meaning of "aunt" consists, at the very least, in the fact that we know how to use the word to refer to people of the appropriate kind.

Most of us know more than this, of course. We know *what it is* that makes a person one of "the appropriate kind." If someone asked, "What does *aunt* mean?" we would probably give an answer like "An aunt is the sister of someone's mother or father." That is, we would list the characteristics or properties that make a person "of the appropriate kind."

The Use theory holds that the meaning of a word is the set of conditions that governs the way the word is used in a language. These conditions (for words that are used to refer, recall) are nothing more than a list or statement of the properties that regulate the word's proper application. The meaning that the word has is thus bound up with the role it plays in a language: with the way or ways in which it is used. To state the meaning of a word is, in effect, to offer a rule for using the word correctly.

But this statement of the Use theory is as abstract as a mathematician's dream. Let's make it more concrete by considering what, in its terms, is involved in answering the question "What is the meaning of the word *aunt?*"

To answer this in terms of the theory, we first have to ask, "What are the conditions that govern the use of the word?" That is, what property (or set of properties) can be named that is such that if a person has it, then the word "aunt" correctly applies to that person?

As we've already mentioned, such a property isn't difficult to specify in this case:

a sister of someone's mother or father.

Anyone who has this property, satisfies this description, can properly be referred to by the word "aunt." The description (property) is a condition that governs how the word is used in English. It is thus the *meaning* of the word "aunt." (As a matter of fact, it's only *a* meaning, because the wife of one's uncle is also called "aunt" sometimes. It's easy to see how this condition could be attached to the other by adding an "or" and writing it out.)

Where do the conditions that govern the use of words like "aunt" come from? They are implicit in our language and are abstracted from our linguistic habits and practices, from the way we talk. Statements of conditions for using words are *reports* about the way or ways that we do use words. So to explain the meaning of an ordinary word is to describe the convention that is followed in the use of it. Anyone who is the sister of someone's mother or father is properly said to be an *aunt* in English. That's just the way that people who speak English employ the word. To tell what the word means consists in reporting this fact.

A swarm of questions buzzes around this brief statement of the Use theory of meaning, and the theory won't be persuasive or clear until we take the time to swat out the answers to a few. Let's take some basic issues one by one in an orderly manner.

Meanings as Arbitrary and as Conventional

The American mathematician Edward Kasner found that in his work he very often had to mention the number 10 raised to the hundredth power. He decided it would be convenient to have a name to refer to this number and, in a moment of whimsy, he asked his small grandson what *he* would call 10^{100}. The little boy said, "Googol." Kasner was satisfied, and he and other mathematicians started to use "googol" as a word.

This is the story of the origin of a word, though it's not a typical story. The word began as a group of sounds that Kasner *arbitrarily* decided to use to refer to the number 10^{100}. Kasner's use caught on, and others started to use "googol" in the same way. Thus, Kasner's *arbitrary* choice became accepted as a *convention*.

Something is *arbitrary* when it is based on nothing more than whim, preference, or caprice. It is *conventional* when it follows a rule, a standard, or customary practice. The use of ordinary words—and hence their meanings—is arbitrary in the sense that at some time or other in a language's remote past people had to make use of sounds to refer to things without precedents to guide them.

There is nothing in the nature of things to demand that "dog" be used to refer to dogs. The Germans do quite well with *Hund* and the French equally well with *chien*. If the history of our language had been different, we ourselves might be using "glick" instead of "dog." Undoubtedly there was an initial arbitrariness in the way that certain sounds were used to refer to certain things. But once the sounds came to be used in the same way by all speakers of the language, once they became words, they were no longer arbitrary. Words were used then in accordance with *conventions*.

To give the meaning of a word is thus not to *make up* a rule for using the word. Rather, it is to identify and state the conventions in accordance with which the word is actually used. So, to ask what the meaning of a certain word is isn't to ask a question so profound that it would take one of the three wise men to answer. Those of us who are speakers of a language are quite accustomed to answering such inquiries. We simply report how we and other speakers use the word in talking. We mention the conditions that govern the word's use: the conventions embedded in practice.

When we learned our language, we learned the conventions that regulate the ways in which words are appropriately used to refer to things, people, actions, states of affairs, and so on. A knowledge of these conventions is an essential part of what it is to know and to be able to speak a language. In fact, without conventions, communication by language would be an impossiblity. We would all make our arbitrary sounds, but without any shared conditions governing their use, we would only be babbling and gabbling. To teach someone the meaning of a word that is unknown to him but known to us, we must make him acquainted with the conventions that we and others have mastered and rely upon.

Time and Meaning

Languages change over time. Grammar becomes altered, new words are added, and old words drop from use. What's more, words change their meanings. Before the twentieth century, the word "plastic" was used only as a modifying adjective to characterize materials that can be formed or molded. In this century, it became a noun used to refer to polymerized carbon compounds synthesized by new chemical processes. Until recent years, the expression "star" applied only to certain lights in the sky, "rock" referred only to chunks of stone, and "off" was a preposition, not a verb.

The meanings of these words altered, for they came to be used in new ways. New conditions for applying the words were introduced, new conventions became accepted. Obviously, to learn what a word means *now* is to learn the conditions which *currently* govern its use.

A word may keep its old meaning and acquire a new and additional one, or its old meaning may be pushed aside and forgotten. In either case, to learn what a word means involves finding out its present uses.

Discovering the way in which a word was used at an earlier time can be a fascinating excursion into history. Who isn't pleased to learn that "methodist" was used in the seventeenth century to refer to anyone who was systematic and methodical and later came to refer almost exclusively to the followers of John Wesley? Students of literature and history find it crucial to learn how words were commonly employed during the period that interests them. But such a discovery doesn't mean that they have located the "true meaning" of a word—even if they have traced it to its first occurrence. It would be as absurd to believe this as to think that the discovery of how people dressed in the seventeenth century reveals the "right way to dress."

How Conditions Can Govern Use

We've said that the meaning of a word can be identified with the set of conditions that governs its use. This means that there is a relationship between a thing's having certain properties and its being correctly designated by a certain word. But the possession of properties can regulate the use of a word in several ways, and we need to be definite about them. Briefly and immediately we'll examine three sorts of conditions that are relevant to an understanding of how words are used. Afterward we'll make it clear just how they *are* relevant.

Sufficient Condition

The word "aunt," as we've said six times, applies to any person who possesses the property of being the sister of someone's mother or father. Having this property can be said to be a *sufficient condition* for being correctly designated by the word. Or, to put the same point in a long-winded way, if the phrase "sister of someone's mother or father" is true of a person, then the word "aunt" properly applies to her as well. Satisfying the description is a sufficient condition for labeling a person "aunt," whether she likes it or not.

We can now abstract and generalize from this example: to say a property or set of properties P is a *sufficient condition* for applying a word to an item is to say that the word is used in such a way that whatever has P is correctly referred to by the word.

Necessary Condition

To the vast relief of many people, not all females are mothers. That is, being female isn't a sufficient condition for being designated by the word "mother." But of course being female has something to do with whether or not a person is called "mother." (At least it does in the most common ordinary use of the word.) Anyone who speaks English knows that the word "mother" doesn't apply to anyone who *isn't* female. Being female, we can say, is a *necessary condition* for being a mother. To put the point the long way, if the word "female" does not apply to a person, then the word "mother" doesn't either.

To generalize: To say a property P is a *necessary condition* for applying a word to an item is to say that the word is used in such a way that whatever *lacks* P is not correctly referred to by the word.

Necessary and Sufficient Condition

The word "mother" doesn't correctly apply to a person who isn't female. Nor does it correctly apply to a person who isn't a parent. Being a female is a necessary (but not sufficient) condition for being a mother, and being a parent is a necessary (but not sufficient) condition for being a mother. But the two properties taken *together* are a sufficient condition for applying the word "mother" to a person. That is, everyone who satisfies the description "female parent" will also be correctly referred to by the word "mother."

A person who lacks either of the characteristics (being female, being a parent) isn't correctly designated by "mother," and a person who has both is. The word thus applies to *all* those who have these characteristics and *only* to those who have them. (Another way of saying this is: "Mother" applies to a person if, and only if, that person is both female and a parent.)

Generalizing from our example: To say a property (or set of properties) P is the *necessary and sufficient condition* for applying a word is to say that the word is used in such a way that whatever lacks P is *not* correctly designated by the word and whatever has P *is* correctly designated by the word.

This is just a way of putting together what we mean when we say P is necessary and P is also sufficient: it's an incorporation of the two explanations we gave before this one.

Now what does all of this heavy technical artillery have to do with the Use theory of meaning? Well, we've said several times that "The meaning of a word is the set of conditions that governs its use." Until now this has been somewhat vague, but we now have ways of characterizing precisely the connections between conditions (having certain properties, satisfying descriptions) and use (referring to certain items). We can speak definitely of the relationship between possessing specific traits or characteristics and being referred to by a certain word. What's more, we can now make sense out of expressions like "has two different meanings," "part of the meaning," and, most importantly, "has a meaning but doesn't refer to anything." But let's keep orderly and not rush ahead.

Conditions and Ordinary Words

Armed with our new keen-edged weapons, let's examine the sorts of conditions that typically govern the use of ordinary words and see if we can't cut away some of the undergrowth that keeps us from getting a clear view of the whole matter of meaning. (Our discussion, remember, is still restricted to words that refer.)

Notice, first of all, that we can find words that are used in accordance with all three sorts of conditions we've distinguished. That is, given any of the types of conditions, we can find words used that way. Our illustrations, in fact, were all common words. What we really want to know is whether there isn't one of the three sorts of conditions that reflects the way in which words are *typically* or *predominantly* used.

Let's start by considering conditions that are necessary and sufficient—N&S conditions, for short. Are words ordinarily used in such a way that the conditions regulating their use are N&S ones? The only suitable procedure for answering this question is just to take a careful look at the way words *are* used. We don't have to go so far as a statistical survey—though one wouldn't be out of place—we can rely instead on our own knowledge of language to enable us to select characteristic cases.

A word used in accordance with N&S conditions, recall, must be one that applies to all and only items that meet the conditions. One such word, as we saw, is "mother." The "female and parent" conditions are separately necessary and jointly sufficient. The same is true, of course, for "father" (male and parent), "sister" (female and sibling), "son" (male and offspring), "brother" (male and sibling), and "daughter" (female and offspring). N&S conditions can be stated to represent the use of a number of words connected with such biological relations as being a father, a daughter, and so on. But of course such relations tend to form a closed and interlocking system. Let's break out, then, and examine some common words that don't seem to fit into such a system.

The word "book" is as ordinary and dull as any other we might arbitrarily select, so let's consider it. Here's what we need to ask: Is there a group of characteristics that is such that all and only books possess that group? If the use of "book" is actually governed by N&S conditions, then we should be able to list the properties that are such that if a thing has them all, it is a book, and if it lacks any of them, it is not. We should be able to do for "book" what we did for "mother" and the rest of the family.

Can we do it? Well, we can try. Since we have to find a group of characteristics that are *necessary* and *sufficient*, the easiest way to start out is to separate these two demands. First, let's try to find a *necessary* condition. That is, let's look for a property of the sort that if something *lacks* it, that thing is not correctly called "book." A person must at least be female to be a mother. Is there a characteristic that something must at least have to be a book?

To answer this, we can't just make up something out of our heads. We have to examine the way in which "book" is used in English, the convention that underlies our practice. Thus, any claims about such and such a property being necessary we can test by considering how we and others who speak the language actually talk.

Let's put a little drama in our inquiry by casting it in the following episode.

> Rachel Reasoner and her Wonder Cat Logos have been taken captive by Mr. Word, a mad lexicographer whose professional disappointments have turned him to a life of revenge. Suspended above the table where Rachel and Logos are strapped down is a gigantic copy of the *American Heritage Diction-ary.* Mr. Word's right hand is wrapped around the lever that controls the hoist mechanism. If Rachel refuses to cooperate with him, she and Logos will be crushed by the weight of words!
> "You and your feline friend have but one chance to live. You know how

the learned world scoffed at me and my theory of meaning. Now you are going to have to prove me right or die trying!''

"What do you want me to do, you word-crazed drudge?''

"You must present me with a characteristic that all things ordinarily called *book* have in common.''

"You mean you want me to give you a necessary condition governing the use of the word *book*?''

"Exactly! I see you are as clever as they say.''

"You may as well drop the dictionary now. You've asked me to perform an impossible task.''

"Nonsense! You are just against me, like the rest of them were.''

"I see I'm going to have to prove it to you. Very well, then. Let's reverse roles. You tell me what you take to be a necessary condition governing the word, and I'll give you a case of something that doesn't have the property but that we still call *book.* If I fail, you can drop the dictionary.''

"I agree, but it must be something we really call *book.* Here's my first condition: a book must be printed.''

"Ridiculous! What about such things as handwritten manuscripts and diaries? We call them books, too, you know.''

"Oh, I suppose you're right. Very well, what about this, a book must be *published.*''

"It's no wonder they kicked you out of the Legion of Lexicographers! You seem to have forgotten that we speak of people who write books that never get published.''

"I guess I did. But that gives me an idea. A book must be *made out of paper.*''

"Ridiculous! You've forgotten about parchment, vellum, stone tablets, and God knows what else. Materials don't have anything to do with whether something is a book or not.''

"Well, Ms. Reasoner, you won't be able to escape from this one. A book must have *words.*''

"You're not just mad; you're stupid. I don't suppose you would consider something that looked exactly like the latest novel but contained nothing but numbers and mathematical formulas a book?''

"I guess I did forget about numbers. So, make it . . . a book requires *symbols.*''

"What about a blank book?''

"A blank book? What's a blank book?''

"It's a book that consists of nothing but blank pages.''

"That's a book? This smells like one of your slimy tricks to me.''

"I'll assure you it's no trick. That's what it's called.''

"All right, then. Mr. Word is a man of his word. I can't think of any more likely characteristics to mention, so I guess I'll have to free you.''

"Thank you. You've shown me once again that, though we may be shackled by a Word, more words of the right sort can free us from bondage.''

Perhaps Mr. Word gave up too easily. Had he been willing to consider more possiblities, maybe he could have found at least one property that is a necessary condition for applying the word "book." Chances are, though, that it would have to be one so general or abstract that it wouldn't ordinarily be regarded as a property that in practice we rely upon in deciding whether or not to use "book" to refer to something. He might have suggested, for example, that to be a book an item must at least have the property of being a *thing*. But to have to mention a characteristic like this as a necessary condition is about the same as saying that in practice there are no necessary conditions that govern the use of "book." For our purposes, in fact, it *is* the same, and we'll count it as such.

It's tedious to give more examples, and anyone who raises the question we've raised about "book" in connection with most other common words is likely to get the same results. Agreeing to take "book" as a representative word, we can draw a conclusion from our examination so far. It's this: *Words as they are used in everyday speech are not typically governed by necessary conditions.*

Imagine that a necessary condition is a thread that runs through everything that is correctly referred to by a word. (Being female is one of the threads that bind all mothers together.) To say that there is no necessary condition for using a word is to deny there is such a thread. It's to say that the way the word is ordinarily used doesn't require that all the things referred to by it have some element in common.

Now, if most words aren't used in ways that make it possible to locate a necessary condition regulating their use, this means that *necessary and sufficient* conditions can't be given either. To be necessary and sufficient, recall, a group of properties has to be *both* necessary and sufficient. Without necessary conditions governing use, we have to give up the attempt to get N&S conditions. So, words as they are ordinarily used are not typically governed by N&S conditions.

That words aren't governed in ordinary life in this way isn't so surprising, really. With a few exceptions like "mother," only technical terms in some special area like mathematics, law, and science are used in ways that can be represented by a list of N&S conditions. The word "octant," for example, is a mathematical term that refers to any one of the eight parts into which a space is divided by three planes intersecting at the same point at right angles to each other. Any section of space that satisfies this description is an octant, and nothing else is.

"Octant" is a technical term, but ordinary words obviously are not. They are used in looser and more elastic ways, and it is this very flexibility that does much to make our language an effective and resourceful instrument of communication. Not only is it not surprising that ordinary words aren't used in accordance with N&S conditions, but from the point of view of communication, it's probably a darned good thing they aren't.

We've now knocked necessary and N&S conditions out of the race to test which of the three original contenders best represents the conditions that typically govern the use of ordinary words. By default, it looks like sufficient condition has won. But we need to keep the contestant running, anyway; otherwise, it won't be clear why it deserves to win. Besides, there are several features of its style that are important and need to be pointed out.

Recall this: there is a sufficient condition governing a word's use when the word is used in such a way that having a certain property (or set of properties) is enough to justify that use. "Aunt" is regulated by a sufficient condition, because whatever is the sister of someone's parent is correctly referred to as an aunt.

Let's go back and pick up the word "book." Mr. Word's attempt to find a necessary condition governing its use was a dismal failure, and this was enough to show us that we couldn't get an N&S condition either. We're left with one big question: Can we find a property or set of properties that will constitute a sufficient condition?

If Mr. Word had given Rachel Reasoner this task, she could have made quick work of it. Here is one sufficient condition, for example: if something is *printed on paper and is bound,* then "book" is properly used to refer to it.

But there's no need to stop here. Here's another sufficient condition: if something is *handwritten on sheets of sheepskin and tied together with strips of leather,* then "book" correctly applies to it.

We don't even have to stop here, but we will. To present a sufficient condition for using a word is to list properties that are such that if a thing has them, then the word properly applies to it. Clearly, then, there can be several sets of conditions sufficient for using a word. The properties listed can be different in each set, but there can also be sets that contain some properties that also occur in other sets.

We can take it as established that sufficient condition won the contest—that it can best represent the way most words are ordinarily used. That's the Big Point we've made in this section. But there are enough confusing points poking out from the big one that anybody who isn't careful might stab himself on them. To avoid this danger, let's go on to the next section and talk about some matters that may blunt them a little.

Inside the Black Box: Some Details of the Use Theory

We've peeked inside the black box of language and seen enough to assure us that the Use theory is the best of the three we've looked at. We've also seen that, generally speaking, words are used in such a way that the conditions governing them are best regarded as sufficient ones. We need to go on now and examine a few of the circuits and hookups so that we can understand just how and why the Use theory works.

We'll examine four points that are concerned with the connections between the use of words and the conditions for use. To help keep things organized, we'll simply talk about these points one by one. After this, we'll finish up by dealing with a matter we've long delayed: namely, explaining how the Use theory can handle words that don't refer.

Sets of Conditions Can Be Put Together in a Single List

Let's start by repeating the point we made about the word "book" in the last section. The point was, recall, that more than one set of properties sufficient for using a word can typically be given. Let's take the word "ball," just to vary things a little.

If something is

spherical in shape,
covered with horsehide,
made of wound fibrous cord,

then "ball" applies to it. Also, if something is

egg-shaped,
made of pigskin,
and contains an inflated rubber bladder,

then "ball" applies to it. What's more, if something is

spherical in shape,
made of wound rubber cord,
covered with dimpled plastic,

then "ball" applies to it. And if something is

spherical in shape,
made of leather,
and contains an inflated rubber bladder,

then "ball" applies to it.

It's possible to go on listing sets of conditions that are sufficient for applying the word "ball" to things that may be in the world. We've presented conditions for picking out or referring to baseballs, footballs, golf balls, and basketballs. We could go on to tennis balls, Ping-Pong balls, pool balls, eyeballs, ball bearings, orbs of office, geographical globes, marbles, soccer balls, handballs, and so on and on.

There is no one specific feature that all objects we refer to by the word "ball" have in common—no thread that runs through them all, no necessary condition for using the word. Instead, there are a number of sets of properties which are sufficient for using the word.

We don't really have to talk about different sets of properties. To some extent this is even misleading, for it suggests that for every word it is possible to find several specific sets of properties regulating its use. When we're dealing with words like "ball," this is pehaps correct, for there's a variety of kinds of balls that are relatively distinct from one another. But this isn't so for words like "charming," "intelligent," "officious," "friendly," and the like.

It isn't even necessary to think of words like "ball" as being associated with several distinct sets of properties. Consider, instead, a single list of properties that are connected with the use of "ball" to refer to things in the world. To keep from repeating the lists and drawing up others, let's just use letters to stand for properties like "made of leather" and so on. Thus, "ball" is associated with, say, properties A, B, C, D, E, F, G, H, I, J, K, L. Each of these properties is a *condition* connected with the ordinary use of "ball." No property is a necessary one, and no *single* property is sufficient. But a *group* of the properties may make up a sufficient condition for using the word. Possessing A, B, C, D, E, for example, may be sufficient for being a ball. So, too, may be possessing A, H, J, L, or E, F, G or some other combination of characteristics.

Consider, as another example, the way we use "shy" as applied to people ("Ford is shy"). There's no single feature that the shy must all share. Rather, there is a large group of characteristics associated with "shy," and if a person has a *sufficient* number of those characteristics, we say he is shy. Someone who hates to meet strangers, answer the telephone, or speak in public is a person to whom we would ordinarily apply the word. The same is true of someone who finds it hard to make conversation, hates walking into a meeting after it has started, and doesn't like to put her own opinions forward.

Words, then, are typically connected with properties in the way that a presidential candidate is connected with registered voters. If a sufficient number of people vote for him, then he wins. But no one certain person has to vote for him, and some of those registered may not vote at all. If a sufficient number don't vote for him, he loses. But that doesn't mean that nobody voted for him.

Or take another analogy. In much the same way that a baseball player must satisfy certain eligibility requirements before being allowed to play, an object has to possess a certain number of properties before a word like "baseball" correctly applies to it. The properties connected with the word function as conditions regulating the word's conventional use, just as the eligibility requirements function as conditions specifying who is eligible to play baseball. Some major differences between these two cases, though, are that the eligibility requirements are few in number, and quite definite, and all must be satisfied. This is *not* so for the conditions governing the use of most of our ordinary words. Let's explore these differences further.

The List of Conditions Is Long and Indefinite

Probably none of us could come close to listing *all* the properties that serve as conditions for using a typical word like "book." To get anything like such a list would take extensive research, for we would have to consider how the word is actually used in a large and representative number of cases.

But just because we can't make up such a list without research doesn't mean we don't know how to use "book" correctly in most instances. We do. It means only that there may be cases in which we *personally* don't count a certain property as a condition governing a word, though at least some other people do. We might not recognize, for example, that being meddlesome is a trait connected with the word "officious." As a consequence, we might hesitate to apply "officious" to a person who is, among other things, meddlesome. Someone else might not pause a moment before doing it.

Most ordinary words have such a large number of characteristics associated with their use that no one person knows them all. So it's always possible for some people to regard a certain characteristic as a *condition* regulating the use of a word, while others don't regard it that way.

We look to linguists and lexicographers to do the research necessary for discovering what speakers of a language *generally* take to be conditions relevant for using a word. Chances are, of course, that their reports won't be exactly accurate. For one thing, the way words are used often becomes altered—new characteristics become associated with them and old ones drop away. No dictionary can keep wholly up to date with a language. For another, a report on the generally acknowledged conditions for use has to ignore special groups—a pipefitter doesn't use "tapped" in the same way that a gambler does. Nevertheless, such reports do succeed in representing the main conditions that constitute the convention in accordance with which a word is ordinarily used. The list of conditions a dictionary provides is, to some extent, indefinite and open-ended. But language itself is indefinite and open-ended, in a sense. Words are often stretched to cover new cases, shrunk to fit a special context, and tailored for a variety of practical purposes.

Suppose you looked out your window early one morning and found that the house across the street had been replaced by an object that appeared to be a gigantic loaf of unsliced bread. Suppose that you felt it, and it felt like bread; smelled it, and it smelled like bread; tasted it, and it tasted like bread. If you called up the police to report what had happened, would you say that the house next door had disappeared and a loaf of bread had taken its place?

It's not clear that "loaf of bread" correctly applies to the giant object, because being of a certain (relatively small) size is one of the conditions ordinarily associated with the phrase. Yet the expression can easily enough be stretched to fit this unusual case. That it can be is just an indication of the open-ended and indefinite lists of conditions associated with words.

No Definite Group of Conditions May Be Sufficient

Suppose that Harry Roth is a man who opens doors for women and offers to carry their packages. For many people these characteristics are ones that serve as conditions for using the phrase "male chauvinist." Possessing one or both of them is something which *counts toward* applying the phrase to a person. Let's suppose they *are* conditions governing the phrase. Do they, taken separately or together, constitute a *sufficient* condition for using the phrase? Most people would say they don't. Harry Roth and other men like him may simply be polite people. Yet others would say they *do:* opening doors and offering to carry packages for a woman is enough to make a man a male chauvinist. There is, then, disagreement about just what conditions are sufficient for correctly applying the term.

"Male chauvinist" is a relatively new term, and it's not strange that the conditions for its appropriate use should still be a matter of contention. But the truth is, the same is so for a great number of established words. Ones like these: competent, intelligent, friendly, accomplished . . . and many more. Such words have associated with them a number of characteristics that are generally acknowledged to be conditions for their use. But some people are more easily pleased than others. That is, some people regard as sufficient groups of conditions that others consider inadequate.

Suppose Charles Osgood has written a book called *How to Pollute and Save Money.* Some people would regard having written a book as a sufficient condition for applying "intelligent" to Osgood. Others wouldn't. If they were told that Osgood earned a B.A. in philosophy, a few more might agree to call him intelligent. But it's likely there would still be holdouts. If it were pointed out that Osgood also earned a Ph.D. in chemistry from Cambridge, others might fall in line.

Osgood might not have enough outstanding traits to convince everyone that he is intelligent, but if it were possible to continue in this vein, there would come a point at which everyone who uses "intelligent" in the ordinary way would have to agree that the word legitimately applies to Osgood. Some set of conditions must be sufficient for using the word. But, of course, this doesn't alter the fact that there isn't a definite set of properties that everyone accepts as the set.

In psychological terms, there are thresholds for use, and some people have lower thresholds than others. Some people lay "intelligent" on almost everyone. Others hold it back like a precious jewel that they intend to award only to the truly outstanding.

Even though individuals have different thresholds for use, there is still an acknowledgment in most instances that some conditions are *more important* than others. Harry Roth, let's say, not only opens doors and carries packages for women, but also

pays women employees less than men,
refuses to promote women to executive jobs,
asserts that women are less intelligent than men.

Now any one of these characteristics will count *more* toward justifying
the use of "male chauvinist" to refer to Roth than will either of the other
two traits. In this sense, the properties are more important conditions
than the other two. Perhaps no single one of them would be regarded as a
sufficient condition, yet in a sense any one of them comes closer to
constituting a sufficient condition than other properties that are also
conditions for using the phrase.

Paradigm Cases

We're all as well acquainted with language as we are with the insides of
our pockets. And this is enough to assure us that the vast majority of words
are used in such a way that there is almost total agreement about when
it's appropriate to apply them and when it's not.

We don't ordinarily go through doubt or anguish, weep or gnash our
teeth, before using words like "lazy," "ghetto," or "rock group." We
may hesitate in some cases, but not many. In fact, it's *as if* there were
associated with most words several clusters of characteristics that everybody recognized as conditions sufficient for applying the word.

The "as if" is necessary here because in using words we typically
don't actually go through the process of *deciding* whether or not a word
applies to a case. We don't *really* have in mind a check list of properties
that are conditions for using the word and consciously run through the
check list to see whether a sufficient number are present.

We've talked rather like this until now, because in doing so we were
able to represent in an explicit way the manner in which conditions can
govern the use of words. In a sense, we've given a picture of what people
can be *represented* as doing in using words.

To be blunt about it, we've suggested that people are rather like slot
machines. The properties of something are fed in, if they are conditions
for using a word, and if a sufficient number of them are present, then
—jackpot—the word applies to the thing.

Where there is doubt or disagreement about whether a word should be
used in a given instance, actual practice resembles the slot-machine
model. "Is that art or a piece of junk?" somebody might ask. "What does
art mean, anyway?" In such cases, we try to be explicit about the conditions for using a word and consciously consider whether they are satisfied or not.

But if the slot-machine or the check-list models aren't literally correct
in most cases, we have a problem. How *do* we account for the fact that
people typically use words *as if* there were cores of characteristics as-

sociated with them that are sufficient for their proper application? If people don't run through a check list, then how is it that they use words as if they did?

It's easier to give a generally correct answer to this question than it is to buy a hamburger at McDonald's on Saturday night. All we have to do is to reflect on our own experience of learning new words.

We master new words by learning how to use them correctly. There are several ways in which we gain such information, but one basic way consists merely in having someone explain to us the meaning of the word. Typically this involves *describing* cases to which the word correctly applies:

> You want to know what *chutzpah* means? All right, I'll tell you. A guy kills his parents. He's caught, tried, and found guilty. "Please, your Honor," he begs. "Have mercy on me. I'm a poor orphan and have no one to help me." That's *chutzpah.*

Such an explanation may also consist in pointing out actual examples:

> You see that dark green stuff floating on top of the pond. Well, that's *algae.*

Such described or actual examples are called *paradigm cases* of a word's use. They are no more than clear-cut instances to which a certain word can be legitimately applied.

Often we learn new words, not by having someone explain their meanings to us, but simply by keeping our eyes and ears open. We notice to what sort of cases a word is applied or in what sort of circumstances a word is used by other people, and we simply follow their use. This is particularly true with rapidly changing slang words. "Groovy," "good vibes," "rip-off," or whatever slang is current, is mastered by observation and imitation.

We often make mistakes in using new words. The paradigm cases that people give us or that we discover for ourselves serve as *guides* for use. But just a case or two is usually not enough to guarantee a grasp of the word's use. The child who calls a rabbit a rat when he goes to the zoo, because he has learned the word "rat" by having animals in the alley or in his apartment building pointed out to him, needs to have his usage polished. By more examples, by cases that are similar but are *not* examples, we can bring his use of a word into conformity with the use of others. When he's reached this point, he's mastered the convention for using a word—he's learned how to use it correctly. He has, in short, learned its meaning.

This way of mastering a word's ordinary use *doesn't* consist in our being given a list of properties which we consult before deciding whether it's proper to use the word in a given case. We don't ordinarily learn words according to the slot-machine model. We learn them by experience. We learn how to *use* words in much the same way as we learn how to *do* anything else—such as riding a bicycle or taking a bus. People explain how a word is used, give examples of use, and put us on our own. We try, make mistakes, get corrected, and finally become smooth users.

The result of the process is that we master the use of words without necessarily being able to give an explicit list of conditions for use. We *know* the conditions, in the sense that we act in accordance with them. But this doesn't mean that we know them in the sense of being able to write them down.

It's both legitimate and useful to try to discover the conditions for using a word that underlie its actual use—to uncover the rule which we unconsciously follow in practice. We've already found that when we do this we learn that a list of conditions is typically long and open-ended. Yet people do often use words, recall, *as if* there were several cores of conditions that everyone acknowledged as sufficient. Paradigm cases make it clear why this is so. People don't ordinarily have any conditions at all in mind when they use a word. They simply use the word because they have *learned* to apply the word in cases like the one they are presently faced with.

It's only from the standpoint of analysis, when we attempt to abstract from practice and discover conditions for use, that there is agreement that various sets of conditions are sufficient ones and that a large number of properties function as conditions governing use.

Words That Don't Refer to Anything

So far we've limited our discussion to words like "dog," "slowly," and "late," which can easily be regarded as referring to objects, actions, or states of affairs. A lot of words do refer, but, as we saw long ago, the meaning of words can't be identified with the classes of objects (and so on) that they refer to. The Reference theory of meaning cracked up on the hard fact that some words obviously have a meaning, even though they don't refer to anything at all. Similarly, the Idea theory shattered into useless fragments when hit with the fact that not all words with a meaning can be plausibly regarded as even referring to ideas. If the Use theory isn't to break up on the same rock as its two competitors, we have to show that some words have a meaning even though they don't refer to anything.

The Reference theory couldn't handle words like "unicorn," "werewolf," and "vampire" because there is nothing for the words to refer to. Adam couldn't have said, "I'll call this creature *werewolf*," because there is no such creature. Nor are there any unicorns or vampires—none of the Count Dracula variety, at any rate. The class of things referred to by these words has no members, so in terms of the Reference theory, the words don't have a meaning. But they obviously *do* have a meaning. It's just that the Reference theory can't explain what it is.

Can the Use theory do better? Yes, it can. All we need to do is ask for a list of conditions that govern the use of each of the words. What does "werewolf" mean? Well, what are the conditions that, if satisfied, justify applying the word "werewolf" to a thing? Here are ones that are probably sufficient:

a person who can change himself into a wolf.

This is the meaning of "werewolf."

So far as we know, no one satisfies this set of conditions. The word "werewolf" then, can't properly be used to refer to anything at all. The same is true of other words like it. They resemble words like "dog," which do refer, but they only purport or appear to refer. In spite of the fact that they can't legitimately be applied to anything, they have a meaning. We learn what "werewolf" means when we learn what properties we should look for when considering whether or not the snarling creature facing us in the alley is to be called a werewolf. Fortunately, we don't learn words like "werewolf" by means of actual paradigm cases.

The Use theory can deal without difficulty with werewolflike words. But the Idea theory can too: the meaning of "werewolf" is the idea of a werewolf that the word stands for. (Of course, if we went on to ask, "what does the idea stand for?" the theory has a big problem.) Only the Reference theory falls wholly to pieces. Still, recall that there are other words which we regard as meaningful that not only don't refer to anything, but don't even *purport* to refer to anything.

"Werewolf" is at least the sort of word that could be applied to something. It just so happens that the world doesn't contain anything for it legitimately to refer to. Words like "though," "a" and "and," however, aren't like that. They don't refer to anything, and it's difficult to imagine what they could even be taken to refer to—not objects, states of affairs, activities, or ideas. Recall that it's with words like these that both the Reference theory *and* the Idea theory collapsed in defeat.

Can the Use theory save the day? Can it account in its own terms for the meaning of these words? Indeed it can. The meaning of such words is, again, the conditions for their use. But since they aren't referring-type words of either the "dog" variety or the "werewolf" variety, the conditions can't consist in *properties* that are relevant to deciding whether or not a word correctly applies to an object. Rather, descriptions of three sorts of matters serve as conditions for the use of nonreferring words.

First, the use of a word like "an" or "also" is governed by the grammatical conventions of the language it belongs to. Second, its use is tied to the context of discourse—to what has been said or taken for granted before. Third, its use is connected with the function that it, as contrasted with other words, serves in the language.

But let's bring down our discussion from the blue skies of abstraction to the brown mud of experience by considering an example. Take the little word "an." It obviously doesn't even purport to refer to anything, so the conditions for its use can't be a set of properties sufficient for applying the word to things. What, then, would we say to explain its meaning? Something like this:

a. "An" is used instead of "a" when it comes before words which begin with a vowel sound ("arsonist," "overkill," "FBI," etc.);
b. "An" is used in contrast with "the" to indicate that we are talking about something not mentioned or noticed before (At first: "There's *an* apple on the table, do you see it?" Then: "Fine, now pick up the apple and eat it.");
c. "An" is used in contrast with "the" to indicate that we are talking about any instance at all of a certain kind and not a specific instance of that kind ("Now suppose an FBI man comes busting through the door . . .").

Observation (a) has to do with the grammar of "an," (b) concerns the context of the discourse, and (c) the function that "an" serves in the language. This three-part description is an account of the use of "an" that reflects the conventions—grammatical and otherwise—that underlie our use of the word. In doing so, it presents us with a set of rules for using the word properly. These conditions express the meaning of "an" in the same way that "sister of one's parent" does for "aunt."

The same sort of account we gave for "an" can also be provided for "also," therefore," "however," and other words that play a nonreferring role in language. Their meaning is the conditions for their correct (conventional) use. The Use theory, in sum, can sail smoothly through the dangerous waters where the other two theories cracked up and sank.

We started long ago with the deceptively simple question "What is the meaning of a word?" In asking it we said we wanted an *analysis* of meaning, of what it is that we can be said to know when we know the meaning of a word. The Reference theory assured us that meaning could be identified with reference and that the meaning of an expression is nothing but the class of things a word refers to. This we found unacceptable: some words don't seem to refer to anything, and some expressions can refer to the same thing but differ in meaning. The Idea theory claimed that a word's meaning is the idea it stands for or represents. This sounded more plausible than the Reference theory, but we found that it too contained fatal flaws: the concept of an idea is not at all clear; different ideas may accompany the same word; different words may be accompanied by the same ideas.

We were left with the Use theory to consider. In its terms, to know the meaning of a word is to know how to use the word correctly. Meaning is learned by mastering the conventions in accordance with which it is used. These conventions, we said, could be investigated, uncovered, and represented as conditions that govern the use of words.

We also pointed out that the slot-machine model is only a way of speaking. In practice it may be hard or even impossible to find all the properties anyone considers relevant to a word's use, and what's more, people sometimes differ about just what conditions make up a group sufficient for using a word. But because words are learned from experience, from paradigm examples, and by practice and correction, there is a high degree of uniformity in the use of most words. When someone knows how to use a word in the way that others who speak the language do, then he knows the meaning of the word. In a sense, then, he knows the conditions governing the word's ordinary use.

The conditions for a word's ordinary, standard, conventional, or usual use can be regarded as constituting the meaning of the word. Most words are used in ways that are not governed by conditions that are necessary or necessary-and-sufficient. The conditions that regulate the use of most words belong to sets of sufficient ones. Moreover, though lists of such conditions are open-ended, there are at least several clusters that are typically taken to be sufficient for applying the word.

The meaning of a word is its use, and that use can be captured by stating the conditions that govern the use of the word. We are thus justified in saying that the meaning of a word is the conditions for its use.

Exercises: The Adventures of Captain Meaning

Once, long ago, in the dark recesses of an abandoned streetcar, an incredibly aged woman—Myra, the Mistress of Meaning—passed on to you the secret that generations of philosophers struggled to discover: THE MEANING OF "MEANING."

"Meaning is use, my child," she said. "Consider this well and ponder it long. Once you understand it, you will see many confusions disappear and many mysteries become solved."

In exchange for the secret, you made a promise to the old woman. You dedicated yourself to the unending fight against linguistic confusion and to the struggle for a universal understanding of the character of linguistic meaning.

To symbolize to the world your commitments to these ends you decided to become . . .

CAPTAIN MEANING!!

Only your small dog Yoyo knows that you are the mysterious figure that dresses in a disposable paper suit overprinted with pages from the *American Heritage Dictionary* and wears a large pair of darkened reading glasses.

Made independently wealthy by the tremendous fortune in priceless made left to you by Myra, you have taken a job as an itinerant peddler of underground newspapers so that you can always be available when questions about meaning arise and your services are needed.

And now, some brief episodes.

Episode 1

"Thanks for coming down, Captain Meaning," said Chief Brown. "We've got a real puzzler on our hands this time, and if anyone can help us with it, you can."

"I'll do what I can, of course. Just what is it that's troubling you?"

"Well, we've got this letter here from the Mad Bomber. You know, the guy that planted a bomb in the city sewer system last month. He says he's willing to give himself up if we would answer just one question for him."

"That's great! Why don't you just answer the question?"

"Answer it! I don't even understand it! That's why we wanted you to help us."

"Very well, what's the question?"

"He says that he has always believed two things. Here they are: (1) that the meanings of words are completely arbitrary, and (2) that whatever meaning a word has is identical with the thing it stands for. He's heard that these beliefs are wrong, and he wants to know why."

"He's willing to give himself up and be put in jail just to increase his knowledge? Maybe he's not such a bad fellow after all."

"Maybe not, but unless you help us he might not ever see a jail."

"His questions are very easy to answer. At least they are for me."

How do you answer these questions for Chief Brown?

Episode 2

"I've really got a problem, Captain Meaning," said Captain Meaning's neighbor Ms. Lieptchitz.

"You know I'm always glad to help. Tell me about it."

"It's my son Larry. He came home yesterday and told me that he had to come up with an example of a word whose use requires the satisfaction of a necessary condition. Also he had to find an example of one that is used in accordance with a set of conditions that's necessary and sufficient. What does all that mean?"

"Please don't panic, Ms. Lieptchitz. I'll be able to help you. Who asked Larry to find such words, if I may ask?"

"It was a gang of neighborhood kids. They said they'd beat him up if he couldn't come up with the right words by tomorrow."

"Hmmm, neighborhood gangs are much more sophisticated than they used to be when I was a kid. But I promised to help, and I will. First I'll explain what those terms 'necessary' and 'necessary and sufficient' mean, then I'll give you the examples you asked for. You'll then be able to help Larry find his own."

"Oh, thank you so very much, Captain Meaning. I wish there were more like you in the world!"

What explanations and examples do you give to Ms. Lieptchitz?

Episode 3

"Please, Captain Meaning, can I talk to you for a moment?"

"Why of course you can, Mr. Larveski. How can I help you?"

"I don't want to get too personal about it, but my wife and I are having a little trouble. She says that we can't really understand one another because the words we use don't ever mean the same to each of us."

"That's strange, but please go on."

"She says we are having a communication breakdown because we each have different ideas that correspond to the same word. For that reason, we can't communicate our ideas to each other."

"Say no more, Mr. Larveski. I can certainly do something to help your situation, if you and your wife are willing to talk about it."

"Oh, we are both anxious to do what we can. Neither of us enjoys being in conflict with the other."

"Fine. Now it seems to me that part of the trouble stems from the fact that your wife holds a theory of meaning that is wrong. If you can get her to see why it is wrong, I think that the two of you will be able to communicate better."

What reasons do you give for saying that Mrs. Larveski holds a theory of meaning that is wrong? Why do you think that accepting the Use theory might improve communication of ideas?

Episode 4

"My boss told me yesterday that I should always be careful to get my facts straight before I accused anyone of anything," said Marge Glower.

"I think that's pretty good advice, Marge."

"I agree, Captain Meaning, but the thing that's been bothering me is that I don't know what a fact is."

"You mean you don't know what the word 'fact' means?"

"I guess that's one way of putting it."

"Suppose, then, that I describe a paradigm case for you."

"Fine, but I don't know what a paradigm case is."

"I'll explain that to you first, then."

What explanation and what paradigm case do you give to Marge?

Episode 5

"Captain Meaning, do you mind if a little kid like me asks you a question?"

"Not at all, Jimmy. I try to help everyone I can, and I'm particularly interested in helping children."

"Thanks a lot. What I wanted to know was this. I've heard a lot of kids talking about goblins, and vampires, and werewolves, and stuff like that, and I asked my brother about them. He said they don't exist."

"That's right; they don't."

"It seems to me, though, that they just must exist in some way. Maybe as ideas or something. Because, after all, we've got those words and those words have to stand for something."

"Your're raising a very good point, Jimmy. But let me explain to you how there can be words that we understand that really don't stand for anything."

What is the explanation that you give Jimmy?

3/A Linguistic Armory

BARD Del Zur swung the great blade at the apparition that loomed in the darkened doorway. A great cry of pain and rage rent the fetid air of the burial chamber, but still the creature came toward him. Its leering face revealed yellowed fangs that Bard knew dripped with venom sufficient to lay waste a hundred men.

Bard fought down his panic and got a firm grip on the spiked mace in his right hand. In his left, he gripped the ivory handle of the stiletto given to him by the dying Stornan.

Now the thing was on him! Its scaly claws slashed towards his belly. But before they met their mark, Bard stiffened his mighty thews and crashed the deadly mace into the center of the hideous head. The needle-bladed dagger he slipped under the horny carapace of the skull and cut the vital artery.

The air was heavy now with red mist, and the only sound was the gibbering of the eldritch fiend lying on the littered floor of the chamber.

This melodramatic passage, in the sword-and-sorcery manner, is here to make a relatively simple general point: namely, to protect yourself from the various monsters of language that produce confusion, misunderstanding, indecision, or even deception, it's necessary to outfit yourself with the proper weapons.

Swords, stilettos, and maces are of little use in the battle against bewitchment by language. Even thews as mighty as those of Bard Del Zur are of no help. We need, of course, appropriate weapons, ones fitted to unraveling the snarls of language and providing protection against error. As we move along through the following chapters, we'll be adding various weapons to our armory, but in this chapter we want only to make a small beginning and introduce a few.

In "Wayward Words" we'll turn the searchlight of attention on linguistic vagueness. We'll discuss the conditions under which we generally regard an expression as vague and point out some of the procedures that can be followed to eliminate vagueness when it's important to do so. We'll end with a discussion of chameleon words, words that can be said to be vague whenever they are used.

The next section will diagnose some of the important ways in which language can be ambiguous and illustrate how ambiguity can result in misunderstanding and a failure of communication. Of course we'll accompany this discussion with some advice about how such trouble can be sidestepped.

In "Power Plus" we'll focus on connotations of words and take the opportunity to notice the difference in persuasive power between two passages with the same content but with different loads of connotation.

It's clear from this preview that the weapons we'll be introducing are not things of shining steel or glittering obsidian. They are concepts and distinctions and hints on how to use them. Dull though they may seem, their edges are sharp. They are weapons of the mind, and in the hands of the skilled they will do good service.

Wayward Words (1): Vagueness

Before getting down to the messy business of talking about vagueness and (in the next section) ambiguity, we need to spend a moment making clear just how big a bite we want to take out of this topic. Let's start from left field with another fragment of a story, this time a gothic one:

> Julian hid himself in the shrubbery that grew thick around the ruins of the old abbey. Tense and watchful, he peered past the edge of a moldering lichen-covered stone block through a ragged clearing in the hanging branches of a giant yew tree. The brightness of the full moon allowed him a clear view of the figure standing by the remains of the shattered altar—it was the Countess Mara!
>
> As he watched with in-drawn breath, the Countess made an *ambiguous* gesture with her hand—was she beckoning someone to come or perhaps indicating that he should stay hidden? All at once, as though coming from nowhere, Julian saw a *vague* form looming in the fog that hovered close to the limits of the encircling forest. Julian knew it must be the vampire Charnak. Julian gave an involuntary shudder at the sight of the dread creature.
>
> "You are here at last," the Countess said. "Where have you come from?"
>
> Charnak made no answer, but waved a hand *vaguely* toward the darkness of the east.
>
> All at once the scene grew dim. Julian looked upward and saw that a heavy cloud was moving across the face of the bright moon. It was a peculiar cloud, black and with an *ambiguous* shape. Looked at one way, it resembled a giant bat; another way, a man in a dark cape. Julian shuddered, and moved by a *vague* feeling of uneasiness, he quietly left his hiding place and started back to brooding and decaying Ravenscroft Castle.
>
> *(Never to be continued.)*

In this passage the words "vague" and "ambiguous" (and forms of them) appear several times. They are used to characterize gestures, forms, shapes, and feelings. Typically, in ordinary life, we also use these words to describe attitudes, suspicions, hunches, figures, photographs, drawings, nods of the head, and so on. Since these various kinds of things are not instances of language, we can say that cases like those in the story fragment involve nonlinguistic ambiguity and vagueness.

Our interest, however, is with language. What we want to know can be put quite simply: What does it mean to say that a word, phrase, expression, or sentence is vague or ambiguous? In short, our concern is with *linguistic* vagueness and *linguistic* ambiguity. This is the bite we want to gnaw out of the general topic.

The theory of meaning that we have developed puts us in an excellent position to understand what it is for language to be vague or ambiguous. And in accordance with the practical principle that forewarned is forearmed, such an understanding ought to provide ways of allowing us to detect and be on guard against these agents of confusion. Now let's move on into the dark region of vagueness.

Three people who have been found guilty of a crime are not necessarily all guilty of the same crime. One may be guilty of murder, another of arson, and the third of burglary. Similarly, we shouldn't assume that when we say a word is vague we always mean the same thing. There are at least two distinct and common ways in which a word can legitimately be said to be vague. We'll discuss each; then we'll turn to a special group of words we'll call "chameleon words."

Comparative Vagueness

One of the greatest inventions of our remote and unknown ancestors was *measurement*. We're so accustomed to dealing with minutes, pounds, feet, miles per hour, and so on that it's difficult for us to appreciate what an incredible achievement it was to make use of standard units and to represent measurements in individual cases in number of units.

Measurement is only a form of description, but its advantage is that it allows us to give very precise descriptions. We can say, "The knife blade was six and a half inches long, and it entered the right side of the chest four inches from the midline," rather than "The knife blade was rather long, and it entered the chest somewhere on the right." Since measurements are expressed in numbers, we say that measurement makes it possible to provide *quantitative* descriptions in place of qualitative ones.

Words are sometimes said to be vague, then, when they lack the precision of a quantitative description. More properly, they are said to be vague when they lack quantitative precision *and* they are used in connection with something we generally consider to be measurable or countable.

Consider the following true-to-life episode:

"Now, Mrs. Willis, we would like for you to tell us just what things were like in the ballroom before you heard the groan and saw the Ambassador slump to the floor."

"I'll try, Inspector, but I'm not much good at these things. There were a *bunch* of people crowded around the Ambassador, and *several* of them had drinks in their hands. *Some,* I think, were also smoking."

"Pardon me, Mrs. Willis, but could you be more specific? Exactly how many people were *by* the Ambassador, and just how many had *drinks,* and how many were *smoking?"*

If Mrs. Willis were merely telling an anecdote about the Ambassador to a few friends, the words she uses would probably be thought perfectly acceptable. No one would object that they are vague and ask to have them replaced by numbers. But since the Inspector may have a murder to investigate, he needs more precise information. Just how many people were near enough to do the Ambassador harm? How many might have had a small but poisonous dart concealed in a hollow cigar? How many might have substituted a poisoned drink for the Ambassador's? Clearly enough, the Inspector regards the italicized words as vague because he needs more precise information and, if Mrs. Willis's memory is good enough, it is possible to get it.

Though quantitative descriptions are important, we have to be careful not to sell ordinary language short. It is in numerous ways a very subtle instrument, one that has been developed over the course of centuries to enable us to deal with a wide variety of situations that we encounter in everyday life. Because of this, it can be used to make distinctions and introduce comparisons of various degrees of refinement.

In cases in which measurements expressible in terms of numbers on some sort of scale are unimportant or impossible, we rely on ordinary language in framing descriptions and providing information. Let's take a case in which measurement is not possible and see how everyday language handles it.

Suppose Eurydice asks Orpheus, "How much do you love me?" It just so happens that at the moment we have no way to measure love, so Orpheus can't answer something like "I love you 128 cupids," in the way he might reply "I weigh 175 pounds." But of course Orpheus isn't at a total loss. He can say, quite naturally, "I love you a tremendous amount" ("a great deal," "a lot") or even "I love you very little" ("hardly at all," "not at all").

These sorts of phrases are used to express comparisons. Obviously "a great deal" indicates more love than does "very little," though we have no way of saying just how much more. We often speak of things like love, hate, charm, goodness, beauty, danger, and health as if they were substances that someone can possess in certain amounts. (We talk about them in other ways too, of course.) Despite the fact that we can't give absolute measures of them, we can at least indicate the relative amounts someone may be said to have them. ("She has a great deal of charm," "He has very little health left," etc.) We wouldn't be likely to accuse someone who says "I love her very much" of using a vague expression. That's just one of the ways we have of indicating how much we love someone, and there simply isn't any way of being more precise about such a matter. This is about the best that can be done.

Let's take another kind of case now, one in which measurement is possible but not important. Suppose you're visiting San Francisco for the first time and having a hard time finding your way around. You stop someone on the street and ask, "How far is it to the Golden Gate Park?" You would be absolutely astounded if you were told, "It's 1,508.6 meters from the spot where you're standing."

Now of course someone could give you an answer like this, if he really wanted to go to the trouble to measure the exact distance and you were willing to wait for him to do it. Chances are, though, he wouldn't want to, and chances are that's not the kind of answer you wanted, anyway. All you wanted or needed to know was something like "It's not far" or "It's a hell of a long way from here, better take the bus."

In cases like this, measurement is possible but it's inconvenient and unnecessary. All we need is a rough-and-ready estimate for the purpose at hand. All we want is a general idea of what things are like. For this reason, we aren't ordinarily inclined to regard expressions like "It's quite heavy" or "It's not far" as vague ones. We rely on ordinary expressions to convey to us information that is precise enough for our aims.

If we need more exact information, of course, we can press for it. We might say, "Can you tell me how many blocks that is?" or "About how long will it take me to walk that?" In short, what we take to be vague in connection with things that can be measured or counted depends to a great extent upon our own purposes and needs. If we intend to take a short walk, it's enough to know it's quite cold outside without knowing the exact temperature. But if we want to know whether to pour concrete, which won't set below freezing, then we need more exact information.

Vagueness in Use

The Talmud is a collection of ancient writings that forms the doctrinal basis for traditional Judaism. The first section of the Talmud, the Mishnah, is a record of early oral interpretations of the Scriptures. A part of the Mishnah is devoted to attempts to understand the Scriptural injunction to sacrifice a red heifer.

A major problem faced by the early rabbis in interpreting this injunction can be put in the form of a question: Just when can a heifer be regarded as red?

The word "heifer" presented no particular difficulty. Though we use the word today to refer to any young cow, in its older use it meant, quite specifically, a cow that has not yet given birth to a calf.

It was the word "red" that faced the rabbis with a problem. It was not, of course, that they didn't know when to call certain colors red. There was no difficulty about that. What they didn't know was when to call a *heifer* red.

Put yourself in their position and you'll appreciate something of the seriouness of their situation. Suppose you are quite religious and wholly committed to carrying out the instructions of God presented in the Scriptures. Not only are you personally committed to doing so, but as a leader of your people, you have an obligation to help them follow God's commandments. One of those commandments is that a red heifer is to be sacrificed.

Now the time comes when you and others must select a heifer to be sacrificed. The first cow brought before you is red but has a white blaze on her forehead. The next is predominately red with a few white hairs around the ears. The third brought out is all white except for a small red patch. Which, if any, of these cows is a red heifer? Probably you wouldn't be inclined to choose the third one, but you might be strongly tempted by one or both of the others. Still, if you picked one of them, chances are that one of the people with you would disagree. "How can you call this a red heifer?" someone might say. "Can't you see that streak of white?"

Presumably if a cow were brought in with a coat that contained no other color but red, then everyone would agree that this was a red heifer. And if a cow were brought in with a coat that was totally white, everyone would agree that this was *not* a red heifer. But for various intermixtures of colors between these two extremes it is likely that there would be a considerable amount of disagreement.

Faced with the difficulty of selecting an animal for sacrifice, you would be most likely to decide after a while that the injunction you are supposed to honor is a vague one. It is vague because the phrase "red heifer" is vague.

Let's leave the rabbis and their problem for a moment and consider another superficially similar case. Suppose you are working as a cowhand on the King Ranch and the foreman says to you, "Ride out and round up the red heifers and herd them back here."

"Why red heifers?" you ask.

"No particular reason," the foreman says. "I just need a bunch of heifers to finish up a shipment to Laredo tomorrow, and I figured if I told you to get the red ones that would be one way of deciding which ones to send."

Now in a case like this, what counts as a red heifer isn't really very important. Not much hangs on it. The foreman only wants a procedure to follow, and he might just as well have selected another one. Consequently, it isn't likely that there will be much debate over whether a heifer is red or not. Since it isn't necessary to come back with an exact number, a few heifers more or less don't make any difference. Chances are, then, heifers will be picked that are *more or less red*. Some will be wholly red, others might have blazes or white patches or a few white hairs on their coats. Nobody much cares.

Because nobody much cares, because there isn't much *reason* to care, then it's not very likely that anyone is going to regard the phrase "red heifer" as vague.

Notice how this contrasts with the situation the rabbis face. There, because of religious beliefs and commitments, what counts as a red heifer is an extremely serious problem, one directly connected with obeying a commandment of God. So far as the rabbis are concerned, matters of the greatest consequence hang upon what is and is not a red heifer. Unlike the cowhand, they regard "red heifer" as vague.

The contrast between the two cases puts us in a better position to understand what it is we mean when we say that a word is vague. The first thing that emerges clearly is a recognition of the fact that words are not *inherently* vague. Since the same word may be regarded as vague in one context but not so in another, it's easy to see that vagueness is not a trait that some words have and others lack. It will do us no good, then, to try to draw up a *list* of vague words.

Such an enterprise is doomed to failure from the start. Almost every ordinary nontechnical word would have to appear on the list. Why? Because there is hardly an ordinary word that cannot *in some situation or other* be seen as vague.

On the other hand, there is hardly an ordinary word that cannot *in some situation or other* be regarded as nonvague.

Vagueness, then, does not lie within words, and we would be wasting our time if we attempted to get a rule to allow us to distinguish vague words from nonvague ones. This would be much like trying to get a rule to distinguish carpenters from bricklayers purely in terms of their human traits. Nobody is inherently a carpenter or bricklayer. Rather, the two are distinguished in terms of *what they do*.

Vagueness attaches to words, becomes a property of words, as they are *used* in specific situations. It is the *use* of the word that we call vague, not the word itself. If we want to understand what vagueness is, then, we have to look at situations in which some word or other is said to be vague.

Let's return to the problem the rabbis faced with the expression "red heifer." There are some aspects of the case that are obvious but important. First, so far as they were concerned, it made a great deal of difference whether a cow was called red or not. The difference was one between obeying and disobeying God. Second, they were faced with cases in which they didn't know whether or not to apply the word "red" (to heifers with white spots, and so on). Third, they were aware of the relevant facts about the cows they considered. That is, they could easily tell whether the coats of the cattle had any colors other than red mixed in, how much of some other color there was, and so on.

It's the first aspect of the situation that's the most important. It is the *seriousness* of the matter of deciding, the importance of the consequence of the decision, that led the rabbis into deliberation. It was because of this that they realized they were faced with cases in which they didn't know whether to apply the word "red" and that their doubt couldn't be resolved by getting more facts.

This is sharply different from the situation of the cowhand. There, decision wasn't important, and because it was trivial, there was no need for deliberation. Consequently, there was no agonizing about picking out red heifers and no tendency to regard "red" as vague.

Using these two cases for guidance, we can now give an account of what we mean when we say that the use of a word in a specific situation is vague. (In the situation, we usually say the *word* is vague, and there's nothing wrong with this, as long as it's clear here that it is the *use* of the word that we're talking about.)

A word is used in a vague way when it is used in a situation which has the following characteristics:

1. whether or not the word applies to given cases makes a substantial (as opposed to a trivial) difference;
2. there is doubt or disagreement about whether the word applies to these cases;
3. the doubt or disagreement is not due to the need for more facts about the cases.

A coat that's too warm for the summer may be quite comfortable in the fall. The coat doesn't change; the seasons do. It would be foolish to brand a coat "too warm" without saying under what circumstances it's too warm. It's similarly foolish to brand a word "vague" without explaining the circumstances that make it so.

The three characteristics above allow us to understand what vagueness is and why it occurs. As important as this is, it's only half the story. To stop at this point is like not revealing the murderer at the end of a mystery novel. We need to go on and discuss how vagueness can be eliminated, or at least mitigated, when it crops up.

One of the features of vagueness that we've already noticed puts us in the way of coming up wih a method for dealing with it. The feature is this: it's the borderline cases that are the problem, the gray area that lies between coal black and snow white.

Recall that in the Mishnah case the rabbis had no difficulty deciding that a heifer that was totally red was a red heifer and that one that was totally white (nonred) was not a red heifer. It was the cows falling between these extremes that made them uneasy and uncertain. It was the cows that were more or less red.

Obviously what we must do, then, is to find some way of dealing with borderline cases. This is *the* problem facing anyone who has to resolve a matter in which the vagueness of some expression causes a crucial difficulty.

When it's practical, the most direct way of eliminating vagueness is to ask for clarification. If you were on a school board and received a petition from a parents' group demanding that all *unqualified* teachers be replaced, the most sensible course of action would be to ask the group to be more specific and say just what they mean by "unqualified." Hopefully, they would supply you with a set of standards that could be employed in a rather straightforward way if you agreed to them. For example: A teacher is unqualified who has received no professional training in the subject taught, and so on.

This, of course, puts the problem into the hands of the parents' group, and they must come up with some means of doing away with the vagueness in their original demand. From our standpoint, then, this way of resolving the problem of vagueness is not solved but only shifted. If we imagine ourselves in the parents' group, the problem is still with us.

Also, it is not always possible to throw the hot potato to someone else. We frequently just have to decide for ourselves how to deal with vagueness in a particular situation. The rabbis, for example, were on their own. God had told them to sacrifice a red heifer, but He was unavailable for comment on just when a heifer could be considered red.

How, then, can we put ourselves in a position to handle borderline cases? The answer is easy in the abstract but hard in the concrete: *We must come up with a set of explicit criteria that will serve as guides for making decisions in doubtful or disputed cases.*

The Mishnah records that in the red heifer case, five different traditions of interpretation grew up. These traditions held that a heifer is red when:

1. one hair is red;
2. some hairs are red;
3. a majority of hairs are red;
4. most (i.e., virtually all) hairs are red;
5. all hairs are red.

Anyone who accepted one of these traditions would be in an easy position to decide when a heifer is red. Doubt and uncertainty, debate and disagreement would all dissipate in the cold light of clarity. Anyone who was not colorblind and could count could make decisions.

There is nothing to applying such straightforward criteria. The trick is in deciding upon them. Is there anything useful that can be said about the business of establishing criteria to turn vagueness into relative clarity?

A quick answer to this question is, yes. But the answer has to be followed by the admission that there are no mechanical rules or procedures to follow. The fact that *five* different criteria were proposed in the rabbinical tradition and that each had its defenders teaches us a lesson: There is no guaranteed way of securing agreement to criteria that are proposed. This is not too surprising, of course, for in all matters reasonable people can differ, even when they have the same aims and have access to the same relevant facts.

But just because there is no automatic and guaranteed procedure for getting criteria doesn't mean that the enterprise is not worthwhile or that nothing helpful can be said about it. In cases in which vagueness holds sway, it is in fact the only hope, and that makes it quite an important topic to discuss. So here we go.

To solve the mystery of getting criteria, we must search the situation in which the problem of borderline cases arises. The clues lie in the answers to questions that, at first sight, seem to have no more to do with eliminating vagueness than does the size of apples in Minneapolis. Here are the questions:

1. What goal or purpose do we want to achieve that requires us to make decisions about whether the word applies?
2. What are the results of applying a proposed criterion likely to be?
3. How willing are we to accept those results?

Let's consider the use that can be made of these questions in deciding upon criteria by looking at an example.

Suppose you are the one in the parents' group who has been given the responsibility for eliminating the vagueness of "unqualified." Once the vagueness has been overcome, then the school board can act on the demand that unqualified teachers be dismissed from the school system.

The situation you are in is one in which some teachers are clearly outstanding—obviously qualified—but many are not. Your purpose (Question 1) is to get rid of teachers who are, in some way or other, unfit for their jobs. This doesn't mean you want to keep only the outstanding teachers. You're willing to keep the competent, perhaps even the mediocre, ones as well. You want to get rid of the really incompetent. But how do you draw the line in borderline cases?

The answer is, make use of criteria. Many possible criteria can be considered and tested by means of answers to the three questions.

For example, you might try: "A teacher who has not written and published a book is unqualified." This is obviously a highly stringent criterion, and the consequences of applying it (the answer to Question 2) are likely to be that you will eliminate as unqualified almost all the teachers in the school system. The criterion might eliminate all those you consider to be borderline cases, but it would also be likely to eliminate many of those you consider to be outstanding.

Are you willing to accept this consequence (Question 3)? Probably not. A criterion that practically wipes out the school system and eliminates teachers regarded as outstanding is clearly not a criterion you would want to employ. Indeed, the fact that it eliminates excellent teachers along with others raises the question as to whether having written a book is sufficiently connected with being a qualified teacher to make the criterion appropriate in terms of your purpose.

Another, weaker criterion seems in order. Perhaps one like this: "A teacher who has not had professional training, or its equivalent, in the subject taught is unqualified." What are the results of this? This can be answered only in an actual situation, of course. Presumably the basketball coach who teaches history but has never had any education in history would be branded unqualified. If he teaches physical education, in which he has had training, then he would not be classed as unqualified. The general consequence of such a criterion would be to eliminate teachers who could not show that they have been trained in the subjects they teach. This seems to be an acceptable consequence, and it is one in keeping with the purpose of making the distinction between qualified and unqualified in the first place.

To some extent, the criterion shifts the problem. After all, a criterion has to be applied. Now the focus is on "professional training or its equivalent," rather than "unqualified."

But there is nothing objectionable about this. Indeed, there is usually something downright satisfactory. The problem of "unqualified" is really much harder to deal with than the expression "professional training or its equivalent." We've *simplified* a difficult problem. Teachers who have degrees or certificates, have taken special courses, attended institutes or been students in teacher-training programs could all be considered to have professional training or its equivalent. If there is difficulty in deciding when this phrase applies, then the same questions relevant to the general problem can be asked here and criteria to resolve its application can be formulated.

It might seem that there is no end to the problem of getting criteria to apply expressions to cases. We try to eliminate a vague expression by formulating criteria and then find we must have criteria to apply the criteria, and then, who knows, criteria to apply even then. We seem to be in the position of having to open up Chinese boxes forever. It's true that *in principle* the process could go on without end. But in practice it really never does. We eventually (usually) reach a point at which we agree that the words in which certain criteria are formulated are clear enough to apply, and starting from this point, we build upward until whatever vague expression that was causing us trouble loses its grip on us.

We have now inched our way through some difficult terrain. We have learned to identify uses that are vague in given situations and considered how to eliminate vagueness by employing three questions that serve as guides in the search for criteria. To complete our discussion of vagueness, we need only take a look at a peculiar group of words that we'll call "chameleon words."

Chameleon Words

In the golden age of radio mysteries, Mr. Chameleon was a detective who was "the master of a thousand disguises." With his faithful assistant Mike Clancey, Mr. Chameleon was able to use his skills at disguise to track down criminals who might otherwise have escaped paying the full penalties of the law.

Languages contain a number of words that, like Mr. Chameleon, can wear various disguises. They can be different things to different people and take on their meanings from the groups that employ them. Has it ever struck you as strange that virtually every country in the world—even Communist ones—applies the word "democratic" to its government?

Since these governments include absolute monarchies, parliamentary monarchies, representative republics, and military dictatorships, this is strong evidence that the word "democratic" is a chameleon word. When people in Canada, Australia, Great Britain, and the United States consider the word "democratic" or "democracy," they generally have in mind governments of a representative kind, ones in which the wishes and wants of the people are expressed by elected officials. Yet when Arab sheiks and the heads of banana republics apply the words to their own countries and governments, they explain that for them democracies are countries in which the interests of the people are served. And of course both of these notions are a far cry from the democracy of the ancient Greeks, which demanded direct participation in decision making by all eligible citizens.

Mr. Chameleon had an identity of his own. It was the one he assumed when he was not wearing one of his thousand disguises. But chameleon words have no identity separate from their disguises. They are what they are made to be by the users of the words.

To put the point less fancifully, we might say that *chameleon words are ones which have no generally accepted conditions governing their use.* There are no examples, then, that will be universally accepted as paradigm cases of their use. Strange as it may seem, there are those who would deny that the United States is a democracy. It is not so strange, of course, that most people in the United States would deny that countries in which rulers have absolute power are democracies. It's as hard to find a country that everybody would agree is a democracy as it is to find a person who everyone would agree is virtuous.

Of course we need not look across the world to find chameleon words. There are plenty of them in our own backyard. Consider those favorites "radical", "liberal," and "conservative." The John Birch Society is very likely to use these words in ways that don't exactly parallel the uses by the *New York Times,* and yet a third set of uses is likely to be found in the writings of the Peace and Freedom Party. A politician or position the Young Americans for Freedom regards as radical will probably be regarded as liberal or conservative by the Progressive Labor Party.

Political terms form the richest lode that can be mined for examples of chameleon words, because politics is, after all, a slippery business. But chameleon words are found in other areas of discourse also. Consider the word "pornography". As used in the pulpit of the First Church of the Solid Rock of the Pentecost, the word is likely to apply to items as diverse as a Bob Hope television special and the film *Animal Lust.* Some people will use the word to refer to films and writings that glory in violence, while others won't apply it to anything at all.

A lot of other words have the same characteristics of gaining the substantial part of their meaning from the person or group that uses them. Consider these, for example: insane, irreligious, un-American, responsible, republic, philosophy, reasonable, logical.

It would be nice if there were some sure and certain sign by means of which chameleon words could be recognized in order that pointless disputes could be avoided and misunderstandings could be averted. Unfortunately, there is no such way. There is, that is, no test procedure that can be employed.

But here, as in life in general, experience is not without its rewards. Anyone who reads carefully and listens critically will, after a time, get to be familiar with a number of words that are chameleon words. Several of them are listed here, and probably most anyone can add to the list. He will feel his nostrils flare at the scent of danger and be ready to ask questions like "Just what sort of thing do you consider to be pornographic?"

Questions such as this are the only appropriate response to situations in which chameleon words play a role of importance. The user must be asked to supply us with the conditions he takes to govern the use of the word. He must, that is, supply us with what he considers an appropriate definition of the word.

When he has done this, we at least know where he stands and can talk with him in a rational fashion. When he has done this, we are in a position to understand what he says. Before this time, we're only guessing.

We might be in a position in which we have to do more than understand, however. If someone is about to mount a campaign against pornography and wants our support, then we might understand what he is saying but wish to convince him that he shouldn't carry out his campaign. We might try to do this by attempting to convince him that the meaning he attributes to "pornography" is too broad and has unacceptable consequences. That is, we might wish to deal with the word "pornography" as a vague word.

When there is reason to do this, when the issue goes beyond mere understanding and becomes one that we regard as important, then we deal with the chameleon word in the same way as we deal with words that are vague in a crucial use. That is, we make use of the weapons that we forged earlier in this section.

Wayward Words (2): Ambiguity

The word "ambiguous" is derived from the Latin for "wandering about," and it has a present meaning still reminiscent of its origins. *An expression is ambiguous when it can be understood in more than one way, and we aren't certain which way is intended.* Like a rat faced with multiple choices in a maze, we wander about between alternatives, unsure of the proper path.

That is what we do when we *detect* the ambiguity. It is just as likely that we will march down a single path because we wrongly believe it to be the only one. Since it may or may not be the one intended, there is a possibility that we will fall into the pit of misunderstanding at the end of the road.

Expressions can open up the paths of ambiguity in different ways, and by focusing on these ways, we can identify some distinct types of ambiguity. We'll consider three major kinds, but this does not necessarily mean there are not more. A gimlet eye and an ardent desire to make distinctions would probably uncover several other types. Yet these three will be quite enough for ordinary purposes of avoiding confusion and greasing the skids of communication.

Word Ambiguity

A standard definition goes like this: "A word is ambiguous when it has more than one meaning." This definition isn't exactly wrong, but it isn't all that right, either. It belongs in the same class as "Man is a featherless biped," about which we want to say, "Well, yes, but . . . ."

The trouble with the definition is that almost every word has more than one meaning. To find a word with *exactly* one meaning just about requires hunting through technical and scientific dictionaries. Take an everyday word like "line," for example. It doesn't take much reflection to come up with several meanings for it: fishing cord, a mark, an arrangement of troops, a string of print, an item in a budget, a winch-cable, and so on.

Most words have multiple meanings, and it's not very helpful to regard them all as ambiguous. We want to save "ambiguous" as a label for cases in which words can generate uncertainty, puzzlement, or confusion of a certain sort. What we need, then, is a more precise definition of "ambiguity" as applied to words and phrases, a definition that will permit us to detect or avoid problem situations.

The best approach, perhaps, is to start with a case in which a word causes confusion of the kind we're concerned with. Suppose you have your first job as a teacher, and whether you are rehired or not depends in part on the responses on the student evaluation forms. One of the items on the form reads: "Instructor uses enough illustrations."

As you read the results on this, you become puzzled. You were quite careful to present numerous examples and clarifying materials in your explanations in class, but you discover that a substantial number of students say that you used no illustrations at all. But suddenly you get a clue as to what is wrong. One student has written in the comment space: "Some portraits and diagrams would help a lot." This same student has checked the box saying you used no illustrations.

What has happened, of course, is that you (and probably some students) took the word "illustrations" to mean "examples, analogies, and clarifying material," whereas many in the class took the word to mean "visual representations, such as drawings, diagrams, and photographs."

Obviously, the responses to this item are not a reliable indicator of whether you used enough examples in class. The ambiguity of "illustrations" has destroyed the value of the question and weakened the usefulness of the entire evaluation.

As this example makes clear, *an expression is ambiguous when it has more than one meaning* and *it is used in a situation or context in which it can be understood in at least two ways.*

Ambiguity, then, is not a mark of Cain that words must forever bear for having more than a single meaning. It is, rather, an outcome or result. Ambiguity is *produced* by using certain words in certain situations. There is no way of telling from the sentence "Instructor uses enough illustrations" on the evaluation form just what meaning of "illustrations" is intended.

Because ambiguity is something that is produced by using words and is not an inherent trait of words, this means that it simply isn't possible to draw up a list of words under the heading "ambiguous" and warn everyone to be on the lookout for them. What we have to do, instead, is to develop an attitude of caution and to acquire the skill needed to *detect* ambiguity when it does occur.

Word ambiguity is not really a major problem of communication, and to some extent it has traditionally received a bum rap. It's not responsible for nearly as much confusion and misunderstanding as is vagueness and general incoherence (see the section "Through a Glass Darkly" in Chapter 10). The reason it does not cause more trouble is just because the contexts in which we use words are almost always adequate to indicate exactly which meaning we intend of several possible ones. Try a simple experiment. Try to think of situations in which the words "bank" and "bark" can be used ambiguously. It can be done, but it's rather difficult. Writers of logic books always nod their heads wisely when warning of the dangers of ambiguity, but they hardly ever come up with genuine and serious cases.

This is not to deny that there *are* such cases, however. Our first example is a serious case, and we can wind up this discussion by considering another one.

Suppose you are the director of a local program that is funded by the Department of Health, Education, and Welfare. You receive a notice that all HEW programs have been subjected to a periodic review and that some have been terminated. Yours is being continued, but the letter informs you

> Your program will be supported at the present level of funding during the next five fiscal years.

Just what does "present level of funding" mean here? There are at least two clear possibilities:

1. the program will receive exactly the same number of dollars for the next five years as it received for the present year;
2. the program will be kept operating in the same way over the next five years as it is operating now.

There is an important difference between these two possible understandings. The first says, in effect, that an absolute limit on the amount of money received will be set. Should inflation continue, this would amount to a budget cut. The second can be read as promising more actual money than is presently being received, if the money is needed to offset increasing expenses and keep the program going in its current manner.

It is this sort of ambiguous case that people get into fights about.

Referential Ambiguity

Croesus, the last king of Lydia, decided in 546 B.C. to extend his kingdom into Persia. Being a careful man and wishing to know his chances of success, he consulted the oracle at Delphi for advice. Should he go to war with Persia or not? The oracle is supposed to have told him:

> If you cross the river Halys, you will destroy a mighty empire.

Croesus interpreted this as a good omen and advanced his troops across the river and into Persia. But he was taken by surprise at the city of Sardis by the army of Cyrus the Great, the king of Persia. The Persian forces easily defeated the Lydians; Croesus was taken prisoner by Cyrus and narrowly escaped death by burning. The great kingdom of Lydia ceased to exist.

The oracle had been right. By going to war with Persia, Croesus destroyed a mighty empire—his own.

The truth is, of course, the oracle would also have been right had Croesus defeated the Persians. The phrase "mighty empire" in the prophecy can be taken to refer either to Lydia or to Persia. Had Croesus been shrewder or less intent on his own purpose, he might have noticed that the oracle failed to make clear what empire was being discussed. The prophecy is a case of *referential ambiguity*, and Croesus was its victim.

Referential ambiguity, as the name indicates, occurs when an expression is used in such a way that it can be understood as referring to or picking out more than one person, place, class, situation, and so on. The expression seems to select just one thing, but it actually selects more than one.

Most common cases of referential ambiguity arise from taking expressions that require a context to make their reference clear and using them without adequately specifying or indicating that context. Pronouns (*I, you, he, they, it, she,* and so on), in particular, depend upon the situation—who is talking to whom about what—to make their reference unambiguous. If you read in *The Chicken Farmer's Monthly,* "We need to decrease our egg production to get higher profits," you know the "we" here is the chicken farmers.

Suppose, though, you are at a party and a police officer comes to the door and takes a quick look around. She talks with the hostess a moment. As she starts to leave, she says quite loudly, "You have to show up at the city detention center within two hours, or I'll be back with help." Does the "you" refer to the hostess only or to all those present? There is no way to tell from the sentence alone. The officer failed to indicate in any way just which of the two possibilities she intends.

Words having to do with time are also responsible for generating ambiguities in reference. Obviously, words like "today," "tomorrow," "yesterday," "in an hour," "a week ago," and so on have to be used in connection with a given time (a *base* time) in order to be understood as intended. A failure to be clear on the base time produces confusion about just what other period is being referred to. This kind of ambiguity is so familiar to all of us that it's not worth illustrating.

One last example is enough to illustrate that referential ambiguity can lead to serious trouble. During the Senate Watergate Hearings on Presidential Campaign Procedures in 1973, James McCord, one of the participants in the burglary of Democratic National Headquarters, claimed that he had been told that the break-in had been approved by "very high authority." McCord testified that he took this phrase to refer to the President or to someone close to the President and that, had he not believed this, he would not have carried out the burglary. But the President and those around him denied that they had ever authorized the Watergate burglary. And others testified that the phrase did not refer to the President and his associates but to high officials not connected with the White House in any way.

It's clear that the context could have been better specified for McCord to eliminate any chance of referential ambiguity. To do that, of course, would have meant a loss of "deniability" for whoever did give the instructions.

Grammatical Ambiguity

The crowd around the booth was tightly packed, but Martha Cervenski pushed her way to the counter. "Take a chance in a raffle for ten cents," the sign said, and Martha passed her money across the counter and got a number in return.

The wheel spun. "Number 248," the operator called out. "Right here!" Martha shouted, pushing up front again to claim her prize.

"Here you are," the operator said. He handed her a dime.

Later, on reflection, Martha decided the experience had been worthwhile. It had taught her to read more carefully.

The sentence "Take a chance in a raffle for ten cents" is a case of grammatical ambiguity. Grammatical ambiguity occurs when a sentence is put together in such a fashion that it can be understood in more than one way. Martha presumably understood the sentence to mean (1) Ten cents buys a chance in this raffle. But it can also be understood as meaning (2) The prize in this raffle is ten cents. (The operator can make use of both of these meanings and charge ten cents for a chance in a raffle in which the prize is ten cents.)

This illustration is something in the nature of a joke, but grammatical ambiguity can produce confusion of a serious kind, also.

Suppose you are the defense attorney for Gertrude Flavia, who has been charged with the murder of Carl Agel. To prepare your case, you read the police report on the incident and meet with the following sentence:

> Flavia started down the stairs with Muhlenburg behind her, yelling, "I'm going to kill that bastard Agel."

The first thing you notice is that the sentence is ambiguous. Read one way, it seems to say that Flavia was doing the yelling. Read another way, it seems to say that Muhlenburg was doing the yelling.

As a defense attorney for Flavia, you will, of course, want to construe the sentence in the second way. If Muhlenburg was threatening to kill Agel, this will help make it unlikely that Flavia killed him. The prosecutor will want to construe the sentence as saying that Flavia was yelling the threat, for this will help strengthen his case against Flavia.

Who would be right, you or the prosecutor?

There is simply no way to answer this question on the basis of the sentence alone. The grammatical structure of the sentence makes it impossible to declare that one understanding of the sentence is correct and the other wrong. There is a sense in which *both* understandings are right. That is, the sentence can be *understood* in more than one way. This does not mean, of course, that both Flavia and Muhlenburg were yelling. It means that the sentence doesn't tell us which one was.

Other parts of the report may provide help in deciding which way the sentence is supposed to be taken, and the author of the report may testify about what he intended to say when he wrote the sentence. It is only information of this kind that will allow us to decide which version of the sentence correctly describes the actual state of affairs.

The ambiguity in this example is due to a grammatical error (a dangling participle, to be specific). That is, the problem is caused by a departure from standard English grammar. But not all grammatical ambiguity is produced by mistakes in grammar. (Nor do all mistakes in grammar produce ambiguity.)

Suppose that a representative of the Millionaire, a man known for his generosity to ordinary mortals, rings your doorbell. He introduces himself and says: "On the condition that you not reveal the source, I am prepared to give the sum of one million dollars to you and to your husband." The grammar here is impeccable, but the ambiguity is obvious. Is the representative presenting one million dollars to *each* of you (for a total of two million) or is the sum for *both* of you. If you want to know for sure, you must ask.

Grammatical ambiguity is most often the result of carelessness and inattention, rather than deliberate deception. Nevertheless, its effects are the same, whatever the motive: puzzlement, error, and confusion.

Special: Two for the Price of One: Ambiguity *and* Vagueness

By the look of things that have gone before, we have drawn a diamond-etched line to separate the sheep of ambiguity from the goats of vagueness. The two have been made to seem as different as earth and sky or night and day.

But even the wise deserve a word of caution here. Earth and sky meet at the horizon, and night and day converge at dawn. Similarly, there are cases that can be viewed as ones *either* of vagueness *or* of ambiguity or *both*. It all depends on where you perceive the greatest problem to be and so how you want to crumble the cookie.

Suppose you are reading a book on Greek culture and you run into a passage like this:

Intellectual life in Athens in the fourth century B.C. was outstandingly active. Aristotle wrote on biology, meteorology, physics, logic, ethics, and numerous other topics. Other Athenians produced books on such practical matters as farming and raising children properly.

After reading this passage, you might say that the last sentence involves word ambiguity. The "books" in that sentence can be understood in at least two different ways:

1. collections of handwritten or printed pages fastened together and bound between protective covers;
2. literary compositions of any sort.

Under ordinary circumstances, you simply would not care which of these meanings is the intended one. Suppose, though, that you are hard at work on a history of book manufacturing. In such a case it *would* make a difference whether the author of the passage meant only that the Greeks composed literary works or whether he meant they produced bound volumes. It's not possible to tell from the passage just which understanding is intended.

Let's suppose the writer goes on to say that "These writings were passed from hand to hand and the wealthy collected them in private libraries." This seems to straighten out the problem of ambiguity, for they were passing *something* from hand to hand. Now does what they were passing around qualify as a book in the first sense given above?

You could say, in this connection, that the word "book" is a vague word. That is, you might know about the physical objects with literary compositions written on them and still not know whether or not to call them books. If, for example, you had to draft a law governing the importation of books from foreign countries, would the productions of the ancient Greeks fall within the scope of the law? Let's assume they were bunches of handwritten sheepskin pages tied together with leather thongs. Are they books? Obviously you would have to develop criteria to deal with cases like this.

In this example we have pointed to a case of ambiguity and showed how, when it is resolved, a case of vagueness may pop up. Well it might be that the ambiguity would never have occurred to you were you not interested in book manufacturing, and only the case of vagueness would have been important. Or it might be that the vagueness would never had been an issue had you not had to draft a law about book imports. And the truth is that unless there is some special interest that is directing your attention and focusing your thoughts, the sentence containing "books" would not be taken to be either vague or ambiguous.

Power Plus: Connotation and Denotation

There are more snares in language than vagueness and ambiguity. Everybody knows that words are not just neutral counters that we push around in the game of communication. Rather, most words are freighted with attitudes and prejudices and loaded with psychological associations. By our choice of words we often, consciously or unconsciously, reveal our approval or disapproval, our admiration or envy, our distaste or delight. Someone who refers to a person as an "old maid" and not as an "unmarried woman" suggests, by the words he uses, that there is something faintly ridiculous or pitiful about the person referred to.

Furthermore, the words we choose to apply to things often serve to connect those things to a web of psychological associations. We come to think of those things in the same way that we think of whatever is associated with them. Different words might produce different associations and so different ways of thinking. Anyone who refers to Hugo Gernsback as "the father of modern science fiction," is obviously encouraging us to think of him in the same respectful (appreciative?) way that fathers are supposed to be thought of. On the other hand, someone who refers to Gernsback as "the first czar of modern science fiction" obviously would like for us to think of him in the harsh way we reserve for dictators.

The constellations of attitudes and associations that swirl around the words we use are generally referred to as the *connotations* of the words. By contrast, that to which the word is applied in a given case is often spoken of as the *denotation* of the word. (These definitions are relatively loose and reflect the use of the terms in literary criticism, where there is a particular need to talk about connotations. The terms have a different and more precise technical meaning in logic, but this is something we don't have reason to deal with here.)

Given this distinction between connotation and denotation, it's easy to see how it is possible for two expressions to have radically different connotations while having the same denotation. Compare these two sentences:

> The legislature restored the death penalty.
> The legislature resurrected the death penalty.

"Restored" is a relatively neutral word, though it does have a slight air of approval about it. "Resurrected," on the other hand, is not neutral at all. It suggests images of graves being opened that ought to be left closed and of the dead being brought back to life. Anyone who chooses "resurrected" over "restored" is obviously going out of his way to indicate his disapproval of the legislature's action. Yet inasmuch as both words can be said to apply to the act of deciding to include the death penalty in laws specifying the punishment for certain crimes, they may both be said to have the same denotation.

Cases like this example make it clear why informal logic should be poking around in corners that are usually the province of English teachers and literary critics. The choice of words, as we've seen, can be used to convey attitudes and suggest associations. But words can also *influence* attitudes and opinions. By encouraging a reader (or listener) to think about a topic in a certain way—the way conveyed by the connotations of words—someone who is presenting a claim or just offering a description is well on the road to getting his audience to accept his point of view.

Informal logic is concerned, among other things, with persuasion—with the acceptance of claims or attitudes. More specifically, it is concerned with *rational* persuasion: that is, with persuasion that consists in gaining agreement by the force of reasons and evidence. There is a morality of persuasion, just as there is a morality of living.

Since language plays the major role in persuasion, it's important to be aware of some of the ways in which it can be used in an unfair or unjustified way. In discussing fallacies we'll have the opportunity to point out some of the specific ways in which deception or error can occur in language used to persuade. Here, though, we need only notice in a general way that the choice of expressions can play a role in influencing attitudes and beliefs. We want merely to recognize how it is that the way in which something is said not only conveys information about the attitude of the one who says it, but also potentially exerts an influence on his audience. An awareness of the possibility of such an influence is like eating a spoonful of butter before drinking a pint of whiskey. It might not keep you from getting drunk, but it helps slow down the process.

So far we've talked about connotation as attaching to particular words. But of course connotations of words in a passage of prose are all likely to hang together and form a net supporting the general point of view expressed in the passage. Each word will have its own connotations, but the connotations of many of the words will be of the same sort.

Along the lines of the connotation-denotation distinction, we can make another distinction between what we'll call the *connotative content* and the *asserted content.* The connotative content is the network of psychological associations and attitudes of approval or disapproval, envy or admiration, and so on that accompanies a piece of prose. The asserted content is the set of claims or assertions made in the passage.

Just as it's possible for two words to have very different connotations and the same denotation, it's possible for two written or spoken passages to have different connotative content and the same asserted content.

From the point of view of logic, our basic interest is in asserted content. We are concerned with claims that are made and with the reasons or evidence (or lack of them) that are put forward to support those claims. Evil is frequently more interesting than good, and from the standpoint of style, the asserted content of a passage is generally far less pleasant to read after it has been (more or less) separated from the connotative content. The advantage gained, though, is that the claims advanced in the passage then stand naked and exposed. It is then possible to ask yourself whether you are justified in accepting them. The danger that powerful and psychologically persuasive language will lead you to agree with what you might not really want to accept is lessened.

Before saying more about connotative and asserted content, let's take a look at a case in which most of the connotative content is removed and the residue of asserted content left.

FROM: Future Tense Public Relations, Inc.
TO: Mr. Abraham Lincoln, White House, Washington, D.C.
SUBJECT: Possible Improvements in the So-called Gettysburg Address

Dear Abe,
   I was sorry to hear that your little talk in Pa. didn't go so hot. Quite frankly, after reading a big chunk of it, I can't say that I'm all that surprised. (I hope

you don't mind me getting to the bottom line right off.) It's a good thing you decided to go into politics and not something where writing talent counts!

Anyway, a bunch of us have been kicking your speech around to see what we could come up with before you let it be published. (That's where you're going to get your biggest audience, after all, so you don't have to feel so bad about not impressing the yokels in Pa.) We think the speech is fundamentally sound, but it needs a little punching up here and there. Also, a few changes in wording would do wonders to help win people over to your side.

I don't want to go through the whole thing without getting an okay from you. So we thought we'd just give you a gander at our revision of the first paragraph to see if you would buy it. Give us the word, and we'll push on.

I had better quote the first paragraph for you. You might not remember it, and since you sent us that envelope, you probably don't have a copy for yourself. Here it is:

Four score and seven years ago our fathers brought forth on this continent a new nation, conceived in liberty, and dedicated to the proposition that all men are created equal.

Now, Abe, I really don't know what you hope to gain from being so long-winded. Why "four score and seven years"? Why not just come right out and say 87 years? I guess that long phrase has a certain grandeur and makes it sound like the country has been around a long time, but it's so cumbersome. Be short and snappy is the rule I follow.

Also, the business about our "fathers." Now you know as well as I do that there aren't going to be very many people who read your speech with fathers (literally speaking) who participated in the Revolutionary War. As a figure of speech, I guess "fathers" is all right, but it seems to me to suggest a closer relationship than the facts warrant. Probably you can leave the word out and make the point another way.

Along those same lines, I'm not sure "conceived" is the word you want. It certainly means something like "thought up," but it also suggests something along the lines of "giving birth." You know what I mean, fathers and mothers conceive children. Why don't we just call them "founders?"

Why do you want to say "brought forth"? This makes it sound like those old guys were godlike and summoned the new nation into existence in the way that Jehovah parted the Red Sea. Don't you think "founded" or "started" would be better? (By the way, I think "nation" is really a good word to use.)

"Dedicated" might be too strong a word here. It suggests, after all, a very strong commitment. Maybe we just ought to say that the founders were committed to certain views. (As you can see, I don't like "proposition" either. It sounds like it stands for something too definite.)

The last part of the sentence I don't like very much at all. Let me tell you why. For one thing, "created" has theological overtones I think you might want to avoid for political reasons. Besides, what you really want to say is that people begin life as equals. (Knowing you, I suspect you also want to say they stay that way. Me, I'm not so sure.) Another thing, I don't know where you stand on this issue, but if you want to keep the women's lib people happy, you might try avoiding "men" as a substitute for "people."

Well, I could go on, but I think I've said enough to give you a fairly good idea of the sort of rewrite we would do for you. The first paragraph, the way we would do it, goes like this:

This nation was founded 87 years ago. The founders believed that all people should be free and equal.

Like it? I betcha do. Notice that nothing of any substance is lost. The content is practically identical with your (pardon me) long-winded and high-flown sentence.

Give us a sign and we'll do the rest for you.

Yours truly,

Burton B. B. Halls

Burton B. B. Halls,
Vice-President

As crass as Halls's letter may seem and as unexciting as his results may be, he is right about one thing: the asserted content of his paragraph is essentially the same as that of the Gettysburg Address. What has been cut out, of course, is the "poetry," the rich and evocative vocabulary of the original. What's left are the two basic assertions of the first paragraph of the address. Dull and dry as the new pagagraph is, it represents just what needs to be done in any passage of prose when there is a question about what is asserted in the passage. In chasing truth, logic must sometimes leave beauty behind.

Is the new paragraph free of connotation? Not really. Nearly all words have some connotation—with the exception of words like "all" and "is" and "the," words that are used to form words into sentences. Consequently, the distinction between connotative content and asserted content is not really one that can be fully realized in practice. It is, at best, an ideal.

In practice, the aim must be to restate passages in words that are as neutral as can be found. Care must be taken, of course, not to betray the asserted content. That is, it would be incorrect to change the claims in a passage in an attempt to reduce the connotative content.

Of course, none of this need be done unless you are concerned with identifying the claims that are made and with evaluating the basis for them. (If you don't want to eat, you can die of starvation.)

There is an additional aspect of connotation that is quite important and worth paying close attention to. Its importance really goes beyond the somewhat narrow interests of informal logic. It's not going too far to say that it concerns living a moral and rational life.

Language, like banks and Fourth of July celebrations, is a social institution. Words acquire their meaning from the ways in which they are used in the society. But they also acquire their connotations from the society. Accordingly, many words have come to embody the prejudices and attitudes that are implicit in the society.

Words like "dago," "nigger," and "kike" are obviously ones that do more than simply pick out people. They are words that drip with the acid of contempt, hatred, or derision. No one would ever think they are neutral, and anyone who chose to use them would be deliberately expressing such an attitude.

There are other words, though, that have connotations that are only dimly recognized as bearing the prejudices of the society itself. Some of these clearly embody attitudes about the proper role of women. As we've already noticed, for example, the expression "old maid" suggests a person who is somewhat ridiculous or pitiful. The word "bachelor" has no such connotation. Indeed, it is often used to express admiration for someone free of family responsibility who is gallant and dashing. Society's attitude is clear in these two cases: women ought to be married, and men who can escape it are lucky and admirable.

Similarly, the words "queer" or "fruit," as applied to homosexuals, do much more than simply identify individuals whose sexual interests or practices differ from those of the general population. They express a social attitude of superior contempt and (particularly the latter) suggest that any person they apply to is somewhat laughable.

Developing a sensitivity to the unwarranted attitudes and prejudices that are built into the connotations of some words is important from both a moral and intellectual point of view. It is one way of becoming aware of beliefs that are taken for granted in a society, and awareness is, of course, a necessary step in subjecting the beliefs to a critical examination. Anyone who is not willing to inherit his beliefs in the same blind way that he inherits the color of his eyes must be prepared to recognize what society is asking him to accept in providing him with a language.

If there are words that we regard as prejudicial or as offensive, either in themselves or because of their connotations, then we are free to avoid their use. In fact, we are perhaps obligated not to use them. Furthermore, we ought to encourage others not to use them.

Is it really true that women who don't marry ought to be regarded as pitiful and ought to be made to suffer the disapproval of society? Anyone who answers yes to this question has the job of showing why we should accept his claim. Anyone who answers no should avoid using the expression "old maid." No matter what the answer is, however, everyone ought to become aware of the fact that beliefs of this sort are often unconsciously endorsed merely by the use of words that have such connotations.

Exercises

Conversations with a Sophist

I generally don't go to Twelfth Street, because it isn't a pleasant neighborhood. Several of the buildings have been blinded by boards nailed across the windows, and in a few places there are only piles of broken bricks to mark where apartment houses once stood. Everyone who can has moved to the better neighborhood to the north.

There's a shop there, though, that sells Indian spices, and every now and then I journey down to replenish my supply of fenugreek, asafetida, and star anise. I'm glad there's a reason for me to go, otherwise I never would have happened on the Sophist.

I never found out his name. "Just call me the Sophist," he told me, "because I love verbal tricks and deceptions the way some people love the truth."

The Sophist's shop was right next door to the Indian grocery, so I could hardly avoid seeing it. I suppose only curiosity, though, led me inside. The sign hanging above the door was hand-lettered with red paint on a white background and gave no clue to the sort of thing you might expect to find inside. I thought it was just one of those cute names like "The Last Tomato" or "Noah's Bark" that gift and antique stores seem addicted to.

No such thing. The sign said "Sophist," and inside was the Sophist.

"I'll make you an offer," the Sophist said, just as I stepped inside the door. "I'll try to convince you of a claim that you know to be absurd, and if you can explain to me in a satisfactory way what's wrong with my reasoning, then I'll pay you a dollar."

"What's the catch?"

"The only catch is if you can't give a satisfactory explanation, then you pay me a dollar. Do you agree?"

"Will I have to have any special scientific knowledge or something like that?"

"Not at all. All you need to know is the English language and the sort of general things that everybody knows. I don't mind telling you, all my tricks are verbal ones that hinge upon ambiguities. Telling you that only establishes the rules for today's game. At some other time I'll introduce you to some other tricks."

That first day I lost five dollars, but I went back several times afterwards. After a month or so I reached a point at which I was breaking even or losing at most only a couple of dollars.

Things got much harder when the Sophist started using all sorts of fallacies and sophistries. I'll tell more about them later. Right now, I'm going to present here some of the verbal tricks that the Sophist used on me at our first meeting. See how you would have done if you had been in my position. You don't stand to lose any money, at least you don't here. But who knows, you might have occasion to meet the Sophist yourself someday.

(1)

"Now," said the Sophist, "I'm going to convince you that you are on the other side of town."

"That's ridiculous; I'm right here, and if I'm right here I can't be on the other side of town."

"Listen a moment. You're on Twelfth Street, I'm sure you'll agree. Now Elm Street is on the other side of town from Twelfth Street, isn't it?"

"Yes, that's right."

"That means then that Twelfth is on the other side of town from Elm. But you've already admitted that you're on Twelfth Street. Therefore, you're on the other side of town."

(2)

"Do you know what is behind that door?" the Sophist asked, pointing to what was apparently a closet.

"No, I have no idea."

"Well," he said, pulling the door open, "it's the man who works in the spice shop next door. I have to conclude that you don't know him."

"That's ridiculous," I said. "Cumwar will tell you that I've known him for at least three years."

"It may be ridiculous," said the Sophist, "but I invite you to explain what is the matter with my argument."

(3)

"Do you like to study?" asked the Sophist.

"Not particularly."

"Good, then you will be happy to have me demonstrate to you that studying is a waste of time."

"I should be interested in hearing that, but don't expect me to be convinced."

"Well, I'm sure you agree that the more you study, the more you learn. And, of course, the more you learn, the more you forget. Clearly, then, the more you study the more you forget, so studying is a waste of time."

(4)

"Do you think that pain is desirable?" the Sophist asked.

"Of course not."

"Well, you don't deny, do you, that there are people that we call masochists that seem to desire pain?"

"There are such people, I'll admit."

"Well, then, since pain is desired, it seems to me that we have to conclude that pain is desirable. After all, something that can be seen is obviously something visible." ·

(5)

"Are lions, tigers, and elephants found in Alaska?" the Sophist asked.

"Of course not," I said, "They are inhabitants of warm places like Africa and Asia. In fact, the lion is found only in Africa."

"That they should live in Alaska would be peculiar, then?"

"It certainly would."

"Well, if they are peculiar to Alaska they must be found there then, for when something is peculiar to a place this means that it is characteristic or typical of it."

(6)

"Have you bought a lottery ticket?" the Sophist asked me.

"Yes, I have. I wanted to be in the first legal lottery the state ran. I would sure like to win that million dollars."

"Don't worry; you're certain to win."

"That's ridiculous; hundreds of thousands of people are buying tickets."

"Well, somebody has to win, doesn't he?"

"Sure."

"Somebody has to win, and you're somebody. Clearly, you have to win."

(7)

"I was just admiring that tooled leather belt you're wearing," the Sophist said. "Did you make it yourself?"

"No, it was a present from a friend."

"It does belong to you, though?"

"Sure."

"Do you think it's a work of art?"

"I'm not sure what others would say, but I think so."

"Then you must have made it."

"Why on earth do you say that?"

"Because it's a work of art and it's yours. Therefore, it must be your work."

(8)

"What's the heaviest substance you know?" asked the Sophist.

"So far as I know, nothing is heavier than lead."

"I see. Well, feathers are heavier than nothing, aren't they?"

"Certainly."

"Well, then you have to agree that feathers are heavier than lead."

(9)

"How are you at mathematics?" the Sophist asked.

"I'm very poor."

"All right, I'll keep things simple. Do you believe that 2 is a number and that 3 is a number, that there are two numbers?"

"Certainly."

"That's what I thought. I'll show you that you're mistaken."

"Impossible!"

"Well, 3 and 2 make 5, don't they?"

"I'm not that bad at math! Of course they do."

"Well, then, 5 is a number. Accordingly, 3 and 2 aren't two numbers, they're one number."

(10)

"You know," said the Sophist, "some time ago we talked about animals in Alaska. That reminded me to give you a warning."

"What's that?"

"I want to tell you that you should be careful never to lose an elephant in this country."

"Well, I don't have one to lose, but why do you say that?"

"Because you would never find it."

"That's ridiculous. It ought to be very easy to locate an elephant in a country as populated as this one."

"So you might think, but if you stop for a moment you'll recognize that I'm right. I'm sure you've read many times that elephants are not found on the North American continent. If you lost one here, then, you would never find it."

The Pride of the Empire

The Second Galactic Empire has endured for a thousand years. Some think its success is due to the high value placed on contemplation, but others believe it is a result of the rigorous training that its children receive in proper reasoning.

The Second Galatians are particularly proud of their ability to recognize a case of ambiguity when they meet up with it. Strangely enough, even after several thousand years they still find useful the ancient classification of ambiguity into the following three kinds:

1. expression (word) ambiguity,
2. grammatical ambiguity,
3. referential ambiguity.

Indeed, their indebtedness to the past goes beyond this. In the same way as inhabitants of the Dark Centuries still employed examples drawn from the Greeks and Medievals, the Second Galatians continue to employ examples that were new when the Empire State Building was still standing.

Below is an exercise taken from an S.G. logic book intended for the use of children. Test your own skill against the Galactic standard of excellence.

A word of explanation is necessary, though. The sentences or passages below do not all involve ambiguities. Many do, however. Here is your job:

1. Identify each case of ambiguity.
2. Explain the ways in which the ambiguous case can be understood.
3. Say what type of ambiguity it involves. (That is, classify the ambiguity in terms of the above scheme.)

1. We are offering a free gift worth $50.00 to our old customers and all new customers who sign contracts for work amounting to $500.00 or more.

Adv. in the *St. Louis Post-Dispatch*

2. Unemployment in California dropped slightly last month, although the number of people out of work increased.

San Francisco Chronicle

3. POSSIBLE CRISIS FORESEEN HERE AS CARE OF NEEDY MUSH-ROOMS

Headline in the Richmond (Va.) *Times-Dispatch*

4. I did not commit perjury. I testified under oath that Johnson went away and returned in the afternoon.

5. White Hawk, a thirtyish toothless veteran of eight years on the road, rises, a snake skull dangling from a leather thong around his neck, a knife stuck in the top of one of his worn fringe boots. He is tripping on mescaline, and he has his dog, Shatunge, stoned too. White Hawk moves toward an approaching tourist, the dog staggering behind him, muttering, "Come on, tourist, I gotta make my bread for today."

Newsweek

6. Ms. Willmina Schama announced yesterday that she will marry a vet and enroll in Mineral Area Community College in the fall.

7. About all that remained after the large group had made its exodus toward home was a dish partially filled with apple sauce, a brown sweater, a maroon sweater and five pounds of butter, some of which will be used at the next picnic in three weeks.

Huntington (Pa.) *Daily News*

8. For the "Quintet in E flat Major, Opus 16," joining Rose will be Miss Elizabeth Gilpatrick, french horn; Glen Vliet, clarinet, Robert Johnson, bassoon, and Dox Carr, pharmacist.

Casper (Wyo.) *Star-Tribune*

9. You can't pay too high a price to win an election.

HARRY TRUMAN

10. Found—Black Puppy, possibly German Shepherd mixed in Brookfield at 8826 Ogden Ave. FL 4-0310. Anyone may have puppy or owner.

La Grange (Ill.) *Advertiser*

11. "WOMEN IN JUNGLE CAN FISH" ANTHROPOLOGIST REPORTS

12. *Encyclopedia of the XXth Century*

13. If the church does not change its policy with respect to ordination, there is a possibility that there will be a significant decline in its leadership.

14. Mrs. Harold Smith, wife of a Jersey City gynecologist, summed up the attitude of many as she shopped at Alexander's.

"No one likes to look better than I do, but it's insane to place so much emphasis on it," she said.

The New York Times

15. 4 bedrm. home custom built for owner. Large trees and a full bath on 1st floor are among the many fine features.

Adv. in the Wilmington (Del.) *News.*

16. Always do right; this will gratify some people and astonish the rest.

MARK TWAIN

17. ZION CHRISTIAN CHILDREN'S HOME

18. In the middle of the 1970s, a Supreme Court decision made it legal for a woman who wished to have an abortion to do so. The ruling, in effect, made unconstitutional numerous state and local laws prohibiting abortion. Not all communities were pleased with the situation, and a number of them, particularly in the Midwest, passed laws forbidding medical abortions to be performed in hospitals supported by public funds over which they had control.

    Often, in small towns, public hospitals were the only medical facilities in the community, and even when this was not so, numerous women could not afford to pay the higher prices of a private hospital. When the mayor of one community was criticized for the city's policy, he did not deny the policy. Instead, he defended it by saying, "Any woman in this town is free to have an abortion. Our policy does not prohibit this."

19. When Pyrrhus, the third-century king of Epirus, asked an oracle for a prophecy about the outcome of an impending battle with the Roman Legions, he was told: "Pyrrhus, I say, the Romans shall subdue."

20. The universe is not only queerer than we imagine—it is queerer than we *can* imagine.

J. B. S. HALDANE

21. It was reported from Washington today that the nation's top lawyer has assailed the President's stance on the use of wiretap information.

22. These two regiments were established by Congress after the Civil War as an "experiment" in the use of blacks in the regular army. Living in substandard quarters and given rigorous duties, Professor Fowler shows how these men nevertheless consistently received excellent ratings in military bearing, discipline and experience.

Publishers' Weekly

23. Introducing of a form of nationalized railway passenger service in the United States on May 1 gives recognition that there is still need for a rapidly deteriorating mode of transit.

Montreal Star

24. Evolution is only a theory and so need not be taken seriously.

25. The author effectively displays a mixture of bitter affection and contempt for all men that will be very appealing to most women readers. At best they're irresponsible children, at worst betraying heels.

From the jacket of The Girls, by Nicola Thorne

Some Simulated Real-Life Cases Involving Vagueness

1. You are the principal of a high school in a community with a very conservative school board. The school board has passed a dress code that applies to all schools in the district, and it has sent a letter to all principals informing them that it is holding them directly responsible for the enforcement of the code.

   A particularly troublesome provision of the code is stated in the following way: "All male students are required to wear their hair cut and styled in an appropriately manly way."

   Now this is a regulation that you must enforce (or accept the consequences for not enforcing).

   Explain why this provision is particularly troublesome. That is, explain why it is a genuine case of vagueness.

   Discuss possible criteria that might be employed to remove the vagueness. (Keep in mind that the criteria must be ones that can be defended to the school board.)

2. You are a member of the United States House of Representatives, and there is considerable talk in the House about the possibility of impeaching the President. It is generally agreed that it would be improper to talk about whether the President ought to be impeached for certain acts he may have committed until a clear understanding of what constitutes an impeachable offense is arrived at.

   The first step is obviously to turn to the Constitution. There it is stated that a President can be impeached if he is guilty of "treason, bribery, or high crimes and misdemeanors."

   Treason and bribery present no particular problems, but what is to be taken as a "high crime or misdemeanor"?

   Some members of the House argue that this expression applies only to acts that involve violations of the criminal law. Others claim that an impeachable offense must be broader than that. It must cover cases that involve actions that are unique to the office of President. For example, they say, the President has the legal power to pardon felons, but what if he suddenly declared that all those found guilty of federal crimes and currently serving prison sentences for them are free? This would be a legal act, but it would seem only reasonable to demand that a President who did such a thing be a prime candidate for impeachment.

As a member of the House, you must make up your own mind about this question, for you will have to vote on issues involving it.

Examine possible criteria and discuss the likely effects of adopting them. Don't fail to consider the consequences that your criteria might have if they are too broad. The discussion must keep in mind the nature of the U.S. constitutional government and the separate and equal legislative, judicial, and executive branches.

3. You are still a member of the House, and you have no sooner settled the problem of criteria for impeachment than you find yourself appointed to the House Judiciary Committee. It will be your job to hear the evidence that is presented and determine on the basis of it whether the President should be impeached.

The very first day the committee meets a serious problem arises. Charges that are brought against the President must be decided on the basis of the evidence. They must be adequately supported by the evidence if they are to be recommended to the entire House for its action.

But what constitutes *adequate* evidence?

No numerical measurement is possible, of course, but it is suggested that it may be possible to get a better understanding of when the evidence is adequate by employing more precise expressions.

Some members argue that the evidence is adequate only when a charge can be established *beyond a reasonable doubt*. This test, you'll recall, is the one used in criminal trials.

Other members argue that the charges are established when they are supported by a *preponderance of* evidence. This is interpreted to mean more evidence for than against the truth of the charge.

Some say the first criterion is too stringent, and others say the second criterion is too weak.

Discuss these two criteria and consider arguments for and against employing them.

Consider the possibility of finding a third criterion that is superior to each of these.

4. You are an ordinary citizen who simply cannot decide about the rightness or wrongness of abortion. You are very much against taking human life, and if abortion involves taking human life, then you are against it. But is an unborn fetus really a human life? If it is not, then you are not against abortion on principle and are perfectly willing to let it be a matter of individual choice.

This is the situation that you (and millions of others) are faced with. What sorts of criteria are relevant and adequate for its resolution?

5. Standard Oil Company announces that it has plans to build a new oil refinery in your town—a small community of 25,000. You are the leader of a group that is initially opposed to this project, and you meet with a representative of Standard Oil to attempt to convince her that the refinery should not be built. When asked to give a reason, you say that the refinery would result in a deterioration of the quality of life in the town.

    The oil company representative insists that you specify just what you mean by the phrase "quality of life," and explain why you believe a refinery would result in its deterioration.

6. You are the Standard Oil representative and you specify what you mean by "quality of life" and explain why a refinery would not result in its decline.

    Is it possible that the you above and the you in this role might reach agreement about criteria that specify what shall count as a violation or satisfaction of the quality-of-life notion?

7. Several years ago, Dr. Arnold Hutshnecker, physician to President Richard Nixon, proposed that psychological tests should be given to all children between the ages of six and eight. Those that were found to have what he called "violent tendencies" that might lead to crime would be sent to special camps for treatment.

    This program, Dr. Hutshnecker claimed, would be "a direct, immediate, effective way of attacking the problem [of crime] at its very origin, by focusing on the criminal mind of the child" and could take the place of slum clearance and social rehabilitation programs.

    Do you see any dangers in Dr. Hutshnecker's proposal? Discuss the proposal with respect to the problem of getting criteria for identifying violent tendencies in children that might be expected to produce adult criminals.

The Face in the Flames

Suppose you are an investigator of psychic phenomena, and the account of the experience given below falls into your hands.

In conducting investigations, you wish to have information as exact as possible about all aspects of the circumstances in which strange events occur. In fact, you're something of a fanatic about this. For this reason, you find the account below unsatisfactory in many respects. You are aware, of course, that not everything can be described in a quantitative way.

To illustrate how unsatisfactory most accounts of psychic phenomena are, you read this account and pick out the expressions that are used in connection with things we regard as measurable, datable, or countable and explain how these vague expressions could be replaced by more exact ones. Also, you locate the words used to indicate comparative amounts (or degrees) that cannot be replaced by quantitative ones.

My name is Mona Selfridge. You will not believe what I say, but I must tell you anyway—not for your sake, but for my own. I must have something real to hold onto, even if it is no more than words on paper.

I had not lived in Boston very long before I heard a very peculiar tale. Lamurial Roberts, a woman I had known at college years before, informed me one day at lunch that the house I had rented was one of several places where murders attributed to the Boston Strangler had taken place.

"I know you're not superstitious," she said, "but there is talk in the neighborhood that strange things still happen here."

I was more amused than frightened. "What sort of things?" I asked.

"I don't know, really, but they say the house is so filled with pain and terror that on some nights the whole atmosphere becomes charged with it. It's as if the sufferings of the poor woman that was killed there have soaked into the structure of the house and are released again when the conditions are right."

"Am I the first person to live there since the crime?"

"No, a number of others have rented it for awhile, but they all moved out. Some, I've heard, were driven mad."

"Well, please don't tell me how the poor creature died. I don't want my imagination playing any tricks on me."

I gave no thought to Lamurial's warning, until a few nights later. During the late evening, after some friends I had invited to dinner had gone, I settled myself comfortably by the fire. A little wine was left in the bottle, and I was finishing it off before going to bed.

I was tired and drowsy and let nothing but the crackle of the fire fill my mind. But then, very softly, above the fire, I heard the distinct sound of whimpering. It was low but pained, desperate. It seemed only a few feet from my chair, perhaps on the hearth.

I told myself it was only a high wind blowing across the chimney. I tried to ignore it, shut it out of my mind, but I couldn't. It stirred me deeply, but it didn't much frighten me.

I became very frightened when the images started. I saw, with my eyes open, swords of flame cut at a limbless, headless torso, saw the light skin char and turn red with rawness. Then, as in a grotesque newsreel, the scene moved past and was replaced by the face of an attractive woman. The face was serene, but only for a moment. Suddenly the hair blossomed into licking flames and the face within the fiery halo became twisted and distorted with agony.

The soft whimpering abruptly changed into a scream of anguish, and the scream was repeated and repeated endlessly.

My eyes were open, staring, but I could see nothing but the hellish image and hear nothing but the awful screams.

Time passed, but I never fainted or lost consciousness. I watched and listened, unwillingly, until a dark shadow seemed to fall between me and the tortured face. It was as though someone had stepped in front of me, some very large man. Then, as suddenly as it had begun, the screaming stopped.

The wineglass still sat at the table by my chair, the wine untasted. The room was still the same, except for one small matter. Even though there were only embers in the fireplace, the fire burned higher and brighter than before.

The Prose of Lester Lapin

Lester Lapin is not an admirable person. He has specialized as a speechwriter in preparing speeches with an astoundingly high number of what we call "chameleon words." Lester's theory is that the more chameleon words you pack into a speech, then the more people will agree with what you say. They will simply assign their own meanings to the words and ignore the fact that these may not be the meanings that the speaker would assign to them. If there is ever any problem of criticism, the speaker can always claim that he's been misunderstood.

Below is a passage from a speech written by Lester to give you an idea of the sort of things that he writes. Go through and pick out all the words that seem to you to be chameleon words. Be prepared to explain the ways in which these words change their meanings in various circumstances.

> It is a distinct privilege to address an organization such as yours that has for so long attempted to see to it that the ideals of democracy and patriotism continue to flourish in this great country of ours.
>
> You know, there was a time when a fool and his money were soon parted. Nowadays, that's something that happens to all of us.
>
> And that's what I want to talk to you about this evening.
>
> From the very beginning, our country has subscribed to a very simple philosophy. We have believed in freedom, justice, and the rights of individuals. It's my belief that we have lost touch with this philosophy, and it's for that reason that we've fallen upon such hard times.
>
> Our country is filled with millions of people who are great successes. But it is also filled with those who are great failures. It is this last group that poses a real and immediate threat to all of us.
>
> These are the people without jobs, with too many children to support, with no skills, no determination, and no interest in working. Those of us who are courageous in our beliefs, unremitting in our labors, and wise in the conduct of our lives are the ones who have to pay such a high penalty for the indolence and greed of others. Our tax dollars go to support those who still have the audacity to complain about having to stand in line to get their relief checks!
>
> We are wise enough to know this sort of thing can't go on forever. We have to take steps to encourage those without motivation to take honest jobs. But we can't hope to do this until we make it more uncomfortable to be on welfare than it is to work for a living.

"Let's Say It Right"

During the time when the United States was deeply involved in the Vietnam war, the U.S. Military Command in Vietnam decided that it didn't like some of the terms that reporters and even its own briefing officers were using.

Certain terms, the Command believed, did not express the proper attitude toward the Viet Cong enemy, the soldiers hired by the U.S. and South Vietnam, and various military programs and operations. To try to put a stop to the use of these terms, the Command issued a directive called "Let's Say It Right." The directive had the effect of forbidding news-briefing officers from using the words. It was hoped that the civilian media would stop using them also.

Take a look at the expressions that the Command labeled "incorrect" and those that it called "correct." Explain why the Command might prefer the "correct" to the "incorrect" in terms of the differences in connotations.

Incorrect	*Correct*
Viet Cong tax collectors	Viet Cong extortionists
People's Liberation Army	Viet Cong
5 O'Clock Follies	Military Assistance Command daily press briefings
U.S. troop withdrawal	Redeployment of forces
Volunteer	Mercenary soldier
Search and destroy	Search and clear

"Irregular Verbs"

Bertrand Russell started a new game when he "conjugated" some "irregular verbs." Here is one of Russell's conjugations:

> I am firm
> You are obstinate
> He is pigheaded

For most purposes, the asserted content can be taken to be the same in each case: the individual referred to continues to hold on to his position. There are, of course, significant differences in connotation.

Explain the differences in connotations in Russell's example and in the cases below. Are there also differences in asserted content? If so, point them out.

1. I am greatly insulted
   You have a right to be annoyed
   He is making a mountain out of a molehill

2. I explain fully
   You are a little verbose
   He rambles on endlessly

3. My fiancée is beautiful
   Yours is quite nice looking
   His has a nice personality

4. I have reconsidered
   You have changed your mind
   He has gone back on his word

5. I was misinformed
   You were mistaken
   He lied

6. I deserve it
   You are fortunate
   He lucked out

7. I am profound
   You are clever
   He is facile

8. I gave it my best effort
   You worked hard
   He barely tried

9. I am justifiably pleased
   You are proud
   He is smug

10. My opinion is carefully considered
    Yours is thoughtful
    His is hasty

Exercise your imagination and make up five examples of your own.

4/ A Fair Exchange: Definition

GOAT: *Antique garbage disposal unit*

It is one of the maxims of the civil law that defi-
nitions are dangerous.

SAMUEL JOHNSON

IN THE last chapter, we witnessed the dangers of connotation and forged weapons from the fires of reason to fight those dread creatures, ambiguity and vagueness. In this chapter, we'll continue our battle against the dark forces of language. We'll devote ourselves to becoming more self-conscious and critical about definitions. In the process, we'll acquire some more sophisticated knowledge about how to avoid the puzzles and confusions of language, and we'll also acquire the tools necessary to present and evaluate definitions.

In "Oil and Water," we'll make a beginning by dividing definitions into two categories. These categories are based upon whether we are reporting what a word means or laying down a rule for using it. "They Laughed" will be our workshop section, and there we'll develop several methods or techniques for defining. At the end we'll see that they are all just variations on a single prime technique that is connected with the view of meaning that we accepted in Chapter 2.

Definitions, like apples and eggs, can be good or bad. But in order to evaluate them we need to have in mind some criteria or standards against which they can be measured. We'll devote "Separating Sheep from Goats" to presenting standards for criticism and evaluation.

In the last section, "Dirty Definitions," we'll talk about the ways in which definitions can be used as tools by the Kingdom of Darkness, about how they can deceive and mislead. There we'll discuss two illegitimate types of definition, persuasive and loaded.

Before doing any of this, though, there is a matter that has to be tended to. We need to say what a definition is before we start talking about definitions. In short, we need a definition of "definition."

A blatant fact that is easily ignored because it causes so few practical difficulties is that definitions are of *words*. They are, of course, also of expressions, phrases, terms, symbols, and so on, but we can easily stretch "word" to cover these as well.

Definitions are *not* appropriate for the things that words refer to, name, describe, characterize, or whatever. Thus we define the word "table" and not the object from which we ate breakfast. No one can eat breakfast at a word, and no one can define a table. We can eat off tables, pound on them, carve our initials on them, or throw them on bonfires, but we cannot define them.

We can define "table," but we can't do any of the things with it that we can do with a table. There are, of course, other things we can do with "table." We can grave it in bronze, shout it from the rooftops, whisper it gently, or write it in blood. We can do none of these things with the objects to which the word refers.

In sum, then, definitions are appropriate only for words and not for the objects or states of affairs that words refer to. And to say this is only to acknowledge the use-mention distinction. (See Chapter 1 for a discussion of the distinction.) To define a word involves talking about the word. That is, it involves mentioning the word, rather than using it. What we want to say about it, of course, is what it means.

After all this to-do about only words being defined, the plain truth is that people don't usually observe logic-book niceties in asking for and in giving definitions. People rarely say such things as "What does the word 'gazebo' mean?"

Such questions are highly unnatural in most ordinary situations. About the only time that anyone asks them is when the word is a foreign one or when he hasn't got the slightest clue as to whether the word refers to a machine, a way of acting, a tasty dessert, or what.

Contrary to the impression given above, then, when most people want a definition they don't ask about the word. They ask about what the word refers to. The ordinary way to ask for a definition of "gazebo" would be to ask "What's a gazebo?"

The typical response wouldn't be to start out with "The word 'gazebo' means . . . ." Rather it would be something like "A gazebo is a small house where one can sit and enjoy a view." More often than not, then, a definition is presented as if it were only a description of whatever is referred to by the word.

There is nothing wrong about giving a definition in this way. Not only is it common practice, but it's a practice we'll sometimes find it convenient to follow. The only real danger in giving definitions in this way is that it's not always clear whether someone is offering a definition of a word or whether he is just mentioning a few facts about what the word refers to.

Suppose someone says, "A hog is an animal that wallows around in the mud a lot." Is he defining "hog" or just making a casual observation about the habits of hogs?

Making the use-mention distinction has the advantage of guaranteeing that we put our cards on the table. When we say, "The word 'hog' means . . . ," then we've made it clear that we are giving a definition of the word. People are then in a position to recognize that we at least claim to be explaining the meaning of a word. They then know how to respond to what we say.

Oil and Water: Stipulative and Reportive Definitions

Oil and water never mix (unless there's detergent present), and neither do the two general types of definition we're going to talk about here. So far as we're concerned, all definitions will be either stipulative ones or reportive ones. That is, they will either lay down a rule for the use of a word or they will report on actual use. Definitions, like people, can't serve two masters. Why this is so will soon be obvious.

Stipulative Definitions

To stipulate is to lay down a condition. Someone might say, for example, "Club regulations expressly stipulate that a dog must wear a collar in order to be served in the dining room." A stipulative definition, then, consists in laying down a condition for using a certain word. It is, in effect, an announcement of the rule that will be followed in using the word.

The word introduced by a stipulative definition may be a newly minted one or it may be one already in common currency that we want to use in a new or special way. Which it is gives us grounds for distinguishing between two kinds of stipulative definitions.

Arbitrary

Let's start by considering a case in which we might want to use a stipulative definition to introduce a brand-new word.

Suppose you were an anthropologist writing a field report on a tribe you had been studying and you found it necessary to refer very often to the last man to return to the village after a hunt who brings no game with him. You might find it convenient to coin a word to refer to the person who is picked out by this long descriptive phrase. Otherwise, you would have to keep using the phrase over and over.

You might, quite arbitrarily, combine a few letters from the description and come up with "lamgam."

Your readers could hardly be expected to know what this means, since you just made it up, so you have to give a definition of the word. You would have to say something like:

> In this report, I shall use the word "lamgam" to mean the same as "the last man to return to the village after a hunt who brings no game with him."

This is, of course, a stipulative definition. It is a resolution or decision to use a certain word in the way indicated by the definition. The definition specifies the rule for using the word. It lays down the condition governing the use of the word "lamgam."

In cases like this, there is a totally free choice as to whether a new term is introduced and, if so, what it is. There is, as we've said, no preexisting standard or rule of use that the definition must report. For this reason, we might call stipulative definitions that introduce wholly new expressions *arbitrary stipulative definitions.*

Newly created technical terms, abbreviations, and symbols are all typically introduced for the first time by means of arbitrary stipulative definitions. Consider these cases:

1. Instead of writing "B.C." after a number, I shall write " $-$ " in front of it to indicate the same thing.
2. By "X" I shall mean "the sum of all values of x."
3. Let "P_1" refer to the first person who enters the room.

Arbitrary stipulative definitions are not reports on standard practices. They can, however, be offered as recommendations to the effect that the expression introduced be *made* a part of standard practice. That is, they can be presented as proposals for general adoption. If a proposal is adopted and the word becomes used, then a report about the meaning of the word ceases to be an arbitrary stipulative definition. It becomes a report about some standard use of the word. In short, the arbitrary meaning of the word becomes a conventional meaning. (See Chapter 2 for further discussion of the distinction between arbitrary and conventional meaning.)

When, for example, Norbert Wiener introduced the new term "cybernetics," he defined it as "the science of communication and control systems." This was an arbitrary stipulative definition. It was an explanation of how he was going to use the term. But in addition to announcing the rule that he was going to follow, Wiener also expressed the hope that others would take up the word and use it in the same way. His hope turned out to be well founded, and a word that began life by means of an arbitrary stipulative definition has now come to have an ordinary or conventional use. Anyone who defines the word nowadays must take the standard meaning of the word into account.

Let's consider a case now in which we might want both to introduce a stipulative definition and to offer it as a proposal for general acceptance. The reason for considering such a case, as we'll see, is to make clear what sort of critical considerations are relevant to evaluating stipulative definitions.

Suppose you were colorblind and couldn't distinguish between red and green. Since both red and green look alike to you, you might see no reason for having the two words "red" and "green." Why have two words to refer to (what would be for you) the same color?

Suppose, further, that you got fed up with linguistic discrimination against the colorblind in our society and formed a CB Liberation group. One of the aims of the group is to get people who aren't colorblind to stop using the words "red" and "green," because their use makes CB people painfully aware of their handicap.

To accomplish this aim, you introduce a new word. The word "reg," you explain, refers to both the color red and the color green. Thus, to those with so-called normal vision, something is reg if it is either red or green. For those in the CB group, who can't detect the difference, both colors are simply reg. They don't even have to say to themselves, as others do, "If it is red or if it is green, then it is reg." They simply recognize a certain color as reg.

In introducing the word "reg," you would be making use of an arbitrary stipulative definition. You would be saying, in effect, "This is the rule in accordance with which the word 'reg' is to be used."

In introducing the word "reg," you would be making use of an arbitrary stipulative definition. You would be saying, in effect, "This is the rule in accordance with which the word 'reg' is to be used."

Since we are the masters of language and not it of us, we are completely free to introduce any new words that we wish to. No one is going to keep us from it. And, as we've already seen, arbitrary stipulative definitions are just the way that new expressions are deliberately introduced.

But, of course, the CB Liberation group is interested in doing more than merely defining a word by stipulating its meaning. It wants to get its definition accepted by society so that the new word will become one used in ordinary life. It wants the word to be adopted and, by its use, to acquire a conventional meaning, one that is the same as the original arbitrary meaning.

The CB group, then, is making a proposal that the word "reg" be accepted in general usage in accordance with the rule that it laid down. Since a proposal is not something that can be true or false, no one could object that in defining "reg" to mean "red or green" you were saying something that wasn't true. On the other hand, no one could say that you were saying something that *was* true either. Truth and falsity simply don't enter the picture.

A proposal can't be true or false, but it can be ill-considered, silly, a bad idea, or something of the kind. That is, a proposal can be evaluated with respect to certain aims or purposes, and it can be judged in terms of how helpful it would be in achieving them.

The proposal that we use "reg" to replace "red" and "green" can undoubtedly be supported by reasons. It is undeniably true that our society is arranged so as to discriminate against people who are red-green colorblind. To take a trivial case, we think it's peculiar for people to wear one red sock and one green sock, and anyone who does it is likely to be ridiculed. More seriously, our traffic lights are based on red and green signals, and the colorblind must try to make use of cues other than color to know what a light is directing them to do.

On the other hand, compared to the many reasons why we find it useful to distinguish between red and green, the proposal that we use "reg" to refer to both colors has little going for it. Not only would most people not want to sing "Reg Grow the Lilacs," but they would point out that having two words permits us to give more refined descriptions. An amateur geologist who had been told that garnets were reg, for example, wouldn't know enough to be surprised should he happen to find a green garnet.

It could be argued, then, that the social justice that would be achieved by ending discrimination against the red-green colorblind by adopting the proposal wouldn't be sufficiently great to outweigh the disadvantages of abandoning "red" and "green" in favor of "reg." Furthermore, it could be said, the discrimination could be ended in other ways without having to alter the language.

Whichever side of this controversy one finds convincing doesn't matter for our purposes. The point is that even though it's not appropriate to talk about stipulative definitions being true or false, this does not mean that they are beyond challenge. We are particularly moved to criticize when an arbitrary stipulative definition is presented to us as a proposal recommended for general adoption. We then examine it in terms of its advantages and disadvantages with respect to certain goals or purposes.

We aren't ordinarily as ready to criticize someone who introduces an arbitrary stipulative definition for his own purposes and doesn't recommend that it be made a general convention. We can do so, however, and sometimes there is good reason for us to do so. If, for example, the writer of a textbook introduces a large number of new words or symbols that we regard as unnecessary or confusing, we have a perfect right to object to them in just those terms. Everyone is free to make use of as many stipulative definitions as he likes; there's no law against it. But this doesn't mean that the definitions are a good idea or that we can't criticize them.

Restricting

Let's turn now to the second type of stipulative definition that we'll be concerned with. This is the kind that involves making special use of a word that already has an ordinary or standard meaning.

Anyone who has ever read his insurance policy carefully, examined his income tax instructions, or listened to a court proceeding is well aware of the fact that a number of rather ordinary and familiar words are used in some quite extraordinary ways.

Words like "dependent," "building," "blind," "income," and "damage" are pulled out of ordinary language and redefined for use in a new context. In ordinary language, for example, the expression "head of household" has a rather broad usage, and the boundaries of its application are rather indefinite. A man or woman who makes all the decisions in a family might correctly be called the head of the household, even though he or she contributes no money for its support. For tax purposes, however, "head of household" is defined as "an unmarried person who furnishes over half the cost of maintaining a household for at least one relative."

The meaning given to the expression by this definition is certainly connected with the ordinary meaning, but the two are not at all the same. Furnishing a majority of the cost of supporting a household is certainly one of the conditions relevant to determining, in ordinary life, whether someone is to be considered the head of a household or not. But it is far from the only relevant condition, and even when it is met we might still not consider such a person the head.

Definitions of this kind involve taking an ordinary word and stipulating what it will be taken to mean in a special context. The redefined word will almost always have a much more narrow or restricted range of application than the word's ordinary usage permits. For this reason, we can call definitions of this sort *restricting stipulative definitions*. (Since the definitions are intended to make the use of the words more precise, they are also sometimes called "precising definitions.")

In our example, it's clear that "head of household" will apply to a much narrower range of cases when the expression is used in accordance with the condition in the stipulative definition than it ordinarily does. Furthermore, by laying down an explicit condition to govern the use of the word, the definition does much to eliminate the possibility of vagueness and ambiguity in the use of the expression. Far fewer problems will arise about just who is to be considered the head of a household.

Indicators that an ordinary word is going to be given a restricted or special meaning by stipulative definition are phrases such as "for the purpose of this contract," "we shall understand a [such and such] to be," and "in this book I shall mean by. . . ." Expressions such as these are a tip-off that the word defined will, in the context, be used in a way that does not conform with all respects to its ordinary meaning.

Words that are made the object of restrictive stipulative definitions don't lose their citizenship in the commonwealth of ordinary language. No matter what the tax laws or the insurance companies say, we are free to continue using words like "income" and "loss" in the way that we always have. Restrictive stipulative definitions, in effect, make technical terms out of ordinary words. Outside of the special situations, however, the words continue to have their old meanings.

It does happen, of course, that restricting definitions come to alter the meaning of ordinary words. That is, the meaning assigned to the word by the definition becomes the generally accepted meaning. In eighteenth-century biology, for example, the word "fish" was defined in such a way as to exclude whales. This was a departure from the common use of the word. (Jonah, according to the Bible, was not swallowed by a whale, but by a big fish.) Our use of the word "fish" today, then, is a result of the modification that made it a technical term narrower in application than it was in ordinary eighteenth-century usage.

Just because we have talked about restricting stipulative definitions in connection with income tax forms, laws, science, and so on doesn't mean that they don't have their uses in other parts of life as well. In fact, all of us rely quite heavily on restrictive stipulative definitions in presenting arguments and engaging in disputes. In order to make ourselves understood more clearly and in order to make our views more precise, we frequently define key words. The definitions we give are generally not reports about how the words are ordinarily used. Rather, they are announcements of how *we* are going to use the words. The meanings that we attribute to the words are usually closely connected with the words' ordinary meanings. However, we attempt to give the words more restricted and exact meanings than their ordinary ones.

If, for example, you were trying to convince someone that our society should provide basic medical care for all who need it, you would probably find it necessary and useful to define "basic medical care." You might say something like, "By 'basic medical care' I mean the treatment and prevention, if possible, of disabling diseases and defects." This is certainly close to what most people would understand by the phrase, though the phrase probably has a wider range of application than this.

In any case, by offering an explicit definition of this sort, you would put yourself in the position to show that the reasons you present to support your position are relevant ones. And, just as important, you leave no doubt about just how your claim is to be understood.

It would be strange to regard the definition of "basic medical care" in such a case as a technical term. It is, however, something *like* a technical term, for it involves assigning a more precise meaning to an ordinary expression.

The most important thing to remember about stipulative definitions, whether they are arbitrary ones or restricting ones, is that they involve *deciding* to use a certain word in a particular way. The definition is, so to speak, a statement of this intention. It is a stipulation of the rule that is going to be followed in using the word. You may hope or propose that others will use the word in the way that you do, but this is a separate matter. Neither a decision nor a proposal can be true or false; yet either can be a candidate for criticism.

Reportive Definitions

If the meanings of words were the same sort of things as stuffed elephants or narwhal horns, Egyptian statuary or Aztec funeral masks, then they could be arranged in displays. There could be a Museum of Meanings in which the meanings of words could be placed on exhibit so that people not familiar with them could stroll through and learn what they are.

There could be a Contemporary section, in which the ordinary meanings of words were exhibited. Then there could be a Technical or Science-and-Industry section, which would be devoted to the meanings of words that are technical terms. Finally, there could be a Historical wing, in which the meanings of old-fashioned words or the old-fashioned meanings of contemporary words were exhibited.

But, obviously, meanings can't be displayed in the way that whalebones, crossbows, and suits of armor are. They simply aren't the sorts of things that can be propped up in museum cases or arranged in dioramas.

How, then, can we deal with the meanings of words? We can handle them easily enough by relying on other words. We can provide words with definitions that explain their meanings by reporting how the words are used. Such definitions present an account of the conditions or rules that govern a word's use. (Such an account may, of course, involve describing paradigm cases of the word's use.)

Definitions that attempt to explain how a word is actually used are intended to be reports about the word's meaning. For that reason, they are called *reportive definitions.*

It's important to notice that reportive definitions are as different from stipulative definitions as chalk is from cheese. A stipulative definition is, in effect, a *decision* to use a word in a certain way, whereas a reportive definition is, in effect, a *claim* that a word is *in fact* used in a certain way. A stipulative definition assigns a meaning to a word; a reportive definition reports that the meaning of a word is such and such.

The difference has a tremendously important consequence. We've already seen that stipulative definitions can't legitimately be said to be true or false. Since they are decisions or proposals, it's not appropriate to talk about them in terms of truth. But the opposite is the case with reportive definitions. They are put forward as accounts of how words are actually used, of what their meanings are, in certain situations. Such an account can be a true one or a false one. Furthermore, it can be accurate or inaccurate in specific respects.

Let's consider an example. In his novel *Breakfast of Champions*, Kurt Vonnegut introduces as a character a science fiction writer named Kilgore Trout. Trout is convinced (or says he is) that mirrors are openings to another universe parallel to our own. They are holes through which the other world can leak in. For this reason, Trout decides to use the word "leak" to refer to mirrors.

This is a little odd, but there's nothing objectionable about it. Trout's decision is, in effect, a stipulative definition. (It's true that his use of the word in ordinary conversation creates some difficulties of communication. We might try to convince him to drop his use of the word because of this. But if he doesn't want to, well . . . it's almost a free country.)

But Trout doesn't stop with his stipulative definition. At one time he tells a truck driver, "Back where I come from we call mirrors *leaks."* Now this is simply not true. Trout purports to be reporting on how the word is ordinarily used "back where he comes from," but the report that he gives is false. Trout is the *only* one who uses the word this way. His stipulative definition of "leak" may or may not be a good idea, but his report on that word's use in his part of the country is simply incorrect.

There is a big gap between exactly right and completely wrong, and it's quite possible for reportive definitions to fall into this massive crack. A report that "heater" means "a device for producing heat or one who heats something" is quite correct *so far as it goes.* The report is incomplete, however, for the word is also used in another way. As a slang expression, the word refers to a revolver.

Similarly, a reportive definition might be defective, not because it is incomplete, but because it inaccurately describes the conditions governing a word's use. If it is reported, for example, that in biology the term "cell wall" is used to refer to the envelope surrounding a cell, a legitimate objection could be raised. The expression "cell wall" is applied only to the envelope around plant cells. The one surrounding bacterial cells, animal cells, and so on is called a "cell membrane." The definition of "cell wall," then, as a report on the use of the term in biology, is inaccurate in a very important respect.

Reportive definitions are factual descriptions. (Or, better, they are *put forward as* factual descriptions.) The facts they are supposed to report are the conditions that regulate the use of a word—the meaning of the word. Reportive definitions, consequently, are not *prescriptions.* That is, they are not statements about how a word *ought* to be used. They aren't laws that must be followed, but descriptions of practices. The word "bimonthly," for example, means "every two months." But, as a matter of fact, it is also used by a large number of people to mean "twice a month." This may be a regrettable fact, but it's a fact, nonetheless. A complete and accurate reportive definition must faithfully record both meanings of this word. (It must, at least, if it is to be a general report about ordinary usage. If the report is limited to the use of the word by such peculiar groups as members of the Modern Language Association, then it may be that only the first meaning is the ordinary one.)

The importance of stipulative definitions is fairly obvious. Everyone recognizes a need, from time to time, to define a word to suit his immediate purposes or to introduce a new term to make his task easier. The importance of reportive definitions, though perhaps less obvious, is at least as great. In the most general terms, they contribute immeasurably to the improvement of communication and to our understanding of language. None of us knows the meanings of all the words in our language. Consequently, when we encounter new words, we need to have a way of finding out what they mean. Reportive definitions provide one way. Similarly, if communication is to be successful, there has to be some consistency or regularity in the way that we use words. Reportive definitions, by telling us how words are standardly used, allow us to model our use on that of others. They are, then, instruments that permit us to share a common language that is considerably more extensive than it would be if we were limited solely to those words that we learn and use in ordinary life.

Furthermore, reportive definitions give us access to technical and historical areas. Without a definition of "cell wall," it would be hard to gain an understanding of plant physiology. It would take a long time to learn the word from its use alone. A reportive definition speeds up the process. Similarly, a knowledge that in Victorian England the word "radical" was used most often to refer to followers of Jeremy Bentham and Utilitarianism makes it much easier to read Victorian history.

We've already suggested by the examples we've used how reportive definitions might be divided into types. Let's become explicit now and separate them into the following three types: lexical, historical, and technical. Enough has been said in connection with other matters to allow us to explain these types in very brief compass.

Lexical

The word "lexical" means "having to do with the vocabulary of a language." The vocabulary of a language is something like the Blob: its pseudopods extend into a variety of places and its outline is indefinite. The vocabulary of a language might, for example, be taken to include the special terms of science, mathematics, grammar, logic, and so on. For our purposes, then, let's make use of a restricting stipulative definition and say that "lexical" has to do with the words of a language *as they are ordinarily used.*

A *lexical definition,* then, is a report on the ordinary meaning of a word. It is an explanation of the ordinary or standard use of a word.

A lexical definition of the word "acute," for example, would include the meanings "having a sharp point," "keenly perceptive," and "of great importance." These are some of the ordinary meanings of the word. It would not include other, more specialized, meanings, which are found in medicine, music, and geometry, to name just three fields.

The use of the word in these fields may be connected with the ordinary meaning of the word, but this is not necessarily the case. In the ordinary use of the word, an acute pain is one that is sharp, but in medical terminology it is a pain of short duration.

When we ask about the meaning of a word, it is most often a lexical definition that we are requesting.

Technical

A technical reportive definition is, obviously, an explanation of the meaning of a word that is used in some special area or discipline. The definition is an account of the use of the word that is standard *in that area.*

Thus, in physics the term "mass" can be defined as "a measure of a body's resistance to acceleration." In terms of a specific version of Newtonian mechanics, "mass" gains its meaning from the equation $F=ma$ ($F=$force, $m=$mass, and $a=$acceleration). In modern relativity physics, mass is no longer regarded as independent of velocity, so in the context of that theory the term takes on a significantly different meaning.

We all speak with many tongues, of course. Our knowledge of words is rarely limited solely to words as they are generally used. Also, we all work at jobs of one kind or another and participate in all kinds of activities ranging from collecting beer cans to skin diving in the Andes, so we get to know the specialized vocabularies in many areas. Consequently, the line between lexical and technical definitions is frequently hard to draw and is sometimes downright arbitrary.

For all that, it is still well to keep in mind the fact that there are many words that have both ordinary and technical meanings. A failure to do this can result in confusions and misunderstandings. An important case of this is the word we used for illustration above: "mass." In ordinary language, we regard "mass" and "weight" as being virtually synonymous. In physics, however, they are quite different. One's mass on the moon, say, remains unchanged, but one's weight is only about one-sixth of that on earth. (This is because the gravity of the moon exerts less force, but one's resistance to change of acceleration remains unaltered.) A failure to realize that "mass" is a technical term in physics that is not equivalent in meaning to the ordinary use of the word, makes it all but impossible to understand even relatively simple physical explanations. In an "age of science" this is a definite handicap.

Though it's true that some words have uses both in technical areas and in ordinary life, this is, of course, not the case for all words. Some words have *only* technical meanings. In either case, a technical reportive definition is an explanation of how a given word is used in some specific area.

Historical

As we've already noticed in discussing theories of meaning, words have a history. Their meanings change over time. Accordingly, a reportive definition of the way that a word is used at present does not necessarily inform us about how it was used in the past. To discover this we must do historical research. We have to read the documents of the time—magazines, court reports, laws, letters, diaries, and so on. In short, we have to try to figure out from the way words were used just what the conditions governing their use might have been.

This kind of knowledge is important for a better understanding of the historical period. Without knowing, for example, that in the eighteenth century the word "flasher" referred to someone of brilliant appearance, it's possible to get a wildly wrong idea about someone who is described by his contemporaries as a flasher. The modern meaning of the term is simply not the one intended.

Similarly, there are words that are now archaic or have passed wholly from use that have to be learned in order to understand the writings of earlier times. If, for example, you don't know what "bathing machine" means, you will not be able to understand the description of one of the "five unmistakable marks" of a snark, because:

The fourth is its fondness for bathing machines.

A historical reportive definition is simply an explanation of the meaning that a word had during some particular historical period. Except for the fact that the period is not the present, the definition does not differ in principle from a lexical definition. (Assuming, that is, that the word is one that was in common use. It is also possible to give an explanation of the past meaning of a technical term. It is important to the history of science to note, for example, that in the eighteenth century the expression "fixed air" was used to refer to what we now call "oxygen.")

What we've said in this section can be briefly summarized. A *reportive definition* is an attempt to explain how a word is actually used. Such a report can be true or false, complete or incomplete, accurate or inaccurate. Since reportive definitions have the status of factual claims, they can be tested against the actual facts of a word's use.

A *lexical* reportive definition is an account of the standard or ordinary use of a word. A *technical* definition is an account of the use of a word that is the standard use in some special area or discipline. A *historical* definition is an explanation of how a word was used during some particular period in the past. The explanation may be of the ordinary or of some technical use of the word.

"They Laughed When I Started to Explain the Meaning of a Word . . ." or How to Define

Nothing can be more embarrassing. You are at a party, or you have to write a report for the boss or even a new textbook on quantum mechanics, and *you have to give a definition.* Perhaps you want to explain the ordinary meaning of a word. Perhaps you want to introduce a special term. You know you must do a good job or face the laughter or derision of your audience.

Here's a promise! If you master the techniques of giving definitions that are described in the pages below, then you will never have to feel embarrassed when you are called on to give a definition.

They may start to laugh, but when they see how well you define, their laughter will turn to smiles of appreciation at a job well done!

AMAZE YOUR FRIENDS! CONFOUND YOUR OPPONENTS!

The promise above is a little too strong, but only a little. Chances are that no one is going to be terribly impressed by the masterful way you give a definition. The truth is, though, that an understanding of some of the more important ways of explaining the meanings of words does make it easier to give clear and precise definitions. And this is undeniably a skill worth acquiring.

We'll discuss only four methods of giving definitions. But in connection with the last method, we'll see that we could multiply this number if we wanted to. In fact, we'll see that all methods of definition can be regarded as no more than variations on one method of explaining the meanings of words by giving an account of the conditions that govern their use. But more of this later.

The specific methods that we'll discuss represent frequent and important ways of defining. They are not wholly free inventions, of course, but are derived from our ordinary practice. Generally speaking, they can be used to give both stipulative and reportive definitions, though we'll mainly be talking of reportive ones.

It's useful to keep in mind that we aren't bound by some universal edict to define words in one particular way. The way we define depends on the reasons we have for explaining a meaning in the first place. Accordingly, there isn't one specific way of defining that's superior to all others and that serves all our purposes.

Methods of defining are thus like methods of transportation. A plane, a bus, or a unicycle may all get you where you want to go, but in a particular situation you will probably have reasons for choosing one way over the others.

Definition by Synonym

Suppose you're reading a novel about life in Greenwich Village that was published in the 1930s. The dialogue, you discover, contains several weird expressions that are completely unfamiliar to you. For example: rubberneck wagon, lip muff, kick the gong around.

As it turns out, these are all slang expressions current in the thirties, and most of them have passed out of use. If you could find somebody who still knows what they mean (can remember how they were used), he might prepare you a list like this:

rubberneck wagon: sightseeing bus
lip muff: moustache
kick the gong around: smoke an opium pipe

The expressions on the right have the same meanings as the ones on the left. That is, they are *synonyms. Definition by synonym* consists merely in providing a word that is equivalent in meaning (or nearly so) to the word being defined. The aim, of course, is to supply a word that someone can be expected to know for one that he may not know.

All the slang expressions above have ordinary English equivalents, and their definition is a rather simple matter. In virtually every case, the slang and the ordinary expression are used in exactly the same way. ("He shaved his lip muff" and "He shaved his moustache," for example.) But when it comes to defining ordinary words by providing other ordinary words as synonyms, we run into a bit of trouble. The trouble is this: There seem to be very few, if any, ordinary words that are exact synonyms. Consider the words "trail" and "path," for example. The two are very close in meaning, and we might say either "He strayed from the trail" or "He strayed from the path." Notice, though, that there are some cases in which we wouldn't regard the two as equivalent in meaning. No one would think that "Hansel and Gretel left a trail of breadcrumbs" means the same as "Hansel and Gretel left a path of breadcrumbs." The second sentence makes it sound as though they left a virtual highway of crumbled bread.

This trouble is not terribly serious, though. What we have to keep in mind is that when we define by offering a synonyn, we have to select a word that is used in the same way *in the same context* as the word defined. The synonymy we have to rely on, then, is that that holds between the uses of two words in the same kind of situation. In some other kind of situation, one of the words might apply and the other not.

To define by offering a synonym is to say, in effect, "The word I'm supplying you is used in the same way in this context as the word I'm defining." Accordingly, a standard for judging definitions by synonym consists in requiring that the word offered as a synonym be as close in use to the word defined as possible. Anyone who offered "dwelling place" as a synonym for "flat" would be open to criticism. It's true that flats are dwelling places, and in some cases it would be just as correct to say "I'm returning to my dwelling place" as "I'm returning to my flat." Yet "dwelling place" has a much broader range of application than "flat." It applies to castles and grand hotels, as well as to huts and hovels. "Apartment" is obviously a better choice, for the two words can be used interchangeably in a greater number of cases.

Definition by Enumeration

If you wanted to count the ways you love someone, you would name them off one by one. To count off or name one by one is to *enumerate.* Just as the proof of a pudding is in the eating, the nature of enumerative definition is in its name. An *enumerative definition* consists in providing a complete list of all the items referred to or named by an expression.

To be successful, an enumerative definition must meet two requirements. First, the list must be a *complete* list. It's not enough merely to provide samples of things referred to by a word. *Everything* denoted by the word must be put on the list. Second, the list cannot contain items that aren't denoted by the word. In sum, then, the list must contain all and only those things that the word being defined picks out or names.

Here are some cases of enumerative definitions:

southwestern state: New Mexico, Arizona, Texas, California, Nevada, Utah, Colorado

solar planet: Mercury, Venus, Earth, Mars, Jupiter, Saturn, Uranus, Neptune, Pluto

transuranic element: neptunium, plutonium, americium, curium, berkelium, californium, einsteinium, fermium, mendelevium, nobelium, lawrencium

An enumerative definition explains the meaning of an expression only in the sense that it lists the items the expression picks out or names. The relation between the expression being defined and the definition of it is not like that between "car" and "automobile" or "father" and "male parent." In these cases, the expressions in each pair can be said to have the same meaning. So far as definition by enumeration is concerned, though, the relation between the expression being defined and the definition is more like that between "New York" and "the largest city in the United States." In this case, the two expressions have different meanings, but refer to or denote the same thing. Similarly, the names of all the southwestern states, taken as a group, refer to all the southwestern states, and the expression "southwestern state" likewise refers to each and every southwestern state.

Since the meaning of a word is not identical with the reference of a word, there is a sense in which enumerative definitions don't explain the meanings of words. Yet in another sense they do. They indicate how a word is used by providing a list of those things that it is correctly used to refer to.

The examples that we've considered make it clear that enumerative definition can be of considerable use. But it's important to notice that when it is used there are several assumptions that are generally taken for granted. For instance, it's usually assumed that the items listed are ones that are picked out by the word *at the present time.* Thus an enumerative definition of "transuranic element" in 1939 would not be the same as one given in 1944, for the simple reason that during that period of time additional elements were discovered. This generally presents us with no practical difficulty, for in most circumstances in which we use enumerative definitions it's the current list that we want anyway. Someone doing the history of physics, however, couldn't rely on a present-day enumerative definition of "transuranic element" if he wanted to understand the expression in the same way as people in, say, 1939.

Also, there are other restrictions on how lists are formed that are usually unstated because of the situation. The phrase "registered voter" might be defined by enumeration by a list of names. Such a list, though, would be for a particular election in a certain state, county, district, and so on. The expression, then, is not given a general definition.

Furthermore, because ordinary words most often pick out things that belong to a potentially unlimited class ("chair," "wolfbane," and so on), the technique is not one that can be used for most words in the language. Its principle use is in supplying stipulative definitions, either of new expressions or of ordinary expressions that are being used in a special or restricted way. This isn't to say that it cannot be used for reportive definitions. It's just that, as a matter of fact, most words don't lend themselves to reportive definition by enumeration.

Definition by Example

Suppose that you are home alone and are comfortably sitting and reading a book when there is a tremendous clap of thunder, a rushing of wind, and a powerful sulfurous smell fills the air. You look up and see standing before you Dark Lucifer. Satan himself!

"I have come to offer you a bargain," he says. "If you can follow the command I shall give you, then I will grant any request that you make. If you cannot, then I shall claim as my property your immortal soul."

After assuring yourself that the command will be one well within the range of normal human abilities, you agree to the offer.

"Very well," his Satanic Majesty says, "I will give you my command. Define the word 'red.' "

"You mean you want me to define it in terms of some theory of electromagnetic radiation—wavelengths in the visible spectrum, stuff like that?"

"No, I don't want a scientific account of the nature of red light. I want a definition of the word as it's ordinarily used. Surely you must be able to do that; after all, the word's been around much longer than these fancy theories."

How could you satisfy Satan's demand? If you could do it, then not only could you save your soul, you could wish for something magnificent—such as the eternal happiness of all mankind.

In this section we'll be considering how such commands can be carried out. We'll be talking about how words like "red" can be defined by making use of examples. We'll find also that many words unlike "red" can be defined by presenting examples.

As we noticed in Chapter 2, the word "paradigm" means "a clear-cut case." Thus somebody who is said to be "a paradigm of virtue" is the very model of virtue. He is, we might say, a prime example: "If there's such a thing as virtue, he's a case of it." A paradigm case or paradigm example of a word's use is a case in which the word definitely and unhesitatingly applies: "If the word 'red' doesn't apply to that delicious apple, then it doesn't apply to anything." In talking about defining words by making use of examples, then, we are talking about using paradigm cases to explain how a word is used.

Paradigm cases can be presented in different ways. That is, there are various ways of explaining just what sorts of things, situations, or people are the appropriate ones for a word to apply to. In this section, we'll talk about three of the more important ways of presenting paradigm cases. At the end you should be able to beat the Devil at his own game.

Ostensive Definition

To broaden the intellectual horizons of some deserving child, we might drag her down to the reptile house of the zoo. We would, of course, want this to be an educational visit and not one given over solely to pleasure. Let's suppose, then, that we decided to teach her the names of some animals.

We decide to start with the gila monster.

Standing outside the display case, we point a finger at the creature sunning itself inside and say in a definite tone of voice, *"That's* a gila monster." Being even more helpful, we might point to the iguana sleeping in the next case and emphatically say, "That's *not* a gila monster."

In pointing and naming we would be giving an *ostensive definition* of the expression "gila monster." The English word "ostensive" borrows its own meaning from the Latin for "to point." An ostensive definition, then, consists in nothing more difficult than pointing to an object that is referred to by a certain word and pronouncing the word. We might just as well call it "pointing definition," but "ostensive" is too well entrenched to be uprooted.

Like most activities, there's a bit of art or skill in giving ostensive definitions. Not a great amount, though, and most of us pick it up quite naturally in childhood. It's most helpful, for example, to explain how a word is used by pointing to more than one object of the sort that it refers to. ("There goes another one," you might say, as a gila monster scurries across the floor of the reptile house.)

Furthermore, it's also useful to indicate other objects to which the word you're defining does not apply. It's only sensible, of course, to point out those objects that rather closely resemble appropriate objects. It's helpful to tell someone that "gila monster" doesn't apply to an iguana or a gecko, but it's not helpful to say that it doesn't apply to a lamppost or a circus tent.

Ostensive definition is a rather crude but effective way of getting someone to understand how a word that is strange to him is used. Of all the ways of defining, it's probably the one most commonly employed in everyday life. It explains what a word means by demonstrating how the word is used. Some people prefer to say that it is a way of teaching words, rather than defining them. But so far as getting an understanding of the meaning of words is concerned, this is not a very important distinction.

Ostensive definition is a rather obvious and straightforward process. The truth is, though, there is a rather complex net of assumptions woven together to support the operation of ostensive definition.

We can use it successfully for many words that we don't know, because there are many words that we already know. We can get clear about what someone is pointing to by asking him questions. ("Do you mean that strange animal, or are you pointing to that cactus thing?") If we didn't share the same language and couldn't ask questions, then ostensive definition would be of doubtful effectiveness.

For example, suppose you just arrived on this planet after a long trip from the fourth planet of Tau Ceti. You know no English and the Extraterrestrial Friendship League assigns a teacher to help you learn the language.

He decides to help you acquire a basic vocabulary by providing you with some ostensive definitions. Accordingly, he points to a dog and says, "Dog." He points to a turtle, shakes his head and says, "Not a dog." A fly is buzzing around the room so he points to the fly and says, "Not a dog."

What are you to think? Are you to believe you've been taught a word that corresponds to a word in your own language for "mammal" or "possesses teeth"? Supposing that the dog was a white Yorkshire terrier, have you been taught a word that corresponds in your language to "white" or "furry," or even "Yorkshire terrier"?

Perhaps by extensive comparisons, coupled with approvals and corrections from your teacher, you might eventually learn that the word "dog" refers to dogs. But the process would be arduous and tedious.

We've assumed also that you, a visitor from a strange planet, are already acquainted with such conventions as head shaking for disapproval and pointing. Perhaps this assumption isn't justified, though. How would you know that when your teacher held out his finger to point at the dog and said "Dog," he wasn't using the word to refer to his finger? Or maybe he was telling you what that position of the hand is called— perhaps you might think he was trying to teach you the word "pointing." Or how do you know that pointing is used to suggest a line running from the fingertip to the object indicated? You might believe that the object referred to was the one encountered by an imaginary line extended in the other direction and ending at some object behind the teacher. Besides, is the teacher pointing to a spot on the dog, the whole dog, the dog's color, just what?

Speculating in this way has a bit of fun attached to it, but it has a serious aspect also. For one thing, it makes it obvious that giving ostensive definitions is not really such a simple matter. On analysis, the procedure turns out to be a rather complex one, though we aren't going to attempt a thorough analysis. Defining by ostension seems simple to us because we already know a language and we understand the conventions that are involved in the process of pointing, naming, affirming, and denying. The language and the conventions we assimilated almost painlessly and unconsciously from our culture. For someone from a culture wholly alien to our own, ostensive definitions would be likely to present problems that for us are unreal.

Furthermore, speculation about the difficulties that such a creature might face not only helps us understand what is involved in giving an ostensive definition; it also helps us see why we might sometimes find such definitions misleading. You don't have to be an alien to wonder when someone points to a part of an electron microscope and says, "Electron gun," whether he is telling you the name of the anode or the grid or the assembly of the two. If you're not sure, you can ask. But you can think you're sure and be dead wrong. That's one of the disadvantages of pointing definitions.

Mentioning Examples

Nobody requires much persuading to agree that giving an ostensive definition by actually pointing to an item designated by a word can be quite inconvenient. Chances are there are no movie stars in your living room. Consequently, to give an ostensive definition of "movie star" by pointing out one or two isn't very practical. You would have to travel to Hollywood, Las Vegas, Cannes, or wherever you might expect to find them, and this seems like an awful lot of trouble to go to just to give a definition.

An obvious alternative is merely to *mention some examples* of people to whom the expression can be applied. You might say, for instance, "By 'movie star' I mean somebody like Woody Allen, Humphrey Bogart, Karen Black, and so on." The people named are ones who are definitely referred to by the expression, and the "and so on" indicates that you don't mean the list to be a complete one. You're only giving *samples* of people designated by the expression.

Since names are no more than verbal fingers, the same woes that beset ostensive definition are found here. This means that in defining by mentioning examples, it's a good idea to present a *variety* of examples. It's also wise to indicate some cases that, though similar, aren't appropriate. You wouldn't want to define "novel," for example, by mentioning only the titles of eighteenth-century novels. Also, it might be a good idea to mention a few biographies or histories to make it clear that "novel" doesn't apply to them.

Defining by mentioning examples is similar to definition by enumeration, but there is one significant difference. In defining by enumeration, it's necessary to list *all* the items to which the word applies. But this is not required of definition by example. It's necessary only to mention *some* of the items. Thus it's possible to define expressions like "odd number" by mentioning only a few numbers. Since there is an infinite series of odd numbers, an enumerative definition of the expression can't be given.

Every silver cloud has its dark lining. The very fact that definition by mentioning examples does *not* involve listing all cases in which a word applies opens up the way for confusion and misunderstanding of the sort discussed earlier. The risk involved is outweighed by the advantages, though, and there are steps that we can take to reduce confusion and misunderstanding. We just have to be prepared to take them.

Defining by Describing Examples

Another obvious alternative to pointing is *describing*. That is, rather than pointing a real finger or a verbal one at an example of a person, place, thing, or situation to which a word applies, you might just paint a verbal picture of an appropriate case.

Suppose, for example, you wanted to define the word "charlatan," and there aren't any charlatans around to point out, and you don't know any you could refer to by name. What can you do? Well, you could describe the sort of person to whom the word applies. You might say something like this: "Do you remember in all those cowboy movies the guy who comes to town to sell snake-oil or some ancient Indian herb medicine? He always claims it's a miraculous cure, but is really lying about it. Well, that sort of person is called a charlatan."

You are saying, in effect, that the word is properly used to apply to a person of this sort. This doesn't mean, of course, that it isn't also used to refer to other sorts of people. You are describing only one kind of case in which it's correctly employed.

Defining by describing cases really has a lot more flexibility than pointing and naming do. After all, life is short and experience is limited, and we can hardly expect actually to be directly acquainted with all the sorts of things, people, and situations to which the words we need to know apply. Descriptions are a pale substitute for experience (as readers of adventure novels know), but they are at least adequate for the purpose of learning many words of a language.

Not all defining by describing is a replacement of experience. We sometimes define words by describing circumstances of the sort in which people typically have certain experiences. The definition is a way of saying "The word applies to the feeling (or sensation or whatever) you have in this kind of situation."

Suppose, for example, that someone didn't know the meaning of the word "depressed" as it is used in a sentence like "I feel depressed." You might try substituting some more or less equivalent expressions in the sentence, but you might also describe the sort of situation in which somebody might be expected to feel depressed. You might say: "Can you imagine how you would feel if you just learned that your girl friend had died of an incurable disease, you had flunked out of school, and your father had cut you off from your inheritance? If you've had things like this happen to you, then you know how you would feel. That's feeling depressed."

Or, to take an easier case, suppose someone is just learning English and doesn't know what "blue" means. You don't know his language so you can't give him a synonym. You might tell him something like this: "Go outside on a clear day and look up at the sky. The color you see is what we call 'blue.' " In this example, you are describing a set of circumstances under which someone can put himself in the position to have the experience that's necessary to learning what the word means.

Despite the disadvantages and possibilities of confusion inherent in all three ways of defining by example that we've discussed, the technique is of primary importance. Not only is it of considerable practical usefulness, but some words seem to require this sort of definition for a proper explanation of their meaning. For example, no one learns to apply color words like "heliotrope" or "puce" or even "red" and "blue" without having the colors they refer to pointed out to him. Or without being told how he can put himself in the position to have the experiences that an understanding of the words requires. Similarly, words like "sweet," "sour," "bitter," and "tart" can be learned only by tasting the sorts of things that can be said to be such. ("You know the taste you get when you bite into a lemon; well, that's a sour taste.") Also the meaning of words like "loud" and "soft" (as applied to sounds) and "blinding" and "bright" (as applied to light) can only be understood from experience. A definition of these words, then, involves indicating in some way examples of cases in which the words are correctly used.

We have not discussed all the ways of using examples to define. Sometimes, for instance, we explain how a word is used by showing someone a picture of the sort of thing that it refers to. That such a technique is effective is one of the reasons that picture books for children are so popular. We could probably include pointing at a picture in the category of ostensive definition. It simply involves an additional convention. Probably, too, we could include in the same category cases in which we actually ask someone to smell something or feel something with his fingers and then tell him what word applies to what he is smelling or feeling. After all, these are definitions that operate on the same principle as pointing.

In any event, it doesn't really matter what we call the subclasses. The important point is that in all such cases we are indicating a way in which a word is properly used by supplying in some way or other examples of the word's use. It is this that is fundamental. The rest is icing on the cake.

Use Definition

This is the last method of definition that we're going to introduce, and it's going to be a peculiar one. What makes it strange is that we're going to include within it all the other methods of defining and leave room to shove in some others besides. It's almost as if somebody said, "In addition to pears, oranges, and tangerines, we also have fruit."

But an explanation of why we're going to use this odd category is in order.

To make sense of the explanation, let's first recall some basic facts. To give a definition is to explain the meaning of a word. But what is the meaning of a word? Since we spent a lot of time answering this question in Chapter 2, there's no need to go into details here. It's enough to say that the meaning of a word is the set of conditions that govern the way the word is used.

Consequently, to explain the meaning of a word is to give an account of the conditions that regulate the word's use. The uses of words—their meanings—are explained in much the same way that the uses of gadgets like can-openers are explained: by presenting an account of the proper circumstances, features, objects, and so on that are associated with and govern their uses.

With this sort of information in hand, it's possible to view the methods of definition that we've been discussing from a more general perspective. We can now see them as merely aspects of one Grand Enterprise.

The Grand Enterprise is explaining the meanings of words by supplying an account of the conditions that govern their use. *The methods of definition are all ways of revealing features of the way that words are used.* (Or are going to be used, when the definition is stipulative.)

That is, the methods are all ways of indicating relevant and important features that function as conditions regulating use. Thus Definition by Example involves describing or pointing out cases of the type that a word applies to. Enumerative definition consists in providing a list of all the cases that a word picks out. And Definition by Synonym relies on the fact that in some situations the uses of different words are often governed by the same conditions.

We could, if we wanted to, create as many methods of definition as there are kinds of conditions associated with the uses of words. In cases in which a certain sort of feature is the most important one for explaining how a word is used, then the best method of definition would be one that focused on that feature.

For example, when the origin of something is an important condition, we could give a genetic definition. So a genetic definition of "igneous rock" would be "rock formed by great heat." When it's what a thing does or is used for that's the most important feature, we could offer a functional definition. Thus we could define "mordant" as "a substance used in dyeing."

We could obviously go on and on until we ended up with a gross or more of definitional methods. We could have "grammatical role" definitions, "social significance" definitions, "legal" definitions, "literary" definitions, and so on. We could, as we've said, create as many methods as there are kinds of conditions that govern the uses of words.

If we did this, though, we would find ourselves with an embarrassment of riches. We would have so many definitional methods that we would tend to lose sight of the whole point and purpose of definition. It's better to stick to a few significant methods and lump together the more specific and limited ones.

Clearly enough, though, Use definition is the Prime Method. It is the theme upon which all other methods are merely variations.

This raises the question, why introduce other methods at all? Though we didn't talk about all possible methods, we did discuss three besides Use.

In truth, there is no really overpowering reason to introduce the specific methods. We would be on firm footing just to say, "There is one method of definition, and that's the one that consists in explaining the conditions that govern a word's use."

The reason we haven't taken this path is because there is a practical advantage in having several methods of definition at one's disposal. Rather than the general order "Give conditions of use," the various methods tell us what *sorts* of conditions we should look for and mention. Thus they supply us with a framework for thinking about conditions of use. This makes it easier to identify relevant conditions and to explain them to others.

The methods of definition are, in effect, specifications of one general method. The specifications offer an additional practical advantage. As we've already seen, certain methods are more suited to specific sorts of words and purposes than others. A definition of "number" can't be given by Enumeration, for example, but this method may be helpful in explaining that an expression like "Pacific state" applies to just those things on a short list.

The specific forms of Use definition, then, supply us with a number of methods from which we can select one that seems best suited for the job at hand. The methods offer us some structured options, and we don't have to flail around trying to discover the best method to use. That is, we don't have to flail around *as much*, because we still have to choose a method.

Quite apart from specific methods, the major point to be emphasized is that to give a definition is to mention the conditions that govern the use of the word. If this single principle is remembered, then long after the names of all the methods have become lost in the fog of time, it will still be possible to realize what's required of us when we face the task of giving or evaluating a definition.

Separating Sheep from Goats: Standards for Definition

We have no laws that explicitly recognize what is good in human conduct, but we have plenty that point out what we regard as bad. When it comes to evaluating definitions, we are in a similar position. It's a lot easier to supply a list of definitional vices than to compose a hymn of definitional virtues. Since the easy path takes us where we want to go, we'll follow it. In this section we'll point out some of the varieties of definitional sin.

There are two matters we ought to get straight on before we begin. First, not all the vices we'll be discussing are ones that can be shared by all the ways of defining that we've discussed. For example, definition by enumeration is a rather straightforward procedure that's not likely to go wrong in any way that can't be put down to simple error (or deliberate deception). Also, in our discussion of definition by example, we've already noticed some of the ways that defining in this fashion can go wrong or be misleading. We won't bother to repeat those observations here.

Second, definitions are given for different purposes and to different people. Consequently, a definition that's satisfactory for one purpose or to one group might not be for others. Someone reading a popular book on astronomy might want to know only that "parsec" can be defined as "a unit of astronomical distance" so he can understand (at least roughly) what it means to say that something is only four parsecs away from earth. But a student of astronomy needs to be told that a parsec is a unit of measuring astronomical distance that is based on the distance from the earth at which the stellar parallax is one second of arc and that it is equal to 1.9×10^{13} miles, or about 3.258 light-years.

The astronomy student would be likely to object to the first definition as intolerably vague, and the ordinary person would likely criticize the second definition as too technical and obscure.

The upshot of this is that any commandment like "Avoid language that is obscure or vague in giving a definition" is totally useless as an absolute command. It's like giving someone a moral rule like "Always do the right thing."

This observation isn't intended to be a counsel of despair, though. The point is that the commandments we'll be discussing have to be interpreted in a liberal and sensible fashion. They are merely guides to the conduct of defining, not rules that guarantee success. It's necessary to keep in mind that the standards, expressed as prohibitions, are ones to be followed relative to the purpose at hand and relative to the audience for whom the definition is intended.

You have to proceed in something like the following way. My job, you say to yourself, is to give an explanation of the meaning of the word "extrasensory perception" as it's used in parapsychology. My audience is composed of professional psychologists who don't know anything about parapsychology. All right, I'm free to use technical terms, and I had better try to give a fairly complete explanation of the term. Now, I'm ready to follow the standards of giving a good definition.

It's at this point that the prohibitions we'll talk about below come into play.

Avoid Complete Circularity

A definition can be said to be circular when it explains the meaning of a word by using the word itself or one of the word's grammatical forms. Here are a couple of circular definitions:

chairperson: a person who chairs
bookbinder: one who binds books.

As they stand, these definitions are unacceptable because they are almost totally uninformative. An explanation that doesn't explain is an explanation not worth having. And you would probably be on good grounds if you suspected that anyone who gave you definitions like these was deliberately trying to keep you from finding out what the words meant. Or, at the very least, was trying to put you off from pressing for a real explanation.

There is an obvious and easy way to repair these definitions. All we need to do is to supply other definitions of the words they use. If, for example, you were also given an explanation of what it is to chair a meeting and to bind a book, then the definitions would be informative.

With these additional definitions in hand, the circularity of the original definitions would be harmless. But without them, those definitions would be useless. We can say that the original definitions when they are not supplemented by additional definitions are completely circular. The commandment, then, is to avoid *complete circularity* in defining.

Perhaps the easiest way to avoid complete circularity is simply to give a definition that does not require an additional definition to explain the meaning of the term that makes it circular in the first place. If, for example, "bookbinder" were defined as "a person who encloses and fastens a book between covers," then there would be no need of the supplementary explanation.

Sometimes, though, it's simply convenient from the standpoint of exposition to give a circular definition and then render the circularity harmless by giving an additional definition. For example, a definition of "welfare recipient" could probably be done most easily by defining the term as "one who receives welfare" and following this with an explanation of what it means to receive welfare. To choose to proceed in this fashion is merely to elect to follow one strategy of explanation rather than another.

A minor warning is in order in connection with circularity. Don't be confused into thinking that a definition is circular because the word being defined is *mentioned* in the definition. This definition is not circular, for example:

damn: The saying of "damn"; a curse.

The word "damn" is mentioned in the definition, but it's not being used. Circularity results only when the word being defined is used in the definition. (Recall that a word in quotation marks is, in effect, a word itself, and it is not the same as the word without those marks. You can't very well have circularity unless some version of the *same* word as that defined appears in the definition.)

Avoid Language That Is Obscure, Ambiguous, or Metaphorical

The primary purpose of a definition is to explain what a word means. Accordingly, anything that gets in the way of a proper understanding of the explanation ought to be avoided. Nothing gets in the way so much as language that is difficult to understand, ambiguous, or not to be taken literally. Let's briefly survey these three sins.

Avoid Obscure Language

The following definition is an excellent example of one that almost dares anyone to understand it:

net: anything reticulated or decussated, at equal distances, with interstices between the intersections.

There isn't anything wrong with this definition in the sense that it contains any errors of reporting on the use of the word. The description it gives of the features that something must have in order for the word "net" to apply to it is perfectly accurate.

From the standpoint of intelligibility, though, there is something terribly wrong with the definition. The language in which it is given is so recondite and obscure that it's hard to imagine that anyone who could understand the definition would have any use for it.

(By the way, the definition is one of the more famous ones in Dr. Samuel Johnson's *Dictionary*. Probably the Great Cham was just exercising his sense of humor, not believing that anyone would really need to be told the meaning of such a simple word.)

For contrast with the above definition, consider this one:

net: an openwork fabric with the threads woven, knotted or twisted together at regular intervals, forming meshes of varying sizes.

The clarity of language here is so obvious that this definition might serve as an example of the kind of language that a definiton ought to contain.

Though we mentioned this earlier, it's worth pointing out again that to say that the language of a definition shouldn't be obscure isn't to say that it can't be technical. A definition of "gram molecular weight," for example, will have to be expressed in terms that are used in chemistry. It is a technical reportive definition:

gram molecular weight: the weight of a compound, expressed in grams, that is numerically equivalent to the mass, expressed in atomic mass units, of one molecule of the compound.

It may well be that no one can understand this definition unless he understands what it means to talk about the mass of a molecule of a compound. This doesn't brand the definition as defective, however. The language is clear and precise.

Someone might complain that this really isn't the sort of definition he wanted. He might have wanted only to be told something that would give him a crude idea of what the term means. In which case, a functional (though still reportive and technical) definition would probably have done the job. For example:

gram molecular weight: That's a way of measuring a compound in amounts that are large enough to use conveniently.

The fact that someone wanted another *sort* of definition doesn't mean that the first sort offered was defective in some way. ("There's nothing wrong with the milkshake; it's just that I wanted beer.")

Avoid Ambiguous Language

If a definition is given that involves any of the three ways of being ambiguous that we distinguished in Chapter 3, then it's defective and ought to be rejected. After all, it's hardly possible to take an explanation as a good one if you aren't even sure how the explanation is to be understood.

The following definition is one that contains an ambiguous word:

playwright: one who produces plays.

The troublesome word is "produces," for it can mean "manufactures" (i.e., writes) or "finances and supervises presentation of a play."

Similarly, the definition below leaves it unclear whether it is literary composition or handwriting that is intended:

minuscule: a form of writing developed during the Middle Ages.

The definition of "vernier" as "an auxiliary device designed to facilitate fine adjustments on precision instruments" is grammatically ambiguous. It's impossible to tell from the sentence alone whether the device is *applied to* precision instruments or is *attached to* them. It's the last interpretation that is intended, and if the phrase "on precision instruments" were moved so it followed "an auxiliary device," the definition would be unobjectionable.

Avoid Metaphorical Language

There is, hopefully, a place in the world for wit and fancy and the playful use of language. Definition is not that place, though. Literal as mud and dry as dust is the only way to give definitions. Otherwise, the aim of explanation is frustrated. When it comes to the crunch, it's better to sacrifice beauty for truth.

It's not likely that anyone who defined "camel" as "the ship of the desert" would be taken seriously. (Of course, somebody who didn't already know what a camel was wouldn't be very enlightened by this supposed definition.) There is a danger, though, that someone might take the definition of "the United States Constitution" as "the rock of American democracy" literally as the *name* of a certain rock. After all, if he has heard of Plymouth Rock and the Rock of Gibraltar, he won't be too surprised to hear that there is another rock called "United States Constitution."

Definitions given in metaphorical language are, at the very best, uninformative. At the worst, they are misleading. Metaphors should be kept locked in their cages and allowed out only when they can peform tricks that are useful as well as amusing. So far as definition is concerned, that time is never.

There's more to be said about metaphors used in definitions, but we'll save it until a later section. Then we'll talk about some of the ways that metaphors and other turns of phrase can be put to work to deceive and mislead, by carelessness or by craft.

Avoid Being Too Broad or Too Narrow

> The Master of the Inner Truth pays a visit to a small Kentucky village. There he announces that he will answer any question put to him.
>
> "What is talent, Master?" a young man asks.
>
> "Talent," he says, "is the ability to compose a beautiful sonnet while taking a bath."

How's that for a definition? Pretty lousy, really, and hardly worthy of a Master of Inner Truth. The major trouble with it is that it has merely presented us with one sort of case in which we would be willing to say someone has talent. (It's possible to say that the case mentioned is a paradigm case, and if the Master goes on to describe other cases, we can let him off the hook.)

A proper definition of "talent" ought to make it clear that the word applies to a wider variety of cases than the one cited by the Master. We want to make sure, for example, that we include people who compose poems other than sonnets, those who write outstanding novels, plays, movie scripts, and propaganda, those who perform such actions as playing the viola or riding the unicycle particularly well, and so on.

The definition the Master gives, we would say, is too *narrow*. It excludes many kinds of cases in which we would regard it as legitimate to apply the word "talent."

Suppose we widen the definition, then. Let's define the word in this way:

talent: the ability to do something.

You don't have to be a Master of Inner Truth to recognize that we've gone too far in our definition. We have broadened the word's range of application to such an extent that anybody who is able to perform anything in any way whatsoever can be said to have talent. The word now applies to both Martha Graham and a dancing bear, to Arthur Clarke and any hack who can put words on paper. It applies to the poor drudge scrubbing the steps and to the person who flips the switch that turns on the computer. The definition now, of course, is too *broad.*

In this case, the definition is too broad because it would lead us to apply "talent" to cases that we wouldn't ordinarily regard as appropriate. You might say here that the definition is just *wrong,* if it's intended to be an explanation of the ordinary meaning of the word.

There is, however, another way of being too broad that doesn't make a definition wrong. It just makes it very unhelpful.

Consider the following definition of "shirt":

shirt: an article of clothing.

Quite correct, right? Right. But the obvious difficulty is that anyone who didn't know what a shirt was in the first place would not be helped very much to be told it's an article of clothing. True, if he had absolutely no idea about what a shirt is, he would be helped a little bit. He would learn that it's not a device that's fed through a computer, it's not something to eat, and it's not something to read while commuting to Oshkosh.

On the other hand, the definition doesn't distinguish a shirt from the fez of the Sultan of Baghdad, the cloak of Captain Marvel, or the turban of Ibis the Invincible. The definition, again, is not wrong, but it's too *broad*. More features need to be added in the definition so that it becomes clear just what sort of thing more specifically *counts* as a shirt.

It should be clear from the three cases we've looked at that a proper definition has to be like Baby Bear's porridge—*just right*. It can be neither too narrow nor too broad.

Fancifully speaking, a definition draws a circle around the things or situations to which the word defined applies. (The circle is rather rough for some words.) Accordingly, you have to be careful to see that the circle doesn't include things to which the word doesn't apply. On the other hand, you have to see that it doesn't leave out things to which the word does apply. Giving a proper definition isn't really all that different from sorting oranges and potatoes.

By the way, the Master could have given a better definition of "talent" had he said something like this:

talent: the natural or acquired ability to do something in a superior way.

If anybody cares, a definition of "shirt" that escapes the crime of being too broad would be one along these lines:

shirt: a garment for the upper part of the body, typically with sleeves, collar, and a front opening, and sometimes worn under a coat or another heavier shirt.

Avoid Using Irrelevant Features

There's no reason to give the Master of Inner Truth a hard time, but there is something else wrong with his definition that ought to be mentioned. You'll recall that he defined "talent" as "the ability to compose a beautiful sonnet while taking a bath."

If we took this definition literally, in the way that a computer or a robot might do, it would have an odd consequence. It would keep us from saying that the author of a beautiful sonnet had talent if he composed it while sitting at his desk or riding on the IRT subway. We could say that he had talent only if he composed it *while taking a bath*.

Clearly no one would intend this, and to suggest they might is just to make a bad joke. Nevertheless, the bad joke has a good point. Mentioning features that are not relevant to the use of the word being defined is to invite confusion and misunderstanding.

It's possible to go from bad to worse and mention *only* features that are irrelevant to the use of the word. Suppose, for example, someone defined

"rock music" in this way: "music played on electrically amplified instruments."

The natural response to this definition would be, "Well, that's not
quite right. Sure, a lot of rock music does use amplification, but that's not
really what makes it rock music."

The definition seems to miss the point. It focuses on features that seem
accidental or irrelevant. After all, if the electricity is turned off, rock
music doesn't have to come to a halt. It can be played on instruments that
aren't amplified and still be rock. A definition would be more on target if
it zeroed in on such features as the themes and beat of the music. These
are what are basic to making it what it is.

In giving a definition, then, we ought to aim at mentioning those
features that are relevant and important to the word's use. We ought to
avoid mentioning those that are irrelevant or trivial. And this is so even if
the features are ones that are always found in those cases in which the
word is used.

For example, let's suppose that all students hate freshman composition. A definition might go like this:

freshman composition: the class that all students hate.

Obviously, even if this were true, it would have nothing to do with
explaining the meaning of the phrase. After all, suppose all students
were to come to love the course, the meaning of the phrase "freshman
composition" wouldn't change. To define the phrase properly we need
to mention those features that are important and relevant to its use.
Something like this:

freshman composition: a college course that aims at improving the writing skills of
    students through practice and criticism.

We could add many more commandments to this list, but since God
needed only ten to cover all aspects of life, we ought to be able to get by
with four to deal with definition. These "rules" are no more mechanical
than an apple, and they can't be applied in an automatic fashion. As with
most rules that deal with real life, they have to be employed with
discretion, judgment, and imagination.

Dirty Definitions

We generally think of definitions as tools to be used to smooth the path of
understanding and open up the road of communication. Such, indeed, is
their legitimate use. But just as the same scalpel that saves lives in the
hands of a surgeon can become an instrument of destruction in the hands
of a maniac, so can definitions become methods of deceit.

In this section, we'll discuss two types of definition that involve
misleading an audience under the guise of presenting a legitimate expla-

nation of the meaning of a word. Sometimes such definitions are presented only in fun, and are not really intended to mislead. Most often, however, they are used to cloud the understanding, to alter attitudes, and to secure agreement on a point of view without troubling to argue for it. Used for these ends, such definitions are morally dirty. If there were a Deceptive Practices Act regulating definitions, they would be outlawed by it.

Persuasive Definitions

In his famous eighteenth-century dictionary, Dr. Johnson defined "lexicographer" as "a maker of dictionaries; a harmless drudge." A lexicographer *is* a maker of dictionaries and he *may* be a harmless drudge, but of course, "harmless drudge" is not part of the usual meaning of the word. After years of exacting labor, Johnson was allowing himself a sardonic comment on his chosen occupation.

Persuasive definitions are definitions that appear to explain the ordinary meaning of a word but are really disguised attempts to influence our attitudes or conduct. Since rhetoric is "the art of persuasion by words," and such definitions try to persuade us to adopt a certain point of view, they are also called *rhetorical definitions*.

Some persuasive definitions attempt to influence our attitudes only in a gentle way. Like Dr. Johnson's definition, they are not intended to deceive us, but they are intended to express an opinion and to get us to share that opinion.

Cardinal Newman's definition of a gentleman as "one who never inflicts pain" was not put forward as a report on how people who speak English use the word "gentleman." Rather, it expressed Newman's belief that a gentleman *ought to be* such a person. Anyone who thought this notion of a gentleman a good one would thus have to conduct himself in the prescribed fashion.

Sir Henry Wotton's charmingly ambiguous definition of an ambassador as "an honest man sent to lie abroad for his country" quite successfully conveys a certain attitude toward diplomacy and diplomats. Similarly, Oscar Wilde's famous definition of foxhunting as "the unspeakable in pursuit of the inedible" leaves no doubt about what he thought of foxhunting. Ezra Pound's quip that nowadays a philosopher is "just a guy too damned lazy to work in a laboratory" makes quite clear Pound's contempt for philosophers.

In spite of the fact that they may look like and read like definitions, cases like the ones above are not really definitions. None of them was ever offered as a serious definition (except for Johnson's), though, no doubt, they were offered seriously for some other purpose.

Sometimes, however, persuasive definitions are not just epigrams or editorials. Some are deliberately designed to be misleading. They are phrased to appeal to prejudices and emotions and to influence behavior and attitudes, while at the same time attempting to pass as legitimate definitions.

Consider these, for example:

1. A Catholic is a person who owes allegiance only to the Pope.
2. A Negro is a person who bears the mark of Cain set on him by God to separate him from the rest of the human race.
3. Jews are an inferior race of people bred from the dregs of other races.

Such definitions are generally offered as correct accounts of the meanings of the words they pretend to be explaining. But they are, of course, only propaganda devices that work by associating the word and what it refers to with a complex of emotionally charged terms.

Not all persuasive definitions must be so virulent or appeal to prejudices and emotions in such a direct fashion as the ones above. Some consist in linking the word supposedly defined with honorific words like "my country," "patriotic," "intelligent," "with it," and so on.

There is obviously a place for strategy in formulating persuasive definitions, and the smart propagandist must know his audience and their values and prejudices so he will know what sort of words to use in framing his "definitions."

He must also decide, of course, whether he wishes them to approve or disapprove of the things referred to by the word he is defining. It is, after all, a poor propagandist who leaves his audience in doubt as to what their opinions ought to be.

Consider the following definitions and notice the kind of appeal made:

liberal: a person who is ahead of his time, one who tries to see future problems before they become crises.

liberal: a person out of touch with the hard realities of the world, one who dreams of utopia and ignores immediate and pressing difficulties.

woman: a person selected by nature to be the mother of children and the assistant of man.

woman: someone who has been forced to bury her talents and sacrifice her intelligence because of a repressive male-dominated society.

Probably few people are taken in by persuasive definitions, unless they are already prepared by their own wishes and prejudices to be misled. Being fooled by a persuasive definition, then, is generally a symptom and not a cause. Yet not all who are misled are willingly misled. So a knowledge of persuasive definition and an awareness of how it works is considerable protection against the dangers of deception.

Loaded Definitions

Loaded definitions are close cousins of persuasive definitions. A loaded definition does undertake to explain the meaning of a word as it is used, but the explanation is expressed in a prejudicial manner. The definition given is thus "loaded" with bias, and what ought to be a straightforward factual account of the use of a word is turned into a propaganda device.

Two famous historical cases of loaded definition are the following, which were given by Samuel Johnson in his eighteenth-century *Dictionary:*

excise: A hateful tax levied upon commodities, and adjudged not by the common judges of property, but by wretches hired by those to whom the tax is paid.

oats: A grain which in England is generally given to horses, but in Scotland supports the people.

An excise tax is one that is levied on the production or consumption of commodities. Dr. Johnson's definition does succeed in conveying about this much, but it also packs into the definition assumptions about the nature of such a tax and about the people who collect it. Someone not knowing the meaning of the word and attempting to learn it from the definition would get the impression that an excise tax is *necessarily* a hateful tax and that the people who collect it are always base and despicable ("wretches"). These assumptions are not a part of the legitimate meaning of the word "excise." Whether people love or hate a certain tax has nothing at all to do with whether or not it's properly called an excise tax. Nor does the character of the people who collect it.

Loaded definitions share with persuasive definitions the frequent technique of employing words with pleasant or unpleasant connotations, words that encourage us to approve or disapprove of whatever they are applied to. The use of the words "hateful" and "wretches" are examples of this practice.

Notice, though, that the second of Dr. Johnson's definitions conveys a low opinion of the people of Scotland without making use of such words. In saying that Scots eat the same food as horses do in England, it invites us to conclude that, compared with the English, they may be like animals in other respects as well. (And, of course, even if it were true that the Scots ate oats and the English didn't, this would have nothing to do with the proper use of the word. It's in no way connected with the meaning of "oats.") Definitions don't have to be loaded, then, solely by the presence in them of emotionally charged words. Suggested comparisons can also do the trick.

The following definitions illustrate both kinds of loading. Furthermore, they give some indication of the ways in which individuals or groups can further their own interests. If the definitions they offer were generally accepted as legitimate, then the viewpoints they represent would be accepted as well.

integrationist: a person committed to the foolish and dangerous doctrine that races of man ought to have equal rights and form one society

welfare assistance: money paid by government agencies to people who are too lazy and shiftless to support themselves

lobbyist: a person who helps make democracy more effective by representing the interests of a group to government officials

As these examples show, loaded definitions, unlike persuasive definitions, do include an account of the standard meaning of the word defined. Persuasive definitions make no attempt at this. For this reason, loaded definitions are perhaps more dangerously misleading than persuasive ones. The grain of truth makes the pound of prejudice easier to swallow.

Concerning the recognition of loaded definitions, a word of caution is in order. Not all definitions that are expressed in evaluative terms are loaded ones. They may be perfectly legitimate accounts of the meanings of ordinary words.

It's an interesting fact about languages that many words have evaluations built into their meanings. This is not at all surprising, for, after all, language is used to express evaluations. Certain words, then, come to apply to persons or situations that display characteristics of which we don't approve, or which we think foolish, imprudent, or irrational. A definition of "evildoer," for example, has to include a value phrase to the effect that an evildoer does evil.

Or, to take a more dramatic example, "murder" has to be defined in such a way as to make it clear that murder consists in *unjustified* killing. (It is this fact, by the way, that makes it nonsensical to ask "Is murder ever right?" The question has to be "Is killing ever right?" We might say that by definition murder can never be right [i.e., justified].)

Similarly, the word "scoundrel" means "a worthless and unprincipled person." Thus we show our disapproval of such a person by calling him a scoundrel, not by defining what he is called in such a way as to display disapproval.

In any event, the explanation of the meaning of a word that correctly reports how a word is used may contain evaluative phrases. So long as the definition does not pack prejudice into the explanation, it is not a loaded one. A loaded definition can be such only in contrast with an unloaded one, and if society or the community of language users does the loading, this is standard use. It's not something we are directly responsible for, at least not so far as giving definitions is concerned. Our job is simply to report the facts of the word's use.

Exercises

The Court of Definition

From your modest beginnings as a Scare-Quote Identifier for Logic, Inc., you have worked your way up to a truly distinguished position in the field of informal logic. The International Logic Association has elected you to serve a term on the Court of Definition.

As a justice on the Definition Court, you are to apply fairly and forthrightly the rules regulating definition. You are to use your best judgment to determine whether the definitions that come before you are guilty of violating the Prohibitions. You are to assume, of course, that the definitions have been offered as reportive definitions.

The Prohibitions, recall, are these:

1. avoid complete circularity;
2. avoid language that is obscure, ambiguous, or metaphorical;
3. avoid being too broad or too narrow;
4. avoid using irrelevant features.

In addition to seeing to it that these Prohibitions are not violated, you are to keep a sharp eye out for those who try to get away with using persuasive or loaded definitions.

All judicial opinions must be defended, of course, so you must be prepared to explain why you regard a Prohibition as being violated or why you decide that a certain definition is persuasive or loaded.

Since not every definition that comes before you will be guilty of some crime against logic and right reasoning, you must be considered in your opinion and be certain that you have good reasons to back it up.

Cases of Definitions To Be Judged

1. Eat: To perform successively (and successfully) the functions of mastication, humectation, and deglutition.

   AMBROSE BIERCE,
   The Devil's Dictionary

2. Pooh-pooh: To say "pooh-pooh," to dismiss without consideration.

3. Time is the moving image of eternity.

   PLATO

4. Poetry is the kind of thing poets write.

   ROBERT FROST

5. An antimetabolite is a substance that antagonizes the action of a metabolite.

   ERWIN DI CYAN,
   Vitamins in Your Life

6. Mysticism is just tomorrow's science dreamed today.

   MARSHALL MCLUHAN,
   Playboy Interview

7. Money: A medium of exchange.

8. A demonstration is a dissenter's device to rally the uncommitted behind him so that by sheer weight of numbers an aura of conviction is projected on his behalf.

SPIRO AGNEW

9. According to the alchemists, "calx" was the ash or fixed part of a substance that remained after it had been burned.

10. A drug is a substance that has an effect upon the body or mind.

National Clearing House for Drug Abuse

11. Balkan states: The states that occupy the Balkan Peninsula: Albania, Bulgaria, Greece, Rumania, and Yugoslovia.

12. Happiness is a warm puppy.

CHARLES SCHULTZ

13. An element is a substance, a sample of matter consisting solely of atoms with the same atomic number.

W. A. KIEFFER,
Chemistry: A Cultural Approach

14. Carbon is the element that is the backbone of life.

15. Ensign: A standard of a military unit.

16. Scientist: One of those scholars who receive the largest amount of federal money in the form of research grants.

17. Policeman: A killer licensed by society to protect the lives and property of the rich.

18. Informal logic: A travel guide to the ordinary world of correct reasoning.

19. Oxygen: A substance ordinarily sold in cylinder-shaped tanks.

20. Harmful: Capable of harming or causing harm.

American Heritage Dictionary

21. Abortion: A form of murder in which an unborn fetus is removed from its mother's womb and allowed to die.

22. [Poetry] is language whose individual lines, either because of their own brilliance or because they focus so powerfully what has gone before, have a higher voltage than most language has. It is language that grows frequently incandescent, giving off both light and heat.

LAURENCE PERRINE,
Sound and Sense

23. Cultivate: To improve and prepare (land), as by plowing or fertilizing, for raising crops; to till.

American Heritage Dictionary

24. Library: A collection of books primarily intended for personal use and not for sale.

25. Singletree: A whiffletree.

American Heritage Dictionary

26. Woman: The sex most discriminated against in present-day society.

27. Intellectual: Any left-leaning crackpot who subscribes to dangerous and unpatriotic ideas.

28. Conservative: A person with both feet firmly planted in the mud.

29. Tea: A beverage that is drunk in England at four o'clock in the afternoon.

30. An egghead is one who stands firmly on both feet in mid-air on both sides of an issue.

SENATOR HOMER FERGUSON

31. Amnesty: The state's magnanimity to those offenders whom it would be too expensive to punish.

AMBROSE BIERCE,
The Devil's Dictionary

32. Yawn: A silent shout.

G. K. CHESTERTON

33. Medicine: The only profession that labours incessantly to destroy the reason for its own existence.

JAMES BRYCE

34. Lawyers: The only persons in whom ignorance of the law is not punished.

JEREMY BENTHAM

35. Tact: Knowing how far we may go too far.

JEAN COCTEAU

In the Def-Class Division

After your term as justice on the Definition Court expires, you are at a loss for another job. But Logic, Inc., comes through again and asks that you serve as a consultant to their Definition Classification Division.

They've accepted some contracts that have faced them with some tough problems in classification, and you agree to help with them.

The standard scheme that you use, recall, is this one:

1. Stipulative
   a. Arbitrary
   b. Restricting

2. Reportive
   a. Lexical
   b. Technical
   c. Historical

You are handed a list of the definitions and you begin work classifying them in your usual careful and competent manner.

1. Siphonostele: A vascular tube surrounding the pith in the stems of certain plants.

2. *Free verse*, by our definition, is not verse at all; that is, it is not metrical. It may be rimed or unrimed. The word *free* means it is free of metrical restrictions.

   LAURENCE PERRINE,
Sound and Sense

3. For our purposes language may be defined as systematized combinations of sounds which have meaning for all persons in a given cultural community.

   THOMAS PYLES,
Origin and Development of the English Language

4. Cure: A method or course of medical treatment used to restore health.

   American Heritage Dictionary

5. I now mean by elements . . . certain primitive and simple or perfectly unmingled bodies, which not being made of any other bodies or of one another, are the ingredients of which all those perfectly mixt bodies are immediately compounded and into which they are ultimately resolved.

   ROBERT BOYLE,
The Sceptical Chemist (1661)

6. By a Fallacy is commonly understood any unsound mode of arguing, which appears to demand our conviction, and to be decisive of the question in hand, when in fairness it is not.

   RICHARD WHATELY,
The Elements of Logic

7. Curette: A surgical instrument shaped like a scoop or spoon, used to remove dead tissue or growths from a bodily cavity.

   American Heritage Dictionary

8. I shall make use of the expression "DSP" to abbreviate "different senses of possible."

   PAUL GOMBERG

9. *Grammar* is the Art of expressing the Relations of Things in Construction; with due Accent in Speaking, and Orthography in Writing, according to the Custom of those whose Language we learn.

   A. FISHER,
Grammar (1788)

10. By an *argument* we mean a system of declarative sentences (of a single

language), one of which is designated as the *conclusion* and the others as *premises*.

BENSON MATES,
Elementary Logic

11. The term "mortgage," when used herein, shall include deed of trust, trust deed, or other security instrument.

American Land Title Association Standard Form 3360

12. Concerning the coverage afforded under Section II of this policy, "occurrence" means an accident, including injurious exposure to conditions, which results, during the policy term, in bodily injury or property damage.

Prudential Policy and Casualty Insurance Company

13. When we review the different institutions in our Western society, we find some that are encompassing to a degree discontinuously greater than the ones next in line. Their encompassing or total character is symbolized by the barrier to social intercourse with the outside and to departure that is often built right into the physical plant, such as locked doors, high walls, barbed wire, cliffs, water, forests, or moors. These establishments I am calling *total institutions*, and it is their general characteristics I want to explore.

ERVING GOFFMAN,
Asylums

14. "Motor vehicle" means a land motor vehicle, trailer or semi-trailer designed for travel on public roads (including any machinery or apparatus attached thereto) but does not include, except when being towed by or carried on a motor vehicle, any of the following, utility, boat, camp, or home trailer, recreational motor vehicle, crawler or farm type tractor, farm implement, or, if not subject to motor vehicle registration, any equipment which is designed for use principally off public roads.

Prudential Policy and Casualty Insurance Company

15. To "barbadoes" a person meant the same in the seventeenth century as to "shanghai" him meant in the nineteenth.

SIDNEY W. MINTZ,
Columbia Forum (Spring, 1970)

A Strange Hobby

To relax from your consulting work with Logic, Inc., you pursue a rather strange hobby. On the principle that it takes one to know one, you spend some of your free time constructing loaded or persuasive definitions. You find that this gives you an opportunity to express your own beliefs and prejudices in a harmless way. It also prepares you to recognize loaded or persuasive definitions when they are used in a serious (or half-serious) way by others.

Here are a few of the expressions that you deliberately define in a dirty and unfair fashion:

1. Physician
2. Food-Stamp Program
3. Homosexual
4. Militant (noun)
5. Intellectual (noun)
6. Politician
7. Women's Liberation
8. State Legislature
9. Pornography
10. Income Tax

Logic, Inc.—Special Assignment

A hermit has been discovered living in a cave high in the Rocky Mountains. He has been there since the atomic tests of the early 1950s, but he has now decided that the world isn't going to be bombed out of existence in the next few years and that he wants to rejoin society again.

The Interior Department has hired Logic, Inc., to assist this man in his return to present-day society. This presents a difficulty for the organization, because four of its Definition Agents are on sick leave with the complaint of eyestrain and acute boredom. They ask if you would be willing to step in and lend a hand.

You readily agree to, of course. The task that you are given involves explaining to the man the recently acquired meanings of the words listed below.

1. What would you say by way of explanation in each case?
2. What method or methods of definition seem to you most useful in giving your explanations?
3. Which words on the list have meanings that were new several years ago but now seem well established? Which have meanings that are not well established, so that a report on them is really a historical definition?

acid	dropout	pad
bag	freak	pill
bread	grass	pot
busing	hangup	rap
bust	head	rock
camp	joint	stoned
demonstration	Mace	topless

5/Climbing Jacob's Ladder: The Uses of Language

ACCORDING to an Old Testament story, while Jacob was on his way to the land of Padanaram to find a wife, he had a strange dream one night. He dreamed he saw a ladder extending from earth and into heaven, and as he watched, he saw angels climbing up and down on the ladder.

We can hardly consider ourselves angels, but otherwise this is a rather good image to represent the transition we are going to make from the earthly support of language to the heavenly realm of argument.

Until now, we have focused on language alone. In Chapter 2 we developed an acceptable theory of meaning, and in Chapter 3 we stocked up our linguistic armory by hammering out weapons to deal with ambiguity, vagueness, and connotation. Finally, in Chapter 4 we took quite a careful and detailed look at types of definitions and at ways of defining.

We've been able to throw some light into the darkened crannies of language, where confusion, doubt, puzzlement, and indecision lurk and hide. This in itself is a task worth doing, but we're ready to make use of the tools we've developed to tackle an even greater project.

The time has arrived to come to grips with *rational persuasion.* This is a label that covers a topic with as many facets as the fabled diamond of Rajipur, and we aren't going to be able to talk about them all at once.

In fact, where we'll start will look at first sight as if it has about as much to do with rational persuasion as dogs have to do with dogmas.

In this chapter, we'll identify and discuss four of the major ways in which we use language. Some of those ways, we'll see, are not closely connected with the business of making claims and giving reasons to back them up. They are not, that is, intimately related to rational persuasion. Consequently, we can ignore them forevermore.

On the other hand, some of the ways are as bound up with rational persuasion as taxes are with money. Once we have identified these, we'll stick with them to the sweet end of the book.

This chapter is the first rung on the ladder that leads up from language considered in its own terms to language used for the purpose of discussion, persuasion, criticism, and evaluation.

In the next chapter we'll climb up to the next rung by turning our attention to the kinds of disputes and disagreements that people get involved in. We'll discuss ways of resolving disputes in a sensible and reasonable fashion. Also, we'll come face to face with arguments for the first time, and we'll discuss how to identify a piece of prose as an argument and how to go about challenging or criticizing the argument if we find ourselves in doubt about accepting it.

But this is all in the future. Now it's time to pull ourselves up to the first rung.

What We Do by Talking: Four Uses of Language

When the anthropologist Malinowski studied the culture of the people of the Trobriand Islands, he described their language as having two major uses. The *pragmatic use* of language was to communicate information and help in arranging the ordinary affairs of life. The *magical use* was to try to bring about desired events.

Malinowski's categories were quite broad and each included numerous more specific uses to which language was put. They were set up in order to get a better understanding of the society of the Trobriand Islanders, and Malinowski regarded them as adequate for this purpose. He was, of course, as aware as anyone else that the two general uses of language that he distinguished were not the *only* uses that could be identified.

Salami can be sliced in many ways—in thick slices or thin, in chunks or strips—and the way it's sliced depends on the use you have in mind for it. Very specific uses of language (telling jokes, ordering a hamburger) can be dumped into a variety of bins. Malinowski's bins aren't suitable for our purposes, because our concern is not with anthropology but with informal logic.

But before setting up our own bins—before distinguishing any general uses of language—we need to have in mind some reason or purpose for making the distinctions. That is, we need to be clear about the *point of view* we will take with regard to language.

Recall that we said in Chapter 1 that informal logic is concerned with a number of familiar activities that are carried out by the use of language: defining a word, presenting and evaluating arguments, using examples and analogies to illustrate a point, and so on. These and similar activities involve language that is in a general way directed toward communication. In fact, it's not going too far simply to state flat out that informal logic is primarily concerned with language as a means of communication.

But communication is a very general use of language, and defining, arguing, and so on are rather specific uses. It's possible to distinguish ways of using language that fall between these two extremes. That is, we can identify some of the general ways in which language is used to communicate.

Why bother to make such middle-of-the-road distinctions? There are two main reasons. First, informal logic is not concerned with *all* the uses of language in communicating. It has virtually nothing to do with poetry writing, proclamations, declarations, or resolutions, and very little to do with storytelling or advising. It's important, then, to have at least a vague understanding of the kinds of uses informal logic deals with in order to understand its aims better and to recognize its limitations.

Second, when some uses of language are confused with one another serious misunderstanding can result. Puzzles, disagreements, and point-less disputes may crop up. Since they might be avoided and discourse kept rational and to the point, in the general interest of improved com-munications it's worth the trouble to make a few obvious distinctions among the uses of language to communicate.

The four uses of language that we'll be discussing are ones that are traditionally dealt with in informal logic. They are useful distinctions, but there's no magic about them. Other distinctions are possible, and these in fact are rather rough ones. No one should feel puzzled or cheated if he can think of cases that don't fall neatly into one of our categories. A sledgehammer isn't needed to swat a fly, and informal logic can do very well without exception-tight categories.

Shut Up: The Directive Use of Language

The American humorist Ring Lardner entitled one of his short stories " 'Shut Up,' He Explained." The title hits a jarring note, and we have to look twice to be sure we've read it correctly. It jars because the two phrases "shut up" and "he explained" simply don't fit together in any way we can grasp. It's just this inconsistency that makes Lardner's title humorous. There is no imaginable context in which someone says "Shut up" *as an explanation.*

"Shut up" is obviously a command or *directive,* not an explanation. Language is used directively in connection with actions. Our general aim is to influence the actions of others in such a way that they will do as we wish. The information that we communicate is, at least, what we want done. But the communication of even this limited amount of information isn't always the main object of using language directively. Its purpose is often to get people to act the way we want them to. Thus the intention behind the language can sometimes be fulfilled even when there is misunderstanding or no understanding at all. A loud scream can usually do the same job as a sentence like "Please get off my foot."

The directive use of language can be described and analyzed with respect to a variety of situations, and directives themselves can be sub-divided into a number of different types. Here are some cases:

a. *Orders.* For example, a policeman to a group of demonstrators: "Keep moving, don't block the sidewalk, keep moving, keep the sidewalk clear."

b. *Demands.* For example, women demonstrators to the Attorney General: "We want the same pay for the same work, and we want the same chances for promotion that men have." Or, an irate tenant to his landlord: "It's been three months since I told you about the rats—you must do something about them."

c. *Directions.* For example, a civil service exam: "Print your name legibly in the space provided at the top of page 1. Put your last name first."

d. *Requirements.* For example, the state welfare office: "You must fill out the pink card before you will be allowed to see a caseworker."

e. *Charges.* For example, judge to a jury: "You have heard the case for both sides, and you now must decide whether the evidence is such as to make you certain beyond a reasonable doubt that the defendent is responsible for firing the shot that put an end to the life of Lamont Cranston."

f. *Injunctions.* For example, Jesus in the New Testament: "A new commandment I give you—Love one another as I have loved you."

g. *Requests.* For example, "Please send five dollars to help pay the costs of publishing this newsletter."

h. *Questions.* For example, "What time is it?"

Perhaps these cases are not all different types of directives. Nevertheless, though all are directives, some are clearly quite distinct from one another. A demonstrator, for example, is in no position to *order* a policeman to do anything. But he can *request* (or even *entreat* or *beg*) that he do something. A tenant may *request* or *demand* that his landlord exterminate the rats in his apartment, but he cannot *charge* or *direct* the landlord to do so.

There are many ways of using language directively, and there are many words typically used to give directions. Moreover, such factors as *who you are* and *to whom you are talking* and *what the situation is* are important in determining the particular sort of directive language you use. It's interesting and illuminating to examine closely the directive use of language, and a number of philosophers have recently devoted themselves to developing a "logic of commands." We would, unfortunately, have to move too far out of the orbit of informal logic to discuss the logic of commands in enough detail to be worthwhile.

Too Bad: The Evaluative Use of Language

Rhadamanthus, in the mythology of the Greeks, was such a fair and just man during his lifetime that after his death the gods made him a judge of the dead in the underworld. Modesty and simple truth keep most of us from comparing ourselves with Rhadamanthus. Who in honesty can claim that he is always just? Nevertheless, we all resemble Rhadamanthus at least to the extent that we are constantly *called upon* to make judgments. Almost never do our judgments have the form of legal pronouncements; rather, they are *evaluations*.

The evaluative use of language is a tangled web, and it's all but impossible to grasp the strands without becoming enmeshed in issues of bewildering complexity. Philosophers have done their best to make the issues clear, but in spite of their efforts there isn't even general agreement about how the evaluative use of language can be characterized. But since our interest in this use is limited by our primary concern with informal logic, we can steer clear of most of the sticky problems of evaluative language and make do with a rather rough characterization of it.

It's enough for our purposes to say that language is used *evaluatively* when it is employed in connection with *values, standards, criteria,* or *rules.* To get a better idea of what this means, let's begin simply by considering the following sentences:

a. The *New York Times* was *right* in publishing the Pentagon Papers.
b. It is not *proper* for a judge to preside in a case in which he has a vested interest in the outcome.
c. *The Valley of the Dolls* is a *dreadful* book.
d. The paper mills in the United States have acted in an *irresponsible* manner in disposing of their waste materials.
e. It is *important* for a government to be honest with its citizens.
f. I'm sorry to have to turn you down for the job, but you didn't make an *adequate* score on the exam.
g. The forests of Oregon are simply *beautiful.*
h. The lakes of this country have been *ruined* by pollution.

In an ordinary sense of the phrase, each of these sentences is a *value judgment.* That is, each of them is an *evaluation* (of some sort) of the subject or state of affairs that it mentions. Such sentences taken alone give no indication of exactly what values, standards, rules, or criteria might have been involved in making the evaluations. The sentences *are* the evaluations. They are decisions, conclusions, judgments, or mere assertions, and any grounds or reasons for them remain unstated. In each case, it would be appropriate to ask such questions as "Why do you say that?" or "What are your reasons for that?"

But our characterization of the evaluative use of language needs to be broadened in one respect. So far we have limited the use to specific evaluations, such as saying things like "The killings at My Lai were wrong" and "Your exam score is inadequate." Such sentences involve particular claims or judgments, but it's more informative about the use of language if we broaden our notion of evaluative use to include also cases in which values, rules, and so on are *themselves* explicitly stated. Thus a sentence like "Killing is wrong" is evaluative in its normal use because it's an expression of a moral belief, attitude, or standard. Such a sentence is not an evaluation of a particular case—like the My Lai incident—but a general statement which covers all cases of that kind. Similarly a sentence like "An examination score of at least 72 is required of every job applicant" is the statement of the standard that will be used in evaluating applicants.

What we've called the "evaluative" use of language is also sometimes called the "normative" use. The word "normative" originated from the Latin word for a carpenter's square or ruler, and it still has a connected meaning in English usage. Something is *normative* when it involves norms, rules, specifications, or standards of some kind.

We have at our disposal a large arsenal of words that are typically (but not always) used to express our values and evaluations. Here are just a few (most have opposites):

beautiful	good	proper
just	should	foul
lovely	honest	ought
attractive	fine	shameful
handsome	pitiful	disreputable
qualified	acceptable	adequate

These words are used in other ways also. There are probably no words which are used *solely* in sentences which make evaluations. For that matter, there are numerous ways of expressing evaluations without using words commonly associated with evaluating. "That simply will not do!" said at the right time in the right place is an evaluation, yet it contains no typical evaluative words.

Though there is no unique class of evaluative words, a glance at the list above is suggestive in one way. Some words seem to be appropriate to the same sort of context, a context to which others on the list aren't appropriate. Words like "lovely," "handsome," and "beautiful" are typically used in the same sort of situations (discussing a painting, a poem, or a person, for example), and the same is so of words like "should," "ought," and "just," and ones like "adequate," "acceptable," and "qualified."

This suggests what is already rather obvious. Namely, that the evaluative use of language is not itself of a single piece. There are different evaluative uses of language that we typically recognize in ordinary life, and the following three categories are one way of distinguishing the more important of them.

Ethical Evaluation ("You shouldn't have done it.")

Sentences like "The internment of citizens of Japanese descent during World War II was wrong" are moral or ethical evaluations. In general, whenever language is used to make the claim that a certain action (or type of action) *ought or ought not* be done, it is being used in an ethical way. Actions, of course, aren't the only sorts of things which we employ language to talk about. Policies, procedures, and states of affairs are also characterized as *wrong* or *bad*, as *right* or *good*. That is, they either ought or ought not be as they are, and language that describes them as such is also being used in an ethical way.

The ethical use of language has faced philosophers with two problems of stupendous difficulty. First, how is the ethical use of language to be interpreted? Suppose someone says, "Killing is wrong" or "You ought not kill." Is he merely making a statement about himself, one which could also be expressed as "I don't like killing" or even as "Killing—Ugh!"? Or is he issuing a kind of directive like "Don't kill!" which he hopes people will follow? Or perhaps he is making a claim that he can justify by appealing to reasons for its acceptance? Maybe, of course, more than one of these interpretations is correct. The interpretation of ethical language—the meaning of ethical terms and the content of ethical sentences—is the job of the area of philosophy called "metaethics."

The second difficulty consists in attempting to answer questions like "What rules or principles ought we to accept for the governance of our lives?" The difficulty is nothing less than that of determining the moral values which we should hold, of deciding what sorts of actions are right and what sorts of life are good. This task is that of *normative ethics.*

Neither of these mammoth difficulties is one that we can deal with here. But there is more than enough reason to mention them. For one thing, they are matters of crucial importance with respect to our ordinary moral evaluations and deserve to be noticed as aspects of the evaluative use of language. More to the point, though, in the next chapter we'll be discussing the resolution of disagreements about evaluations, and it will be useful to keep these two difficulties in mind.

Aesthetic Evaluation ("It's beautiful!")

We say about movies, novels, poems, plays, dances, and musical compositions that they are beautiful, brilliant, and well done or that they are bad, impoverished, and lousy. In doing so we are passing judgment on them from an aesthetic point of view. We are presenting an *aesthetic evaluation.* Generally speaking, language is used in an aesthetically evaluative way whenever it is employed to express the claim that a work of art (or a natural object) does or does not meet certain standards or possess certain qualities. Words like "lovely," "beautiful," "bad," and "inconsequential" are those typically taken to represent aesthetic standards or qualities, and to apply such terms to objects is to make an aesthetic evaluation.

Aesthetically evaluative language presents philosophical problems similar in content and difficulty to the ethical use of language. How, for example, are we to interpret words like "beautiful" when they are used evaluatively? Does "Picasso's *White Clown* is beautiful" mean simply "I like that painting"? Does the sentence make a claim that can be backed up by reasons and evidence? To mention another difficulty, how is the evaluative use of words like "beautiful" connected with the use of nonevaluative words like "red" and "straight-line"?

Pragmatic Evaluation ("That does it.")

Suppose that, times being hard, you are working at a poultry farm. It's your job to grade eggs according to size. Since it's a small concern, there is no automatic machinery, and you have to do the grading personally. You stand in front of a slowly moving belt covered with eggs. Beside you there are three egg crates, and you must sort the eggs into small, medium, and large sizes and put them into the crates. An egg is small you're told, when its diameter (at the largest place) is about 1½ inches, medium when the diameter is around 1⅝ inches, and large when it's around 1¾ inches.

As you stand in front of the belt sorting eggs, you are evaluating. You are making decisions based upon a criterion or standard. If you put your decisions into words, you might say such things as "This egg will not do as a large" or "This is definitely a small egg."

Language is used in a pragmatically evaluative way whenever it is employed to express the decision that something will or will not do, is or is not acceptable, is or is not important, in accordance with a standard or rule relating to some practice, function, or purpose.

Sentences like "Green plants are the most important part of the biosphere" are evaluations that can be supported by facts about the biosphere and the role played by green plants in it. The importance of plants is connected with the functions they serve—trapping energy from the sun, being food for many forms of life, producing oxygen, and so on.

An evaluation like "Most people on welfare are not employable" is based on what we take to be minimum qualifications (standards) that a person must meet before we consider him able to work at a normal job. This and similar evaluations are more complex than grading eggs, but in principle they are quite similar.

Pragmatic evaluations are different from moral evaluations, but the two sorts can be intimately connected. Whether a person is suitable for a job or not can be regarded as simply a pragmatic evaluation—Does he satisfy standards A, B, and C? But the standards which are used may be called into question. That is, we may ask,' "Are these the standards which *ought* to be used?" Suppose to qualify for a job a person could not be either black or female. There's no great trick in making the pragmatic evaluation, but the rule in accordance with which decisions are reached is certainly open to criticism from a moral point of view.

Gee Whillikers: The Expressive Use of Language

Flash Gordon has just hurled one of the clay people over the edge of a bottomless pit. As the creature plummets to the bottom a shriek rends the air: ARRRGGHHHhhh!

The cry of the clay creature is an example of the expressive use of language, or at least it would be if a shriek were language. To express (ex-press) in a root sense is to squeeze out, and language is used expressively when it is used to represent a certain feeling, emotion, or attitude—one presumably squeezed out from the depths. For example:

"How awful!"—as spoken by someone watching films of the torture of war prisoners.
"Poor dear!"—as spoken by a man to his wife who has just lost her job.
"That'll show them!"—as spoken by someone who has just heard of the shooting of five students by government troops.

In the expressive use of language , the medium is the message. Words are used for the purpose of exhibiting or giving vent to attitudes or emotions. Exactly *what* is said is generally of secondary importance—"terrible," "atrocious," "shameful" (or merely turning away in disgust) will do the same expressive job as "how awful!" What is communicated is primarily that the speaker feels a certain way or holds a certain sort of attitude.

Some philosophers, as we noticed above, have suggested that the sentences we use to make ethical and aesthetic evaluations can best be interpreted as cases of the expressive use of language. That is, they have argued that what we generally call value judgments aren't really judgments at all. They are just special instances of language used expressively. (No one has said that this is so of pragmatic evaluations, however.)

Sentences like "You shouldn't have done that" are thus regarded as no more than expressions of disapproval. The person who says such a thing is expressing his attitude about what was done. Perhaps also he is trying to get whoever performed the action to share his attitude and not to do such a thing again.

This way of interpreting the evaluative use of language is appealing on the surface. For, after all, when we say of actions that they are wrong or of novels that they are bad we are expressing our attitude towards them. We are making our feelings known. But a difficulty with the view comes after we've recognized this. Here it is: Are our moral and aesthetic claims *only* ways of making our feelings known?

The issues connected with this question are too many for us to explore. Notice, though, that when we say such things as "It is wrong of you to kill those people" we don't act as if we were *merely* expressing our feelings. Rather, when pressed, we go on to present reasons and grounds for what we say. That is, we treat our evaluations as *claims* which need to be *argued for* and justified. We act as if our sentences have a content over and above the fact that they also express our feelings and attitudes.

Bees Have No Knees: The Informative Use of Language

Fantastic Facts

- Most people change position every seven to eight minutes while asleep.
- Snakes cannot hear, but they are sensitive to odors and heat.
- Erastosthenes of Cyrene (284-192 B.C.) estimated the circumference of the earth to a value which is only fifty miles off from the one we now accept as correct.

The sentences that express the "fantastic facts" in the above list are all examples of the informative use of language. Language is used *informatively* when it is employed to make a factual claim. The claim made need not be true, so far as the use of language is concerned. For example, "All women are ten feet tall" may be used to make a factual claim, and even though the claim is false, language is still being used in the way we'll call "informative." (With more justice this might be called the "misinformative" use, but there's no great advantage in multiplying labels.) So language is informatively employed when it's used to convey information *or* misinformation.

Also, just to keep the record straight, language is used in an informative way even when the factual claims it expresses are not all that fantastic. "Some cars are blue" and "Grass is sometimes green" make factual assertions that are trivial and wholly uninteresting, yet the language used to make them is being used informatively.

Claims put forward in this way are correct or incorrect, true or false, depending upon some matter of fact. That is, some actual state of affairs, some fact about the world, wholly separate from the claim, is what makes it true or false. To take the simplest possible sort of case, if someone says, "Snow is white," then his assertion is correct if *as a matter of fact* snow is actually white. Such matters are ones that require that we examine the world, find out the facts. This, of course, is not always so easy to do, and there are many difficulties connected with establishing factual claims.

The informative use of language seems simple enough, but difficulties frequently arise in particular cases. Suppose someone is looking at a painting and says, "The shading of the figure is quite delicate." Has he made a factual claim or an evaluative claim? There's no simple way to answer the question, for we have made no sharp distinction between language used informatively and language used evaluatively. We needn't be particularly worried about this, though. Chances are we would proceed in the same way no matter how we classified the use of the sentence. We would ask questions like "What do you mean by that?"

(i.e., what features count as conditions governing the use of "delicate"?) and "What reason do you have for saying that?" (i.e., what are the features actually found in the painting that support your claim?).

Three Sidelights on Use

Every good director knows that the proper lighting can make a scene more effective and increase an audience's appreciation of it. The same is true of intellectual matters, in the sense that illuminating different aspects of a topic can often increase our understanding of it.

Having distinguished four major ways in which language is used, in this section we will consider three matters that are connected with use. Hopefully, our discussion will provide the light that will dispel whatever darkness may still linger around our main topic.

Grammar and Use

It might seem odd that we've been talking about the *uses* of language rather than, say, about the grammatical forms of sentences. Like pussyfooting Victorians who can't bring themselves to talk about sex openly, we may seem to be avoiding coming into direct contact with language by talking about its uses.

Not so. Hopefully, it will be obvious by now that a study of the ways in which language is used can be important and illuminating. And it's crucial that the *use* of language not be confused with something that is often closely associated with use.

The "something" that's most likely to cause confusion is grammar, so we will be well advised to see why the two, though they sometimes go hand in hand, are not really the same.

A seventh-grade "language arts" textbook is likely to divide the sentences of English into four kinds:

Interrogative: What can we do to eliminate poverty?
Imperative: Eliminate poverty.
Declarative: We can eliminate poverty.
Exclamatory: What poverty!

It's tempting to assume that the grammatical forms of sentences can be identified with the uses to which they are put. The world might be simpler if this were so, but it isn't. Sometimes grammar is a *clue* to use. But the clue to a use is not the use, anymore than the clue that leads to a murderer is itself the murderer.

Declarative sentences are generally used informatively: "The Acropolis is in Greece." But they may also be used evaluatively: "The Acropolis is beautiful."

An interrogative sentence may be used in a directive way: "When did the police arrive?" is a polite way of giving the directive "Tell me when the police arrived."

Exclamatory sentences are frequently evaluative as well as expressive: "How beautiful!"

What's more, it's easy to imagine situations in which the same sentence has different uses. Consider the sentence "Raleigh smokes" and how it might be used:

Directively: An ad in *Playgirl* picturing a man in Elizabethan clothes smoking a cigarette in obvious enjoyment, with the caption Raleigh Smokes."

Evaluatively: President of the Anti-Smoking League explaining why Raleigh wasn't given a job: "Raleigh smokes."

Expressively: The V-P of the League upon hearing that the President has been a secret smoker for years: "Raleigh smokes!"

Informatively: The response of the League V-P to a reporter who has asked if anyone in the organization smokes: "Raleigh smokes."

The point to these examples is that, just as there are no words that are associated solely with the uses we distinguished, so there are no grammatical forms that correspond exactly with those uses. Anybody who doesn't feel that the "Raleigh smokes" case is persuasive should consider the sentence we mentioned in·our earlier discussion. "This will not do" can obviously be used in all the ways we've distinguished and probably others as well.

Multiple Modes, or Doing Several Things at Once

Our categories of uses of language aren't logic-tight (or ratproof), but this is not at all a drawback. Rather, it's quite useful, because it permits us to describe and analyze cases in which the same sentence is used to do several things at the same time.

"I'd like to have a nice sirloin steak" said in a lifeboat adrift in the middle of the Atlantic is likely to be merely a piece of autobiographical information or the expression of a desire. But the same sentence spoken to the waiter at the Old Homestead Steakhouse is not *just* an informative or expressive sentence. It is also a directive.

Similarly, "Malcom X's autobiography is one of the best life stories written in his generation" is both informative and evaluative. It says that Malcolm X wrote an autobiography *and* that it's one of the best.

Poetry is the extreme example of language pushed to its limits and made to perform in ways that are uncommon as well as familiar. It is an extraordinary and powerful form of discourse, one that turns language into an instrument of unusual subtlety. But there is at least a little poetry in our ordinary speech, and it's not odd for us to use language to serve multiple purposes.

In fact, this is the rule, not the exception. For ordinary communication we often have to be careful that we don't use language that does too much. If we are attempting to give a straightforward informative account of a street fight that we saw, we have to be very cautious in our description. We have to avoid making evaluative claims about who was responsible for starting the fight and whether it could have been avoided or not. Of course, we may not want to give a straightforward informative account. We may be interested in placing blame or expressing our feelings about what we saw as well as providing information. Language can do either job, but it's often important that we be clear in our own minds just what it is that we are doing with language.

Questions and Uses

If somebody says, "Oh, damn!" it would be very strange indeed to ask "Is that true?" In such a case, it's wholly inappropriate to ask about truth, for the sentence is bèing used in a purely expressive way. We might ask, "Why did you say that?" or "What's the matter?" We might say, "Sorry" or "Too bad," depending on the circumstances. But we would *not* ask "Is that true?"

Obviously, certain questions can sensibly be asked about sentences used in one way that cannot be asked about sentences used in other ways. "Is that true?" isn't sensibly asked about an expressive use, but it isn't sensibly asked about a directive use, either. It would be ludicrous to ask someone, "Is that true?" when he has just said, "Shut the door." It would be perfectly proper, though, to ask all sorts of other questions: Why should I? Who are you to give me orders? These are suitable and sensible questions as responses to a command.

Anybody who uses language informatively is clearly open to the question "Is that true?" If he says, "The alligator is in the bedroom," the question is a natural one. But it's not the only appropriate question. We might also ask ones like "How do you know?" or "What's your evidence for that?" or "How did you find out?" If he wants us to accept what he says, then he has to be prepared to answer such questions.

It's harder to say what questions are appropriate about language that's used to make evaluative claims. Claims that are evaluative in a pragmatic fashion can usually be prodded and questioned in the same way that sentences that make factual claims are. If somebody says, "Trees are our most important natural resource," then it's quite natural to ask "Is that right?" (or true, or correct, or accurate, etc.). It's easy to imagine the kinds of facts that we could offer to back this up.

Similarly, whether or not someones satisfies a standard or rule for getting a job or drawing welfare payments or whatever, is mostly a matter to be settled by finding out the facts in the case. (Of course, whether the standard is right or fair is a matter of moral evaluation.)

This is all clear enough, but what are we to say about sentences that are used to make ethical or aesthetic evaluations? Suppose Quinn says to

Tolton, "You really shouldn't have looted that store." The natural question for Tolton to ask is "Why?" And Quinn's natural answer is likely to be "Because it's wrong to steal."

If Tolton accepts this, then she'll probably agree that she did the wrong thing. But suppose she doesn't. Does it make any sense for her to ask "Is it *true* that it's wrong to steal?" That is, is it appropriate to question the truth of a moral claim in the way that we question the truth of a factual claim?

There isn't any settled answer to this question. Some philosophers believe that it makes as much sense to talk about the truth of moral claims as about factual ones. Others say the question of truth is inappropriate, because moral rules are guides or goads for conduct of a certain kind. Moral evaluations, then, are according to this view more like commands or statements of standards than like factual claims.

There is agreement on one matter, though. When somebody offers a moral evaluation or presents a moral rule, it's appropiate to ask him to give *reasons* for what he says. It's certainly not immediately obvious to everyone, for example, that stealing is always wrong or that it's wrong in some particular case. It would be quite proper for Tolton to ask Quinn to *justify* his evaluation. If Quinn justifies it by appealing to the general rule "Stealing is wrong," then Tolton can ask why she should accept the rule.

We can and do come to agreement in matters of evaluation. Not always, of course, but often enough to make it reasonable and worth the effort to try to get someone to accept our claims or point of view. We come to agreement because we all recognize that it makes sense to ask people for the grounds or reasons for what they say. If we find those reasons convincing, then we concur by accepting the evaluative claim that they make.

Aesthetic evaluations resemble ethical ones with respect to the matter of providing reasons. The person who says, "Hank Williams was a marvelous songwriter" is open to the question "Why do you think so?" Our inclination is to tell him to put up his reasons or shut up about his evaluation. If we could never reach agreement in such cases, we wouldn't bother to argue about them. Nobody ever tries to convince anybody else that chocolate ice cream is the best ever made, but people do try to convince others that Hank Williams was a marvelous songwriter.

The four ways of using language that we've been discussing provide us with some instruments to understand the process of communication. They allow us to recognize what may be at issue in a given case and point out what kinds of questions it's appropriate for us to ask.

This is not an accomplishment to be sneered at. But informal logic is also after bigger game. It's concerned not only with effective communication but with rational persuasion. It's interested, that is, in the ways in which claims are backed up by evidence and reasons. This is the topic that will dominate our attention in most of the following chapters—recall that this chapter is the first rung on the ladder leading up to persuasion by rational argument.

Given the focus of informal logic, it's clear that only two uses of language fall within the spotlight—the *informative* and the *evaluative.* Language used in either of these ways involves making an assertion or claim—either stating that something is a fact or presenting an evaluation of some sort. Typically, this isn't the end of things, either. In a response to a challenge or in an effort to be convincing, we usually go on and attempt to justify our assertions. That is, we present reasons, grounds, facts, or evidence that we think support our claims. When this occurs, we are then in the business of rational persuasion. And when we are in that business, we become involved in the business of informal logic.

The directive and expressive uses of language don't result in claims. Though we may ask for a command to be justified or for an expression to be explained, neither use involves making an assertion. It's a primary task of informal logic to scrutinize the ways in which we support claims and to state clearly the standards we use to judge support. From here on then, the directive and expressive uses of language will be of minimum concern to us, and the evaluative and informative uses will be of paramount importance.

Exercises

Name Those Uses!

The top-rated television show "Name Those Uses!" has decided to devote an entire program to the uses of language. Because of your position with Logic, Inc., the show's producer asks you to serve as an expert consultant. The fee isn't very large, but then you get your name in lights. (At least you get your name on the crawl at the end of the program, where it will be seen by over twelve million people.)

The format of the show is this: contestants will be given a sentence (or a passage with underlined sentences), and they must then indicate the way in which its use may be best described.

Your job is to go through the sentences and passages supplied to you by the show's staff and identify the best characterization of use in each case. In short, you must supply what will be considered the right answers in the quiz. Unlike the contestants, though, you must also be prepared to give reasons for categorizing the sentences as you do. To be fair, you also must indicate why, in some cases, answers other than your own might be plausible.

At your suggestion, the categories used on the show will be the ones developed at Logic, Inc.: Expressive, Informative, Evaluative (Moral, Aesthetic, Pragmatic), and Directive.

1. To die for one's theological beliefs is the worst use a man can make of his life.

   OSCAR WILDE

2. According to the operon model, both gene induction and repression operate at the transcription level.

3. And hence no force, however great, can draw a cord, however fine, into a horizontal line which shall be absolutely straight.

   WILLIAM WHEWELL

4. Tell me not, in mournful numbers,
   Life is but an empty dream!

   HENRY WADSWORTH LONGFELLOW

5. "I can't" is the saddest sentence there is.

6. Come live with me and be my love,
   And we will some new pleasures prove. . . .

   JOHN DONNE

7. Regard it as the greatest wrong to prefer life to honor and, for life's sake, to lose the reasons for living.

   JUVENAL

8. What dire offense from amorous causes springs!
   What mighty contests rise from trivial things!

   ALEXANDER POPE

9. Formal logic represents thought at its best. The heat of argument is drained away, and all that is left is the pure and abstract form of frozen thought. There is icy beauty!

10. *Lloyd Cambell was standing outside the bar watching all the straights move down the street.* They kept their eyes lowered and their heads bowed toward the ground.

    "Jesus Christ," he said in a loud voice, *"this place is a sure 'nough freak show."*

    The policeman across the street looked across and caught Cambell's eye. Cambell stared back, and the cop walked over and stood beside him.

    "Get the hell out of here, slimeball," the cop said.

    Cambell started to explode, but he held himself back. *"I ain't breaking no law,"* he said.

    "You're smelling up the air," the cop said. *"Now move!"*

    Cambell moved. He walked away without anger. It had been replaced by cold hatred.

11. *Phobos was faintly visible, but Deimos had not risen.* Frieda Cohen was happy now, now that she had seen her first moonrise on Mars. It was worth the years of study and competition, the months of training and the weeks of grueling constant acceleration that the trip required. In

the domed shelter it was warm and peaceful and she felt relaxed, more relaxed than at any time she could remember.

"Jerry," she said to her second in command, *"do you mind checking the oxygen level in here?"*

"Check it yourself," he said. "I can't turn loose of this capacitor or we'll never get radio contact established."

Frieda did it herself. *Jerry was an excellent electronics engineer.* It was too bad he was such an unpleasant person. His worry over equipment, his constant checking and rechecking had almost driven her crazy during the trip out. But perhaps she should be thankful. They made it, and *that was the important thing.*

"*This capacitor is defective,*" Jerry said. "All our equipment is fourth-rate. It's a wonder we ever got here."

"Just do the best you can."

"You should have refused to obey Control's order to touch down."

"On what grounds, cowardice?"

"We're not cowards. We just don't have good sense or we would have refused to get into the lander in the first place. *It's not safe.* Ever since Congress cut back on the space program we've had to try to get along on inferior equipment."

The red sand kept up its relentless scratching at the face of the fragile plastic bubble. Eventually it would scratch its way through, but, of course, the oxygen would be depleted long years before that happened.

You're right, Jerry, Frieda thought, the lander is unsafe. But then I never intended to return. *Too bad about you.*

Getting Your Hands Dirty

1. Describe situations in which the same sentence might be used in all of the ways we've talked about.

2. Pick an article in a newspaper or magazine. Select a paragraph at random, then go through the paragraph and discuss the way (or ways) in which each sentence is used.

3. Write a short passage in which you include all four uses of language. (You might also try for all three kinds of the evaluative use.) Feel free to use dialogue or to tell part of a story.

6/The Dynamic Duo: Disagreement and Argument

This man is trying to fly.

This man is trying to keep from hanging.

W E ARE still climbing Jacob's ladder, from the ground of language to the heavenly realm of argument. In the last chapter, we took the first step by distinguishing four major uses of language and announcing that our prime concern will be with only two of them. In this chapter, we will pull ourselves up another few rungs.

In "Disagreeable People," we'll consider the kinds of disputes or disagreements that reasonable people have with one another. We'll talk about the steps to take to resolve disagreements in a friendly and reasonable way, and this will be another rung on the way up to rational persuasion by means of arguments.

In "There's One Now!" we'll stare into the face of the Gorgon head of argument itself without being turned to stone. More prosaically, we'll define the notion of argument as it appears in logic and provide some practical pointers on recognizing arguments, even though they are wrapped in various disguises.

Having introduced and practiced the art of identifying arguments, we'll move on to the last section, "On Guard!" to discuss some of the general ways in which arguments can be put to the test. This examination of the grounds for challenging arguments will lead us directly into the next chapter. There we'll pull out all the stops and engage in an orgy of discussion of deductive and inductive arguments. But more of this later.

There we have Jacob's ladder. From the use of language to make claims, to disputes about claims that are made. From disputes about claims, to the identification of arguments—in which claims are made and reasons are given to back them up. From identifying arguments, to challenging them. Finally, in the next chapter, to a more detailed consideration of deductive and inductive arguments. And there we are in heaven itself.

Disagreeable People

We are all disagreeable people. At least we are in the sense that we are often willing to dispute what someone says.

When language is used to make a claim, there is no power on earth or in the heavens that requires us to accept the claim that is made. We can question it, challenge it, ask for reasons for it. We can ask that the vagueness be cleared up and the ambiguity removed—if it suffers from these ailments. We can simply dig in our heels, refuse to accept the claim, and push forward instead a claim of our own.

A disagreement is, at the very least, a failure to agree. More illuminatingly, it is a situation in which there is a conflict between two apparently opposing claims. In such a situation, we generally attempt to resolve the conflict by discussing and debating what we consider to be the relevant matters at issue.

Our general aim is to secure agreement by persuading the other person to accept our point of view and renounce his own. We aren't interested in getting people to agree with us by any means, fair or foul. We want them to be convinced and to accept our view voluntarily. For this reason, we are going to be concerned only with *rational* persuasion.

In this section, we'll build a set of boxes into which we can dump most ordinary disputes. That is, we'll construct a scheme of classification. This will not be an end in itself, of course. Our reason for doing so is that it will help us get clear about what sorts of matters can be at issue when we disagree with someone.

By examining some of the ways in which we disagree (that is, kinds of disagreements), we can put ourselves in a better position to spot what kind of issue is in contention in our ordinary disputes and to realize what has to be done to move in the direction of agreement.

Recognizing the way in which we are disagreeing with someone may not settle a dispute, but it keeps us from engaging in trivial and pointless wrangles. It also permits us to see why we must sometimes merely agree to differ.

But now it's time to build our boxes.

Factual Disagreement

Suppose a man named Steere says, "*The Sirens of Titan* was written by Isaac Asimov," and we say, "No it wasn't." The fight is on, and we can't both be right. But how can we go about settling a dispute like this? It can't be done just by having Steere or us restate what was said in clearer terms and a louder voice. "*The Sirens of Titan* is a novel, and I'm saying that Isaac Asimov wrote it." The response to this can be made just as clear and just as loud: "I know *The Sirens of Titan* is a novel, and I know what you're saying. What *I'm* saying is that Isaac Asimov *didn't* write it." We are no closer to resolution, and getting progressively louder or even adding threats and gestures doesn't help settle the issue.

The disagreement doesn't result from a failure in understanding what is said or anything of the kind. The dispute is about a *matter of fact:* Who *did* write *The Sirens of Titan?* The only way to settle the dispute is to find out what the facts are. Just because someone *says* something is so doesn't make it so, and just because someone says something is *not* so doesn't mean it is not so. The disagreement can be ended only by examining facts which are independent of what anyone says. If we produce a copy of *The Sirens of Titan* and Kurt Vonnegut, Jr.'s name is listed on the title page as author, this would ordinarily put an end to the dispute.

It wouldn't necessarily do this, though. Steere might not be convinced. He might say, "You just had that title page printed with Vonnegut's name on it to fool me. I still say Asimov wrote *The Sirens of Titan.*" Or he might say, "That title page proves nothing. 'Vonnegut' is the pseudonym under which Asimov publishes a lot of the books he writes." The disagreement is still on, but the way in which it has to be settled hasn't changed. It is still a dispute about a matter of fact, and the facts of the matter are what must be learned to answer the question "Who wrote *The Sirens of Titan?*" If we presented fact after fact showing that Vonnegut was the author and all of them were accepted, Steere could still *claim* that Asimov was the author. But all the evidence would be against him, and after a while it would be irrational for him to hang on to his claim.

Settling a dispute about who wrote a book is ordinarily a very simple matter. Unlike our example, people rarely cling to their claims with such tenacity that they perversely make up stories to explain why the information we present is not adequate or refuse to change their opinions in the face of overwhelming contrary evidence. Yet not all disagreements about facts are so simple, and there can often continue to be grounds for reasonable disagreement when supporting evidence is inadequate. Consider the claim that Advanced Australopithecus, a prehuman ancestor species which lived about a million and a half years ago, fashioned tools. The evidence for this is scanty and difficult to obtain. Some anthropologists believe that he did, and some believe that he didn't, even when they agree on what constitutes a tool. The dispute is about a matter of fact and in principle it is no different from a dispute about the author of a particular book. But the available information is not sufficient to settle the question beyond *reasonable* doubt. The important thing, of course, is that anthropologists recognize what sort of disagreement they have on their hands. Knowing this, they know just what is involved in moving in the direction of a settlement. They are free to turn their attention to research, to "getting the facts," and don't have to waste their energies in bootless squabbles.

There are extremely complex cases of what might be regarded as disagreements about facts. They are made complex because the "facts" in dispute are bound up with a scientific theory and expressed in its terms. If a physicist says, "The atom consists of a positively charged nucleus, about which negatively charged particles rotate in various orbits," there is obviously no simple way of seeing whether this is right or not. And there is no simple way of settling a dispute about it. It is necessary to consider the theory which embodies the claim and the range and variety of evidence which supports the entire theoretical structure within which the claim is made. Even then the matter might not be settled, for not only might the evidence not be compelling in one direction or another, but there might be a rival theory which has some basis of support. "Getting the facts" and "disagreements about the facts" in such cases present logical, philosophical, and scientific problems of great complexity and difficulty. It might be better to call such disagreements as the one about atomic structure "disputes about theories" and save the phrase "disputes about facts" to apply to more straightforward cases of disagreement.

We can see how to go about settling disputes about whether dogs have sweat glands, whether Addis Ababa is the capital of Ethiopia, whether Luther said, "Here I stand, I can do no other," and so on. It may, of course, be *very* difficult to put an end to disputes about such matters. It is notoriously hard to learn the facts in numerous sorts of cases. (Imagine trying to find out the exact words which Goethe spoke on his deathbed or the name of George Washington's horse.) But the difficulties are practical ones. They are ones which arise from attempts to get the information needed to resolve the dispute. *In principle* disagreements about facts can be settled, even though *in practice* they might not be.

Verbal Disagreement

The time is 1971, and you are attending a rally called to protest United States involvement in Vietnam. One speaker, who is opposed to the purpose of the rally, addresses the group and declares, "The U.S. is not now and has never been at war in Vietnam."

The statement is met with jeers and catcalls, and the entire group is convinced that either the speaker is being ironic or he is out of touch with things. Or that he is simply crazy. In any case, his assertion is heatedly denied.

Those hoping to get him to agree that he is wrong point out that United States troops were sent to Vietnam in the early 1960s, they mention the bombing raids flown by the Air Force, they tell him about the casualty figures on each side, and so on.

He agrees that all of this is true; yet he still insists that the United States has never been at war in Vietnam. What could be going on here? Why does he still refuse to admit that he is wrong? Is he simply being irrational and refusing to accept overwhelming evidence as adequate? Not necessarily.

The dispute may hinge on a word— the word "war." So far as those who disagree with him are concerned, the United States is at war when it is engaged in sustained military operations against some other power.

So far as the speaker is concerned, the United States can be at war only when the Congress *declares* war. And war was never declared in Vietnam.

The point in contention, then, is a purely verbal one. Once the words are straightened out, it's easy to see that both parties to the dispute can be right. In fact there is, in a sense, no real disagreement between *what is said* in each case, because the same word is being given two different and compatible meanings. The dispute is a phony one, if by this we mean there is no real difference between the contenders. Of course there *appears* to be a real and fundamental difference, but quite literally there is only a misunderstanding.

A *verbal disagreement* is a dispute which results when one or more crucial words are taken to have different and incompatible meanings by the disputing parties and neither of them realizes this. It's common to say such disputes are "about words," but this is misleading to a slight extent. Such controversy is not really *about* words in the sense that a denial of the claim that " 'Wanderoo' is derived from Sanskrit" would be a controversy about words. When people say a dispute is about words, what they want to stress is that there is no genuine disagreement but that there seems to be because it is a word that is the burr under the saddle. Once the offensive word is located, agreement can be reached by having everybody put his meanings on the table. With meanings in plain view the disagreement vanishes.

Disagreements which hinge upon different interpretations of key words can never be harmoniously concluded until the source is recognized. Carloads of facts count for nothing towards a settlement. Focus of attention has to be on the very words by which the claim and counterclaim are expressed. The meaning of each crucial term has to be stated until it can be discovered which ones are being assigned different meanings. If none is, then the dispute is not a verbal one, and grounds for agreement have to be sought elsewhere. To *reveal* a disagreement as a verbal one and to *avoid* such disputes, definition of important words is the best instrument to employ. The ancient demand of "Define your terms!" expresses a good piece of advice for sidestepping and settling pointless quarrels.

Here is a little tale illustrating a dispute which turns upon a word. For all the world it seems like a fascinating and important difference of opinion, yet it is not:

> Several years ago, I was seated with a half dozen or so friends around the fireplace in one of New York's more fashionable clubs. The wintry wind was whistling outside, and the dinner had been excellent. Brandy and port were making their way around the small circle. Altogether it seemed a fine evening to discuss matters of a sort which the daily press of events keeps us from reflecting upon. Before long, I suspected, someone would bring up some philosophical topic or other, and the chase would start.
>
> After a few desultory remarks about the unkindness of the weather, the

excellence of the brandy, and the "slightly musty" taste of the port, my expectations were satisfied. Soames, a man known best to the public for his three expeditions up the Zambesi River, led off.

"You know," he began, "few people realize the rather astonishing fact that when the water tumbles down Victoria Falls and there is no one around to hear it, then it makes no sound."

Noakes, a physician whom we all admired for the scientific calibre of his thinking, quickly rose to Soames' challenge. "Come, come, Soames," he expostulated. "Surely you can't be serious."

"I assure you I am quite serious," Soames replied, apparently somewhat vexed that he should be thought frivolous in his opinions.

"Well, you ought not be," Noakes said gruffly. "You have absolutely no way to support your absurd claim."

Soames stiffened slightly, as if he were preparing to meet a bodily rush from his opponent. "Indeed I do have a way to support what I say," he responded. "Any reasonable man can easily see that if there were no one by to hear the water splash over the falls, then the water would make no sound."

"Stuff and nonsense," said Noakes, with more force than I thought proper to the occasion. "That's no reason at all, only a repetition of what you've already said. Because of that, it's just as silly."

"Then perhaps," said Soames icily, "you will be so kind as to tell me why I should believe that the water *does* make a sound when it hits the Zambesi after its drop from the precipice."

Noakes seemed delighted by the opportunity and quickly seized upon it. "Indeed I shall. It requires only a bit of scientific thinking. Suppose you put a tape recorder by the falls, turned it on, and went away. When you replayed the tape you would have the sound which the falling water makes when there is no one by. It's as simple as that."

Soames smiled a little. "I applaud your ingenuity, of course, but I fear it is *not* as simple as all that. What you would hear would be noises from a tape. What you would *not* hear would be the sound of the waterfall when no one is there. There can be, I repeat, no such sounds."

I saw Noakes redden slightly, and I feared a violent outburst of some kind. The other members of our little group remained silent and gave no sign of imminent participation in the dispute. I decided, then, that the time had arrived for me to adjudicate in order to preserve the tranquility and harmony which we all treasured so much.

"If you will permit me," I began in what I hoped was a conciliatory tone, "I think I can see what is at issue here, and I may be able to bring satisfaction to both parties."

Noakes glowered at me, and Soames fixed me with his icy stare. The other faces mirrored relief, however, and, drawing courage from them, I continued.

"See here," I said, "the bone of contention you two have been chewing is just the little word 'sound.' Noakes, you in your scientific fashion mean by 'sound' the physical disturbance in the air which the water makes when it crashes on the rocks below the falls. It's for that reason you would find a tape recording made in the absence of any human being conclusive proof that a sound is made by the falling water. Is that so?"

"Certainly it is so," Noakes answered. "Sound is nothing more than vibrations in some medium such as air. Tape recorders can record them, and people can hear them, if they should be around."

"Quite so," I said. "Now" —I turned toward Soames —"if I have understood correctly, so far as you are concerned a sound is nothing other than an auditory sensation. Thus nothing can be a sound unless it is actually heard. For that reason you deny that the waterfall makes a *sound* when there is no one there to hear it. You further deny, on the same grounds, that one could record the sounds when nobody is around, for if nobody is around, on your definition, there can be no sounds. Have I represented you correctly?"

"Indeed you have," said Soames.

"To continue then, Soames, let me ask you this. You do not deny that falling water creates a physical disturbance in the air when no one is about, do you?"

"Certainly not," Soames answered.

"Very well, then," said I. "Now, Noakes, you do not, I trust, deny that there can be no auditory sensation produced by a waterfall when there is no one close enough to be affected by the sound waves."

"Of course not," Noakes responded.

"Then, gentlemen, I think we can conclude that you are both in agreement and have no quarrel with one another. It is only the fact that you each assigned to 'sound' different meanings that gave the appearance of a dispute. I now suggest that we each have another glass and turn our conversation towards literature for a while."

A verbal dispute doesn't have to be resolved by showing that someone is in some way *misusing* a word or giving a meaning to it which doesn't reflect its ordinary use. Neither of the parties has to be found guilty of a crime against language. The important thing is to recognize the joker in the deck—the rogue word which incites disagreement where none need be present.

Verbal disputes are vexing because they are hard to discover. People may disagree in earnest and at length and perhaps never discover that different meanings given to the same word are the only barrier that separates them. But verbal disputes have a pleasant feature as well. It is possible to resolve a disagreement about words without anyone's having to change his opinion and without anyone's having to be wrong. Everyone wins, and no one loses.

Evaluative Disagreement

A quite mortal bard by the name of F. D. Hemans presented the waiting world with a poem beginning with these lines:

> The boy stood on the burning deck,
> Whence all but he had fled;
> The flame that lit the battle's wreck
> Shone round him o'er the dead.

Very unsurprisingly, there are many people who regard this as execrable poetry, but there are others who don't share this view. They think, in fact, "Casabianca" is a rather good poem. Two from opposing camps (say Boggs and Diggs) may disagree with one another, even when they agree about the facts involved and about the meanings of all crucial terms. Both readily admit that it's proper to call "Casabianca" a "poem," that it was written by Hemans, and that it's about the bravery shown by a boy during a naval battle. They might even agree that a good poem can be defined as "one which can be reread many times, with new discoveries on each occasion." Still they fail to be in accord. Their disagreement is about the *evaluation* of the poem. Boggs claims that the work is perfectly atrocious, not one which fits the meaning of "good poem" at all. Diggs denies this and asserts that, on the contrary, "Casabianca" is indeed a good poem.

The difference of opinion between Boggs and Diggs is not one which can be resolved by shopping around for more facts about the poem's author, the historical event (the Battle of the Nile) which it was based on, or anything of the sort. Meanings are not in dispute, neither the meaning of any of the words in the poem, nor any of the words used to talk about the poem, so definition will not settle the difference. The keystone in the arch of dispute is whether or not "Casabianca" can properly be called a "good poem," though there is total agreement about what this means.

How may agreement be secured, if it can be? Must Boggs and Diggs just say their say, shake their heads in the realization of hopelessness, and walk away? Of course not. People rarely act this way. What happens, rather, is that each tries to *persuade* the other that his opinion is the correct one. Like courtroom lawyers, each one presents his case and does his best to convince his opponent to accept the view he advocates. Diggs may try to get Boggs to see that "Casabianca" is filled with vivid images of battle and chaos, that the reader is pulled into the scene and made to feel *aware* of what a naval engagement was like and to appreciate the cool courage shown by the boy in the heat of the battle. Boggs attempts to get Diggs to realize how mawkishly sentimental the poem is, how it doesn't present individual responses but only standardized, conventional, and wholly predictable ones. Even the battle images, Boggs might say, are wholly trite; there are no unsuspected observations, no personal perspectives, no effective metaphors.

So the dialetic would proceed, each pointing out unnoticed or unappreciated aspects of the poem to the other, each trying to make his case the more persuasive one. No score can be kept, and it is not possible to total up points at the end of the dispute. In fact, the dispute may not come to an end, except in the sense that the two just get tired of trying to convince one another. They may simply have to agree to differ, neither having been persuaded of the correctness of the other's position and the incorrectness of his own.

Of course we all regard ourselves as *open* to persuasion, and sometimes this is even true. On occasion we do change the evaluations which we make of poems, movies, novels, plays, and people. In disagreements about evaluations, both parties of the dispute must play the roles of defense attorney, prosecuting attorney, jury, and judge. We must try to show why our evaluation ought to be accepted and why the contrary one is wrong. But at the same time we must act like a jury and weigh the evidence on both sides. Finally we must judge whether our opinion is so weakly supported that we can no longer hold it in comfort, whether our opponent's opinion is so strongly supported that we must accept it, or whether we now simply don't know what to think.

It often happens, of course, that we think we haven't made a good case for our point of view or that our antagonist has presented a better one, and yet we remain unconvinced. We aren't necessarily being irrational, for in evaluation there is never *conclusive proof* that one position or another is the correct one. We may, after all, still entertain doubts about a man's guilt or innocence after the trial is over, the jury's verdict is in, and the judge's pronouncement has been made. In the legal system decisions have to be made, sooner or later, and a judgment issued. But it's not that way in ordinary disagreements about evaluation. To this extent, our analogy is misleading. If either Boggs or Diggs remains unpersuaded, even after all has been said by each to sway the other, then there is still a difference of opinion between them. It may be one which will never be resolved.

Evaluative disagreements can be quite complex and can involve sub-disagreements about facts, words, and other evaluations. Before the main difference can be settled, the component ones generally have to be resolved. Boggs and Diggs might not agree about the meaning of "trite images," and even if they do, they might not agree that the images in "Casabianca" are trite. Many levels of disagreement might have to be worked through and laid to rest in the process of trying to secure a unanimous opinion. Some subdisagreements may be about matters so serious that a failure of accord concerning them makes argument on the major issue impossible. If Boggs and Diggs both believed that no poem can be a good one unless it expresses a personal, as opposed to a stereotyped, point of view, then if they can't agree as to whether "Casabianca" has or lacks this characteristic, they also will be unable to agree as to its value as a poem. On the other hand, if they believe that employing effective metaphors is just a feature typical of most good poems, but not one which a poem must have to be good, then they can continue to disagree about "Casabianca's" metaphors, even though they reach accord on the basic question of its value.

It would be very peculiar, but quite possible, for Boggs and Diggs to agree on every subissue raised and still disagree on the main one. The reason this would be odd is that we generally move towards agreement by settling our differences with respect to what both parties to the dispute take to be constituent issues of it. The hope and the expectation is that a sufficient number of agreements on these issues will result in agreement concerning the one big issue of which they are parts. More often than not, and happily so, this turns out to be the case.

Special cases of evaluative disagreements can sometimes be settled by transforming them into ones which may be ended by an appeal to known or discoverable facts. This can be done when both disputants agree on some more fundamental value, and the resolution of the dispute about an evaluation hinges upon whether this fundamental value is or is not being realized. If Boggs and Diggs disagree about the desirability of legalizing the sale of LSD but can agree that drugs which produce harmful psychological or physiological side effects ought to be illegal, then a way is open for settling their dispute on factual grounds. Information about LSD which indicates that it has damaging consequences may move them towards agreeing that the drug ought not be made generally available. Contrary information may move them in a contrary direction. (Even in this case, Boggs and Diggs may dispute the facts and the evaluation of effects as damaging or safe.)

Interpretative Disagreement

There is a fourth manner of disagreeing which it is handy to distinguish. To give it a name, it is *interpretative disagreement*. It can arise when neither facts, nor the meaning of words, nor evaluations are in dispute or involved. When people disagree about the meaning or theme of a movie, play, poem, or novel, or about how the action of a real or fictional person should be construed, or about the correct understanding of an event or work of art, their difference of opinion is one concerning interpretation.

Consider some examples.

1. Hamlet, apparently thinking himself alone, delivers a soliloquy which begins:

> To be, or not to be: that is the question.
> Whether 'tis nobler in the mind to suffer
> The slings and arrows of outrageous fortune,
> Or to take arms against a sea of troubles,
> And by opposing end them. To die; to sleep;
> No more; and by a sleep to say we end
> The heart-ache and the thousand natural shocks
> That flesh is heir to. 'Tis a consummation
> Devoutly to be wish'd.

All of Shakespeare, and *Hamlet* in particular, has always been food for hungry critics. This passage, in the context of the play, has been interpreted in many ways. Some ways are consistent with others and some are not. Here are just a few:

a. Hamlet, convinced that his uncle murdered his father, is disgusted and disillusioned about life and is contemplating suicide.
b. Hamlet is meditating on suicide, and his inability to decide whether it is better for him to live or die reveals the general irresoluteness of his character.
c. Hamlet is not really alone and he realizes that he is not. He says what he does to make it appear that he is going mad so that his uncle, the King, will be put off guard and not suspect him of plotting revenge for the death of his father.
d. Stage directions make it clear that Hamlet has a book with him. He is reading from the book, not meditating on suicide.

2. **BECK:** George Smiley is such a polite and generous man. The last time he paid me a visit he seemed to be quite interested in what I said about Etruscan pottery and promised to make me a present of a piece from his own collection.

   DOBBS: He certainly doesn't strike me as polite and generous. I think he is fawning, unctuous, and niggardly.

3. **ROE:** In "Fire and Ice" Robert Frost uses the two agents of destruction named in the title of the poem to stand for out-and-out world war and a cold war, respectively. His speaker gives his opinion about which of these two is more likely to bring about the end of the world. He decides, in the first stanza, that fire is the more likely candidate. But in the second stanza he tells us that ice, or the cold war, also has a great potential for destruction, one sufficient to bring about our end.

   MEYER: That seems basically wrong to me. In that poem, Frost uses two theories about the way in which the world will end—one religious, the other scientific—to suggest that whatever may become of the terrestrial globe, certain human emotions—like desire and hate—destroy the world for individuals every day.

4. **CHADWICK:** In all of his movies Bogart always portrays a man who is hard and unyielding, individualistic, and competent, who hates pretense and sentimentality and yet is fundamentally human and decent.

   SIMPSON: I can go with you part of the way, but in my opinion you go much too far. A number of characters are played in that way, but by no means all of them.

How can diputes like these be settled? Persuasion again seems to be the road leading to accord. The blackjack, thumbscrew, and pistol? No, at least not among amicable and reasonable people. The persuasion must be of a much gentler sort than these harsh devices make possible. It has to be persuasion of the kind which is often instrumental in settling evaluative disagreements. Basically it consists in getting someone to see a point of view, and to accept it. It involves "making a case" for an interpretation. In the final analysis each person has to decide for himself whether to accept or reject an interpretation, but this doesn't mean he has to decide without consideration, that he must grope in the dark and shun offers of light. He can be open to persuasion and listen to the case which is made for an interpretation. What's more, if he has a different interpretation, he can try his hand at making a case for it and at trying to convince his opponent.

The most important interplay in settling interpretative disagreements is probably between *plausibility* and *implausibility*. The person offering an interpretation can't simply preach it like the gospel and let matters rest there. If he expects someone who doubts or disagrees to give assent, then he has to *develop* his interpretation. He has to show that it is consistent with features or facts about the matter interpreted, that it doesn't contradict what is already agreed upon. The interpretation, in addition, must not ignore features of a work of art or an action simply because they don't fit into the interpretation. There are many interpretations of works and events which suffer the fatal flaw of ignoring significant and recognized features. Finally, a unified way of looking at what is being interpreted has to be supplied, a way that suggests the connections which various traits or features have with one another. The interpretation ought to present a framework within which each significant trait finds a place. The result should be a coherent pattern that "makes sense" out of the work, event, or action, either in whole or in part. An interpretation gains its plausibility from the extent to which it does make sense, is coherent, is consistent, and is complete. The interpreter has to convince the doubter or the challenger that this view of things is plausible in this sense, that it does all of these jobs. If there is an alternative interpretation under consideration in the disagreement, then he must show that his does a better job than the alternative.

In the last dispute above, Chadwick must mount a defense. He must set out to convince Simpson that the interpretation of Bogart characterizations which he offers is plausible. Taking as examples Sam Spade in *The Maltese Falcon* and Philip Marlowe in *The Big Sleep*, he may discuss the traits which these characters have—their perceptiveness, intelligence, and sense of justice. Most of these traits, he may point out, are also possessed by the individuals Bogart portrayed in *The African Queen*, *High Sierra*, and *The Petrified Forest*. There is, he may claim, a core of such traits that is revealed in every figure which Bogart played. Bogart's accomplishment as an actor was that he could imbue diverse and often unsavory characters with these fundamental human traits.

Simpson may not be at all convinced. He may point out that Captain Queeg was a character played by Bogart and Queeg certainly lacks some of the traits Chadwick claimed to be present in all Bogart portrayals. If Chadwick agrees to this, then Simpson has succeeded in showing that the interpretation is faulty. Queeg doesn't fit the pattern which Chadwick claimed holds for all Bogart movies. Chadwick could modify what he said, of course. He could say that he only meant his interpretation to be *generally* true, not true in all cases. But, Simpson might continue, what about the prospector in *The Treasure of Sierra Madre?* He doesn't fit the pattern either. And so on. If Simpson can find the ammunition to keep firing he might succeed in shooting down Chadwick's interpretation. Each shot that scores a hit makes the interpretation less plausible. If he is not convinced by Chadwick's case, Chadwick may be convinced by his. There are cases that count in Chadwick's favor and ones that count in Simpson's favor, and eventually each must decide which case is the stronger. They may have to agree to differ.

Chadwick need not sit by with a hopeless look while Simpson brings up cases that he says count against the interpretation. Simpson's claim that Queeg or some other character doesn't fit the pattern may be challenged. If this happens, then a new interpretative disagreement is opened up at a lower level. How is the character of Queeg, and so on, to be interpreted? The subgame is played in the same way as the main event.

A value generally accepted for judging interpretations of novels, poems, movies, and many other kinds of works of art is that the interpretation be *interesting*. One that is plausible, unifying, and consistent with the facts may be so obvious and dull that it is not worth considering. It may be little more than rehash of the plot or a description of the work. A good interpretation not only is plausible and keeps all the traits of the work in focus, but it makes our sight more acute. It allows us to glimpse features and connections which escaped our attention, and it increases our understanding and appreciation of factors that we have noticed before but have regarded as puzzling or unimportant. A good interpretation should give us a *new view* of a work.

Some disagreements that seem to be about the interpretation of events or actions are often just disguised factual disagreements. Consider this one: Calvin Thompson and George Hecht are hanging around Times Square. From a tobacco shop at the corner of 42nd Street and Broadway, a man dressed in a dark topcoat and wearing a homburg steps out and walks to the curb. He glances down Broadway, raises his hat, and replaces it again. Thompson and Hecht see him do this and discuss it.

THOMPSON: People in New York are politer than I thought. Did you see that guy tip his hat to that fat woman wearing an American flag?

HECHT: Jesus, anybody can tell you're from out of town. He wasn't being polite. He's obviously in the numbers racket, and he was giving a signal to that hard-looking guy standing behind the fat woman. The one with the hat probably just made a pickup at the cigar store, and the other one might be his bodyguard.

Was the man in the black coat merely tipping his hat out of politeness or was he doing it as a signal to a confederate? Both Thompson and Hecht might be said to be *interpreting* the man's behavior, but their disagreement is one which can be settled by ascertainable facts. They may be in no position to get the facts required, of course. Yet to determine whether one or the other of them is right or whether they are both wrong, only a bill of facts will turn the trick. They must, if they really want to know, investigate the man in the hat, his business, and his associates. They have to learn who the fat woman is (perhaps she was an accomplice) and who the other man is. If the facts show Hecht to be right, then they show that his interpretation is right. So too for Thompson, although he and Hecht can't both be right.

Had Thompson merely said, "That man in the black coat lifted his hat and then replaced it on his head," we wouldn't ordinarily say this was an *interpretation* of what he saw. We would just say Thompson described what he saw. The truth is, though, there is nothing like a "natural" distinction between describing and interpreting with respect to actions and events. In practice we tend to make the distinction only on a comparative basis. An account which seems to us to involve a number of assumptions about what was happening we call an "interpretation" in contrast with a more straightforward account which we see might be given. On most occasions, though, if Thompson had been asked to describe what he saw and he reported, "I saw a man tip his hat to a fat woman wrapped in an American flag," we would regard this as a description of what he saw. It's only when we compare this with the rather more neutral "A man lifted his hat and replaced it" that we are inclined to say Thompson *interpreted* what he saw. Despite recognizable differences between them, both descriptions are of facts. In one case, though, to know that Thompson's description is correct we need only know that the man took off his hat and put it back on. In the other case, to know that the description is correct we must know this as well, but we must also learn *why* the black-coated man behaved in this way. That is, we have to find out about the background conditions and relationships.

Disagreements about the meaning or interpretation of a piece of behavior are almost always to be resolved by finding out the facts. Just because we sometimes make a distinction between "describing" and "interpreting" may make it appear that more often than not there is something else involved in settling disputes about such interpretations. But this is not so. It is just that it is necessary to find out more facts to resolve disagreements over "interpretations" than to resolve ones over "descriptions."

"Almost always" is a phrase which weasels out of saying "all." Some events and some behavior we do *interpret* in much the same way that we interpret works of art. The interpretation comes in after all facts considered relevant are known and individuals simply have to make up their minds about how to construe what someone says or does. If, after dinner with George Smiley, Beck and Dobbs are discussing how Smiley acted and Beck says he was polite and Dobbs says he was boorish, then this is a disagreement that can't be settled by an appeal to the facts. Each must make a case for his contention and try to persuade the other to accept his interpretation. In doing so they may, of course, appeal to facts which both already know and accept. Beck may point out that Smiley listened to the conversation, didn't interrupt when someone else was speaking, and was generally agreeable. Dobbs may ask Beck to recall how Smiley slurped his consommé, discussed embalming during dinner, and gulped his port afterwards. Each uses the facts to make his case, and they do not require, nor could they use, any new facts. Of course if they were disagreeing about whether Smiley was in general a boor or a polite person, rather than about whether on the one occasion he acted boorishly or politely, then they would need a great many facts not available in a single instance. They would have to know or learn what Smiley's behavior is like as a rule.

There is some difficulty, too, in distinguishing evaluative disputes from interpretative ones. The reason for this is simply that we often simultaneously interpret *and* evaluate an event or whatever. Frequently we do so by using words to interpret that have built-in evaluations. If someone says, for example, "Nixon and his staff ran the government as a dictatorship," he is at one and the same time interpreting the facts of the Nixon presidency and evaluating them. The word "dictatorship" has an evaluation associated with its use, for we disapprove of dictatorships. But all this means is that disagreement may arise on two fronts. Finding an exact category for a particular dispute is not all that important. Realizing what is involved is.

Clear-cut cases of disagreements about interpretation are ones in which it is possible to ask about evaluation after the issue at dispute is settled. For example, somebody might say that D. W. Griffith had a tremendous influence on the development of film techniques. Somebody else may disagree. But after they have agreed (if they do) on the question of influence, they may still disagree about whether Griffith's influence (or lack of it) was a good thing or a bad one, whether we ought to approve of it or disapprove of it.

Some disagreements are pure and simple disputes about facts, words, evaluations, or interpretations. But real disputes typically are not. They involve disagreements of all four sorts or at least of two or three sorts. They are not *purely* about facts, and they are not about a single *simple* issue. By contrast with pure and simple disagreements, they are impure and complex. A radical who says: "The corrupt and fascist government of the United States must be replaced by one responsive to the voice of its citizens" opens the lid on a box of bees. The issues are multiple, some obvious and some submerged, and there is room for disagreement of all kinds on all constituent questions. "What do 'corrupt,' 'fascist,' 'responsive' mean?" "Is the United States corrupt?" "What are the facts that show that it is?" "How are the facts to be interpreted?" "Should the government be replaced?" "What does it mean to 'replace' a government, anyway?" And so on and on in a way familiar to us all.

The ways of disagreement which we have listed are merely helps for untangling the threads of real disputes. They are distinctions which it is useful to keep in mind in exploring just what sorts of matters are in dispute.

There's One Now!: Identifying Arguments

"In my youth" said Father William, "I took to the law,
And argued each case with my wife;
And the muscular strength, which it gave to my jaw,
Has lasted the rest of my life."

LEWIS CARROLL,
Alice in Wonderland

The most important and satisfactory way of resolving the majority of disagreements is by presenting someone with an argument that he finds persuasive. Arguments are the most important weapons in the arsenal of rational persuasion. They are used not only in contexts in which there is disagreement, but in situations in which someone wishes to convince us to accept a claim, to win us to his position, and to avoid disagreement.

But what is an argument? How can we recognize one when we see it? And how can we state it in the clearest way so that we can evaluate it and determine whether we want to accept it or not? Those are the questions we'll be concerned with in this section.

Wrangles, disputes, quarrels, altercations, debates, spats, controversies, and squabbles are all among the things which we usually feel free to call arguments. They aren't the only things, though. Each book of Milton's *Paradise Lost* is introduced by a section entitled "argument," and there Milton presents in prose form a summary of the book's contents. ("The consultation begun, Satan debates whether another Battle be to be hazarded for the recovery of Heaven. . . .") More generally, the argument of an epic poem is the gist or plot of the work, and the point, thesis, main idea, claim, or conclusion of an article, paper, essay, book, or play is often spoken of as its "argument." ("The argument of Sorely's book is that some people have the power to transform themselves into wolves.")

It's undeniably legitimate to apply the word "argument" to these sorts of cases, and there are even more varieties which could be brushed off for inspection. Logic and arguments are usually thought of as connected as closely as bees and honey or dogs and bones, and so they are. But for all that, logic is not especially concerned with any and every kind of thing which is called an argument. Rather, the word "argument" is used in a somewhat technical sense in logic. Its use is restricted in such a way that it picks out only *some* of the things commonly said to be arguments.

To speak directly, so far as logic is concerned an *argument* consists in making a claim or advancing a thesis and offering reasons or evidence for its acceptance. Since we both express our claims and offer evidence by means of declarative sentences, we can rephrase our definition along these lines: *An argument is the written or spoken assertion of a sentence on the basis of some other sentence or sentences.*

An argument, as a group of sentences, can be divided into two parts. The sentence asserted is called the *conclusion* of the argument, and the other sentences are known as the *premises* of the argument. When an argument is offered, the premises are understood as being put forward to provide justification or support for the conclusion. That is, they are supposed to provide grounds of some sort for asserting the conclusion. Here is an example of an argument:

PREMISE: Demonstrations and protests frequently end in violence.

PREMISE: In spite of that fact, they represent the free expression of opinion.

PREMISES: It is more important to us, as Americans, that people should be free to express their opinions, even when violence might be involved, than it is that violence should be avoided at all costs.

CONCLUSION: Demonstrations and protests must be allowed.

An unfortunate but real fact of life is that arguments don't often confront us shorn of extraneous verbiage and with premises and conclusion neatly labeled. Generally they are intricate verbal arabesques which blend passing observations, indignant asides, and character estimations with sentences intended to serve as premises. Conclusions are sometimes stated before the premises upon which they are supposed to stand are supplied, and sometimes only those with the sharp eyes of Argus can spot the conclusion in a welter of sentences.

Chunks of writing and stretches of discourse which are thought or claimed to be arguments have to be subjected to close scrutiny. The premises have to be extricated from whatever extraneous matters twine around them, and the conclusion has to be identified. Obviously before we can ask whether an argument is a sound one or not we have to know what it is. This can be a formidable task, and it's made even more difficult by the fact that not *every* group of sentences is an argument. Perhaps the sentences only express an opinion or an attitude, one for which no support is given or intended. Consequently, there is no guarantee that we will be able to isolate premises and conclusion in a piece of prose.

Knowing when a bunch of sentences contains an argument and finding out exactly what it is, is a very tricky business. No one could possibly think this is an argument:

> At night I think of the east wind, blowing in from the Orient. If my senses were only keener, I imagine, I could smell the odors of spices and tea, of jasmine and incense. But I smell nothing. Nothing but the harsh odor of exhaust fumes and the stink of rubber burning at high speed down the highway.

But what about this:

> "Goodbye, till we meet again," [Alice] said as cheerfully as she could.
>
> "I shouldn't know you again if we *did* meet," Humpty Dumpty replied in a discontented tone, giving her one of his fingers to shake: "You're so exactly like other people."
>
> "The face is what one goes by, generally," Alice remarked in a thoughtful tone.
>
> "That's just what I complain of," said Humpty Dumpty. "Your face is the same as everybody has—the two eyes, so—"(marking their places in the air with his thumb) "nose in the middle, mouth under. It's always the same. Now if you had the two eyes on the same side of the nose, for instance—or the mouth on the top—that would be *some* help."
>
> LEWIS CARROLL,
Through the Looking Glass

This certainly doesn't seem to be an argument at first glimpse. Yet if we take a very close look at what Humpty Dumpty says, we can detect an argument lurking in his words. A short form of it would be:

PREMISE: Your face is the same as everyone's face.

PREMISE: It is impossible to recognize a person whose face is the same as everyone else's.

CONCLUSION: I wouldn't recognize you if we met again.

Humpty Dumpty's argument is not a good one, of course. When we talk about faces being alike, we mean they resemble one another in specific detail, not just that they have those features which make them faces at all ("two eyes," etc.). Humpty Dumpty's argument gets what little plausibility it has from his word play with "same." Still, it *is* an argument.

Conclusions of arguments, as a rule, are not difficult to spot. There is a small group of words which often serve as indicators that a conclusion is about to be stated. They are flags which wave to mark conclusions. Paying attention to these words and to what follows them makes it relatively easy to locate a conclusion even in difficult and obscure passages. Some of the tip-off words are: thus, so, therefore, hence, consequently, so we see, we may conclude, etc. Here's how they are typically used:

(a) Peter took either acid or speed. I know he didn't have any acid, *so* he must have taken speed.
(b) No one in this country who desires a college education should be denied one. Many can't afford it, however. *Thus,* the government, national or state, must see to it that those who have the desire but lack the money are provided for.

A conclusion is sometimes stated before the premises are. When this is done, there are several words which are often used to indicate that what follows is to be taken as *justifying* or *supporting* the conclusion. When the conclusion is stated first, "for," "since," or "because" usually appears between it and its premises. As in this case:

> We must change our tax system, *because* as things stand now middle-income people pay more than do the very rich, and this is grossly unfair.

Such words don't always appear flanked by conclusion and premises, though. Sometimes they show up as the first word in a sentence. When this happens, the premises usually come right after them, and then there is a comma or a word like "therefore" or "then" and finally the conclusion. To illustrate:

> *Because* new and more stringent demands are being made on our state universities and the money alloted to them is less than adequate to fulfill the demands satisfactorily, the state legislatures must realize that budget increases are imperative.

The crude, the careless, dastards, and deceivers are known to drop in conclusion-indicating words where they don't really belong. A word like "therefore" displays a banner inscribed "Premises have been given, conclusion follows," and when such words are present we have every reason to expect that what appears before them supplies grounds for what follows them. We are, sadly enough, often disappointed. Untutored or unpracticed writers have a terrible habit of using "thus" and "therefore" as if they were bridge words like "moreover," "now consider," or "one final point." These writers offer such unsavory bits as:

> Our cities are in real trouble. Housing is inadequate for numerous families, and the inner-city is fast becoming a ghetto. *Thus,* food prices are higher there than in the suburbs.

Quite often people slip in conclusion words when they don't really intend anyone to take what they say as an argument. In this example, the sentence following the "thus" is just another item which could be mentioned along with the others characterizing the plight of our cities. Of course the "thus" justifies us in *treating* the group of sentences as an argument. If we do, then on the basis of what is said, we would have to point out that it's not a convincing argument, for no clear-cut reasons are given for why food prices are higher in the inner city. (It might be a disguised or telegraphed argument, of course. If we suspected this, we would have to ask that the hidden premises be uncovered.)

Most likely, and on the side of tolerance, we would generally recognize that such a case is not really offered as an argument, even though it's dressed up like one. It's just a case of bad writing, we would assume. But in writing "thus" and "so," we are inviting others to judge what we say as an argument, even if we didn't intend for it to be taken that way. The moral is: Don't point a "therefore" at someone unless you really mean it. Conclusion indicators are not merely transition words. They are much stronger, and when we use them we make a commitment we ought to be prepared to back up.

Conclusion words are useful tools for shrewd deceivers. If we read with one eye or listen with half an ear, we can easily be duped into thinking that grounds or reasons have already been given when someone says "therefore" and then pronounces a conclusion. Those intent on gaining our agreement may slur over their reasons or only pretend they have some, then come down hard on their conclusion. In all cases, we have to pull back and take a look at what is being said and the grounds given for asserting it. We have to locate the premises and spot the conclusion, then evaluate the argument. Most importantly, we always have to keep in mind that just because someone says, "so we see," we don't have to agree that we do.

That arguments are often hidden in the midst of piles of sentences shouldn't be overemphasized. Almost as often arguments are telegraphed by means of a very few sentences that don't actually state the complete argument. Consider this case, which, though not an argument, is similar to a telegraphed argument precisely because more is involved than what is actually said: The CIA has put us to keeping a close watch on a man named George Bell, a prominent businessman suspected of having radical views about income distribution. On a telephone tap we hear Bell tell his broker, "I have decided to do it, so go ahead." What has Bell decided? What is the broker supposed to do? If all we know is what we have heard, there is no way we can answer these questions. Bell and his broker aren't in any doubt, though. They aren't because, on the day before, the two of them met for lunch, and on that occasion Bell mentioned that he was considering selling all he owned and giving everything to the poor. He then promised the broker that he would call him on the next day and let him know the decision. If we knew this background information, then we would know what Bell had decided and what the broker was being told to do. Without it we can't say.

Arguments are frequently much like this in their presentation. Propounders of arguments often take it for granted that there are certain things that are just too obvious to be worth mentioning or that there are some matters that are already agreed upon and don't have to be mentioned. As a consequence, what is handed to us as an argument may not be a *complete* argument but only a rough sketch for one. It is left for us to fill in the details, if we wish to, and produce a finished portrait. The roots that support a tree are mostly underground. Similarly, an argument may have only its conclusion and a premise or so actually stated, while other premises are merely assumed or taken for granted.

Good advice to follow, particularly when dealing with arguments which smell a little fishy to us, is to take truncated or elliptical arguments and try to set them out in full. This is sometimes difficult to do because it is often hard to know just what *has* been taken to be so obvious that it didn't need stating. It's not possible to give any general rules for digging out the premises of an argument when they aren't given, because how an argument is stated depends a great deal upon the person to whom the argument is delivered, what the arguer thinks that person knows or needs to know, what the arguer and the receiver have been discussing and what they agree upon, and so on.

Consider this sketch of an argument:

Gregg and Mettler have been discussing the problem of environmental pollution, and they have both agreed that immediate steps need to be taken to halt pollution and to clean up the environment. Gregg says, "I think that business and industry should bear the greater part of the financial burden of repairing damage to our environment. After all, they are the groups which have profited most from its destruction."

Gregg is presenting Mettler with a shorthand version of an argument. What he actually says can be written out this way:

> PREMISE: Business and industry have profited most from practices which have been destructive of the environment.
> _____
> CONCLUSION: Business and industry should bear most of the costs involved in repairing environmental damage.

Yet these are only the bare bones of Gregg's argument, and chances are that Mettler doesn't need to have it fleshed out for him. But if it were presented in a more complete form, it would be something like this:

> PREMISE: The natural environment has been damaged in many ways.
>
> PREMISE: Steps ought to be taken to repair the damage.
>
> PREMISE: Business and industry have profited most from practices which have been destructive of the environment.

PREMISE: Groups which have profited from environmental destruction ought to be the ones which bear most of the costs involved in repairing the damage.

CONCLUSION: Business and industry should bear most of the costs involved in repairing environmental damage.

Not only might Mettler not need to have the argument spelled out for him, but he might not even be able to spell it out for himself. Some of its premises might be so obvious to him that, if he were asked to present the argument in a full form, it might not even occur to him to mention them. It sometimes takes a sharp eye and a quick mind to spot premises which are floating unremarked beneath the surface. This is particularly true when we are not looking from a distance but doing our scrutinizing close at hand.

The point to all of this is simply that arguments are ordinarily given in some context. The context generally determines what is taken to be obvious and what is assumed. In filling out an argument sketch we have to disassociate ourselves from the context sufficiently to be able to recognize what is being taken for granted that ought to be stated explicity as a premise of the argument.

In analyzing pieces of writing or stretches of speaking with an eye to identifying the arguments and putting them before the judgment bar, it's useful to write out the arguments in a standard form. The pattern conventionally followed (as above) is to write down each of the premises separately, then draw a line under them to indicate that the grounds offered for the conclusion are finished. Next, the sentence stating the conclusion is written under the line. With this form to follow it's not necessary to label each sentence as "premise" or "conclusion." The line is enough to indicate which is what.

There are obviously no sentences which have "premise" indelibly stamped across their faces, and there are obviously no sentences which must eternally wear the brand "conclusion." A sentence is a premise only in some given argument. It's a premise of *that* argument. A sentence which is a conclusion is a conclusion of a particular argument, not in itself or for *any* argument. Clearly, then, a sentence which is a premise of some argument may be the conclusion of another or vice versa. As in this case:

The U.S. is committed to the principle of tolerating and protecting the moral and religious beliefs of its citizens.

The draft laws often force individuals to act contrary to their moral and religious beliefs.

CONCLUSION: The draft laws are not consistent with tolerating and protecting moral and religious beliefs.

Any law that is not consistent with the fundamental principles of American democracy ought to be changed.

The toleration and protection of moral and religious beliefs is a fundamental principle of American democracy.

PREMISE: The draft laws are not consistent with tolerating and protecting moral and religious beliefs.

The draft laws ought to be changed.

It is, of course, in this familiar manner that we construct chains of arguments. Our primary interest may be in establishing the last conclusion, but in order to do that we may have to offer some more arguments, ones which purport to establish one or more of the premises in our final argument.

Logic and Arguments

It's no secret that logic in its various forms is fundamentally concerned with arguments. But shipwrights and sailors, hosiers and clothiers, ironmongers and victualers, and everyone else are also concerned with arguments. People in all trades and on their own free time and for myriad reasons offer, criticize, accept, and reject arguments. The question becomes this: In what ways, from a logical point of view, do we take an interest in arguments? Well, we use them, certainly, but so does everyone else. The distinction that makes a difference is that from the perspective of logic we concentrate our attention on arguments as arguments. Arguments are not only devices we employ, they are part of our *subject matter*. We focus on arguments, scrutinize, examine, criticize, describe, and classify them. To abandon the generalities, there are two major ways in which we are concerned with arguments when we are "being logical."

1. We are interested, first of all, in characterizing and clarifying the nature of the relations that may hold between the premises and conclusions of arguments. In trying to get a conclusion accepted, there are at least two different sorts of claims which people may make about the connection between their conclusion and the sentences they offer as premises. Sometimes a conclusion is said to *follow from* or be guaranteed by the premises. In other cases the premises are said merely to offer some support for the conclusion; though the premises are not said to guarantee the conclusion, they are claimed to provide at least some reason or evidence to accept it. Obviously enough, we will expect different things from an argument when we are told that its conclusion follows from its premises than we will expect if we are told that the conclusion is just

supported by the premises. Expecting different things, we will judge arguments in a different way, depending upon what claim is made for them. But what exactly are the relationships between premises and conclusions of arguments that words like "guarantees" or "follows from" and "supports" or "confirms" are supposed to characterize? This is certainly a question that falls within the scope of logic, and we will try to answer it in the next chapter.

2. Noticing that there is often an important distinction between the arguments that people offer and the claims that they make for them brings out a second interest in arguments from the logical point of view. We would like to have some rules or criteria for evaluating arguments. We need to know what makes an argument a good one, and we need to be able to spot bad or risky arguments. Even if we can't get an explicit and firm set of rules to help us do this, then we can at least try to discover what sort of practical considerations are relevant to estimating the worth of arguments. "Grass is green; therefore, the United States should support higher education" is an atrocious argument. No one would ever think otherwise. But can we say what makes it a bad argument? If someone offered it to us, on what grounds could we object to it? Well, we need to find out. The next section of this chapter is on objecting to arguments, and the matter of evaluation is (in part) discussed there. But as we've already seen, arguments are not always of the same kind. Some are said to have premises that guarantee the conclusions, and some are said to have premises that merely support the conclusions. We certainly won't and don't evaluate both kinds the same way. How we evaluate each, along with the first question we raised, we'll examine in the chapter following this one.

"God was not so sparing of man that He only made him two-legged and left it to Aristotle to make him rational." The point of John Locke's quip is that people could spot bad arguments and recognize good ones long before Aristotle wrote down formal logical rules. Locke's point ought not be forgotten, because it applies to anything we may say about arguments.

There is no Bureau of Argument that has the job of laying down laws of arguments. In numerous cases we know a bad argument when we see it, and we don't need any rules or logic books to tell us not to accept it. The same is true of good arguments. There are, of course, many times when we are unable to decide whether an argument is worthless or excellent. But because we *sometimes* can't decide doesn't mean that we can *never* decide it.

In investigating the ways in which conclusions may be connected with their premises and in trying to get standards for weighing the worth of arguments, we are far from starting in the dark. One of the jobs of logic is to bring out into the open and clearly state many of the relevant considerations which we ordinarily take for granted or are not even fully conscious of when we present, accept, and evaluate arguments. We *recognize* the distinction between an argument whose conclusion follows from the premises and one whose conclusion doesn't. But logic aims at more than this. It wants to state clearly and analyze fully the difference. We already know how to estimate the worth of many arguments, but logic attempts to make explicit the criteria which we implicitly assume when we accept an argument as a good one or reject it as bad. In short, the rules and distinctions of the logic of arguments are not ones which descend upon us from above. They are not things imposed upon us without our leave, nor are they ones which are made up fresh and whole from the fevered brains of logicians and philosophers. They are produced by a reflection upon and a refinement of what we do in practice, of what we do when we accept, reject, and criticize arguments.

The logic of argument is a description of arguments and of how we deal with them. But only in a certain sense. In practice we may sometimes be careless, unrefined, or inconsistent in our formulations and appraisals of arguments. Logic not only strives to bring our submerged presuppositions and criteria to the surface but tries to harmonize them. Logical distinctions and criteria may then come to be instruments. They may, then, come to modify the very practice that they, in part, reflect. But the rules and distinctions themselves are still judged by our practice. If someone presents us with a rule that would result in our having to accept arguments that we regard as bad, then we are free to reject the argument and the rule. We could, on the other hand, decide to keep them both. We are the masters of the rules, not they of us.

The advantages of having a set of instruments, in the form of distinctions and criteria, for dealing with arguments are mostly obvious. One which might be overlooked is that once we are armed with our logical weapons we are in a good strategic position to face up to those arguments whose worth we doubt. We use standards tested in many cases and find that they characterize arguments as bad or good in the same way that we do without the standards. We can then approach new and unexamined arguments with our rules in hand and feel that we have firm ground on which to erect our opinions about them.

We have now climbed up Jacob's ladder high enough to meet with arguments face to face. We have learned what an argument is and in what ways logic is concerned with arguments. We've also discovered that one of the greatest difficulties that faces us in dealing with arguments in ordinary life is in *identifying* them—in discovering just when a piece of prose is an argument and going on to locate its premises and conclusion.

This is a matter that takes a good bit of practice to do well. Though this is a case in which practice never leads to perfection, it does lead to a considerable increase in skill and to the development of a critical attitude that is well worth cultivating.

On Guard!: Challenging Arguments

Once we have identified an argument, either by having someone neatly lay it out for us or by the harder method of discovering premises and a conclusion by ourselves, the game is only half over. We still have to decide whether we ought to accept the argument or not.

This means that we have to be prepared to probe at the argument, to look for its weak spots and its downright flaws. If the argument can be answered and our objections satisfied, then we are free to accept the argument.

On the other hand, if our doubts can't be resolved and we are under no pressure to make a decision, we might quite sensibly decide merely to suspend judgment. Or we may discover that the argument is so obviously unsatisfactory that we ought to reject it on the spot.

Also, if we know something about the subject of the argument and can detect a flaw in the argument, we might not be content to sit still and ask questions. We might decide instead to present a counterargument to establish a conclusion incompatible with that of the original argument. What we do, then, depends not only on the argument we are faced with, but upon the context and our own knowledge and inclinations.

In this section, we'll discuss four of the ways in which we typically question, cast doubt on, and challenge arguments. They are all important ways, but of course they aren't the only ways. Since it's the premises of an argument that are presented to support or justify the conclusion, all of our ways of challenging will focus on certain aspects of the premises. After all, if the premises collapse in a pile of dusty rubble, then so does the conclusion.

Before jumping head first into our discussion, there is one question that we've sidestepped that needs answering. It's this: Why distinguish ways of challenging arguments? Well, there's a certain intellectual pleasure in doing so. The ways of challenging that we'll be talking about are very common ones, and as you might expect, they aren't spun out of thin air but are abstracted from our ordinary practices. This means that we can learn something about ourselves and the way we do things.

But the reasons for making the distinctions go beyond this. To do a better job in evaluating arguments, it's useful to become self-conscious and critical about the ways in which we can test and question them. An argument that looks safe and sound at first glance may turn out to be rotten and untrustworthy at second sight.

Getting clearer about the ways in which arguments can be probed, questioned, criticized, and challenged doesn't always save us from making mistakes or accepting bad arguments. But it helps a little.

Challenging the Truth of the Premises

It sometimes happens that we find an argument utterly convincing—

except for the crucial fact that we doubt the truth of at least one of the premises. Or perhaps we even know that one of them is false.

If someone presented us with this argument:

> The United States should treat all Communist governments alike.
>
> The United States has not diplomatically recognized the U.S.S.R.
> _____
> Therefore, the United States should not recognize Communist China.

we wouldn't be prepared to assent to the conclusion on the basis of the premises offered, because we know that the second premise is false. We might accept the first premise and we might believe that the conclusion could be established on other grounds, but we would for certain not regard this argument as a good one.

In a more complicated kind of case, we might just cast doubt on one of the premises. Though we are not at all sure it is false, neither are we at all sure it is true. Suppose a follower of Konrad Lorenz argued:

> Our legal and social codes rest on the assumption that human behavior is never the result of instinct.
>
> If this were ever shown to be otherwise, far-reaching changes would have to be made in those codes.
>
> It has now been shown that man has an aggressive instinct.
> _____
> Therefore, changes must be made in our legal and social codes.

We might, again, be delighted to accept this argument as a sound one, if it were not for the uncomfortable fact that we are not at all convinced of the correctness of the third premise. It is, then, this premise that we challenge on the grounds of truth. It is up to the arguer either to show that he can get along without the premise—that it is superfluous—or to convince us that it is well enough supported for us to take it as true. To accomplish the last, he might have to present us with another argument which has the disputed premise as its conclusion. If we were persuaded by the new argument, then the way would be open for us to accept the original one. If we were not persuaded, then we would not at all be obliged to agree that he had given adequate grounds for the original conclusion.

This would be a typical sort of case, but not all cases are like this. There are some assertions which can be used as premises and which are such that we would not expect anyone to try to argue for them or offer any evidence for them. If someone said, "This is a cat," and pointed to a cat right in front of him, then even if he went on to use the sentence in some argument, we wouldn't expect him to be able to present *evidence* for his assertion on demand. If we were there and challenged that premise, he wouldn't deal with us by giving us another argument which has "This is a cat" for a conclusion. Rather, he would try to find out why we were doubtful. Have we seen cats before? he might ask. Do we know what "cat" means? Did we see what he was pointing at? Unless we are joking or playing some kind of philosophical game, we just don't challenge the truth of sentences like "This is a cat" unless we are confused or puzzled in a way that questions such as these can uncover. There are just some things which we know that we don't require evidence for. Once our confusions have been straightened out, we accept the truth of such claims without argument or evidence to convince us. In short, when we challenge the truth of some premises an additional argument to persuade us to accept it is not always appropriate. We may just have to be helped a little.

We may be better informed about the lack of grounds for accepting a premise to do more than just question it. Openly and actively we may challenge it by giving reasons for *not* accepting it. Sometimes we don't just sit and wait to be convinced. We counterattack. We ourselves supply an argument *against* the premise we think false. We might claim, for example, that it is not only doubtful that people have an aggressive instinct, but it is certain that they don't. The burden of proof for the assertion that human beings are instinctively aggressive (in some sense) rests with the person who wants to use it to establish some other conclusion.

Solomon-like, we are free to sit back in Rhadamanthine judgment and demand to be shown. But we may not wish to take this easier path. We may choose to assume the more difficult task of showing that the claim is wrong and ought not be accepted. If, by our own argument, we can show this, then we will have supplied an even better reason for not accepting the original argument. We will be in a position to ask for more than merely suspended judgment. We can demand rejection of the argument and its conclusion.

Challenging the Relevance of the Premises

The premises of an argument are offered as reasons or grounds for accepting the conclusion. We are then perfectly within our rights to demand that the premises present reasons or evidence that are *relevant* to the conclusion. Precisely characterizing the notion of relevance with respect to the premises of arguments is a task of Byzantine complexity, one which anyone would be ill-advised to attempt if he didn't intend to do a thorough job of it.

Of course just because we don't have a philosophical theory of relevance doesn't mean that we are unable to determine in a great variety of cases whether a reason or bit of evidence is relevant to a conclusion or not. If we didn't already make decisions about relevance, a philosophical account of it would have no place to start. The philosophical account presupposes that we do judge the appositeness of premises, that we know how to do it, and that we usually do a fairly good job of it. "What is the correct *analysis* of our appraisals of relevance?" is the philosophical question, but fortunately it's not the practical question in case-by-case decision making.

So, without pretending that we have an exact and adequate philosophical theory of relevance, we can just limit ourselves to saying that a premise is relevant to a conclusion when it is *pertinent to, bears upon,* or is *germane to* the conclusion. For every premise of every argument we have to ask the question "Is this pertinent to the conclusion?"

Suppose someone calmly and sincerely argued, "Marijuana really ought to be legalized, because almost half of our population is now under thirty." We might agree with the conclusion heart and soul, body and boots, and if so we will have all the more reason to lament that a poor argument for it has been given. Another argument might establish the conclusion solidly, but this one doesn't. The premise of the argument is as true as can be—which is to say it's true—but the lamentable and damnable fact is that the premise is not at all relevant to the conclusion.

If all or none of the population was under thirty, or if 20 or 75 per cent of it was, the premise would not be a bit more pertinent to the conclusion. In deciding whether or not the possession and use of marijuana ought to be made legal, the proportion of the population under thirty matters not a jot or a tittle. It wouldn't even matter if the group under thirty was the main or sole consumer. (It's possible, of course, to *imagine* a situation in which the proportion of the population under thirty would be relevant. But we can imagine anything. Relevance has to be relevance to the situation as it is.)

What does matter are such things as the effects of marijuana on the physical health of users, its psychological effects, the results of long-term use, and so on. More general considerations, like whether governments do or don't have the right to impose prohibitions and punishments in areas which might be left to individual decision making, or whether or not governments have the responsibility to protect their citizens from possibly harmful commodities at the expense of limiting their freedom of choice, are also relevant. So the challenge to this argument is not to the truth of the premise but to the pertinence of the premise.

A challenge is not a rebuttal, and we may sometimes boldly claim that a premise is irrelevant to the conclusion of an argument only to learn that we are dead wrong. Out of confusion or out of ignorance we may take exception to a premise. Rising to the challenge the arguer may successfully demonstrate to us that the premise does have a bearing upon the conclusion, one which we failed to recognize. Suppose Jane Marsh, a specialist in Middle English literature, presented us with this argument:

> The last story that appears in the *The Canterbury Tales* is the *Parson's Tale.* Thus, in spite of the fact that *The Canterbury Tales* appears to be a disjointed and disorganized collection of individual narratives, it is really a unified work.

If we had never read the *Tales*, or had never thought about the issue of unity, or were not well acquainted with the details of the work, Marsh's premise would most likely appear quite irrelevant to us. We simply wouldn't be able to see what bearing it has on her conclusion. But if she explains to us that the *Parson's Tale* is presented as a sermon that shows life to be a pilgrimage to salvation through repentance, then we can see that the premise is at least pertinent to her conclusion, even though it may not adequately support it.

The relevance of a premise may be a matter of contention between us and the arguer. We may insist that he present us with an additional argument showing that the premise that we challenge has a bearing upon the conclusion. Or, as when truth is at issue, we may be so convinced that the premise has nothing to do with the conclusion that we ourselves enter the field. We don't just query the relevance of the premise, we argue that it is *irrelevant and impertinent.* The outcome of one or both of these contests may then play a decisive role in our acceptance or rejection of the challenged argument.

Quite often the question of relevance can be settled merely by having the arguer supply us with additional premises. Premises may appear beside the point of the conclusion simply because the argument is of the telegraphed or truncated sort, in which the arguer takes for granted some premises which need to be set down openly. This is the way it is with Marsh's argument above.

Challenging the Adequacy of the Premises

A happy situation it is when we meet with an argument which has premises that are true and, what's more, relevant to its conclusion. But even into this apparent paradise there is room for the ugly serpent of *doubt* to crawl. "Do the premises present *adequate* grounds for embracing the conclusion?" is the question our intellectual conscience whispers to us. The answer quite often has to be a resounding No. A man who says, "I just met a Turk yesterday; he was a Zen Buddhist; consequently, we must conclude that all Turks are Zen Buddhists," can hardly expect us to join with him in his conclusion. His premise is relevant, unquestionably, and we may assume it's true, but it's certainly not adequate evidence for his claim.

People have a bad habit of making claims for which they offer only the briefest and shakiest justification. Our own bad habits are burden enough to bear, and we ought not let ourselves be euchred into accepting an ill-founded conclusion because of someone else's. The rule to follow is this: Demand adequate evidence and accept no substitute.

Sad to say, but quite true, the rub comes here. When is the justification offered in the premises adequate for the conclusion of an argument? Except for cases of deductive arguments, in which (as we shall see later) the truth of premises guarantees the truth of a conclusion derived from them, there is no general answer to this question. Much—very much—is packed away in it, and we can't unpack it all here. But there are a few things, perhaps useful, which can be said to bring out some of what is hidden when we query the adequacy of premises.

Premises are supposed to supply relevant and adequate *reasons* for the conclusion. Facts, like "Bangkok is in Thailand," can be counted as reasons. So too can sentences like "Killing is wrong" and "Ross Mac-Donald is not as good a writer as Conan Doyle," which are not ordinarily regarded as stating facts or making factual claims. Suppose, to improve our focus on adequacy, we limit our scope to arguments whose conclusions are established by mentioning facts and are, if established, themselves counted as facts. Talking about adequacy in arguments of other kinds is perhaps a more difficult job. But it's a task which we will just have to shirk here, because even the "simpler" course we've chosen is full of obstacles and rough spots.

The evidence presented in the premises of arguments which have supposed facts as their conclusions doesn't come in neat packages. We have to dig it out, dust it off, and assemble it. It's always fragmentary or partial. The adequacy of the evidence is a matter of degree, and there is never a point at which we can say, "Now we can rest; *all* the evidence is in." Yet often there is a point at which we can and do say, "The evidence is now *adequate*."

Let's take a very simple case. Suppose that someone claims that in the United States it always snows more days in January than in the other months of the year. As a premise for his conclusion he mentions that in 1965 snow fell more days in January than in the other months. The truth of the premise, let's assume, is in no doubt. It's true and it's relevant to the conclusion. But no one would be happy with the argument, because we feel that the slim premise is being made to bear too heavy a weight. The record of what the weather was like during a single year *counts toward* establishing the conclusion. It *confirms* or *supports* the conclusion, but not to the extent that we would be comfortable in accepting it. We are always doubting Thomases, and we would demand that a record of the days of snow per month for a number of years be put in evidence. More favorable information has to be deposited in the evidence bank before we are willing to withdraw the conclusion.

Exactly how many years we would have to examine, though, is an open question. More than one or two, certainly. Less than a thousand (assuming we could), probably. In each case examined, we would have to discover that it snowed more days in January than it did during each of the other eleven months. Each time we discovered that it did, this would be another bit of evidence to confirm the conclusion that this is what *always* happens. Each favorable report could be another premise, and each premise would make the conclusion more and more plausible.

Notice, though, the *one* report about a year in which January did *not* have more days of snow than some other month delivers a deathblow to the assertion that it *always* does. No matter how many other years have been investigated and have presented us with favorable evidence, one unfavorable report destroys the carefully built up plausibility that January always has more days of snow. We learn at a blow that this claim is false, and knowing it is false we can't still regard it as plausible. Such a report *disconfirms* and *falsifies* the conclusion of the argument.

When this happens the person offering the argument has to surrender his strong conclusion about what "always" happens. But he might choose to retrench and say something like "Well, it usually or *generally* snows on more days in January than in other months." The game has started again, but the argument is different now because the conclusion is weaker. "Usually" or "generally" goes in for "always." All the evidence that was favorable to what always happens in January will continue to support what generally happens in January. Reports like "In January 1970 there were not as many days of snow as there were in February of that year" *count against* what usually happens. They are disconfirming evidence, but just one such report can't falsify the new conclusion. With "usually" in the conclusion we have to balance the favorable information we have collected against the unfavorable.

If the evidence is overwhelming in one direction or another we have no trouble deciding what to do. When we examine a hundred years and discover that in all of that time January has never had more days of snow than the other months, we lose no time rejecting the conclusion. If, on the other hand, we find that there are only three years in which some other months had more snowy days, we jump at the conclusion with alacrity.

But here we are again. What if the hundred years split 40 to 60 in favor of the conclusion? Do we accept it? Well, in part it depends upon what we understand by "usually." If we take it to mean "over half," then we might accept the conclusion without agonizing over the matter. Of course the closer and closer the ratio of favorable to unfavorable evidence comes to a 50-50 split, the more uncomfortable we will be.

It may reach a point at which, unless we just have to, we are not willing to say whether the premises present adequate evidence for the conclusion or not. Or we may just drop the "always" and the "generally" and limit ourselves to describing what our investigation has uncovered in terms of the ratio of the years in which January was the snowiest month and the years in which it was not.

There's another crucial matter which hasn't been mentioned, though. If we confine ourselves to weighing up the merit of a particular argument, we tend to focus our attention just on the premises and conclusion. But in raising the question about the adequacy of the evidence supplied by the premises, we have to move to a broader context. We can't just restrict ourselves to considering the premises and the conclusion. We have to ask, "Do we need to examine more cases before deciding whether or not to *accept* this argument and its conclusion?" Are we prepared to say it generally snows more often in January after we have examined the weather records of fifty years? All available records? When do we have *enough* information to decide about the conclusion?

This is another one of those uncomfortable questions that can't be given a swift, succinct, and satisfactory answer. It's like the question "When do we arrive?" No single answer can be given, but in a particular case, when we know how fast we're traveling and how far we've got to go, we can give a fairly good answer to the question. We judge the adequacy of evidence, too, in a similar way. When we know what is at stake, whether or not additional information is available, and what hangs upon our acceptance or rejection of the argument's conclusion, these influence the decision we make. Evidence we consider adequate in one case we may not regard as such in another. A decision we are willing to make in one situation we would prefer to withhold in another.

Suppose that Glimpson, a biologist, was using rats to test Murato, a new vaccine for use on horses. Suppose also that in addition to whatever beneficial results it might produce, he wanted to argue that it causes no ill effects on horses treated with it. After giving measured doses to a hundred rats during the course of two months and discovering no fatal cases and no cases of sickness, Glimpson might feel rather confident in concluding that Murato is safe for use on horses. The evidence is adequate to conclude this, but what about Murato's use on *people?* It's very unlikely that Glimpson or we would feel the evidence sufficient to establish the conclusion "Murato is safe for human beings." As much as we like horses, we value ourselves more. And because we do we have higher standards for safety with respect to ourselves. We would require that Glimpson produce more favorable evidence acquired over a longer period before we would be willing to allow people to be vaccinated with Murato. In sum, the values we hold often enter into our deliberations about the adequacy of evidence.

It sometimes happens under the stress and strain of circumstances that we have to decide to accept or reject a conclusion at once. We must act immediately because we just haven't time to wait around to see whether new information is going to change the picture. In such cases, we are more or less limited to considering just the premises and the conclusion available at the time we have to decide.

Suppose that in December we learn that we must mount an emergency rescue operation into the depths of Antarctica in January or in February. Either month will be acceptable, but after that it will be too late for those who need help. We have to choose one month or the other. After considering the organizational and logistical problems, the crucial question becomes "Which of the months has the fewest days of bad weather?" Whichever it is, that's the month we will choose, for it will give us a better chance of reaching the other party. A task force is put to work ransacking the weather record for information. It turns out that an examination of reports for fifty years supports the conclusion "The weather in February is generally better than the weather in January."

But what would the records show if we went back twenty-five years more? What will they show five years from now? We lack the time to have the records searched for more than fifty years back and we simply can't wait for future information. We must decide simply on the basis of available and obtainable information. All other things being equal, we would have to conclude that we ought to go in February. The data we have *more adequately* support the conclusion that the weather will be better then, than they support the conclusion that the weather will be better in January. It may turn out, of course, that it was a mistake to leave in February, because the weather in January was better. But this doesn't change the fact that at the time we decided, we had more reason to leave when we did than to go in January.

If we were meteorologists and not leaders of an Antarctic trek we could afford to view the question in a more disinterested fashion. We might regard the evidence as inadequate to conclude one way or the other. We could just withhold decision until the records had been examined, and even then we might say that the information doesn't clearly support one claim or the other. We might be content just to wait until there is a preponderance of evidence on one side. If that never happens, then not having to, we never decide. We might, of course, be forced into deciding. In such a case we are, like everyone else, plunged into a tangle of circumstances. We might have *to decide,* but again like everyone else, we might want to point out that the claim we favor is not necessarily one which we accept as *true*. It's just the one which we regard as being *best supported by the available evidence at the time* we have to decide.

We accept the conclusions of many arguments even though we don't believe that the premises supply evidence which is adequate to establish the *truth* of the conclusion. Life goes on and we can't always afford the Olympian luxury of suspended judgment. Still, the information expressed in the premises of an argument may make it more likely that the conclusion is true than that some other claim is true. We often have to gamble on the truth, and we have to place our bets where we are most likely to win.

We may lose, of course. In any argument in which the conclusion does not deductively follow from the premises we stand the chance of losing. If we had perfect records of the weather going back a thousand years and January had always been the snowiest month in every year, it still might perversely happen that the very next January has less days of snow than the other months. What we accepted as true thus turns out to be false. But this doesn't mean that we did the wrong thing in placing our money where we did. We did exactly the right thing, and it would have been silly to do anything else. It's just that the world is a mysterious place, and we don't have any unbreakable guarantees about how it's going to behave.

Challenging the Fairness of the Premises

Once upon a time there was a man named James Hartman. Hartman was an upright and just man who loved good and eschewed evil. Though extremely rich, he lived simply and devoted his time to working for worthy causes. He was widely known and respected for his many philanthropies. The only dark incident in his life occurred as he was leaving a restaurant in San Francisco. Hartman was unaccustomed to consuming alcohol, and while at dinner he had drunk two martinis, a bottle of Burgundy, and two brandies. In walking to the curb to hail a taxi, he realized that he was totally inebriated, for his steps were unsteady and he had no control over his body. A policeman saw him staggering about and arrested him for public drunkenness. Hartman was fined and given a suspended sentence. He continued his good works, and nothing resembling this incident ever happened to him again.

When Hartman died twenty-three years later, the following obituary notice appeared in a San Francisco paper:

> JAMES CLEMENT HARTMAN (1909-1969): Died of a stroke on April 26. A multimillionaire; once arrested for public drunkenness.

Hartman's family and friends were furious, and understandably so. Everything said in the obituary was true, but nonetheless it gave a distorted picture. The notice made it appear that Hartman was a rich profligate, whereas he was not. The obituary did not give a *fair* account of Hartman's life but selected facts in such a way as to amount to a misrepresentation. Nothing was mentioned of Hartman's life that was favorable, only an isolated and atypical incident.

There are many matters about which we have Great Expectations. We expect obituaries to be fair to the facts of a man's life, and we expect arguments to represent fairly the reasons and evidence relevant to their conclusions. To present only facts that support a claim, when knowing about others that count against it, is to side with Satan and sin against fairness. It is a device of sophists and tricksters, of charlatans and rhetoricians, of all those who are concerned with getting someone to accept a conclusion and don't scruple to use any means that will do the job.

We don't take kindly to people who paint pretty pictures by leaving out ugly but very important facts. We want to know how things really are. We are aware that *all* facts and *all* reasons—pro and con, favorable and unfavorable, for and against—can't be given in the premises of an argument, and we don't demand the impossible. All we want is a just representation of the relevant and important considerations. Anyone can establish "All roses are red" as a conclusion if his premises mention only red roses and if he ignores white and pink ones. Any bureaucrat worth his pension can show that the program he administers is "by and large successful" if he judiciously selects the right sort of cases and closes his eyes to the wrong sort.

Not *all* arguments in which relevant and significant considerations fail to appear are the result of deliberate trickery, of course. Sometimes the arguer may not mention a matter because *he* does not consider it relevant or important. If someone else claims that it is, then this is a question which the two may have to settle before going on to discuss the original argument. At other times an arguer may not bring up certain considerations in his argument because he has already dealt with them in a prior argument, or he intends to deal with them in an additional argument. Accident or ignorance, inattention or carelessness, rather than duplicity or double-dealing, may also be responsible for the omission of relevant facts in an argument, for a violation of fairness.

Consider a straightforward and honest case, one without chicanery and trickery, let's assume. Suppose Carl Baker and Henry Market have been working for the Department of Health and Welfare in Chicago for over three years. During that time both of them have become quite familiar with the problems of drug addiction and hold strong views on the subject. One evening after work they discuss what might be done to deal with the problem of addiction and crime, and Baker argues in the following way:

> Drug addiction is undoubtedly responsible for a great amount of the crime in this city. The addict must have large sums of money to support his habit, and he can usually get them only by illegal means. What's more, crime syndicates like the Mafia flourish only because they can supply an addict with what he needs. They take his money and plow back their profits into other enterprises. The whole system operates only because the addict can't obtain drugs openly and at a fair price. It seems to me, therefore, that in order to reduce crime in this country, we ought to repeal those laws which keep people from buying narcotics without a prescription.

No great leap of imagination is required to see how Market might challenge Baker's argument. Suppose he is perfectly willing to admit that Baker's premises are true and are relevant to his conclusion. To be generous, suppose Market also believes that Baker's conclusion ought to be accepted and that the premises, taken apart from other considerations, supply adequate grounds for accepting it. Still, Market can challenge the argument, because it is just the "other considerations" which may be so crucial. Quite rightly he may be unhappy with Baker's argument for not taking them into account. To challenge the argument, Market need only call attention to the way in which it fails to represent fairly the way things are:

> I'm inclined to agree with you, Baker, but it seems to me that we also have to consider the other consequences that a completely free and legal purchase of narcotics is likely to have. If everyone could buy heroin openly and without a prescription, chances are great that the number of addicts would increase sharply. Laws apparently have at least some effects on curbing addiction. Your proposal might reduce crime, but it would do so only at a terrible price, and you fail to take this into consideration.

To make his argument convincing, Baker has to refurbish it. He has to include important matters that he omitted and try to establish that "even so"—even taking them into account—laws against the sale of narcotics ought to be repealed. Of course it may be that Market's objection never occurred to him and he doesn't see how it can be met. He might, reluctantly, have to give up his argument, even though he is still inclined to believe his conclusion is correct. Or it may be that he finds the objection so serious and unanswerable that he feels compelled to abandon his argument and to reject his conclusion, because he decides it is wrong.

Nobody should take these four ways of challenging arguments in the way that Mohammedans take the Koran—as the inspired word of God. They are far from deserving such honor. Like other distinctions we've made in the past, they are no more than instruments to be used to help us with the task of coping with the problems presented to us by rational discourse and rational persuasion. They shouldn't be idolized, but only respected in the same way as a good shovel is respected.

We began this chapter with disagreement (though, I hope, not disagreeably). Then we noticed that disagreements in ordinary life are frequently resolved by rational persuasion, by means of convincing arguments. This led us into a discussion of arguments, and we outlined the notion of argument and indicated the ways in which logic is concerned with it. We also considered some of the clues that can be relied on in trying to identify arguments in a stream of talk or a chunk of writing. Once we identified an argument, we saw that a perfectly ordinary question to ask is whether we ought to accept it or not. This involved us in a discussion of challenging arguments in order to test their strength and worth. We also noticed that, particularly in connection with the issues of the adequacy of evidence, there are a number of rather sticky details associated with the context of an argument that we have to consider in deciding whether we ought to accept the conclusion or not.

This takes us full circle, from the first of the chapter to right here. We are now ready to move on to take a more detailed and formal look at arguments in the next chapter.

Exercises

The Dispute Parlor

Let's suppose that times are hard and you desperately need a job. The only job you can find is as a referee in a Dispute Parlor down in one of the seamier parts of town. The Dispute Parlor is a place where people go who get their kicks out of disagreeing with other people. The management doesn't like to let things get out of hand, though, so they hire referees to step in once a dispute is underway. The referee's job is to break in and tell the disputants what kind of disagreement they are engaged in and how they might be able to settle it.

To get the job, you have to pass the employment test. It has the following instructions:

1. Take a look at the following short disputes and tell what is at issue in each one. That is, is the disagreement factual, verbal, evaluative, or interpretative?
2. If more than one sort of disagreement is involved, specify which ones.
3. Explain how you would advise the parties to the dispute to go about resolving it and reaching agreement.

1. **GORMAN:** The Postal Department's opening of letters sent abroad by private citizens is a violation of individual rights.

   HONIGFORT: Nonsense. The Postal Department is operating quite within the law. Only a short time ago Congress acted to grant it that power.

2. **BROWN:** Columbus was the first European to land on North American soil.

   McCORD: You are quite wrong about that. The Vikings reached North America long before Columbus did.

3. **ARNOWITZ:** Climpson has just bought an extremely beautiful painting by some totally unknown New York artist.

   SANGUINET: He didn't buy a painting, he bought a lithograph. It's a perfectly awful piece of work too. The man responsible for it is, in fact, very well known in art circles. How he could have created that abomination is a mystery to me. By the way, he's from Chicago, not New York.

4. **ROSENBACH:** Homer's *Odyssey* is the story of the adventures that befall a man after he leaves the Peloponnesian War and tries to make it home to Crete.

   ADAMS: I see that you didn't have the benefit of a classical education. Odysseus, the hero of the *Odyssey,* left the Trojan War. And his home was not in Crete, but in Ithaca.

5. **FIFTHIAN:** The wave of bombings during the late '60s by dissident and disaffected people was indicative of the unresponsiveness of our political system. Had the system paid heed to the peaceful protests and demonstrations, individuals would not have been driven to take such desperate action.

   LANGE: Such a view is far from correct. The system was more than responsive. The trouble was, it had been too lenient. By failing to punish protesters and preachers of sedition it created an "anything goes" atmosphere. Those who protested with impunity thought they could also bomb without hindrance.

6. **ROSS:** T. S. Eliot is nothing but a poetaster.

   MARELLO: I certainly disagree with that view. He is, in my opinion, among the best poets of our century.

7. **DEMASTES:** English is a language entirely without proclitics.

   HOENER: You're quite wrong. No doubt many other languages have more proclitics than English does, but it certainly has some.

8. **GUARDADO:** Dickens's *Hard Times* is primarily concerned with depicting the condition of the British working class and their exploitation by the rising class of factory managers and owners.

   PEVRILL: Well, that's part of its concern but not its main one. Its fundamental thesis is that the utilitarianism of Bentham, the Mills, and the Philosophical Radicals is both heartless and absurd. As a practical and social policy, it generates misery, rather than alleviates it.

9. **BRAKETHORN:** President Lyndon Johnson was repeatedly impeached for the way in which he conducted the war in Vietnam.

   HARRIS: That's simply false. No action against Johnson was ever initiated in Congress during his entire term of office.

10. **LYND:** Lord Lucan's conduct during the charge of the light brigade

that he commanded is best characterized as stupid and negligent. By far Lucan was the worst officer on the field that day.

BRANOSKI: On the contrary, Lord Lucan conducted himself in an exemplary way. The orders he was given were stupid, but his execution of them was heroic. In spite of his lack of military experience, he was an excellent officer.

11. **LANE:** *Easy Rider* is the best Hollywood movie made in the last ten years.

BRYANT: I certainly didn't think it was a very good movie. Besides, if by "Hollywood movie" you mean it was made by one of the big studios, you're wrong. It was made independently.

12. **RABINOWITZ:** Ezra Pound's *Cantos*, which was published in 1940, has been the most influential book of poetry in the twentieth century.

BRIGGS: You're quite wrong about that date. But, more important, you are wrong about Pound's influence. It has been quite negligible.

13. **WALSH:** "Stone walls do not a prison make" is one of the silliest things said in prose or poetry. The man who is in prison is not free. Period.

WATSON: It is quite possible for a man both to be in prison and to be free.

14. **SHAPIRO:** Lady Mary had never met me before, but she treated me like an old friend. She talked to me about my novel and asked quite interesting questions about the archeological work I've been doing in my spare time. She was very charming to me.

HAWKINS: I think she treated you abysmally. You must be a total idiot if you can't recognize when someone is being condescending.

15. **GRZYB:** Belafonte and Poitier have always been treated by Hollywood as idealized blacks. They are handsome and aloof and are always depicted as having great physical courage and sensitivity.

KASTERBAUM: That's really not correct. It's just that they are given roles that call for that kind of person. They may be idealized, but they are not idealized as blacks but as people.

16. **LUNDSTRUM:** It has been clear to me since I was old enough to think for myself that there has to be a genuine social reform in this country. There are too many people living in slavery, and that must be stopped.

DURTINI: I agree with what you say about the need for social change, but your reason for it I just can't buy. I'm surprised to hear that you don't know that there is no slavery in this country. The whole institution was abolished when Lincoln signed the Emancipation Proclamation.

17. **STERNBERG:** Copernicus had few followers in his own time. Nevertheless, he is responsbile for what is perhaps the most significant
revolution in history.

   WILCOX: I've never heard of Copernicus, but even so I'm prepared to
say that you're wrong. The American Revolution was, to my mind,
the most important social and political change in the history of the
world.

18. **DELSMAN:** You probably don't know it, but the Danish national anthem is a piece called "Rolf Krage," which was composed by Her-
man Ewald in the nineteenth century.

   BICKLER: I hate people who try to show off and then make fools of
themselves. The Danish national anthem is "King Christian Stood
by the Lofty Mast." It was written by *Johannes* Ewald in the
eighteenth century.

19. **COLENDRA:** Did you know that "posh" is an acronym for "port out,
starboard home"? It was used by English steamship companies that
sailed between England and India. The better and more expensive
cabins were on the shady side.

   LEADLOVE: What nonsense! That's just false, I'm sure. What reasons
do you have to believe such a silly thing is true?

Doing It Yourself

One of the best ways to familiarize yourself with the kinds of disagreements that we talked about is to make up some for yourself. You should
write up an example of each kind as a "pure" case and compose a few
more that are mixed. By putting yourself in the position of having to
think about clear-cut cases, you will also be forcing yourself to think
about the kinds of issues that crop up in ordinary disagreements.

Making Yourself Disagreeable

1. Suppose you are assigned the job of trying to convince someone who
believes that the Washington Monument is in Mount Vernon that it is
really in Washington, D.C. What would you say to persuade him you
are right? (By the way, why *do* you believe it's in Washington?)

2. A woman stops you on the street late at night. She tells you that she is
convinced that a senator from her state is an evil man and poses a
genuine threat to the well-being of the country. She explains that she
cares nothing for her own life, if by the losing of it she can make the
world a better place. She intends to kill the senator. What do you tell
her to make her change her mind?

3. You have a teacher who tells you that in his opinion movies are not an art form at all. They are merely cheap entertainment for those who are too lazy or too stupid to want to have to think. You tell him you believe otherwise. What possible reason could you have for believing that? he asks. You tell him your reasons and try to convince him to change his opinion.

4. Your next-door neighbor tells you one morning that she believes that most of the troubles that our society faces are due to the activities of a number of Communist agents that have infiltrated. These agents agitate racial troubles, encourage the acceptance of homosexuality as a matter of individual choice, and are behind the movement of women to seek equal rights. How do you convince her she is wrong?

Project: Identification

Let's suppose that Logic, Inc. has hired you part time to work on one of their special projects. The project involves collecting arguments of an ordinary sort and subjecting them to critical examination to discover just how—and how well—people argue. To acquire a large store of arguments, the organization has advertised that it will pay one dollar for every argument (good or bad) that is sent in to it.

Your title is "Argument Identifier" and, as the name suggests, it's your job to sort through the various passages of prose that people send in and determine whether they contain arguments or not. As you might expect, some of the passages contain arguments and some do not. Moreover, some contain more than one argument.

The organization expects a little more of you than this, however. Here are the complete instructions they give you for dealing with the little pieces of prose that you have to deal with:

1. Identify the passages that present at least one argument.
2. Peel away the inessential rhetorical and literary husks and explicitly state the premises and conclusions of the arguments as they are offered in the passages. Feel free to paraphrase (state in other words) the actual sentences of the passages, but be careful not to change their meanings.
3. If it seems to you that only a sketch for an argument is being given, you should indicate what other "obvious" and unstated premises need to be made explicit to turn the sketch into a finished argument. (You'll have to exercise judgment here. You're not allowed just to invent a premise, of course. You must have some reason or evidence to believe the premise is just being taken for granted.)

The first half-hour or so on the job you feel very depressed. There are so many instructions, and you really haven't had much experience at doing this sort of thing before. But then you discover before the hour is up that it's really sort of fun.

1. The age of innocent faith in science and technology may be over. We were given a spectacular signal of this change on a night in November 1965. On that night all electric power in an 80,000 square-mile area of the northeastern United States and Canada failed. The breakdown was a total surprise. For hours engineers and power officials were unable to turn the lights on again; for days no one could explain why they went out; even now no one can promise that it won't happen again.

BARRY COMMONER,
Science and Survival

2. A man's time, when well husbanded, is like a cultivated field of which a few acres produce more of what is useful to life than extensive provinces, even the richest soil, when overrun with weeds and brambles.

DAVID HUME,
Enquiry Concerning the Principles of Morals

3. The abolishment of exclusiveness is involved in the love-relation required between all believers by the express injunction of Christ and the apostles, and by the whole tenor of the New Testament. "The new commandment is, that we love one another," and that, not by pairs, as in the world, but *en masse*. We are required to love one another fervently. The fashion of the world forbids a man and woman who are otherwise appropriated, to love one another fervently. But if they obey Christ they must do this; and whoever would allow them to do this, and yet would forbid them (on any other ground than that of present expediency), to express their unity, would "strain at a gnat and swallow a camel"; for unity of hearts is as much more important than any external expression of it, as a camel is larger than a gnat.

JOHN H. NOYES,
A Theory of Sexual Sharing

4. The increase in the world population is one of the determinants of the ecological crisis and indeed may be at its root. But few persons realize that the dangers posed by overpopulation are more grave and more immediate in the U.S. than in less industrialized countries. This is due in part to the fact that each U.S. citizen uses more of the world's natural resources than any other human being and destroys them more rapidly, thereby contributing massively to the pollution of his own surroundings and of the earth as a whole. . . . Another reason is that the destructive impact of each U.S. citizen on the physical, biological, and human environment is enormously magnified by the variety of gadgets and the amount of energy at his disposal.

RENÉ DUBOS,
The Limits of Adaptability

5. While universities are democratic organizations in the sense that individuals have a broad array of personal rights within them, and that there is a play of opinion inside them which has a massive effect on their evolution, they are not democratic organizations in the sense that majority rule applies to them. For within a university there are acceptable procedures by which people can be graded in accordance with their competence, and grading people this way is essential to the conduct of the university's special business. The egalitarian ideal does not apply across the board in universities any more than it does in any other field where *skill* is the essence of the issue.

CHARLES FRANKEL,
Education and the Barricades

6. The principal characteristic of human culture today is the rapidity with which, under the impetus of science, it is changing. A man of seventy years, unless exceptionally devoted to learning, was educated in a world of fifty years ago, a world of unbelievable cultural antiquity in terms of all we do and prize today. Man has thus worked himself into an evolutionary dilemma of appalling dimensions. He must, to save himself, develop new ways of prolonging education throughout life, or renewing it periodically, and of retaining his mental educability; or else he must curb the impetuous and probably uncontrollable forces of his own scientific and technological enterprise.

BENTLEY GLASS,
Science and Ethical Values

7. If you're not happy, Tipton's not in business. And we're very much in business.

8. Around Harlem, the narcotics squad detectives didn't take long to find out I was selling reefers, and occasionally one of them would follow me. Many a peddler was in jail because he had been caught with the evidence on his person; I figured a way to avoid that. The law specified that if the evidence wasn't actually in your possession, you couldn't be arrested. Hollowed-out shoe heels, fake hat-linings, these things were old-stuff to the detectives.

MALCOLM X,
Autobiography

9. The professor knows that even his fragment of the student's time must be competitively protected. If he does not make tangible, time-consuming demands the student diverts time to courses which do make such demands. It becomes almost impossible to set a reflective, contemplative, deliberate pace in a single course. The tendency is to over-assign work, with the expectation that it will probably not all be done. The cumulative effect on the student is brutal. To survive

he must learn how to not do his work; he is forced into the adoption of the strategies of studentship; he learns to read too fast, to write and speak with mere plausibility.

JOSEPH TUSSMAN,
Experiment at Berkeley

10. The bigger the burger the better the burger. The burgers are bigger at Burger King.

11. Suicide, if anyone considers the nature and not the name of it, evidently lacks the most essential characteristic of murder, namely the *hurt* and *injury* done to one's neighbor, in depriving him of life, as well as to others by the *insecurity* they are in consequence liable to feel. And since no one can, strictly speaking, do *injustice* to himself, he cannot, in the literal and primary sense of the words, be said either to rob or to murder himself.

RICHARD WHATELY,
Adapted from *Elements of Logic*

12. Statistics are beginning to show that we are rapidly becoming a nation of middle-aged to older people and that the youth culture will one day be overwhelmed by mere force of numbers. It is high time that we concentrated more of our energies on understanding the problems of the aging in an urban technological society so that the lives of older citizens may be useful and valuable not only to themselves, but to the whole society. There are 20 million aged today who deserve to be treated as more than a "contentious minority."

NEH Grant Profiles, 1974

13. The "New Wave" science fiction is filled with a general sense of defeat, a wish to turn away from the hard realities of this world, and perhaps [its] obsession with vulgarities is just one result of this. It does not make for great literature, though, and it certainly does not take the sf genre forward.

SAM J. LUNDWALL,
Science Fiction: What It's All About

14. No matter how vast and impersonal its province, science itself is the creation of man. The creation of science is now part of the history of man, and as such it belongs to the whole of mankind. Science may have suppressed poetry or supplanted it, or made our need of it greater than ever before. It may have earned the poet's admiration or aroused his bitter hostility, but it can hardly leave him indifferent.

SAMUEL DEVONS,
Columbia Forum (Fall, 1968)

15. You only go around once in this life, so you better grab all the gusto you can. Grab a Schlitz.

16. One Manhattan actor who spent a weekend in Scientology—and was

immediately disenchanted because the night before the first course they had called him to take *more* courses—tried to make it clear that he did not want to receive the incessant phone calls and letters to which a Scientology friend of his had been subjected. The Scientologists told him to tell this to the "Student Examiner," but when he did, he was hounded to reveal the name of his friend. When he refused, he was "escorted" to the Ethics Officer, who again pressed him for the name of that friend who had complained about the phone calls so that they could "call him and talk with him about it."

PAULETTE COOPER,
The Scandal of Scientology

17. What Danton Walker has done is valuable from another point of view. While he recounts, with apparent amusement, any number of seemingly successful efforts to contact the spirit world, using some unknown force through a Ouija Board, by automatic writing, in seance rooms or through other channels, he also cites several incidents that brought mere dabblers in the supernatural into serious emotional difficulties. Thus, with a sense of responsibility doubtless based on close observations, he cautions the reader against careless dabbling of his own.

MARTIN EBON, Introduction to DANTON WALKER,
I Believe in Ghosts

18. In the chiropractic colleges it is common lore among the students that some states have "easy" exam standards and that other states are "tough." Some students establish residency in "easy" states in order to take the exams there; they can then achieve licensure through reciprocity in other states where reciprocal licensing arrangements have been established. Thus, for example, a Palmer student from Tennessee told a reporter that he planned to take his basic science exams in Alabama and then obtain reciprocity in Tennessee, because Alabama's examinations were known to be easier.

RALPH LEE SMITH,
At Your Own Risk: The Case Against Chiropractic

19. The disease known as alcaptonuria is a very dramatic one. Those who suffer from the disease excrete urine that contains homogentisic acid, a substance that turns black on exposure to the air. In 1909 a British physician named Garrod noticed that the level of homogentisic acid in the urine was increased when foods containing the chemical substances phenylaline or tyrosine were eaten in an increased quantity. This observation led him to suggest that the acid in the urine was caused by the absence of an enzyme required to metabolize it. Geneticists later showed that the disease was inherited in a way that was consistent with its being the result of a homozygous recessive gene (a/a). In 1914 sufferers were shown to lack the enzyme homogentisic acid oxidase. Thus the recessive form

of a gene was demonstrated to be associated with a particular enzyme defect.

20. "Dave Lowry could have escaped," the Lone Ranger said. "There were a number of times when he could have shot me from ambush. He didn't do it, even though he knew that it would mean freedom. And there was a time when I was trapped by a landslide. Dave saved my life. He didn't have to do that. He could have ridden off and left me there to die. But, instead, he saved my life, though he knew I would go on and capture him. Does that sound like the act of a hardened killer?"

> FRAN STRIKER,
> *The Lone Ranger on Powderhorn Trail*

21. Beauty is only skin deep so you'd better be careful.

22. To obtain a particular impression the print-maker must be able to determine those places where the one surface will come into contact with the ink. The various processes of print-making have been developed as a result of the quest of the print-maker to obtain such control: each process offers a different way in which control is maintained over those areas which will print and those which will not. These two types of areas are the essence of the print, and they form the factor by which the artist must be guided in conceiving a print. Thus the different processes of print-making become for the artist and for us different methods of expression inasmuch as they allow the artist various means of controlling what will or will not print.

> JOSHUA C. TAYLOR,
> *Learning to Look*

23. As the marijuana market and subculture have expanded, purchases have become larger in bulk. In the 1930s and 1940s, buying individual joints was common. A few years ago, the nickel bag became popular. Now, the smoker buys an ounce, so each cigarette costs him between 25 and 40 cents, not a dollar. Obviously, economy is part of the motivation: the larger the size of the purchase, the lower the unit cost. But the purchaser also wishes to minimize the number of his transactions: the more frequently he buys, the greater the chance of coming into contact with an undercover police agent—and being arrested. Thus, the appearance of the typical ounce purchase, the cost of which may not be considered the "retail" price.

> ERICH GOODE,
> *Columbia Forum* (Winter 1969)

24. Personally, I would be glad to sell it to you without making any profit, but business is business.

25. Dramatists extended the time-line of the Resurrection play back to the beginning of time and forward to the Last Judgment. Did this extension occur in one step or as a result of gradual aggregation? The

play that is usually considered an example of a transitional work, halfway between liturgical drama and the cycles, is the *Mystère d'Adam*. Upon inspection, however, the Adam and Cain episodes prove to be associated arbitrarily, because of the responsory that was their source, rather than because they are the first episodes of an incomplete drama of redemption. A transition cycle is, after all, a contradiction in terms. Either the author thinks of his work as having unity or he thinks of it as a series of separate plays. Thus the evidence favors the idea that the movement from isolated play to cycle was brought about by a new way of regarding the subject matter rather than by a gradual, unconscious process of aggregation.

O. B. HARDISON, JR.,
Adapted from *Christian Rite and Christian Drama in the Middle Ages*

26. It is time to stop giving lip service to the idea that there are no battles left to be fought for women in America, that women's rights have already been won. It is ridiculous to tell girls to keep quiet when they enter a new field or an old one, so the men will not notice they are there. In almost every professional field, in business and in the arts and sciences, women are still treated as second-class citizens. It would be a great service to tell girls who plan to work in society to expect this subtle, uncomfortable discrimination—tell them not to be quiet, and hope it will go away, but fight it. A girl should not expect special privileges because of her sex, but neither should she "adjust" to prejudices and discrimination.

BETTY FRIEDAN,
The Feminine Mystique

Getting Straight

In ordinary everyday life the word "argument" is probably used most commonly to apply to quarrels and slanging matches in which the participants snarl and curse at one another. By now, of course, nobody is likely to have any doubts that "argument" is used in a different and somewhat technical sense in logic.

To help fix this difference in mind, though, it would be useful to write about a paragraph in which you define "argument" as it is used in logic and distinguish this from its ordinary use.

You might, by the way, ask yourself if there is not some connection between arguments-quarrels and arguments-logical. After all, quarrels aren't generally about *nothing*.

Field Trip

About the only way to gain real skill in identifying arguments is to acquire some experience in looking for them. The arguments given in

"Project: Identification" provide a little experience, but they are only exercises and not terribly realistic. Though the world is jammed full of arguments (and nonarguments) they don't come in neat little packages. They have to be plucked like diamonds from the mass of gray prose that surrounds them and expresses them.

In truth, then, the most valuable exercise in identifying arguments involves venturing out into the world. It requires looking with a sharp eye at books, newspapers, magazines, political pamphlets, and religious tracts. It requires listening carefully to what people say in conversations, debates, or news conferences.

For a real-world exercise, then, try to locate five or so arguments in a realistic context.

Being Argumentative

A slightly more creative way of acquiring some sensitivity to arguments is to spend some time making them up yourself. If you can teach yourself to write arguments, then the job of recognizing those presented by others becomes a lot easier.

For practice, then, try composing one each of the following sorts of things:

1. An argument in which the premises and conclusions are explicitly stated. (Rely on your own judgment to present one that seems to you a complete and persuasive argument for the claim that you make.)
2. An argument that is incomplete because of an "understood" premise. (To do this well, you will have to imagine a situation in which it would be natural not to state a certain premise or premises. Be prepared yourself to say what's been left out of your formulation.)
3. A formulation several sentences in length that is clearly not an argument.

In the Arena

A hush falls over the expectant crowd in the stands. Then it breaks into thunderous applause. Rachel Reasoner, holder of the World's Title in Argument Challenging, has just taken her place at the microphone in the center of the arena.

You don't applaud. Not out of a lack of respect, but for a far different reason. *This* is your opponent. You've fought long and hard in preliminary matches, and now this is the big one.

While the opening ceremonies are continuing, you again read over the sheet outlining the conditions of the match:

The match is admittedly artificial (you read). No one ever challenges arguments in a vacuum and just because he's been told to. We challenge arguments in definite situations when the subject matter of the discussion is something that we care about enough not to begrudge it a little thought.

Furthermore, almost no example of reasonable length can present reasons or evidence that anybody would regard as *adequate* for a conclusion. So challenge on this ground is almost always possible. What's more, the *truth* of all but the most trivial claims ("Snow is often white") is always open to question.

Though the artificiality of the match cannot be overcome at all, the other limitations can be overcome in part by relying on the rather vague notion of being *obvious*.

The Challenger should recognize that, while every premise of an argument *can* be challenged, he should challenge only those that are *obviously* defective in some way. Thus the truth of every premise *might* be queried, but in this match a challenge is appropriate only when the premise is *obviously* false. Similarly, a challenge on the grounds of adequacy is possible only when a conclusion is *obviously* unsupported.

The Challenger must use his judgment to determine what is obvious and what is not. He should consider the arguments presented by the Title Holder and indicate the way (or ways) in which each is open to obvious doubt or dispute.

Your discretion and judgment have served you well so far. Hopefully, they won't let you down now.

You listen carefully as Rachel Reasoner reads the first argument:

1. Liquor can be the source of much relaxation and pleasure. Certainly everyone is entitled to this. Thus, people of any age ought to be allowed to buy liquor legally in all states.

2. A person who loves his country will not be critical of it. The best thing for this country would be for all those who are critical of it to leave. I'm sick of long-haired creeps and girls dressed like men telling me what to think. Consequently, everybody ought to have to sign a patriotism oath, and anybody who refused to sign it ought to be kicked out of the country.

3. The *New York Times* recently reported the case of a man who got enough money from the State Welfare Office to buy an air conditioner for his apartment and to take a trip to the Bahamas during the winter. This case is enough to show just how unfair to the working taxpayer the whole welfare system is.

4. Mr. Stewart is genuinely fond of children. He would undoubtedly make a good teacher in a kindergarten or a day-care center.

5. Cordelia Frankenmuir has the stern manner and distinguished looks generally associated with judges. There is no doubt, then, that she is well qualified to sit on the federal bench.

6. Women are less intelligent than men. In positions of authority, they cannot be trusted to act responsibly. For these reasons, with respect to men, the proper role of women should be one of subservience.

7. The only contribution that organized religion makes to our society is that is gives lonely people a place to go on Sunday morning. With its tax-exempt status, though, it cheats us out of millions of dollars in property taxes. If it were not such a lucrative business, it would wither away. It seems clear, then, that organized religion should be deprived of its tax benefits.

8. During the last decade or so, blacks in our society have had every advantage open to anyone else. Consequently, if they haven't made any social advances, it's their own fault.

9. When there is full employment, the labor market is highly competitive. This drives up wages, and this drives up prices. The result is inflation. Inflation is not a desirable economic condition for a society to be in. Therefore, to eliminate inflation, steps ought to be taken to cut back on employment.

10. The Indians were living in this country long before the Europeans came. They just happened to be here when the Constitution and the Bill of Rights that it included was ratified by the states. Clearly, then, the Bill of Rights does not apply to the Indians who live in the country in the present day.

11. The film is not in Technicolor nor in Cinemascope. The actors are, for the most part, nonprofessionals, and what is more, it is the first full-length feature made by the director John Hammerlove. For these reasons, no one should have any doubts about its deserving a C-grade.

12. Alligator hide is tough and durable. It takes dye quite well and polishes to a beautiful finish. Anyone who has ever delighted in a pair of alligator shoes, a belt, or wallet will readily agree that the conservationists have gone too far in insisting that no alligators be killed for their skins.

13. World population is at an all-time high, and crop failure or marginal yields in many countries have threatened the inhabitants with severe food shortages. It must not be forgotten, though, that food prices in this country are quite high. By not exporting foodstuffs they can be lowered or, at least, kept from rising higher. Consequently, the United States should stop all exports of food and food products to other countries.

14. Jews in the United States sent more money to Israel than did those in any other country. Had that money been kept here it could have been used to expand production, and we would all have benefited from it. A law should be passed limiting the amount of money that can be sent out of the country.

15. Steps should be taken to see to it that holders of public office are properly qualified. Of the last two senators elected in this state, one was an Italian and one was a woman.

Two in One

Finding ways to challenge fairly short and clearly stated arguments is not such a hard job. The task becomes more difficult when you are faced with a longer stretch of prose. First of all, you have to be able to spot the argument or arguments, and formulate them (at least to yourself) explicitly. Only then are you in a position to challenge what you take the arguments to be. Both processes have to be carried out competently, otherwise you may find yourself either totally confused about what's at issue or agreeing to a position that might not be legitimately and sufficiently supported.

As a bit of practice, wade into the passage below, find the arguments, and decide in what way or ways they are most obviously open to challenge:

No elementary school, junior or high school, college, or university that receives public support should be permitted to teach the theory of evolution in any form. The great majority of people in this country are Christians, and a great many more endorse the Bible (the Old Testament, at least) as being the inspired word of God. Consequently, the opinion of this group is the dominant opinion. Since we live in a democracy, the dominant opinion is the one that ought to prevail.

What is this opinion? It is that the words of scripture are true words. What, then, does scripture say about the origin of animals and plants and of man himself? It says in the most direct and simple terms that God created them all. So far as man goes, "In His own image created He him." There's no ambiguity or doubt about that.

Now if the Bible is right, which it is, then the theory of evolution is false. No one wants a false doctrine taught in any educational institution, and for this reason alone, the theory of evolution ought not be taught.

But there is an answer for those unbelievers and mockers who hold that man is nothing but an animal and that all the world came into being through blind forces. The answer is, very well, you are entitled to your opinion, wrong as it is, but you are not entitled to inflict it upon children and students. The dominant opinion is that creationism is correct. The dominant group pays the greatest share of taxes. Therefore its opinion ought to prevail. The teaching of evolution ought to be outlawed.

Leaving Yourself Open

People sometimes say things like "You don't know what it was like during the depression in the '30s. You have to experience things like that to understand them." There's a bit of truth in statements like this, and we can take advantage of it. To acquire a better appreciation of how arguments can be questioned, doubted, and challenged, construct for yourself an argument that you believe can best be challenged on the grounds of: (a) Truth, (b) Relevance, (c) Fairness, (d) Adequacy.

7/Castor and Pollux: Deductive and Inductive Arguments

This womans legs are in the grass.
The grass is growing out of the earth.
The woman is walking on the ground.

So FAR we've talked about arguments with the same sort of easy familiarity that we use when we talk about everyday things like cars and clothes. And it's quite right that we should, because arguments *are* everyday things.

But in this chapter we're going to ascend to a slightly higher realm and take a look at some of the aspects of arguments that professional logicians have concerned themselves with for the last twenty-three centuries or so. In doing this, we'll also be extending our discussion of evaluating arguments with an eye to accepting or rejecting them, which we first took up in connection with challenging arguments.

In "A Distinction with a Difference," we'll make a quick beginning by drawing the distinction between deductive and inductive arguments. This is a distinction as old as the bones of Aristotle, and nearly everybody knows about it. Quite often, though, there is confusion about just how it can be made, and we'll try to dispel a couple of misconceptions about it.

We'll then zero in on deductive arguments alone. In "Certain Conclusions Can Be Drawn," we'll talk about truth and validity, and in "Minding Your P's and Q's," we'll discuss a fragment of formal deductive logic. The main point to this is to take the mystery out of it. But also our discussion ought to give a glimpse of the potential power of modern formal logic.

In the last section we'll concentrate on inductive arguments. There we'll find that there aren't any generally usable formal techniques for determining the worth of most inductive arguments that we meet with. But we will present a few rough-and-ready rules that can serve as guides for evaluation.

A Distinction with a Difference

The rock-bottomed and copper-sheathed distinction between deductive and inductive arguments is a fundamental one in logic. As we'll see later, the distinction is closely connected with how we go about evaluating arguments and what characteristics are relevant for us to consider. For now, though, we can limit ourselves merely to a few preliminary notes about the difference between them. This is just the preview of the main attractions.

A *deductive argument* is an argument in which the premises supply an *irrevocable guarantee* for the conclusion. That is, the premises provide *conclusive grounds* for the conclusion. This means that if the premises are accepted, then the conclusion must be accepted as well.

Look carefully at these examples of deductive arguments and see if you can recognize how the premises absolutely guarantee the conclusion:

All government agencies are subject to political pressures.

HEW is a government agency.
_____

HEW is subject to political pressures.

We will not be able both to maintain a large number of military bases around the world and also to solve our domestic problems.

We will continue to maintain a large number of military bases.
_____

We will not be able to solve our domestic problems.

To grant the premise or premises of a valid deductive argument is also to grant the conclusion. This is sometimes hard to see when there are a lot of premises. So we can look at a rather peculiar case that, for all its peculiarity, is a perfectly acceptable deductive argument. Here it is:

Nixon was the only U.S. President ever to resign.
_____

Nixon was the only U.S. President ever to resign.

It's certainly clear enough in this case that if you accept the premise you must accept the conclusion. Of course, most deductive arguments aren't this trivial.

An *inductive argument* is an argument in which the premises offer some grounds for accepting the conclusion. But the premises of even the very best inductive argument don't supply conclusive grounds for the conclusion. They supply only incomplete or partial ones. Of course, the evidence or reasons offered in the premises may be *adequate* for accepting the conclusion, but the premises don't guarantee the conclusion. This means that to grant the premises is not necessarily to grant the conclusion, as is the case with deductive arguments.

Consider these examples of inductive arguments and contrast them with the cases of deductive arguments we gave above. It's often helpful to try to "see" a difference, before anybody steps in to tell you about it. Here they are:

> Right is a laundry detergent containing phosphate, and Right has been found to be a water pollutant.
>
> Buzz, Bright, and Sharp are also laundry detergents containing phosphate, and each of them has been found to be a water pollutant.
> ---
> All laundry detergents containing phosphate are water pollutants.

> We have examined 85 model Ka-10 radios manufactured by the Brace Company and discovered that all of them pose shock hazards.
> ---
> All model Ka-10 radios manufactured by the Brace Company pose shock hazards.

In each of these arguments the premises present reasons for accepting the conclusion. But the reasons aren't conclusive reasons. The evidence is not *complete* evidence, and, in fact, some might not regard the evidence as even adequate for accepting the conclusion.

There are two fundamental misconceptions about the difference between deductive and inductive arguments that ought to be chased away at once, just in case anybody is likely to be a victim of them.

> *Misconception 1:* "A deductive argument involves reasoning from the premises to the conclusion, and an inductive argument involves reasoning from the conclusion to the premises."

The first thing to notice is that the misconception is blatantly wrong in characterizing arguments. Both inductive and deductive arguments involve premises and a conclusion. That's what an argument is, after all. But what's more, both inductive and deductive arguments rely upon the premises to *establish* the conclusion, to provide the grounds or reasons for it. It is just plain nonsense to talk about the conclusion of an argument being used to establish the premises.

It's possible to exercise our imaginations and guess how this misconception arose in the first place. Once we can see how it might have originated, it should be easier to avoid it.

It's obvious that sentences that are established as the conclusion of an inductive argument can be used in other situations. In fact, they can be used as a premise in a deductive argument. If, for example, we examined a number of field mice in northern New Jersey and found that they all had a high proportion of DDT in their tissues, we might use this evidence in the premises of an inductive argument to establish the conclusion "All field mice in northern New Jersey have a high proportion of DDT in their tissues."

We might then take the sentence that we've established and use it as a *premise* in a *deductive* argument. Like this one:

All field mice in northern New Jersey have a high proportion of DDT in their tissues.

This field mouse was caught in northern New Jersey.

This field mouse has a high proportion of DDT in its tissues.

As you can see, this is a case of teaming up inductive and deductive arguments. This is a fairly common thing to do, for we often want to know just what conclusions can be deduced from a sentence when it is connected with other premises. Just because the sentence is one that is the conclusion of an inductive argument doesn't matter one way or the other.

It's possible in considering cases like this one to see how people can get confused. But what the case *does not* at all show is that an inductive argument in any way establishes its own premises. That's as impossible as being older than yourself.

Misconception 2: "A deductive argument involves reasoning from the general to the specific, and an inductive argument involves reasoning from the specific to the general."

Sometimes this is true, and sometimes it's not. Sometimes it doesn't even make sense to talk about "specific" and "general." Consider this argument:

Simms is on welfare, and Simms can't afford an adequate diet.

Bradley is on welfare, and Bradley can't afford an adequate diet.

Hanson is on welfare, and Hanson can't afford an adequate diet.

All who are on welfare can't afford an adequate diet.

This inductive argument does involve reasoning from specific cases of individual people on welfare to the general case of all people on welfare. And we can formulate a deductive argument which goes from the general case of people on welfare to the specific case of a particular person:

All who are on welfare can't afford an adequate diet.

Glaston is on welfare.

Glaston can't afford an adequate diet.

So far as these two arguments and others like them are concerned, then, there is no misconception about going from the specific to the general and the general to the specific as being characteristic of inductive and deductive arguments. But there are other arguments about which this is a misconception. Look at this inductive argument:

All copper conducts electricity.

All iron conducts electricity.

All tin conducts electricity.

Copper, iron, and tin are metals.

All metals conduct electricity.

With respect to a particular piece of copper, "all copper" is general, and the same is so for pieces of iron, and tin. There are no "specifics" in the first one. There's nothing but "general" terms: "all copper," "all iron," "all tin." It's impossible, then, to move from "the specific to the general."

Of course there is a sense in which "all metals" is more general than "all copper" and the rest. So someone might say "an inductive argument always involves moving from the *less* general to the *more* general." But it's quite easy to show that even this is not *always* the case. All we have to do is to present an inductive argument in which we reason from the "specific" to the "specific." Here's one:

The chocolate cake I bought at Tom's Bakery was stale.

The coconut cake I bought at Tom's Bakery was stale.

The next cake I buy from Tom's bakery will be stale.

On the same premises we might want to assert, "All cakes bought from Tom's Bakery will be stale," but we don't have to. We are perfectly justified in stating the "specific" conclusion, rather than the "general" one.

To deliver the *coup de grâce* to the misconception we have been mauling, take a look at this deductive argument. It's one in which it's not possible even to make the distinction between the "general" and "specific" which the misconception relies upon.

If public school teachers do not receive a wage increase, then they will be forced to strike.

They will not receive a wage increase.

They will be forced to strike.

With tongue in cheek we can summarize in this way: the misconception is a misconception, not because it's not true in some specific cases, but because it is not true in general, that is, in *all* cases.

We've now been introduced to both deductive and inductive arguments. And though we still don't know them well, we're at least on speaking terms with them. Perhaps just as important, we've spiked two guns that might have blasted us into confusion.

Now it's time to take a more careful and detailed look at each type of argument. Deductive argument will be the first specimen under our microscope.

"Certain Conclusions Can Be Drawn": Deductive Arguments

There can be no two ways about it. Either the premises of an argument *absolutely guarantee* the conclusion or they do not. If they do guarantee it, then the argument is a *valid* deductive argument. If they don't, then the argument is *invalid* and no amount of wailing and gnashing of teeth can change this fact.

But there is another way of putting this point that may be easier to catch hold of. At any rate, it's more revealing in certain respects.

An argument is correctly said to be *valid* only when the conclusion *follows* from the premises. Fine, you might say, but what does "follow from the premises" mean? Well, it's extremely difficult to *say* what this does mean, although it's very often quite easy to see that a conclusion does follow from the premises of an argument.

We can say at least a little, though. We can say that the conclusion follows from the premises when it would be *contradictory* to assert the premises and deny the conclusion. This doesn't exactly say what "follows from" means, but it does provide a way of determining *when* the conclusion follows from the premises. Yet even this isn't very helpful unless we also say what it means to be contradictory.

Fortunately this is a very easy task. A *contradiction* is both the assertion and the denial of the same thing, and two sentences are *contradictory* when one asserts what the other denies. Thus "Bears eat honey" contradicts "Bears do not eat honey." If we make one compound sentence out of the two separate sentences, we get the contradictory sentence "Bears eat honey, and bears do not eat honey." This sentence asserts and denies the same thing about bears. (Of course, it could also be expressed in a different way, such as "Bears both do and do not eat honey.")

Now let's see how this test for validity works by considering the least complicated argument possible:

Elizabeth is the Queen of England.
_____
Elizabeth is the Queen of England.

An argument is a valid argument, we said, if the conclusion follows from the premises. The conclusion follows from the premises, we also said, if a contradiction would result from asserting the premises and denying the conclusion. So let's see if this argument is valid or invalid.

An assertion of the premise would be "Elizabeth is the Queen of England." A denial of the conclusion would be "Elizabeth is not the Queen of England." These sentences obviously contradict one another. The two together produce the contradiction "Elizabeth is the Queen of England, and Elizabeth is not the Queen of England." Just in case we had any doubt about it, we can now confidently assert that the argument is a valid one. The conclusion does follow from the premise.

This example is, of course, an incredibly trivial one, one that nobody would ever seriously use in ordinary life. But for all that, the point it illustrates applies far and wide to all possible arguments. Obviously, it's not always so easy to use the contradiction test as it is in our example. Generally, it's necessary to go through very complex procedures to determine whether a contradiction can be found when the conclusion of the argument is denied and its premises are asserted.

(To keep the record straight, it's worth mentioning that if a contradiction never turns up when we apply our test, we can't say that the argument is *invalid*. It may be that we just haven't been successful in uncovering a contradiction that's really there. Or it may be that there's no contradiction to be found. We just have to suspend judgment in such a case.)

To get an idea of how difficult it can be to apply the contradiction test to arguments that are more or less like those we actually use in ordinary life, go back and take a look at some of the examples that we gave earlier. Can you spot a contradiction by asserting the premises and denying the conclusion?

An obvious question about valid deductive arguments immediately pops up when we think about them at all. Just why is it that the premises of such arguments irrevocably guarantee their conclusions? After all, to find certainty of any kind in this very unreliable world is a strange and startling thing.

Unfortunately, there isn't a Grade-A, certified, philosophically acceptable, and universally acknowledged answer that can be given. Any answer that we gave would be highly controversial, and a number of philosophers and logicians would prefer becoming exiles in Tibet to accepting it. Instead of trying to give an adequate and defensible answer, perhaps the best thing to do is just to hint at an answer by relying on an old and useful metaphor.

The juice that we squeeze from an orange is already contained in the orange. Similarly, the conclusion of a valid deductive argument is already contained in the premises. We are certainly immediately aware of it when the conclusion is the *same* as a premise. More often, though, the conclusion is only *implicitly* contained in the premises, and that it follows from the premises is not at all obvious at first sight. Deduction in such a case consists in making *explicit* information that is already in the premises in an unobvious or hidden fashion. (This is similar to the way that finding the sum of a column of figures makes explicit the number that was "hidden" in the column.)

The premises of an argument can't yield more information than they contain, but a good hard deductive squeeze may produce much that no one suspected was there. The ancient adage to keep in mind is this: There can be nothing in the conclusion of a deductive argument that was not first in the premises. The trick, of course, is knowing when this is so.

Our metaphor also helps make it clear why a contradiction results if the conclusion of a valid deductive argument is denied at the same time that the premises are asserted. If the conclusion is already "contained in" the premises, then to deny it is to deny something claimed in the premises. Obviously, then, we are both asserting and denying the same thing. If no contradiction results, then it must be that what we are denying wasn't in the premises in the first place. In which case, the conclusion doesn't follow, and the argument is invalid.

Truth and Validity

All we've talked about so far is the validity of deductive arguments, and we've tried to make clear what it means to say that a valid argument is one in which the conclusion follows from the premises. But it's important not to confuse the *validity* of a deductive argument with the *truth* of the sentences that make up its conclusion and premises. As we'll see, it's possible for an argument to be valid even when some or all of its sentences are false. But let's talk about some cases now.

When All the Sentences Are True

An argument is valid when there is a certain kind of *relationship* between its premises and its conclusion. The relationship, as we've said, is the "follows from" one, so an argument is valid when the conclusion *follows from* the premises.

Given the need for satisfying this relationship, it's perfectly possible for all the sentences in an argument to be true and yet for the argument to be invalid. The conclusion just does not follow from the premises, and that's all there is to it. Here's such an argument:

All postal workers are federal employees.

All F.B.I. agents are federal employees.

All C.I.A. agents are federal employees.

It's obvious in this case that although the two premises and the conclusion are true, the premises in no way guarantee the conclusion.

Sometimes when we know that all the sentences in an argument are true, we're inclined to accept the argument as valid when it isn't. This is particularly so when the argument resembles some other argument that *is* valid. Consider this argument, for example:

All United States senators live in Washington, D.C.

Stuart Symington lives in Washington, D.C.
___

Stuart Symington is a United States senator.

Because all of the sentences in the argument are true, we're tempted to say the argument is valid. But it's not.

Our temptation is made even stronger by the fact that the invalid argument resembles this valid one:

All United States senators live in Washington, D.C.

Stuart Symington is a United States senator.
___

Stuart Symington lives in Washington, D.C.

When you look at these two cases, it's easy to see how the same true sentences can be put together in a way that yields an *invalid* argument and also in a way that yields a *valid* argument.

When All the Sentences Are False

After what we've said already, it doesn't come as much of a surprise to learn that the conclusion of an argument can *follow from* the premises even though all the sentences in the argument are false. Here is an example of a valid deductive argument that contains only false sentences:

All streets in New York are paved with gold.

The Empire State Building is a street in New York.
___

The Empire State Building is paved with gold.

With such arguments as these, we're likely to fall into the trap of thinking that they are invalid because we know for sure that the conclusion and the premises are false. But the truth is, some of them are valid and some of them are not. It all depends upon (you guessed it) whether the conclusion does or does not follow from the premises.

When Some Sentences Are True and Some Are False

A valid argument can have a mixture of true and false sentences. If one or more of the premises is false and the conclusion is true, it's still possible for the argument to be valid. Here's such a case:

All cats are green. (false)

All things that are green have paws. (false)

All cats have paws. (true)

But, of course, just to make things more complicated, invalid arguments can also have false premises and a true conclusion. Take this case:

All Communists are United States Supreme Court Justices. (false)

Joseph Stalin was a United States Supreme Court Justice. (false)

Joseph Stalin was a Communist. (true)

There is a way, though, in which a valid deductive argument *cannot* have a mixture of true and false sentences. If the premises of a deductive argument are all true, then the conclusion of the argument must be true as well. Otherwise it's not a valid argument. The metaphor we used earlier will help make clear why this has to be so.

The conclusion of a valid argument is already contained in the premises. Consequently, if the premises are true, then the conclusion must be true also, *because* the conclusion is only a restatement of something already stated in the premises. So if the conclusion is false and the premises are true, the conclusion is *not* just an expression of information already in the premises. It goes beyond the premises and says something not in them. The following valid argument has true premises and so it must also have a true conclusion:

All government officials are subject to the law. (true)

The President of the United States is a government official. (true)

The President of the United States is subject to the law. (true)

There are two things that it's important to keep in mind about truth and validity. First, validity is a relationship ("follows from"), and the mere presence of false sentences doesn't mean that an argument is necessarily invalid. Second, no valid argument can have true premises and a false conclusion.

Sound Arguments

In the fields of life that surround the groves of academic logic, validity alone is not of much interest. We are mostly concerned with arguments that are valid and *also* have true premises. Arguments that meet these two conditions are usually given a name to distinguish them from arguments that are valid but may contain false sentences.

Arguments that are valid and have true premises and a true conclusion are called *sound arguments.* So all sound arguments are valid, but not all valid arguments are sound. Or we might put our definition this way: Soundness = truth of all sentences in the argument + validity of the argument.

Why be concerned with arguments that aren't sound? The reason is simple enough. More often than not, we aren't in a position to say whether the premises of an argument are true or not. But we may still want to know what conclusions follow from them.

Often we "grant" premises just to see what can be deduced from them. What's more, we may make use of this technique to test the premises of our argument. Let's consider briefly how this can be done by making use of the example that we mentioned earlier.

Suppose we collect information about field mice in northern New Jersey. We haven't examined all of them, but we've studied a number of them. On the basis of our information, we formulate an inductive argument that has the conclusion "All field mice in northern New Jersey have DDT in their tissues." The premises of the inductive argument don't guarantee the conclusion, and it could be wrong. It might be that there are field mice that we didn't examine that have a low amount of DDT in their tissues.

We go out and catch a field mouse, but before examining it we work out the following argument:

All field mice in northern New Jersey have a high proportion of DDT in their tissues.

This field mouse is from northern New Jersey.

This field mouse has a high proportion of DDT in its tissues.

The argument is a *valid* argument, but is it a *sound* one? Well, we can't say, because we don't know whether the first premise is true or not.

Suppose we then examine the mouse and find that its DDT content is high. This discovery adds another bit of information which, in an inductive argument, supports the claim made in the first premise. If we had learned that the mouse had a *low* proportion of DDT, then this would mean that the first premise of the argument would be false. That is, it would be false that *all* mice in the area had such DDT deposits. (Our deductive argument would still be valid, of course.) But even as we've imagined the situation, we still don't know whether or not the deductive argument is *sound.*

It's easy to see from just this simple case that valid deductive arguments can be of great use and importance, even if we aren't in a position to say whether or not they are sound. The world would be a terribly dull place if we had to restrict ourselves to formulating only sound arguments.

Enthymemes

The validity or invalidity of an argument is a purely local affair. It concerns the premises and the conclusion of an argument and *that's all.* It's quite illegitimate to appeal to, assume, use, rely upon, or take for granted information that isn't in the premises. Even if the information is obvious or well-known, it is *still* illegitimate.

An argument that is valid must be so because its conclusion follows from its premises *as actually stated,* not as they are charitably supplemented or assumed or imagined. Accordingly, this argument is invalid:

Thomas Glant is a murderer.
_____
Thomas Glant ought to be arrested.

This conclusion is not guaranteed by the premise. It doesn't follow from the premise.

Of course it's easy to see how to make a new argument that has the same conclusion and uses the same premise and yet will be valid. All we have to do is to supply the obvious premise "All murderers ought to be arrested." When we add this additional premise, the conclusion is guaranteed:

Thomas Glant is a murderer.

All murderers ought to be arrested.
_____
Thomas Glant ought to be arrested.

In the last chapter, we talked about "telegraphed" arguments, ones that take for granted information needed to complete the argument. Such arguments are traditionally called "enthymemes." An enthymeme is just a sketch for an argument, with the premises taken to be obvious left unstated. Strangely enough, some enthymemes even leave the conclusion unstated.

To be tough about it, all enthymemes are invalid arguments. After all, it's the very nature of enthymemes to leave out premises or conclusions.

But we are generally more charitable than this, and when it *is* obvious what sentences have to be supplied, we automatically supply them.

There's a danger to doing this, though. Sometimes we don't immediately see how an argument sketch has to be filled in to yield a valid argument, and we put in premises that weren't intended. Also, sometimes the premises that have to be supplied are ones that we wouldn't want to accept if we realized that they were necessary. As a result, we might find ourselves accepting an argument as sound when it really isn't.

A good practice to follow in evaluating arguments is to get all of the "obvious" premises stated. Only then are we in a position to determine the validity of the argument, and only then are we in a position to decide whether or not to challenge the premises.

Here are a couple of enthymemes that can be turned into valid arguments by supplying some missing sentences:

Groups victimized by society deserve special treatment.

American Indians deserve special treatment.

(Missing premise: American Indians have been victimized. . . .)

All bureaucrats will give you the run-around.

And Charlie Dobbs is a bureaucrat.

(Missing conclusion: Charlie Dobbs will give you the run-around.)

In real life, of course, arguments aren't laid out quite this neatly. Consequently, it's harder to detect what we're supposed to take as "obvious." This is just something that has to be judged by the context, and nobody can provide any golden rule for doing it.

Minding Your Ps and Qs: Formal Deductive Logic

In the first half of the nineteenth century, it was generally agreed that everything important about logic had already been said by Aristotle over two thousand years earlier. All that was left for logicians to do was to work out a few of the details.

Before the century was over, however, men like George Boole and Gottlob Frege showed that there was more to logic than Aristotle had dreamed of in his philosophy. They demonstrated that it was possible to deal with arguments in the same abstract and highly formal way that had previously been associated only with mathematics. In taking this road, they made areas once remote accessible to logical techniques and introduced new and more powerful ways of dealing with arguments.

It's not possible for us to discuss formal logic here in anything like an adequate way. Nevertheless, it's worthwhile to spend a little time examining a fragment of it. Like archeologists who learn something about a culture by studying a shard from a broken pot, our examination of a fragment of formal logic ought to provide at least some idea of what it's all about.

The fragment that we'll be discussing is a part of what is called "sentential logic." "Sentential" means "having to do with sentences." Sentential logic, as the name suggests, is the part of formal logic that is concerned with arguments that are valid because of the ways in which the simple sentences that make them up are put together. It treats simple noncompound sentences as units and doesn't deal with words or phrases that are parts of such sentences.

This may seem more puzzling than enlightening at the moment, but daylight will come dazzling in when we get down to the business of dealing with arguments. We'll start by considering the notion of an argument form and explore how forms are connected with validity. Then we'll discuss what's involved in a deductive proof or demonstration. But one step at a time is enough.

Sentential Form

Consider this argument:

If Simpson is at least sixty-five, then he is eligible to collect Social Security payments.

Simpson is at least sixty-five.

Simpson is eligible to collect Social Security payments.

Now examine this one:

If the chemical 2,4,5-T is used as a defoliant, then damage to human health will result.

The chemical 2,4,5-T is used as a defoliant.

Damage to human health will result.

Both of these arguments are obviously valid. If their premises are granted, then their conclusions must be granted also. If their premises are true, then their conclusions are also true. But they have another important feature in common that might be easily overlooked.

A close scrutiny of both arguments shows that, in spite of their different subject matter, they have the same *form*. The first premise in each is a compound sentence that begins with "if" followed by a complete sentence. Next, still in the first premise, there is a "then" that is followed by another complete sentence. The second premise in each is just a repetition of the sentence that appeared after the "if" in the first premise, and the conclusion is a repetition of the sentence that appeared after the "then." If we used letters to stand for the two sentences that make up the first premise in each argument, we could represent the form of both arguments in this way:

If P, then Q
P
_____
Q

We got this form by replacing the component sentences in each argument with letters. If we make the replacement in a different way we can get a different form. We might, for example, replace every sentence in the argument with a different letter and ignore the fact that the first premise is a compound sentence made up of two complete sentences. If we did this, each of our examples would have the form:

P
Q
___
R

We get this form, to repeat, by disregarding the fact that, in each of our examples, the sentences which make up the second premise and the conclusion are parts of the compound sentence that is the first premise. There are three different sentences in the argument, and we represent them by three different letters.

Because there are different ways of replacing the sentences in an argument, an argument can be regarded as having different forms. But not all forms of an argument are of interest in logic. Formal logic is primarily concerned only with the replacement that preserves the validity of valid arguments and the invalidity of invalid arguments. This means that its interest is in replacement that recognizes the importance of words and phrases like "If . . . , then . . ." in making arguments valid. The kind of replacement which serves this purpose is one that replaces each simple, noncompound sentence in an argument with a letter and keeps expressions (or symbols for them) like "If . . . , then . . . ," "either one or the other, but not both," "if and only if," "and" (the conjunction), and so on. This way of replacement produces what is called the *sentential* (i.e., "sentence") *form* of an argument. The first form given in our examples above is the sentential form, but the second is not.

It's easy to see that any argument which has the sentential form of our example will be a valid argument. Yet the same is not true for the other form. Some arguments that have that form will be valid, and some will not. Here's an invalid one which has the form P, Q / Therefore, R:

Apollo Twelve was a successful mission.

The king is in the counting house.

Barry Commoner wrote *Science and Survival.*

This form ignores the crucial importance of the "If . . . , then . . ." and the way in which the component noncompound sentences in our examples are related to one another by means of it.

If we take our sentential argument form

If P, then Q.
P
———
Q

and, starting from the other direction, allow any declarative sentences to replace the letters P and Q, then we can produce a virtually unlimited number of arguments. As long as we have sentences to plug into the argument form, we can generate arguments. Each argument that we produce in this way is called, in the jargon of logic, a *substitution instance* of the argument form. Each argument is a case or *instance* of the form, which we get by the *substitution* of sentences for letters in the form.

We can divide argument forms, as well as arguments, into valid ones and invalid ones. A *valid argument* form is one that has nothing but valid arguments as substitution instances. Or, to put the matter another way, none of its substitution instances is an argument that has true premises and a false conclusion. An *invalid argument* form is simply an argument form that doesn't meet this test. That is, an argument form is invalid if it has at least one substitution instance which has true premises and a false conclusion. The argument form that we have been using as an example of a sentential form is valid. The nonsentential form we've been talking about is invalid, and here is an invalid sentential form:

If P, then Q
Q
———
P

Just to see that this form is invalid, here is an invalid argument which is a substitution instance of the form:

If James D. Watson wrote *Babbitt,* then he wrote *The Double Helix.*

James D. Watson wrote *The Double Helix.*

James D. Watson wrote *Babbitt.*

Formal logic, as its name indicates, is an enterprise that is chiefly concerned with argument *forms*. It has very little interest in arguments as such and virtually no interest in sound arguments. One of its fundamental tasks is to develop procedures for distinguishing valid deductive argument forms from invalid ones. Since there are apparently unlimited numbers of substitution instances for any argument form, this obviously cannot be done by examining each and every substitution instance and determining whether or not it is a valid argument. The great accomplishment of contemporary formal logic has been the development of several methods for determining the validity of argument forms. What the various methods are we shall here leave shrouded in a tantalizing mystery, for to explain them would lead us too far afield. Our discussion of informal logic would go by the boards, and we would find ourselves enmeshed in the complex machinery of formal logic.

The ability to distinguish valid from invalid argument forms (without examining all possible substitution instances) has its use and is not merely an arcane pastime of logicians. If an argument form can be proved to be valid, then all arguments which have that form will be valid. Accordingly, in order to prove that a given argument is a valid one, all that has to be done is to show that it has a valid form—that it is a substitution instance of a valid form. Is this a valid argument?:

> If the government will not pay the total costs of R.O.T.C. programs, then most universities will do away with their current programs.
>
> The government will not pay the total costs of R.O.T.C. programs.
> ___
> Most universities will do away with their current programs.

Yes it is, because it has the valid form "If P, then Q, P / Therefore, Q."

To prove that a supposedly valid argument is in fact *invalid*, all that has to be done is to show that it has the form of an invalid argument—that it is a substitution instance of an invalid form. Is this argument valid?:

> If Jane Audley takes birth control pills, then she doesn't have to worry about pregnancy.
>
> She doesn't have to worry about pregnancy.
> ___
> Jane Audley takes birth control pills.

No, it's not. It has the invalid form "If P, then Q, Q/Therefore, P." (This form is called "the fallacy of asserting the consequent.")

Obviously not every argument which is proved to be valid by showing that it has a valid form is also proved to be a *sound* argument. As we've already discussed, truth and validity are connected only to the extent that no valid argument can have true premises and a false conclusion. Since a valid argument may contain one or more or even all false sentences, proving that an argument is valid is not the same as proving that it is sound. To prove an argument is sound an extra step has to be taken. After the argument has been shown to be valid, it then has to be shown that the premises are *true*.

Deductive Proofs

No matter how much we squint our eyes and wrack our brains, sometimes it's just not possible to take a close look at an argument and tell whether its conclusion follows from its premises or not. There are technical devices in sentential logic to assure us when an argument is valid, though we aren't going to talk about them. But even when they are used, we still might not be able to *see* how or why the conclusion can be deduced from the premises.

Here, for example, is an argument that is valid, but it's not at all obvious that its conclusion is already "contained in" its premises:

1. If the United States sells wheat to China, then our grain supplies will be lowered.
2. If the United States sells wheat to China and our grain supplies are lowered, then either we will have a shortage or we will have to buy wheat from some other country.
3. If we either have a shortage or have to buy wheat from some other country, then we will have severe economic problems.
4. If we have severe economic problems, then either the rate of inflation will rise or unemployment will rise.
5. If we buy wheat from some other country, then the rate of inflation will rise.
6. If the rate of inflation rises or unemployment rises, then people will lose confidence in the government.
7. If the rate of inflation rises, the elderly and the poor will suffer.
8. Corporations seek profits for their stockholders.
9. If the United States sells wheat to China, we will not have a shortage.
10. If corporations seek profits for their stockholders, the United States will sell wheat to China.

Therefore, people will lose confidence in the government, and the elderly and the poor will suffer.

To show that the conclusion of this argument *does* follow from the premises, we can use an ingenious but basically simple process.

The basic idea behind the process is that we can use some of the premises of the original argument to construct other valid arguments that are much shorter. Since the conclusions of these arguments follow from some of the premises belonging to the original argument, we are free to use these conclusions as if they were extra premises.

If we keep using the process and continue to use our new conclusions to expand our set of premises, we ought at least to be able to see how we can frame a final short argument that will have as its conclusion the sentence that is the conclusion of the original argument.

Ordinarily it's not a good idea to start out by formulating just any short arguments to establish any conclusion. We can do this, but it's not good strategy. Good strategy demands that we first take a look at the conclusion that we want to establish. Then we look through the set of premises and see what interim conclusions might be useful in deducing our final conclusion. When we spot the interim conclusions, we then construct short arguments to try to establish them.

But all of this is too abstract to be very useful. The best approach is to consider by example how the process works. It's necessary to follow along very closely, though, and not lose sight of the original argument.

After looking at the conclusion of our argument, we look at premise 7. We see that if we could establish "The rate of inflation rises" (or "will rise"), then we could assert the rest of the sentence in 7: "The elderly and the poor will suffer." Since this is half our conclusion, it makes sense to try to get a short argument to establish the first sentence as an interim conclusion.

When we look for the other half of our main conclusion ("People will lose confidence in the government"), we see it in premise 6. Clearly, if we could establish the first component in premise 6 ("The rate of inflation rises or unemployment rises") as an interim conclusion, then we could assert the second component that we need. If we can get it, then all we need to do is to stick it together with "The elderly and the poor will suffer," and we will have deduced the conclusion that we're looking for.

But can we get the sentences necessary to frame the short arguments to get the conclusions we need to establish our main conclusion? Well, we just have to work our way backwards and try to find what short arguments we can construct out of the premises (plus the new conclusions) that will have those sentences as *their* conclusion.

If we persist long enough, we can get a sequence of short arguments and make use of the conclusions of each to move towards a final short argument that will have as its conclusion the sentence that is the conclusion of the whole argument. In the sequence below, the sentences with the arabic numbers are the original premises and those with letters are conclusions that can then be used as premises:

(1)   10. If corporations seek profits for their stockholders, the United States will sell wheat to China.

      8. Corporations seek profits for their stockholders.

      a. The United States will sell wheat to China.

(2)   1. If the United States sells wheat to China, then our grain supplies will be lowered.

a. The United States will sell wheat to China.

b. Our grain supplies will be lowered.

(3)   a. The United States will sell wheat to China.

b. Our grain supples will be lowered.

c. The United States will sell wheat to China and our grain supplies will be lowered.

(4)   2. If the United States sells wheat to China and our grain supplies are lowered, then either we will have a shortage or we will have to buy wheat from some other country.

c. The United States will sell wheat to China and our grain supplies will be lowered.

d. Either we will have a shortage or we will have to buy wheat from some other country.

(5)   3. If we either have a shortage or have to buy wheat from some other country, then we will have severe economic problems.

d. Either we (will) have a shortage or we will have to buy wheat from some other country.

e. We will have severe economic problems.

(6)   4. If we have severe economic problems, then either the rate of inflation will rise or unemployment will rise.

e. We will have severe economic problems.

f. Either the rate of inflation will rise or unemployment will rise.

(7)   6. If the rate of inflation rises or unemployment rises, then people will lose confidence in the government.

f. Either the rate of inflation will rise or unemployment will rise.

*g. People will lose confidence in the government.

At this point (with g), we've established half our conclusion. Now all we have to do is to keep up the same process until we get the other half.

(8) 9. If the United States sells wheat to China, we will not have a shortage.

a. The United States will sell wheat to China.

---

h. We will not have a shortage.

(9) d. Either we will have a shortage or we will have to buy wheat from some other country.

h. We will not have a shortage.

---

i. We will have to buy wheat from some other country.

(10) 5. If we buy wheat from some other country, then the rate of inflation will rise.

i. We will buy wheat from some other country.

---

j. The rate of inflation will rise.

(11) 7. If the rate of inflation rises, the elderly and the poor will suffer.

j. The rate of inflation will rise.

---

*k. The elderly and the poor will suffer.

With this argument, we now have both conclusions. All we have to do is to take one more step and put them together.

(12) g. People will lose confidence in the government.

k. The elderly and the poor will suffer.

THEREFORE: People will lose confidence in the government, and the elderly and the poor will suffer.

We've made use of a round dozen of short arguments to show that the conclusion that was asserted on the basis of the premises does indeed *follow from* the premises. Each link in the chain of twelve arguments is itself a valid argument. Accordingly, the whole chain of arguments constitutes a single valid argument.

In our example, each of the interim conclusions played a part, as a premise in some other short argument, in leading to our final conclusion. This is not a necessary feature of such chains, though. Even if we had had some short arguments that led nowhere, so long as they were valid, this wouldn't have mattered. The result wouldn't have been so elegant, of course. It's always more impressive to go straight to your destination than to turn down blind alleys. But elegance isn't everything. Deducing the conclusion is more important.

The chain of arguments leading to the final conclusion constitutes a *deductive proof* of the validity of the original argument. We have now shown that the conclusion does follow from the premises by using a sequence of elementary valid arguments. At the outset of this example, we assumed that we already knew that the argument was valid. The questions asked then were "How does the conclusion follow from the premises?" and "How can it be shown that the conclusion is already 'contained in' the premises?" The questions were answered by constructing the proof. Had we not known at the beginning that the argument was valid, the formulation of our proof would have established that it was. Deductive proofs, then, can be developed to prove the validity of an argument.

By the way, though, we don't always deduce conclusions from premises with an eye towards deducing some particular conclusion, just so we can prove that the argument that has that conclusion is valid. Sometimes we are just curious about what sentences we can deduce from a set of sentences taken as premises. Surprising and unsuspected conclusions can sometimes be drawn from a set of familiar sentences. Scientific theories, explicitly expressed as a group of sentences (theoretical laws or principles), often yield information which no one guessed was there. We can construct proofs of validity by means of deduction, but the construction of such proofs is certainly not the sole use of deduction.

Formal logic, rather than making use of valid arguments to construct deductive proofs, relies upon valid argument *forms*. (An argument can be proved to be valid, recall, if it can be shown to have a valid form.) Looking back at the dozen short arguments we used in our proof, it's easy to see that among the arguments we employed only three argument forms are to be found. They are the following:

Modus Ponens (MP)	(1) If P, then Q.	E.g.:	If corporations seek profits for their stockholders, then the United States will sell wheat to China.
	P		Corporations seek profits for their stockholders.
	Q		The United States will sell wheat to China.

Disjunctive Syllogism (DS)	(2) Either P or Q.	E.g.:	Either we will have a shortage or we will buy wheat from another country.
	Not-P		We will not have a shortage.
	Q		We will buy from another country.

Conjunction	(3) P		E.g.: People will lose confidence.
(Conj.)	Q		The elderly and the poor will suffer.
	P and Q		People will lose confidence and the elderly and the poor will suffer.

Argument forms such as these (each has been given its traditional name and common abbreviation) can be used as *rules*. In accordance with them, each conclusion reached can be justified. Thus, conclusion (a) is established by deducing it from premises 8 and 10 in accordance with the Modus Ponens rule. This means that we don't really have to write out each of the individual short arguments in the chain. We can just indicate what sentences are being used as premises and what rule (what valid argument form) justifies a conclusion. The premises and the interim conclusions can simply be listed one after the other. Out to the side of the list we can supply the name of the rule and the numbers of the sentences involved, to establish each conclusion. Our proof will look like this, then, because we don't have to keep repeating the sentences we are using:

PREMISES:
1. If the United States sells wheat to China, then our grain supplies will be lowered.
2. If the United States sells wheat to China and our grain supplies are lowered, then either we will have a shortage or we will have to buy wheat from some other country.
3. If we either have a shortage or have to buy wheat from some other country, then we will have severe economic problems.
4. If we have severe economic problems, then either the rate of inflation will rise or unemployment will rise.
5. If we buy wheat from some other country, then the rate of inflation will rise.
6. If the rate of inflation rises or unemployment rises, then people will lose confidence in the government.
7. If the rate of inflation rises, the elderly and the poor will suffer.
8. Corporations seek profits for their stockholders.
9. If the United States sells wheat to China, we will not have a shortage.

10. If corporations seek profits for their stock-
    holders, the United States will sell wheat
    to China.

---

11. The United States will sell wheat to China.	10, 8 MP
12. Our grain supplies will be lowered.	1, 11 MP
13. The United States will sell wheat to China and our grain supplies will be lowered.	11, 12 Conj.
14. Either we will have a shortage or we will have to buy wheat from some other country.	2, 13 MP
15. We will have severe economic problems.	3, 14 MP
16. Either the rate of inflation will rise or unemployment will rise.	4, 15 MP
17. People will lose confidence in the government.	6, 16 MP
18. We will not have a shortage.	9, 11 MP
19. We will have to buy wheat from some other country.	14, 18 DS
20. The rate of inflation will rise.	5, 19 MP
21. The elderly and the poor will suffer.	7, 20 MP
22. People will lose confidence in the government, and the elderly and the poor will suffer.	17, 21 Conj.

In the proof (or "deductive demonstration") as we've written it now, each sentence in the list is either a premise or one that follows from the sentences above it as the conclusion of a short valid argument. Rather than working out each of the short arguments, we've done basically the same thing by referring to a valid argument form and the sentences that are to be used as premises in the short arguments.

The valid argument forms that we used are generally called "rules of inference," for they can be used to infer (or conclude) conclusions from premises. Many more such rules could be given, and there is really no limit to the number of valid argument forms there are. Any argument form that has been proved valid can be used as a rule of inference in the way that we've used MP, DS, and Conj. As a matter of fact, only somewhere between 12 and 20 such rules are commonly used in formal logic. Any less makes it hard to construct proofs, and any more makes it hard to keep them all in mind.

That really concludes our brief survey of a fragment of formal logic. In the exercises, more information and more rules are presented so that anyone who wants to gain just a little more sophistication in the area can do so.

Before leaving the topic, though, we ought to point out the severe limitation of the fragment of formal logic we've been considering. Notice that an argument like this:

All public service workers are underpaid.

Sally Chung is a public service worker.

Sally Chung is underpaid.

has to be considered invalid in terms of sentential logic. It has the invalid form P, Q / Therefore R, because there are three distinct sentences involved.

But, of course, it *isn't* invalid. Anybody can see that. It's just that its validity depends on the way that the word "all" functions to put public service workers in the class of those who are underpaid. That is, its validity depends on an expression that occurs *within* a sentence. And sentential logic, recall, can deal only with arguments whose validity depends solely upon the ways in which simple component sentences are put together.

It's impossible, then, for sentential logic to show that this valid argument is valid. That's the limitation of sentential logic. And that's why it has to be extended by what is called "predicate" or "quantifier" logic. We're not going to do the extending, but you should know that it's necessary.

Living Dangerously: Inductive Arguments

By its very nature an inductive argument is one that is invalid as a deductive argument. The conclusion does *not* follow from the premises. There is no guarantee, then, that if the premises of an inductive argument are true, the conclusion will be true as well. Neither implicitly nor explicitly is the conclusion of an inductive argument contained in the premises. The conclusion always *goes beyond* the premises. Thus, the premises of a valid deductive argument irrevocably guarantee or prove the conclusion, but the premises of an inductive argument do not. They only support, make likely, give some reasons or evidence for, or confirm the conclusion.

When we offer an inductive argument we quite literally *hazard* the conclusion. Since the conclusion always commits us to more than is in the premises, there is a *logical gap* between the premises and conclusion of an inductive argument. It is a gap that can't be bridged by deduction. The only way to get from the premises to the conclusion is to leap the chasm. This is the famous *inductive leap,* fabled in song, story, and logic book. If we jump from doubtful or shaky or wholly inadequate premises, we run a terrible risk of falling into the abyss. The conclusion may turn out to be false. Unfortunately, even if we jump to a conclusion from well-grounded, or true, or what we think are adequate premises, the conclusion may still turn out to be false. In short, though the chance of falling into the abyss is greater in some cases than it is in others, it is nonetheless everpresent. The deducer has reason to be happy. If his premises are true and his argument valid, then his conclusion will be true also. The inducer has to live dangerously. The only way he can reach any conclusion at all is by taking a risk.

A deductive argument is valid or invalid, period. But inductive arguments don't fall into such a neat dichotomy. There are, to be sure, good inductive arguments and bad ones. Yet there are many shades that lie between these bold colors. The premises of an inductive argument are supposed to supply grounds or reasons for its conclusion. The premises *support* the conclusion, and obviously enough, the support they provide can range from "none at all," through "moderate," to "overwhelming." To recognize that there is a range of support which the premises of inductive arguments offer for their conclusions, some philosophers and logicians choose to talk about the *degree of confirmation* of conclusions. When the premises of an argument provide very strong support for its conclusion, the conclusion is said to have a "high degree of confirmation," and the conclusion of an argument whose premises provide only weak support for the conclusion is said to have a "low degree of confirmation." For example, the conclusion of this argument

Almost every American is in favor of publicly supported education.

Arthur Kuhn is an American.
_____
Arthur Kuhn is in favor of publicly supported education.

is highly confirmed by its premises. (Notice, by the way, that it is an invalid deductive argument. It would be valid only if *every* American was said to be in favor of such support.) The conclusion of *this* argument has a very low degree of confirmation with respect to its premise:

The effort of conservationists to keep an airport from being built in the Everglades was successful.
_____
All efforts of conservationists will be successful.

Rather than talking in vague qualitative terms of "high," "low," and "moderate" degrees of confirmation, some logicians have attempted to formulate ways of expressing in a precise quantified way the degree of confirmation that a sentence has with respect to some specified group of sentences that are offered as providing reasons or evidence for it. That is, they have tried to specify not only what it means to say that a premise P confirms a conclusion C, but also the way in which a numerical value might be assigned. The numerical value would be the degree of confirmation of C on the basis of P. The issues involved are abstruse and technical and go far beyond the general characterization of inductive arguments which concern us.

There is more to evaluating inductive arguments than merely determining whether or not the premises confirm the conclusion to such a degree that we would be comfortable in accepting the conclusion. As we've already discussed in talking about ways in which arguments can be challenged, various questions can be raised about the premises themselves. We might summarize what we expect of an adequate or good inductive argument by referring briefly to several matters which have already been mentioned.

1. *There must be sufficient reason to accept the premises of an inductive argument.* Ideally, we would like to know that the premises are true. Sometimes, when a premise is a sentence like "The first person interviewed expressed a preference for living in the city rather than in the suburbs" our desires are satisfied. Such sentences we can accept as true with few qualms. Yet premises are not always like this. For example, "Almost every American is in favor of publicly supported education" is itself likely to be the conclusion of an inductive argument. If it is used as a premise, we may question the adequacy of the evidence which supports it. After all, if its truth is highly doubtful we would generally have little wish of basing further conclusions on it. If, however, we regard the evidence supporting it to be sufficient to accept it as true, ordinarily we would have little hesitation about using the sentence as a premise in an argument to establish another conclusion. In short, before we are willing to say of an inductive argument that it is adequate, we demand that its premises be accepted as adequately grounded.

2. *The premises must be relevant to the conclusion.* If the premises of an inductive argument had nothing to do with its conclusion, then we couldn't even talk about them as confirming the conclusion. To confirm the conclusion, they have to count *for* it, and in order to do this they have to be pertinent to it. An irrelevant premise doesn't *disconfirm* the conclusion, but it doesn't confirm it either. It just doesn't count either way. It's neutral, adiaphorous, impertinent.

3. *The evidence or reasons supplied by the premises must be adequate for the acceptance of the conclusion.* It's easy enough to say that a good inductive argument has an adequately supported conclusion, but as we've already remarked, that's just about all that can be said. Exactly when, *in general*, the premises supply sufficient grounds is impossible to say. Yet we can and do say when the evidence is adequate in many specific cases, and, in practice, we accept some inductive arguments as good ones and reject others as bad. Sometimes, of course, we just don't know what to think. Recall, too, that sometimes we just have to decide whether to accept or reject a conclusion on the evidence available at the time and in present circumstances. In such a case, we may realize that the evidence is inadequate, that the argument is not an adequate inductive argument; yet for some reason or other we can't afford to delay judgment. So there is sometimes a distinction between accepting the conclusion of

an argument and regarding the conclusion as adequately established or established as true.

4. *In judging the adequacy of an inductive argument we have to take into account relevant information which might make a difference in our conclusion.* Ideally, we would take into account *all* relevant information. But that's generally impossible simply because of practical limitations in collecting information. What's more, if we formulate inductive arguments at all, then we have to offer them at *some* given time, and we can't just wait around until "all the evidence is in." In some cases, all the evidence can never be in because there's always future evidence to consider, and there's an inexhaustible amount of it. We could never get *all possible evidence* for the simple claim "New York is always more humid than Chicago," for example.

Relevant information available at the time an argument is offered has to be considered because it may provide a reason for rejecting or modifying the conclusion of our inductive argument. An argument may have a conclusion that is highly confirmed by its premises and still be an inadequate and unacceptable argument. This can happen simply because all information which would disconfirm the conclusion of the argument has been ignored. If we start out with a hypothesis about what "every" American believes, then the first case we run into of an American who doesn't believe what we say every American believes forces us to modify our hypothesis. We have to change it to something like "almost every American." If we run into several more disconfirming cases, we have to retreat another step, to what "most Americans" believe. The more contrary cases we encounter the further we have to retreat: "many," "some," "a few," "at least one," and finally, "no Americans." That is, we have to keep weakening our claim, and we may finally have to abandon it. An inductive argument which considered only favorable cases would have a highly confirmed conclusion and give every appearance of being adequate. But it would give this appearance only by ignoring disconfirming cases and thus "loading" its premises. To judge the adequacy of an inductive argument, then, we have to step outside of the premises and ask whether they are fair.

The four characteristics which we have discussed here and in the section on ways of challenging arguments are all marks of adequate inductive arguments. In quick summary, an adequate inductive argument is one that has (1) adequately established premises; (2) premises that are relevant to the conclusion; (3) premises that confirm the conclusion to an acceptable degree (whatever this may be); and (4) premises that represent fairly the relevant information. This is not, by a long book, all that needs to be said about judging the adequacy of inductive arguments.

Questions about how relatively simple conclusions are established by inductive arguments shade off into major questions about the establishment of scientific laws and theories, statistical arguments, and probability theories. Even raising the questions would demand a long foray into the philosophy of science.

The time has come for some radical honesty. The truth of the matter is that most of the discussion of inductive arguments has been somewhat jaundiced up to this point. We've talked of inductive arguments as if they always involved gathering evidence to support such conclusions as "All blacks feel resentment towards American society" or "The next sheik we meet will be wearing a turban." Thus, it's possible that the impression has been created that inductive arguments always have conclusions that make factual claims and premises that cite alleged facts to support those claims. A great number of arguments that are not deductive ones are, indeed, of this kind. What's more, some logicians and philosophers typically use the phrase "inductive argument" to refer only to them. Yet there are many àrguments that neither purport to be deductive nor purport to establish factual claims. For example:

> The space program is costing the American government fantastic sums of money.

> Its only tangible outcome has been to contribute to American prestige.

> Our domestic problems are enormous and immediate.

> Much could be done to solve our domestic difficulties, if the money currently spent on space exploration was severely reduced.

> Therefore, much of the money now committed to the space program should be reallocated to programs which would help overcome our domestic crisis.

The conclusion of this argument doesn't follow from the premises, but the premises do provide reasons or grounds for accepting the conclusion. In accordance with our original definition, such arguments are just as much inductive arguments as those which have factual conclusions like "Lithium hydroxide has a crystalline structure." If, for some reason, the "inductive" label is saved for arguments with (allegedly) factual premises and conclusions, then rather than dividing all arguments into deductive and inductive, we can assure a complete division by simply making a distinction between deductive arguments and *nondeductive* arguments. Thus, all arguments that have conclusions that don't follow from the premises are nondeductive, no matter whether the conclusion is a factual claim or not.

But all of this is just a matter of choosing terms and is not very important. "Deductive/ Inductive" will serve us very well as a name for the distinction, just as we made it originally. What *is* important is that we not overlook or slight arguments that don't have alleged facts as conclusions. The premises of such arguments, like those of the other sort, are put forward in an effort to make the conclusion plausible and thus acceptable. Sentences that might appear as conclusions of such arguments are ones like "C.P. Snow is a much better novelist than the critics have claimed," "Every adult American ought to have a guaranteed annual income of at least $5,000," "Dogs make much nicer pets than cats do," "J. Robert Oppenheimer was the man best qualified to head the Los Alamos project," "Marlowe's Faustus is a much more complex character than Goethe's Faust," "Truman was the best President of any so far in this century," "Hitler made a strategic mistake in withdrawing troops from the Russian front," "There is no one outlook or consistent set of values expressed in Frost's poetry," "Ernest Jones's attempt to apply Freudian theory to the character of Hamlet produced convincing results." And so on and on and on.

It's easy to see why arguments with such conclusions ought not be neglected. They constitute the greatest bulk of the arguments that we ordinarily employ. Rarely do we give straightforward deductive arguments, and not too frequently do we try to establish inductive conclusions of a factual kind. The sciences are typically concerned with each, but this is not at all the case with everyday life. We use, present, listen to, criticize, accept, and reject arguments quite often. But most of our arguments are ones about the evaluation and interpretation of some situation or state of affairs. We offer arguments to get people to see our point of view and to get them to adopt it. We make a case for our position. In doing so, we face them with arguments. Not with deductive arguments, and not with arguments that have factual claims for conclusions, but still with arguments whose premises express reasons for accepting the conclusion we offer. We try to make our claims about interpretation and evaluation and action plausible. In fact, we try to make them *so* plausible that it would seem foolish of anyone not to accept them.

The premises of such arguments may state facts like "Eldridge Cleaver wrote *Soul on Ice*" or "Small diamonds are ordinarily miter cut," even though their conclusions don't allege any facts. Sometimes, as we saw earlier, facts count as reasons for accepting some claim that is not itself factual. In every case in which we assert that something ought to be done, or that something is ridiculous, stupid, ugly, brutal, sad, well-executed, immoral, pornographic, or uplifting, in every case in which we try to get somebody to accept a point of view, a course of action, or a way of looking at an event, novel, play, poem, or film, some facts are always *relevant*. If someone argued that the quality of F. Scott Fitzgerald's writing declined in his later years, it would certainly be pertinent to mention the *fact* that *The Great Gatsby*, generally regarded as an excellent novel, was written rather early in his career and that *The Crack-Up*, a collage of some good and some mediocre pieces, was written late in his career. Or, to go back to an example already used, if someone wanted to establish the claim that the vast amount of money spent on the space program would be better spent in refurbishing our cities, then it is certainly relevant to his arguments that the space program does, *as a matter of fact,* have an enormous budget.

Not all premises may be ones that are factual, even though they supply reasons or grounds for the conclusion. We don't usually regard sentences like "The rights of women as citizens ought to be recognized and protected" as stating *facts.* Rather, we take such sentences to express *values* or *commitments* that we make. (Of course it may be fact that most people in our society accept the same commitment. But that doesn't turn the commitment into a fact. It's the acceptance of the commitment that is the fact.) Such sentences can certainly appear as premises in arguments, and they have just as much right to be there as factual premises do. Here is such an argument which involves a premise which makes a commitment to a value (what ought to be) and a premise which alleges a fact:

The rights of women as citizens ought to be recognized and protected.

Women are discriminated against in the hiring practices of many businesses and industries.

Steps should be taken to guarantee that women have job opportunities equal to those of men.

Similarly, sentences which put forward or make a commitment to an interpretation can also appear as premises:

Hamlet is a weak and irresolute character.

Thus, though he is the main character of the play, he is not the *hero* of the play.

In ordinary life, the arguments we are most apt to meet with are very complex affairs. The premises are likely to be congeries of sentences making factual claims and evaluative ones, or factual ones and interpretative ones, or sometimes factual *and* evaluative *and* interpretative ones. Consider this simple argument:

1. Fitzgerald wrote *The Great Gatsby.*
2. *The Great Gatsby* is an excellent novel.
3. Fitzgerald wrote *Tender Is the Night.*
4. *Tender Is the Night* is a fine book.
5. *The Great Gatsby* and *Tender Is the Night* were written rather early in Fitzgerald's career.
6. Fitzgerald wrote *The Crack-Up.*
7. In general, the writing in *The Crack-Up* does not stand comparison with the other two books mentioned.

8. *The Crack-Up* was written during the latter part of Fitzgerald's career.

Thus, Fitzgerald's early work is better than his later work.

Premises 1, 3, 5, 6, and 8 are factual ones, ones that state facts relevant to the conclusion. Premises 2, 4, and 7 are ones that express evaluations about particular works by Fitzgerald. The argument's conclusion is an evaluation of all his works that were written during two broad periods in his life.

Here, as another example, is an argument that involves premises that allege facts, express values, and make commitments to interpretations of facts and events.

1. Florence Nightingale showed great courage when fighting broke out in the immediate vicinity of the hospital she had established. (fact and interpretation)
2. Her determination and capacity for work made the hospital a success. (fact and interpretation)
3. Government officials and the army had done much to thwart her plans to set up a field hospital in the Crimea. (fact)
4. She ought to have received more help from the army than she did. (value expression)
5. Without Florence Nightingale and her nurses, casualties, diseases, and infections in the Crimean campaign would have been much greater than they were. (fact)

Thus, by her action and example, and without the help and encouragement due her, Florence Nightingale showed her critics that women could stand up to the rigors of an army field hospital and perform their tasks with skill and diligence.

We earlier spoke of the *confirmation* of the conclusion by the premises. The examples of inductive arguments taken were ones that had premises or conclusions that were crudely quantitative. From an examination of a hundred or so field mice in a meadow, for instance, we saw that we might present an inductive argument with the conclusion "All field mice in this area have a high proportion of DDT in their tissues." Or starting from the premise "Almost every American favors state supported education" we saw that we might argue that this premise makes it very likely that a particular American (one randomly selected whose opinion we don't know) favors state support. The examples mentioned in the present discussion of inductive arguments, though, are clearly of a different sort.

A quick glance at the list of sentences that were said to be of the sort typical of the conclusions of many arguments shows that words like "all," "almost all," "each," and so on are not there. Generally, the conclusions are of the kind that don't permit cases or objects (like field mice) to be examined and then counted as evidence for a conclusion. These conclusions are of the kind that most people simply call "opinion" to condemn it or to suggest that there's no need to take it seriously. People tend to say such things as "Well, that's just your opinion." To talk this way assumes that an opinion is just a personal preference or idiosyncrasy which can be ignored or dismissed without examination. But this is far from being true in the case of every claim of the opinion type. There are, after all, opinions that are well-grounded, well-supported, and well-argued. There are opinions that there are *good reasons* to accept, and ones for which there are even *adequate* or *overwhelming* reasons. Then, of course, there are ill-supported opinions, poorly argued ones, and ones for which there are no good or adequate reasons. Consequently, though the sentence presented as the conclusion of an argument may be one that is of the sort we say "expresses an opinion," this doesn't mean it's *just* or *merely* an opinion. The premises of an argument are put forward to provide grounds for it, to give reasons for it. The reasons have to be considered, for an argument is not just a conclusion, even when the conclusion is an opinion-type sentence.

Ought we to say in such cases that the premises *confirm* the conclusion and confirm it to some degree or other (strongly, weakly, very little, etc.)? There's no reason why we shouldn't talk this way, if we want to. But some philosophers prefer to save the word "confirm" for use in arguments whose conclusions seem best regarded as belonging to the "factual" rather than the "opinion" variety.

An alternative to "confirm" is the word mentioned earlier: "plausible." The premises of an inductive argument supply grounds or reasons which in no case completely prove or guarantee the conclusion. They do, however, make the conclusion plausible and, perhaps, worthy of acceptance. Even when we are attempting to persuade someone to accept an evaluation or interpretation, to follow an order or fulfill a request, to embrace a point of view or act in a certain way, we employ arguments. The arguments we offer are typically nondeductive ones, and in presenting them we are generally trying to show that there are sufficient reasons to accept what we say or to do what we ask. We try to demonstrate that the conclusion is *plausible,* that it *ought* to be accepted, that the reasons for accepting it are *good enough*. So if we want to use "confirm" only in cases like " 'Twenty Englishmen interviewed were prejudiced against Catholics' confirms 'All Englishmen are prejudiced against Catholics' to a greater degree than 'One Englishman interviewed was prejudiced against Catholics,' " then we can use the more general term "plausible." "Plausible" can cover all cases of nondeductive argument.

The evaluation of nondeductive arguments with conclusions that make no factual claims is not fundamentally different from the evaluation of those that do. The primary difference is that the premises of the nonfactual type typically include sentences which are themselves non-factual ones. Sentences like "Free medical care should be available for all who cannot afford to pay for it," for example, might appear as a premise. Still, the principles of evaluation are unchanged. We must still ask the usual questions:

1. Is there adequate reason to accept each premise in the argument? If the premises contain factual claims, we must ask whether the evidence for them is sufficient to believe they are true. If a premise is nonfactual and expresses a value commitment or interpretation, etc., then we must ask whether there is adequate reason to accept the commitment or interpretation.
2. Are the premises relevant to the conclusion?
3. Do the premises make the conclusion plausible, plausible enough to accept?
4. Are there reasons not mentioned in the premises which make the conclusion implausible, doubtful, or unacceptable? That is, do the premises adequately represent the relevant information or are they slanted in favor of the conclusion?

Nondeductive arguments are notoriously difficult to judge. Being wary, being informed, careful, cautious, and thorough are not guarantees against being wrong. But they are of more help than ignorance, haste, and carelessness. Our discussion of what to look for in evaluating inductive arguments and what rough standards to follow in formulating them goes little beyond what we all do as a matter of course. Yet it's helpful to reflect on just what it is that we do and to try to describe it in explicit, even if imprecise, terms. If nothing else this helps us to become more self-conscious and critical of our activities. We can then remind ourselves to look for certain marks and to ask certain questions.

We've spent quite a bit of effort in this chapter talking about what makes an argument a good argument. Since evil is often more interesting than good (that's why we read murder mysteries and not lives of the saints), it will be a nice change of pace to go to the next chapter and consider some very bad arguments.

Exercises

Deductive Arguments

Sentential Form

The directions to follow here are simple ones indeed: Write the arguments below in their sentential form.

But nothing in this world is quite that simple, so here are some subdirections to follow:

(a) Use the letters that are given after each argument to abbreviate (stand in the place of) the simple sentences of the argument.

(b) Use the ordinary English words "if . . ., then . . .," "or," "and," and "not" to show the way the simple sentences are put together in the compound sentences. Follow this convention, though: Instead of allowing a "not" to stay inside a sentence, put it in front of the sentence. Thus, if the sentence is "Flash Gordon is not a friend of Ming the Merciless," instead of letting F abbreviate the sentence, let Not-F do the job instead.

That's all there is to it, so far as directions are concerned. But a little advice might also be helpful. As a practical matter, the easiest approach to take in discovering the sentential form of an argument is to start by locating the simple sentences that make up the compound ones. Putting parentheses around the simple sentences is helpful in keeping track of them. For example: If (Flash and Dale are missing), then (Ming is to blame).

Also, be careful to notice that in English we use a lot of pronouns so we don't have to keep repeating whatever it is they stand for. You will want to replace the pronouns (at least in your head) so you can recognize two sentences as being fundamentally the same. For example, the sentence "If the ship landed on Vesta, then the crew is in danger" has "the ship landed on Vesta" as a component. If, later in the argument, you see "It landed on Vesta," you have to be able to recognize that this is the same as the component sentence and not another simple sentence.

Finally, notice that we sometimes don't repeat a verb, so that what looks like one simple sentence can really be broken into two (or more). For example: Either he fell into the Pit of Serpents or into the Well of Dragons. This really breaks down into "Either he fell into the Pit of Serpents or *he fell* into the Well of Dragons."

It just takes practice.

1. If Doc Savage is brilliant, then he must be rich.

    Doc Savage is brilliant.
    _____
    He must be rich. (D, R)

2. Either the fabled Jewel of Opahr is priceless or it is a fake.

    It is not a fake.
    _____
    It is priceless.   (P, F)

3. If John Carter rescued the Princess of Mars, then she is grateful.

    The Princess is not grateful.
    _____
    John Carter did not rescue the Princess of Mars.   (J, G)

4. If *The Skylark of Space* is a bad book, then E. E. Smith is a bad writer.

   If he is a bad writer, then he is justly ignored by critics.

   ___

   If *The Skylark of Space* is a bad book, E. E. Smith is justly ignored by the critics.   (S, E, J)

5. Silverberg has changed his writing style.

   Sheckley has stopped writing satire.

   ___

   Silverberg has changed his writing style, and Sheckley has stopped writing satire.   (S, W)

6. *Slan* involved a new idea or the idea was old and the treatment was new.

   If it involved a new idea, then the treatment was not new.

   The treatment was new.

   ___

   The idea was an old one.   (N, O, T)

7. *Time for the Stars* was written for juveniles.

   If it was written for juveniles or for adults, it is enjoyable.

   ___

   It is enjoyable. (J, A, E)

8. If Cambell gave advice, then if writers listened to him, their work was influenced.

   Cambell gave advice.

   The work of writers was not influenced.

   ___

   Writers did not listen to him.   (C, L, I)

Replacement of Connectives

Until now we've used ordinary English words to indicate the ways that the simple sentences are put together to make compound ones. Because words like "and" and "either . . . or . . ." connect simple sentences into compound ones (and compound ones into even greater compounds), they are called *connectives*. "Not" doesn't connect anything, but it's always included with them for convenience.

We're now ready to make use of a kind of dictionary that will allow us to replace the ordinary English connectives with logical symbols. (The logical symbols are not always exactly the same as the words they replace, for the symbols are few and words are many. The symbols can't catch the nuances, but they make up in precision what is lost in subtlety.)

Using this dictionary, go back and rewrite the sentential forms of the arguments above. Replace the English connectives with symbols.

English	Symbol	Name
either . . . or. . .	v	Disjunction
or		
and		
but, yet	·	Conjunction
if . . ., then . . .	⊃	Implication
not		
(and other ways of denying)	~	Negation

Except for the symbol for "not," all the symbols are used to connect two sentences. This means a sentence on the left side (or its abbreviation), a symbol in the middle, then a sentence on the right side (or its abbreviation). So "Either R or S" is written "R v S".

The symbol for "not" goes in front of the sentence.

Some Rules for Deduction

One of the ways of testing the validity of an argument, recall, is by deducing the conclusion from the premises. That is, by constructing a deductive proof or demonstration. The proof proceeds step by step, and every step is justified by an inference rule.

In a moment we'll list the inference rules that we'll be using in the rest of this exercise. But first, we're going to present *another* set of rules.

These rules are Equivalence Rules. They will allow us to rewrite sentences in ways that will not alter their truth. If a sentence is true, it will stay that way and will not be made false by our monkeying around with its structure.

As we'll see in constructing proofs, it is wonderfully useful to have rules of equivalence. They permit us to get sentences in forms in which the inference rules are stated. That, in turn, lets us assert conclusions in accordance with the rules. And that's what deduction is all about.

We'll use the symbol "=" to mean "can be rewritten as." When we put it between two expressions, it means that the expressions on *either* side can be transformed into the one on the other side.

Equivalence Rules

1. Double Negation (DN)

$$P = \sim \sim P$$

This is the simplest of the rules. It merely says that if there are two "nots" in front of a sentence you may erase them or, if you wish, you may *put* two in front.

For example, (A v B) may be rewritten as $\sim \sim$ (A v B).

2. Tautology (Taut.)
   P = (P v P)
   P = (P · P)
This is the second simplest rule. It just says that when two parts of a compound sentence are the same and they are connected with a "v" or a "·", then one of the parts can be dropped off. (Again, you can do the reverse, if you want to.)

3. Commutation (Com.)
   (P v Q) = (Q v P)
   (P · Q) = (Q · P)
Actually, this may be the second simplest rule. It merely tells you that when two sentences are connected with a "v" or a "·", then you may switch them from one side of the symbol to the other. (Notice, this isn't allowed for symbols other than these two. In other cases, order makes a difference.)

4. Definition of Implication (Imp.)
   (P $\supset$ Q) = ($\sim$P v Q)
These two forms aren't so obviously equivalent as the others. Consider, though, that a sentence like "If Flash is dead, then Ming killed him" does depict an either/or situation. It says, in fact, "Either Flash is not dead or Ming killed him." (You don't really have to understand a rule to use it, though. Understanding often comes *after* use.)

This rule is not as easy to use as the others, either. Anyone who tries to transform a sentence like $\sim$ (A · B) $\supset$ F is likely to get confused. Fortunately, this can be done in a purely mechanical way.

Here's how. (For brevity, let's call the presence or absence of "$\sim$" the "sign" of a sentence.)
   a. Change the sign of the sentence on the left.
   b. Change the "$\supset$" to a "v" (or the "v" to a " $\supset$", depending on the form you want).
   c. Leave the sentence on the right unchanged.
So our hard case above is rewritten as: (A · B) v F.

5. De Morgan's Rules (DM)
   $\sim$ (P · Q) = ($\sim$ P v $\sim$ Q)
   $\sim$ (P v Q) = ($\sim$ P · $\sim$ Q)
This is undoubtedly the hardest of our rules. And to make things worse, there are two of them. It is possible to "see" that the forms in each case are equivalent. (Try this: "It is false that Flash is dead and that Dale is dead." This says that both of the component sentences are not true, and maybe neither is. So we can write: Either Flash is not dead or Dale is not dead. If neither is dead, the first sentence is still true.)

Fortunately, "seeing" is not necessary here, and we don't even have to pay attention to the fact that there are two rules. We can use another mechanical procedure:

    a. Change the sign of the sentence as a whole.
    b. Change the signs of both components.
    c. Change the "v" to a "·" (or vice versa).

Thus the complicated-looking $\sim (\sim F \cdot R)$ very easily gets transformed into the equivalent $(F \text{ v} \sim R)$.

Unlike inference rules, our equivalence rules can be applied to whole sentences or to sentences that are parts of larger sentences. If, for example, you were faced with a really terrible looking sentence like

$$[(A \text{ v } D) \cdot (\sim A \cdot S)] \supset \sim (S \text{ v } D)$$

you would have a lot of possibilities for rewriting. You could focus on the two compound sentences in the brackets that are connected by the "·" and change the "·" to "v" or you could change either of them separately. You could change the " $\supset$ " to a "v" or you could change the "v" to a "·" in the farthest compound sentence on the right.

You wouldn't have to stop there, of course. You could just keep applying the rules and rewriting your rewrites. You might eventually hit on some form that you could use in connection with your inference rules.

These five rules are all that are needed to do the exercises in this book. But some other rules are needed to show that certain valid arguments are in fact valid and to make some proofs easier. We can cover both these bases by three more rules.

6. Exportation (Exp.)
    $[(P \cdot Q) \supset R] = [P \supset (Q \supset R)]$
To "export" something is to send it out. This rule tells us we can "send out" one of the sentences in a conjunction that appears in the "if" clause of an "if. . ., then . . ." sentence. We can get rid of the conjunction and rewrite the sentence by using "$\supset$"s. (We can go the other way also, of course. We can get rid of a "$\supset$" by using a conjunction.)
    In accordance with the rule, we can rewrite a sentence like
    $(\sim T \cdot C) \supset (F \text{ v } A)$ as $\sim T \supset [C \supset (F \text{ v } A)]$.

7. Association (Assoc.)
    $[P \text{ v } (Q \text{ v } R)] = [(P \text{ v } Q) \text{ v } R]$
    $[P \cdot (Q \cdot R)] = [(P \cdot Q) \cdot R]$

This is a simple rule. It says, in its first version, that it doesn't matter how sentences connected by "or" are grouped together. The second version says the same thing about sentences connected by "and."
    Of course you have to be careful to notice that a sentence has "or" (or

"and") as its main connective and has a component sentence joined by the same connective.

A hard-looking case like (F ⊃ V) v (T v ~ C) is easily changed when you see that "v" is the main connective and that one of the other sentences also has this as its connective. The sentence can thus be rewritten as [(F ⊃ V) v T] v ~ C.

8. Distribution (Dist.)

[P · (Q v R)] = [(P · Q) v (P ·R)]
[P v (Q · R)] = [(P v Q) · (P v R)]

It's easy to get confused when using this rule. Here are the two basic things to remember: (1) the main connective changes to the connective of the component sentence (and vice versa); (2) the first sentence from the left—the one in the P's position—is the one distributed (or "gathered" if the rewrite is in the other direction).

How do you rewrite (A ⊃ B) · (C v D)? Easy. You see that the main connective will become "v" and that (A ⊃ B) is the sentence you have to distribute. So: [(A ⊃ B) · C] v [(A ⊃ B) · D] .

A word of caution needs to be dropped here. When a sentence has a "not" in front of it, the sentence has to be regarded as a unit. Its *parts* (the component sentences) can't be distributed. So when you see a case like A · ~ (C v D) you aren't permitted to ignore the "~" and distribute as you would if it weren't there. You can't distribute in this case.

Perhaps before we go on to the inference rules, it would be a good idea to spend a little time mastering the use of the equivalence rules. Since Double Negation, Tautology, and Commutation are too simple to cause trouble, we'll just concentrate on the last five rules. (It is perfectly acceptable to use the mechanical methods of applying the rules.)

1. Use Imp. to rewrite the following sentences. When it's possible, transform the entire sentence and its component sentences. It's best to do this one step at a time.
   a.   (A · D) ⊃ (~ C v P)
   b.   ~ (F ⊃ Y) ⊃ (Y ⊃ F)
   c.   (E v G) v G
   d.   ~ (T ⊃ V) · (D ⊃ T)
   e.   [(H ⊃ I) v (I ⊃ H)] · (H v I)

2. Use DM to rewrite the sentences below. Again, when it is possible, transform both the entire sentence and the component sentences.
   a.   ~ R · S
   b.   ~ (T v ~ Q)
   c.   (F v C) · [~ (F · C) v (F v C)]
   d.   (~ S · ~ T) v (S v F)
   e.   [(E v C) · ~ T] v ~ E

3. Use Exp. to rewrite the following sentences. Apply the rule more than once (in separate steps) where possible.
   a. (A · B) ⊃ A
   b. [(E v C) · D] ⊃ S
   c. (T v Q) ⊃ [(~ S v T) ⊃ F]
   d. C ⊃ [(T ⊃ S) ⊃ A]
   e. [(F ⊃ D) · (A ⊃ C)] ⊃ [(C · D) ⊃ (Q · T)]

4. Use Assoc. to rewrite the following sentences. Apply the rule as often as possible in each case.
   a. [A v (C ⊃ D)] v B   d. [(T v U) v T] v (T ⊃ U)
   b. (C ⊃ D) v (S v T)   e. [(A · ~ B) · ~ A] ⊃ (R · S)
   c. (S · T) · (~ F v C)

5. Use Dist. to rewrite the following. Do the usual about repeated application of the rule.
   a. (L ⊃ M) v (L · M)   d. (N v S) v (N · C)
   b. (L ⊃ M) · (L v M)   e. (~ S · T) v ~ (T v ~ T)
   c. [(S ⊃ T) v T] · (S v T)

Inference Rules

Most of the inference rules that we'll be using in the exercises are ones that we've already met with in the discussion of deductive proofs. Recall, the rules are no more than elementary valid argument forms that we can use to construct "chains" of arguments. To prove that a conclusion follows from a set of premises by the rules is to show that the conclusion is the last link in such a chain.

Rather than discuss the inference rules in detail, we'll just present them, along with a brief example in each case. Our earlier discussion should have made it clear enough how they work.

1. Modus Ponens (MP)

   P ⊃ Q   If this is Mesklin, then we are lost.

   P   This is Mesklin.
   ─────   ──────────────────────────────────
   Q   We are lost.

2. Modus Tollens (MT)

   P ⊃ Q   If this is Mesklin, then we are lost.

   ~ Q   We are not lost.
   ─────   ──────────────────────────────────
   ~ P   This is not Mesklin.

3. Hypothetical Syllogism (HS)

P ⊃ Q	If population continues to increase, then the world food supply will be inadequate.
Q ⊃ R	If the food supply is inadequate, then millions will starve.
P ⊃ R	If population continues to increase, then millions will starve.

4. Disjunctive Syllogism (DS)

P v Q	Either we reduce our standard of living or we must accept pollution and its results.
~ P	We will not reduce our standard of living.
Q	We must accept pollution and its results.

5. Simplification (Simp.)

P · Q	Unemployment is rising, and crime is increasing.
P	Unemployment is rising.

6. Conjunction (Conj.)

P	Unemployment is rising.
Q	Crime is increasing.
P · Q	Unemployment is rising, and crime is increasing.

7. Addition (Add.)

P	We must protect the rights of minorities.
P v Q	Either we must protect the rights of minorities or we must accept an unjust society.

8. Constructive Dilemma (CD)

(P ⊃ Q)·(R ⊃ S)	If Clarke participated in the coverup, he should be jailed. And if he failed to report it, he should be disbarred.
P v R	Clarke either participated in the coverup or failed to report it.
Q v S	Either Clarke should be jailed or Clarke should be disbarred.

These inference rules are quite easy to use, but it's important to keep one thing in mind: the Ps and the Qs are stand-ins for *whole* sentences. The sentences may have other sentences as components, but the connectives in our rules represent the major connectives. Thus, to use MP you have to find two lines, and one of the lines has to have "⊃" as the connective that joins two sentences into the compound sentence that makes up the line. On the other line, you have to have the sentence that occupies the P's position in the rules and *nothing else.* In short, you can't use parts of lines in applying the rules of inference.

All of this will become very obvious with practice. So let's turn to some exercises using both the equivalence rules and the inference rules.

Here's the procedure to follow in the exercises. First, write the sentential form of the argument. In doing this, use the letters that are given as abbreviations for the simple sentences. Second, using both sets of rules, construct a proof or demonstration of the validity of the argument. That is, apply the rules and deduce the conclusion from the premises. Cite a rule to justify each step that you take. Do this by writing the abbreviation of the rule and the line number or numbers that are involved. Put this information on the right side, opposite the line you are justifying.

Also, to help keep matters clear, apply only one rule at a time. At the end of the process, every line ought to be either a premise or a line rewritten in accordance with our equivalence rules or a conclusion justified by our inference rules.

Every argument given here is valid so your real job is to show that it is by constructing a proof.

1. (For an easy beginning, go back and do proofs for arguments 6, 7, and 8 on page 249.)

2. If William Bligh is made Captain of the *Bounty*, then he will be unhappy if Fletcher Christian is not made First Mate. He will be made Captain, and Christian will not be made First Mate. So Captain Bligh will be unhappy. (B, U, F)

3. If the wolf is a canine, then the dog is a canine, and if the dog is a canine, then the wolf is a canine. It is false that either the wolf is a canine or the bear is a canine. Therefore, it is false that either the dog is a canine or the bear is. (W, D, B)

4. If lead melts at a lower temperature than copper, then if mercury melts at a lower temperature than lead, the substance in this tube is mercury. Mercury does melt at a lower temperature than lead, but the substance in this tube is not mercury. Thus, it is false that lead melts at a lower temperature than copper. (L, M, S)

5. If Mendel's results had been published and if proper notice had been taken of them, Darwin's *Origin* would contain an adequate theory of

genetics. Mendel's results were published, yet Darwin's book does not contain an adequate account of genetics. Hence, proper notice was not taken of Mendel's results.   (M, P, D)

6. Either the structure was a helix or it was a double helix and earlier speculation was wrong. If it was a helix, then earlier speculation was not wrong. However, that speculation was wrong. The structure, therefore, was a double helix.   (S, D, W)

7. If Tycho believed in a geocentric universe, then he also believed in epicycles, and if he accepted the sun's apparent motion as real, then he believed in a geocentric universe. He did accept that motion as real. Thus, he also believed in epicycles.   (T, E, A)

8. Either the author of *Pearl* also wrote *Purity* or they were written by two different people. The style of *Pearl* is like that of *Sir Gawain*, and the style of *Purity* is like that of *Patience*. Yet the style of *Patience* is like that of *Pearl*. If the style of *Patience* is like *Pearl*'s, then the style of *Patience* is like *Sir Gawain*'s. If *Patience*'s style is like *Sir Gawain*'s, then *Pearl* and *Purity* were not written by two different people. So the author of *Pearl* also wrote *Purity*, the style of *Purity* is like that of *Patience*, and the style of *Patience* is like that of *Pearl*.   (P, D, S, T, Y, L)

9. Environmental pollution can be stopped only if people are made aware of the problem. They can be made aware of the problem only if biologists participate in public education, and they will do this only if they are encouraged to by the academic community. Thus, if the academic community does not encourage biologists to participate, environmental pollution cannot be stopped.   (E, P, B, A)

10. If the tendency towards aggression is an innate behavior mechanism, either aggression is spontaneously released or it is released by environmental stimuli. If it is spontaneously released, then it is not subject to control. If this is so, then it is not subject to moral and legal evaluation. It is not released by environmental stimuli, and the tendency is an innate behavior mechanism. If aggression is spontaneously released and is not subject to moral and legal evaluation, then many of our laws and attitudes about aggression fail to recognize its character. If they fail to recognize its character, they are wrong. We must conclude, then, that aggression is not subject to moral and legal evaluation and that many of our laws and attitudes about it are wrong.   (T, S, R, C, A, L, W)

Inductive Arguments

The real world is the place to go to get some real live nondeductive arguments to evaluate. A logic-book exercise can in no way take the place of the evaluations made in cases in which the arguments are set out at length and you really care about whether the arguments are acceptable or not.

Also, because there are no mechanical rules for evaluating inductive arguments, their worth has to be discussed and considered at some length—preferably in the company of someone who has already acquired some skills in evaluation. This feature also makes them bad subjects for logic-book exercises.

Recognizing all of this, we'll just have to do what we can. And what we can do is worthwhile, if not ideal.

1. Turn back to the exercises in identifying arguments (pp. 201-207) and deal with the arguments there in the following way:

    a. Reduce the argument to its essentials (locating premises and conclusion, just as in identifying arguments).

    b. Evaluate the acceptability of the arguments in terms of the standards we developed in this chapter.

    c. Discuss how the arguments could be improved (weakening the conclusion, adding supporting premises, and so on).

2. Find *five* inductive arguments of a real-life kind. Look for them in books, magazines, newspapers, and so on. (Try to get *important* arguments about important matters.) Treat them in the same way as above. (Prepare yourself to discuss—and present arguments about—their worth.)

8/Whited Sepulchres:
Fallacies and Sophistries

CONSIDER this fragment from a detective story:

> I saw Clarence enter the ruined house with a mysterious object over his shoulder. It seemed like a rolled carpet, but much heavier and thicker. I realized then I had been guilty of the fallacy of believing Clarence to be innocent of the murder of Major Coalheaver.

The word "fallacy" here is used to mean something like "error" or "mistaken belief." In this sense of the word, it's a fallacy to think that drugs aren't dangerous or that the poor have the same opportunities as the rich. This use of the term is common and totally unobjectionable. It wouldn't even be worth calling attention to it if it weren't for the fact that in informal logic the word "fallacy" has a more restricted meaning.

Broadly speaking, in logic the term "fallacy" refers to any kind of argument that rests on a mistake. In this sense, all arguments that are invalid or that have premises that do not adequately support their conclusions are fallacies. It's probably not going too far to say that, in this sense, "fallacy" and "bad argument" have approximately the same meaning.

Obviously, there are innumerable ways in which an argument can go wrong. That is, there are innumerable kinds of bad arguments. But some kinds occur more frequently than others, some are harder to detect, and some are more tempting to believe. These are the sorts of bad arguments that are of most interest to informal logic, because they are the ones that exert most influence on the reasoning that takes place in ordinary life.

A sizable number of fallacies are discussed in this chapter, but they are only representative of the vast number that could be presented. The ones singled out are all frequently committed and psychologically tempting. But no one should think that just because an argument doesn't commit one of *these* fallacies it doesn't commit *any*. There are more fallacies in heaven and earth than are written down in this book.

Three other points should also be kept in mind. First, because an argument is fallacious doesn't mean that its conclusion is false. It may be possible to establish the same conclusion by another nonfallacious argument. Second, "one to a customer" is a supermarket sales rule that's not observed by bad arguments. An argument may be bad because it commits two, three, or more fallacies at one and the same time. Finally, honest people can err, as the Internal Revenue Service reminds us once a year. Fallacies are frequently associated with double-dyed deceivers who set out, fallacies in hand, to eucher the public by their tricks. The association is accurate, of course, for there are those who deliberately use bad arguments for the purpose of deception. Yet not everyone who commits a fallacy intends to do so. He may well believe that he is offering an honest argument, but by error or by ignorance he argues fallaciously. Studying fallacies not only helps protect us from the bad arguments of others, it also helps protect us from our own.

Biologists who do taxonomy are classified by their colleagues into two categories: the splitters and the lumpers. The splitters are ones who divide animals and plants into a number of small categories, whereas the lumpers are ones who dump them into a few big ones. When it comes to the classification of fallacies, there are also splitters and lumpers. Some set up a number of smaller boxes within bigger boxes, while others make do with a few large bins.

There's no particular magic in any of the common schemes of classification, and they all have good points. Lumping has the disadvantage of failing to call attention to certain distinctive features of fallacies. On the other hand, splitting has the disadvantage of creating so many distinct categories that they can't all be kept in mind.

Since the primary purpose of talking about fallacies in this book is to warn people about recurrent kinds of bad arguments and to help them detect such arguments in ordinary affairs, it's perhaps better to lump than to split. In any case, that's what will be done, and before talking about the fallacies themselves, we need to take a quick look at how they are going to be lumped.

"Fallacies of Irrelevance" and "Fallacies of Evidence" are given over to fallacies that are most often involved in *making a case* for a position. "Fallacies of Irrelevance" deals primarily with specific ways in which the premises of an argument may be irrelevant to the conclusion. "Fallacies of Evidence" is concerned with ways in which the premises fail to give appropriate sorts of evidence or grounds for the conclusion. Both of these general types of fallacies have historically been called *material* fallacies because each concerns the relevance or adequacy of the material (facts or reasons) mentioned in the premises.

Material fallacies are frequently distinguished from linguistic fallacies, which are bad arguments resulting from the incorrect or improper use of language. If, for example, an ambiguous word is used in one way in the premises of an argument and another way in the conclusion, this is a particular kind of linguistic fallacy. Linguistic fallacies aren't discussed at all in this chapter. Even though it goes against tradition to omit them, the truth of the matter is they occur in ordinary arguments so seldom that an adequate treatment of them is hardly worth the time.

All fallacies discussed are informal or inductive fallacies. Deductive fallacies are mistakes in arguments that can be traced to an argument's logical form. Deductive fallacies are, in fact, just invalid argument forms. (See the preceding chapter on the matter of an argument's form.) Most ordinary arguments aren't deductive ones, and accordingly, most ordinary fallacies aren't deductive ones. So for the same reason that informal linguistic fallacies aren't discussed—their rarity—formal or deductive fallacies aren't discussed either.

These first two sections deal with errors of argument that are committed in making a case for a claim, in arguing for a position. "Sophistical Refutations" and "Sophistical Defenses" have a different orientation. "Sophistical Refutations" is concerned with illegitimate ways of criticizing or attempting to refute a claim. That is, the interest is in *counterarguments,* arguments *against* a position. Most of the fallacies discussed are ones which *could* be used in arguing for a positive claim, so they could be put among the fallacies in the first two sections. But because as a matter of fact they are most often used to refute some positive claim, it seems better to group them together and apart.

"Sophistical Defenses" deals with illegitimate techniques used in defending a claim against counterarguments. The techniques really aren't arguments, and technically it's not correct to call them fallacies, for to be a fallacious argument something must first be an argument. Yet devices of defense are so closely tied to arguments that there is good reason to talk about them in that connection. As a matter of fact, not all of the techniques of criticism and attack in "Sophistical Refutations" are arguments, either. Accordingly, the more general term "sophistries" seems best suited to refer to both sorts of illegitimate procedures.

Most of the fallacies and some of the sophistries have traditional Latin names. It's useful to know these names simply because they are ones that are known and used by most people who talk about arguments. (No one should think, by the way, that errors in reasoning with Latin names belong to the medieval era and are out of fashion today. They are still very much with us, as a careful look at the newspapers and at textbooks will show. They are still included in books of informal logic because they are persistent and frequent errors of argument, not out of piety. Our physics may be better than that of the medievals, but our reasoning, or lack of it, seems to be about the same.)

The advantage of having names is that they help us to keep in mind the things named and to identify them when we see them. Names, English or Latin, aren't of basic importance, though. What is important is the ability to detect flawed arguments and sophistries. This chapter can be regarded as an exhibit of such materials, and reading it as one way of gaining familiarity with them. In the same way that a geology museum displays labeled examples of common minerals, this chapter displays labeled examples of common errors of reasoning.

Fallacies of Irrelevance

"Goodness had nothing to do with it."

MAE WEST

The premises of an argument are supposed to provide reasons or evidence for asserting the conclusion. That is, a conclusion is supposed to be supported or justified by the premises. One way of challenging arguments, which we have already talked about, consists in raising an objection on the grounds that an argument's premises are not relevant to the conclusion. The premises don't support the conclusion because they aren't connected with it in any way. They neither count for it nor against it. They are impertinent, irrelevant, and beside the point.

Just as there are a variety of ways in which an argument can be bad, so there are a variety of ways in which the premises of an argument can be irrelevant. The fallacies discussed below are ones that involve making specific sorts of irrelevant appeals. The kind of irrelevant material appealed to gives each fallacy its name. Since there are certain materials which, though irrelevant, are more likely to *seem* relevant or to influence our judgment in favor of an argument's conclusion, fallacies that depend on such materials are the ones we will consider.

Appeal to Ignorance

Argumentum ad Ignorantiam (Argument to Ignorance)

Item from the *The Iceberg,* official publication of the Cryogenics Society:

> Mr. Morton M. Miller, one of the charter members of the Society, addressed the Duluth chapter last Tuesday evening. "Few people realize at present," Mr. Miller said in his talk, "that cryogenic preservation and eventual restoration is a real alternative to bodily death. No one has ever conclusively demonstrated that the maintenance of a body at low temperatures and its eventual restoration to normal functioning is an impossibility. Scientific evidence is on our side, and the gibes of scoffers we can afford to dismiss as the brayings of uninformed asses."

Mr. Miller has, wittingly or unwittingly, committed the *ad ignorantiam* fallacy. He has argued this way: Claim C hasn't been shown to be false, therefore C is true. He has used the failure to find evidence against a claim as evidence *for* the claim. In doing so, Mr. Miller is shirking his duty. The person who takes a position, as Mr. Miller does, bears the burden of proof, and he must come up with reasons and evidence that support his claim. It's quite illegitimate for him to say he regards his claim as true just because no one has *disproved* it. We want to know the reasons *for* it—why we should accept it—not merely be told that there aren't any reasons against it.

The Appeal to Ignorance has two forms, actually. The first was the one in Mr. Miller's argument:

1. Claim C is true, because it has not been shown to be false.

The second form is just the opposite of this:

2. Claim C is false, because it has not been shown to be true.

The second form involves the assumption that a lack of evidence for a claim is the same as evidence against it. In general, this is obviously absurd. "Mars has a molten core" is a claim for which there is no evidence. Is the claim false? Who knows? There's no evidence one way or the other. If the question can ever be investigated, it may turn out to be false. But it's certainly not false because we don't have any evidence that it's true! If the question could be settled in this way, we could save a great deal of money on space exploration.

But there is a problematic aspect to the second form. It's this: For certain kinds of claims we do take a lack of evidence for them as evidence against them. Suppose Lyons spends eight years in the Himalayas investigating the claim, "There is a manlike creature, the *yeti,* or abominable snowman, that inhabits the mountains." After repeated failure to find any evidence supporting this claim, Lyons would be justified in concluding, "There is no abominable snowman in the Himalayas."

Or, to take an absurd case, it's not fallacious to conclude that there is no seal in your bathtub on the grounds that you have looked in the bathtub and found no seal there. Generally speaking, then, after efforts have been made to discover and examine any evidence that *would* be available if a claim. Typically, it comes in a jumble of arguments, some of which may that the claim is false. Notice, though, that this is quite different from asserting that a claim is false when no effort to investigate the claim has been made.

The Appeal to Ignorance is hardly ever used as the sole argument for a claim. Typically it comes in a jumble of arguments, some of which may not be fallacies. Its job is usually only to try to add a bit more persuasiveness to a position. And more often than not, the *ad ignorantiam* is committed in a futile attempt to provide a reason for something which people would like to believe. "After all," people say to themselves and others, "we don't know all there is to know. Nobody has ever shown that there *isn't* any orgone energy, or that telepathy is *impossible,* that God *doesn't* exist, that spirits *don't* speak to the living, that the stars have *no* influence on human life" and so on and on. The *ad ignorantiam* is a straw in the wind which the desperate grasp in lieu of a sturdier support.

Appeal to Authority
Argumentum ad Verecundiam (Argument to Veneration)

A couple of decades ago it was fashionable to smile superciliously at scholars in the Middle Ages who relied upon Aristotle for information about how many teeth a horse has. Supposedly these scholars were so unscientific and so awed by Aristotle's authority that it never occurred to them to go out and count a horse's teeth. But when we ask ourselves certain questions we quickly realize that the way we acquire most of our information is not so different:

- How do we know the structure of the DNA molecule is a double helix?
- How do we know that Alpha Centauri is the star nearest to our solar system?
- How do we know that Caesar crossed the Rubicon?

Most of us believe these things to be true, but how many of us have at our command the evidence needed to demonstrate them? How many of us have *collected* such evidence? Very few. We believe them because they are handed down to us from people who are in a position to know, from people who have collected and evaluated evidence. It's probably no exaggeration to say that the greatest proportion of knowledge that each of has about the world has been acquired from some authority or other. Life is short, and the world is large. We can't learn everything by ourselves.

If authority is so important in determining what we claim to know, then why is it a fallacy to appeal to authority in argument? Well, it's not always illegitimate to cite authorities in support of a claim, but it sometimes is. It's important to notice under what conditions an appeal is appropriate and under what conditions it's not.

An authority, roughly speaking, is a person who is particularly knowledgeable in some field. Because of his education, training, or experience, he has acquired a special competence. In usual terms, he is an expert. He is someone whose opinion counts for more than does an ordinary opinion. But it's here that we must be careful. His opinion counts for more than other opinions *in the field in which he is an expert*.

Plato pointed out around twenty-three hundred years ago that men who are experts in one area are typically inclined to believe they are experts in all areas. This is an understandable foible of people who take themselves very seriously. Movie actors on TV talk shows are forever handing down expert opinions on psychoanalysis, the value of genetic research, and myriad other matters which fall wholly outside the scope of their competence. A host of M.D.s have behaved for years as if the practice of general medicine also makes them experts in clinical psychology, nutritional biology, archeology, and ethics. Hardly any person expert in any field hasn't also fancied himself expert in philosophy.

The world is filled with experts, and one of the ways that the *ad verecundiam* fallacy is committed is this: An expert in field F makes an assertion A about a matter belonging to field G and the only reason he gives for A is the implied reason that he is an expert in F.

Consider the opinion of Harold Hitt, M.D., a specialist in internal medicine:

> It has been clear to me for some time that the social problems of ghetto dwellers are due primarily to the matriarchal family structure.

We are supposed to accept such claims as these for no other reason than that they are uttered by an expert of some kind or other. Oddly enough, people often *do* accept them. So overimpressed are we by any sort of expert that sometimes he need only speak for us to believe. But Dr. Hitt can't legitimately sit back on his prestige and hand down social scientific generalizations with no more grounds for them than his own opinion. He has committed the expert's version of the fallacy of appealing to authority.

Here is the way that we, the nonexperts, commit the fallacy: As grounds or reasons for the assertion A about a matter belonging to field G, we cite the opinion of an expert in field F. For example:

> The social problems of ghetto dwellers are due primarily to the matriarchal family structure. This has been clearly stated as so by medical expert Dr. Harold Hitt. Thus, taking this as established. . .

These ways of arguing are fallacious for the grounds for the conclusions are really no grounds at all. The fact that a person is an expert in F is not relevant to establishing a claim not belonging to F. Such an appeal to authority gives no more support to an assertion than repeating it in a loud voice does.

Yet there is a similar way of arguing by appealing to authority that is legitimate. Obviously it's this: As grounds or reasons for an assertion A about a matter belonging to field F, we cite the opinion of an expert in field F. Thus, if asked to supply a reason for believing that the genetic material DNA has the structure of a double helix (like two rubber bands twisted together), we might quite legitimately cite the authority of James D. Watson , Francis Crick, or any other reputable biochemist or molecular biologist. We take the authority of such people as grounds for our assertions only because they are in a position to provide reasons and evidence to back them up. In a sense, we let their authority act as a stand-in for evidence. We make an assertion on their authority, and to this extent we act for them. We repeat what they have said. Upon challenge to the claim, they are the ones who must put up, not us. We escape our responsibilities in such cases, for we are not in a position to know. They are in a position, and like a blind man leaning on the arm of a friend, we lean on the experts.

Needless to say, it's a different game for the expert. He isn't free to make assertions to his fellow experts and expect them to take his word for it. It would be ludicrous for James D. Watson to say to Linus Pauling, "DNA has the structure of a double helix; I say this on my own expert authority." To others who are also in a position to judge, the expert has to present the grounds for his claims. The promissory notes which he issues to laymen are called in by other experts. If on demand he can't put up, then he must shut up.

The grounds which we as nonexperts have for accepting an assertion may be that it has the *imprimatur* of an authority. This may justify *our* acceptance, but it clearly doesn't justify the assertion in general. Like any other claim, it must be supported by argument. In appealing to a proper authority, we are merely admitting that we are not competent to decide the matter for ourselves.

But what shall we do when the doctors disagree? When a claim about a specialized matter is supported by the unanimous opinion of authorities in the appropriate area, an appeal to this opinion is forceful support for relying on the claim. But issues constantly arise in which diversity of opinion reigns. Expert speaks against expert. One says that our continuing to spew fluorocarbons into the atmosphere will result in an ecological disaster. Another says the practice is basically harmless. One says that underground atomic explosions will produce dangerously high levels of radiation in the atmosphere. Another says the levels will be quite safe. What are we to do?

Very little can be done. The best thing possible, perhaps, is to avoid appeals to authority to support claims in areas where there are no established and generally accepted views. But if push comes to shove and it is necessary to cite an expert, then it's important to pay close attention to who he is. First, does he occupy a position of professional prestige, one that he wouldn't hold if his fellow experts didn't have a high opinion of his qualifications and competence? Professional reputation isn't so important in technical matters not under dispute. Settled doctrines can be assumed to be known to all people in a field. But disputed questions should make us more careful *which* experts we listen to.

Second, and most important in controversial matters, is the expert cited one who is disinterested? That is, is he free from any suspicion of prejudice about the matter which is under dispute? A scientist who works for the Atomic Energy Commission may be just as honest and competent as one who doesn't. Yet the fact that he works for the AEC does mean that there is a possibility that what he says about the lack of hazard in atomic testing may be influenced, consciously or unconsciously, in a way favorable to the AEC. Not necessarily, just possibly. And just because of this possibility, he would not be the best expert to appeal to on issues of radiation dangers. Someone with similar qualifications not employed by the AEC or by an other governmental agency would be a better source. Even experts are subject to political pressures.

People sophisticated enough in argument to avoid the *ad verecundiam* fallacy often hurl themselves into another fallacy. They assume that if a man is an authority in one field and he is arguing for a claim in another field, then what he says is of no value. For example:

> I've heard what Truman Capote has to say about prison reform. But the man is only a writer! If he wants to give advice about literature, I'll listen. Otherwise I won't.

Such a dismissal is only a special form of the *ad hominem* (see below) fallacy. It consists in dismissing a claim because of the personal characteristics of the person who presents the argument. But all arguments must be judged in their own terms. The expert cannot call upon his authority when arguing a matter not in the area of his expertise, but this doesn't mean that he has to remain silent on such matters. Rather, his argument for a claim must be judged in the same way as anyone else's is. His authority shouldn't add any extra strength to his argument, nor should it count against it. It is irrelevant in both directions.

Nicholas Murray Butler unintentionally contributed to the world's storehouse of clichés when he defined an expert as "a man who knows more and more about less and less." The cliché hits close to the truth, and keeping in mind the limitations of experts may help to avoid illegitimate appeals to authority. An authority is an authority in the relevant sense only when he speaks from the chair of his own field. Otherwise he's just like the rest of us incompetents.

Appeal to Pity
Argumentum ad Misericordiam (Argument to Pity)

"Pity melts the mind," said the poet Dryden. As human beings we are as capable of sympathizing with the pains of others as we are of rational thought—even Scrooge turned out to be more than a cash register in the shape of a man. Consequently, our ability to recognize and empathize with the sorrows and circumstances of other people sometimes leads us to be moved by considerations which are, strictly speaking, irrelevant to a topic being discussed. The *ad misericordiam* involves playing on this tendency. It consists in attempting to persuade someone to accept a claim by mentioning factors which might be expected to influence his sympathies.

Around schools and colleges the all-time favorite appeal to pity runs something like this.

> If I don't pass this course, I won't be able to graduate in the Spring, and I don't have enough money to go to summer school. Really, Professor Ruston, you just *have* to give me a C.

In the wider forest outside the groves of Academe, arguments like this aren't uncommon.

> Economic conditions are very tough at the moment. Our quarterly profits are down, and stockholders are beginning to put pressure on management. We

already spend more than a half-million dollars a year on pollution control. It's not reasonable to ask us to spend more at this point in time.

Apparently we are supposed to feel pity for the corporate person—the company—but, of course, it's really the persons representing the company, those responsible for its operation, that offer themselves as objects of pity. How could we be so callous and unfeeling as to want to make their jobs harder by demanding that they put an end to their company's pollution? Besides, Chem Products, Hi-Pro Oil and Refining, and so on are such *nice*, warm, friendly companies that, if they are having problems now, it seems cruel to put them to even more trouble. Generating sympathy for a business corporation may be a hard job, but there are professionals who devote themselves to it. It's all a part of image making. It pays dividends, too, and quite literally so.

Probably ever since men have put one another on trial, the *ad misericordiam* has played a role in both defense and prosecution. Fallacy it may be, but this doesn't mean that it can't be used effectively in the hands of a skillful lawyer. Here is an example which gives an idea of its force.

> I want you to consider that whatever these men may have done, they did it out of a sincere desire to help us all. They wanted their candidate to win, because they thought it was in the best interest of the country. Shall we punish them now for their concern for us? Shall we take them away from their wives and children, lock them up with muggers and rapists? What a poor show of gratitude that would be!
>
> I don't think you will be able to find in your hearts the callousness and ingratitude necessary to send these men to prison. They have suffered so much now, that I know you will not want them to suffer more.

The *ad misericordiam* is a particularly tough fallacy to identify in some cases. Not all mention of factors which appeal to our sympathies is irrelevant, and the trick is to distinguish legitimate appeals from spurious ones. Suppose someone argued, for example, that our system of welfare payments ought to be changed because it produces much misery and suffering. As evidence, he describes cases in which people on welfare are harshly and unfairly treated. The situation he presents is a moving one, but is he guilty of using an *ad misericordiam* argument? Not necessarily. One of the standards by which social policies and institutions are judged is the extent to which they alleviate human suffering. Accordingly, the fact that people are made miserable by a system not only elicits our pity; it counts as a reason for altering the system. It would be quite relevant in an argument demanding a change in welfare policies and practices.

Consider another case. A seventeen-year-old boy is arrested on a narcotics charge. At the trial his attorney paints a bleak picture of the young man's life: homeless since the age of ten, abandoned by his mother, raised in poverty by a distant cousin, unable to keep a job because of illness, and so on. The attorney argues that the boy should be given a suspended sentence and put in a program of counseling and job training. Are these sympathy-inducing facts *irrelevant* to this conclusion? Of course not. They are mitigating circumstances, ones that have a direct bearing on the kind of sentence the defendent should receive if he is guilty. They are not precisely excusing conditions, but they are factors which, given the aims of society and the laws of society, are relevant in deciding how his case should be dealt with.

There is no easy way to determine when an appeal to pity is being made. A risk to be avoided is assuming that the fallacy is being committed just because an argument has premises that mention matters that do elicit our pity. As the examples above show, not all such arguments are fallacious. The only true test is the quite general one: Are the premises relevant to the conclusion, or do they *only* appeal to our feelings of pity?

Appeal to Force
Argumentum ad Baculum (Argument to the Rod)

"When reason is against a man, a man will be against reason," Thomas Hobbes observed. Hobbes' dictum is much too strong, but nonetheless, it's often illustrated in practice. Attempts at rational persuasion have no guaranteed success, and after a person has failed to get someone to accept a claim on the basis of argument, he may be inclined to try other means. The *ad baculum* fallacy is committed when force or the threat of force is used to coerce someone into acting in accordance with a certain claim or policy. For example:

> I have exhausted my patience with you, Mr. Findley. I have done all I can to persuade you that selling the plans for the bombsight to my government would be the right thing for you to do. I'm afraid you now leave me no choice. Let me tell you this, if you do not give us the plans, your crippled wife, your blind daughter, and your poor bedridden mother will be—shall we say—sent to a happier place. Now what do you say, American pig?

The *ad baculum* is a rather peculiar sort of fallacy. Unlike most other fallacies, it doesn't involve an attempt to get people to *believe* a conclusion by presenting irrelevant or inadequate reasons. Its aim is merely to get people to *behave* in a certain way: namely, in the way that they would if they were convinced of the truth of the conclusion.

The Appeal to Force is used in fashions more subtle than our crude example above suggests. It's the subtle uses that are more widespread, for appeals to self-interest are quite often expressed in *ad baculum* fashion. Consider:

> (a) As you may know, Governor, there are very many suburban land-owners who would be quite disappointed if you vetoed the bill prohibiting welfare housing developments in their areas. They represent, I suppose, one of the most influential political groups in the state.

(b) Mr. Chancellor, my advice to you is to expel the students involved in the disturbance without a hearing. Otherwise, the Board is certain to step in and question the way you've handled the situation.

What is said in these two cases counts for nothing in establishing the claims: (a) *You should not veto the bill,* and (b) *The students should be expelled without a hearing.* The reasons given for the acceptance of the conclusions are irrelevant ones, and the point of each of the arguments is to get someone to act in a particular way. Again, unlike most arguments, even fallacious ones, the *ad baculum* doesn't aim at persuading someone to *believe* a conclusion, but only in getting him to *behave* in the same way as he would if he did believe it. Persuasion is directed toward action, not belief.

Appeal to Popular Attitudes
Argumentum ad Populum (Argument to the People)

Samuel Butler rather cynically observed that "The public buys its opinions as it buys its milk, on the principle that it is cheaper to do so than to keep a cow." People are undeniably inclined to buy opinions that conform to what they already believe or would like to believe. An automatic acceptance of claims that fit in comfortably with attitudes already held saves the pain and effort of critical thought.

The loves and hates, the fears and hopes, the prejudices and attitudes of a group of people constitute crucial raw material for the demagogue and the double-dealer. Manipulation of the materials can encourage the acceptance of a claim by a considerable part of the group. The *ad populum* fallacy is committed by appealing to a group's prejudices and attitudes, rather than to relevant reasons and evidence.

Precisely what attitudes are chosen for use in such a way depends upon the group. The attitudes of the Jewish Defense League are obviously not the same as those of the American Nazi Party. An argument that suggested that a political candidate should be rejected because he is Jewish could hardly be expected to persuade Arthur Goldberg. No Black Panther is likely to be moved by an appeal based on the outstanding characteristics of the white man. In short, the *ad populum* arguer must be careful to tailor his argumet to fit the group it's addressed to. If he chooses the wrong approach, counts on an attitude that's not there, he is likely to do more harm than good for his position.

Some arguments are addressed to the public at large, of course. General or widespread attitudes and prejudices are thus the ones appealed to. The object is to hit the ones that move the largest number of people. The most frequent sorts of popular sentiments to be milked are probably these:

a. Patriotism (including love of democracy, hatred of communism, fascism, etc.)

b. Dislike of change (including love of tradition, the "old ways," veneration of people associated with the old ways, etc.)
c. Dislike of the eccentric or unusual (strange clothes, uncommon habits, peculiar beliefs, etc.)
d. Taking obligations seriously (doing a job, caring for a family, carrying out orders, etc.)
e. Racial, religious, social prejudices

These are general categories, of course, and the specific way in which an appeal is pitched depends upon immediate circumstances. Patriotism, for example, is no longer appealed to in the blatant jingoistic manner that it once was (well, at least not as often). Appeals are now phrased in a more sophisticated fashion:

> No one should oppose the President's economic policies. We are in great economic difficulties, and if we expect to overcome them, we must group together and give our wholehearted support to the man who has the job of leading us.

No longer do demagogic politicians who want to maintain a good image refer openly to niggers, kikes, wops, spicks, and the like. Instead they make oblique or "coded" references to racial or religious groups and attempt to exploit the prejudices of their audiences without being too obvious about it:

> We are opposed to building the federal drug treatment center here in River Oaks, because we feel it would bring in too many outsiders, and this would tend to destroy the unity of our community.

"Outsiders," of course, are usually the Black, the Spanish-speaking, and the poor.

The use of code words generally means that the reason the arguer offers for his conclusion is not the *real* reason he has in mind. The code word or words in the premises help him convey his real reason in a disguised form. That is, they supply hints that awaken prejudices and tap the audience's attitudes. The hints are a tip-off to the group that the arguer shares their attitudes, that he's one of them. "This plan will bring outsiders into our community" may mean "This plan will bring Blacks into our community, and we certainly don't want that." But the arguer also presents an apparently legitimate reason ("It will destroy the unity of our community"), so a member of a group addressed can assuage his rational conscience at the same time as he satisfies his prejudices. What's more, the arguer has given him grounds he can use in arguing with others, grounds that allow him to avoid looking like a bigot or sounding like a fool.

Almost every argument about matters of social importance has *ad populum* aspects. Who could argue that racial discrimination ought to be ended without appealing to sentiments of justice and fair treatment? A totally bloodless argument would be all but impossible. An *ad populum* appeal does not, by itself, destroy the value of an argument. The argument is a fallacy when it rests on *nothing more* than an appeal to the attitudes and prejudices of a group.

Fallacy of Stress

The nineteenth-century legal philosopher Jeremy Bentham is supposed to have deliberately hired as a reader a man who spoke only in a monotonous monotone. Bentham was willing to bear the tedium of listening to the man, because he was afraid that a more dramatic reader would mislead him by emphasizing certain words. As Bentham realized, one of the features of natural languages like English is that when stress is laid on different words in the same sentence its meaning often changes. The stress indicates how a sentence is to be understood, and stressing different words allows the same sentence to be used to make different claims or to imply different things about a situation.

Consider the brief sentence "Eat your soup." No matter where the stress is laid, or even if there is virtually no stress, the sentence is a command to eat your soup. Yet stress can be used to imply various things about the context in which it is spoken. If the "eat" is stressed ("EAT your soup"), this suggests there is only one appropriate thing for you to do with your soup and you aren't doing it. The stress doesn't imply that you are washing your fingers in your soup or merely contemplating it, but it does imply that you are doing something besides eating it. Emphasizing the "your" ("Eat YOUR soup") implies that it's not proper for you to eat anyone else's soup and the correct thing to do is to eat your own. "Eat your SOUP" suggests you are eating the wrong dish and you ought to be eating soup.

It's easy to imagine situations in which each of the three words of "Eat your soup" would be stressed with the intent of expressing more or less what these three interpretations do. Too, it's possible to imagine cases in which the stress would be used to imply something different from the interpretations. But the point of importance here is only that by emphasizing different words the same sentence can be made to imply different things.

Strictly speaking, merely stressing a word in a sentence or failing to stress one doesn't constitute an argument. Yet because it's possible to alter the meaning of a sentence by changing or adding stress and because stress does influence what a sentence implies, stress can become a device for fallacious argument. The fallacy of stress is committed when a sentence whose meaning has been altered by stress is used in an argument. Since the significance of the original sentence is changed by altering stress, then the altered sentence is irrelevant to the argument's conclusion.

One way of committing the fallacy of stress involves perverting the meaning of a sentence and making it imply what it was not intended to imply. This is done often in connection with generally accepted social and moral principles. For example:

> Our form of government rests on the principle that all men are BORN equal. It is, thus, perfectly in accord with this principle to hold that only those who have acquired a certain amount of property or achieved a certain level or income should be permitted to vote in Presidential elections.

The stress on "born" in the premise of this argument is used to make it appear that the principle "All men are born equal" applies only to people at the time of birth and not throughout life. On this interpretation, all people start out equal but as some become richer than others, inequalities develop. These inequalities, it's suggested, can then serve as a basis for determining who is eligible to vote for a President. Supposedly this way of deciding doesn't violate the principle, for the inequalities are ones which develop long after birth. But this argument that the principle is not violated rests on a perversion of the principle. Its intended meaning is that in matters such as deciding who shall govern the nation, all citizens are born with *and retain* equal rights.

A second way of committing the fallacy of stress involves the familiar device of quoting out of context. The stress in such cases is not vocal emphasis, but it is still verbal emphasis. A quotation may be pared in such a way that its author is represented as holding a position he didn't express. Or by being jerked out of its surroundings, a quotation may seem to imply something the author never intended to imply. The use of such quotations in an argument constitutes the fallacy of stress just as much as does verbal emphasis.

Chopping up sentences and paragraphs from reviews of movies, plays, and books to make it appear the reviewer has a high opinion of the work is an all too familiar practice. Such dirty work goes on often enough to make everyone aware of this form of the stress fallacy, and it requires little to illustrate it. Everyone is acquainted with cases in which sentences like "*The Ragged Edge* is a movie everyone ought to see if he wants to appreciate what happens when a crew of incompetent writers teams up with an incompetent director" become ones like "*The Ragged Edge* is a movie everyone ought to see . . . ."

Just as familiar is the slightly more subtle practice of lifting out a sentence from its surroundings. Out of the matrix of the sentences that set the tone and catalogue qualifications, a sentence taken alone may represent a point of view quite different from the one the author intended. Richard Schickel, in reviewing a movie called *Doctors' Wives,* for example, wrote, "George Schaefer's direction is every bit as witty and urbane as the script." Read alone, this ordinarily would be taken to mean Schaefer's direction is witty and urbane and so is the script. But in the context of the review it's easy to see that the sentence is ironic. It appears after a discussion which stresses the imbecility of the script, and without the benefit of this discussion, it's not possible to detect the sentence's ironic tone.

Quotations out of context, in general, are more often than not used only as incomplete or unformulated arguments. Thus, "The critic John Hicks said, '*The Ragged Edge* is a movie everyone ought to see' " suggests an argument along this line:

A movie critic is an expert appraiser of movies.

It's a good policy to follow expert advice.

John Hicks is a critic who believes everyone ought to see *The Ragged Edge*.

Therefore, you ought to see *The Ragged Edge*.

Of course no one in real life ever actually formulates such an argument, even to himself. Nevertheless, quoting someone whose opinion is valued is generally understood as presenting a reason for doing or not doing something. Thus it's possible to see such quotations as crypto-arguments. In this respect, quotation out of context commits the fallacy of stress, even though the quotation doesn't appear as a premise in an explicit argument.

Fallacies of Evidence

> *Just the place for a Snark! I have said it thrice:*
> *What I tell you three times is true.*
>
> LEWIS CARROLL
> *The Hunting of the Snark*

Contrary to what Lewis Carroll's Bellman appears to believe, merely saying something, even saying it three times, doesn't amount to a sufficient reason to accept what is said. To assume that it does is to fall prey to a fallacy concerning the ground (or lack of it) on which a claim rests. An argument fails, as we just saw in the last section, if its premises are *irrelevant* to its conclusion in one of many possible ways. Irrelevance is connected with the reasons or evidence put forward to support a claim, but irrelevance isn't the only type of failure connected with reasons and evidence. In discussing ways of challenging arguments, we've already mentioned that, with respect to acceptable arguments, there is an implicit demand that the premises should provide *adequate* support for the conclusion and that they should represent relevant information *fairly*. Here we need to describe a few of the specific ways in which the evidence or reasons expressed in the premises can fail to provide adequate or appropriate support for the conclusion and thus produce flawed arguments—fallacies of evidence.

False Cause
Post hoc, ergo propter hoc. (After this, therefore because of this.)

A GREEK MYTH

Orpheus played his lyre so beautifully that all things on the earth and above it and below it were moved by his music. Every morning he sat on a hillside facing the sea and played, and the power of his playing was such that it caused the sun to rise in the heavens.

If we took this myth quite literally, we could say that it embodies the fallacy of False Cause. The control over the sun ascribed to Orpheus' playing is based on the observation that *after* he played, the sun came up. The *post hoc* fallacy is committed by arguing that just because an event A is followed by (or accompanied by) an event B, then A is the cause of B. Thus, to say that Orpheus' playing *caused* the sun to rise is to argue fallaciously. (Not that anybody ever intended the myth to be interpreted in such a dull and literal-minded way.)

Causal arguments, even ones about ordinary events, are quite intricate. This isn't the place to try to analyze them in detail, but a couple of points need to be considered just to show why the *post hoc* is a fallacy.

The claim that a particular event A (striking a match) under certain conditions (in a gas-filled room) *caused* a particular event B (an explosion) goes beyond the immediate situation. The claim really rests on the more general claim "Whenever an event of kind A occurs under conditions of kind C, then an event of kind B will occur." (Of course it's possible, and sometimes necessary to be more precise than this. Exactly how much gas has to be in the room, for example? And if an explosion doesn't occur, why didn't it?)

General statements of this sort are causal laws. Though we may never explicitly state them to ourselves, we still rely on them in an implicit way. We are able to identify causal connections between events only by means of experience, only because we have learned that events of a certain type are always followed by events of another type when the conditions are right. If our experiences didn't repeat themselves in a general way, if each event was unique in every respect, then we would never be able to grasp causal connections. Like the proverbial goose who wakes up in a new world every morning, we would have no understanding of cause and effect relations.

The fact that an event of kind B follows an event of kind A is certainly relevant to establishing a causal relation between events of the two kinds. But it's not *adequate*. It's just a single case, and in that one case we have no guarantee that the relation between the two is not wholly accidental—like having the phone ring when you just happen to be pointing at it. We want to be assured that there are a number of cases which will support a general claim like "Whenever an event of kind A occurs under circumstances C, an event of kind B follows." If the phone rang every time you pointed your finger at it, it would start to look like pointing your finger caused the phone to ring. In any case, only when we have adequate evidence for accepting the general claim can we start to feel justified in saying that A is the cause of B.

The requirement that there must be a constant connection between events of the two types gives us an assurance that they aren't merely gratuitously associated. This requirement is enough to indicate why the *post hoc* is a fallacy: It is simply not true that in every case in which one event follows another, the first is the cause of the second.

Here, in this old joke, is an example of the *post hoc* fallacy. The case is one in which two events are clearly arbitrarily associated:

> A farmer was traveling with his wife on a train when he saw a man across the aisle take something out of a bag and begin eating it. "Say Mister," he asked, "what's that thing you're eating?"
> "It's a banana," the man said. "Here, try one."
> The farmer took it, peeled it, and just as he swallowed the first bite, the train roared into a tunnel.
> "Don't eat any, Maude," he yelled to his wife. "It'll make you go blind!"

There are tests for causal connections other than mere repetition. For example, does an event of the second kind occur when the situation is the same as usual except that an event of the first kind doesn't take place? If it does, then the first isn't the cause of the second, even though it always precedes it. The sun would rise even if Orpheus didn't play his lyre.

In the "age of science" *post hoc* fallacies are perhaps not as frequent as they once were. But they have by no means completely disappeared from the scene. There are still people who believe that the stars direct their lives just because every now and then a vaguely phrased horoscope accidently coincides with what actually happens to them. Faith healers still attract thousands of adherents just because some people recover from their ailments after the healer has laid on his hands.

The *post hoc* fallacy is also committed when two traits which are merely associated with one another are said to be causally related. For years the *Wall Street Journal* has claimed that "Men who get ahead in business read the *Wall Street Journal*," in the same way as we might say "Men who get ahead in business have five fingers on each hand." A fact, perhaps, but a rather trivial one. Obviously, of course, this isn't the way the slogan is intended to be interpreted. We're clearly asked to believe that "Men who get ahead in business do so *because* they read the *Wall Street Journal*." If we bought this claim, then any sensible man who wanted to be a success in business would immediately take out a subscription to the *Wall Street Journal*. But should we buy it? Probably not. The connection between business success and reading the *Wall Street Journal* is not likely to be a causal one. It's much more likely that the characteristics that make people successful in business are also ones that incline them to read the *Wall Street Journal*. In any case, there's obviously more to becoming successful than reading a newspaper.

Causal arguments are slippery and difficult to judge. But in spite of this, avoiding the *post hoc* fallacy isn't all that difficult. It's necessary only to keep in mind that simple sequence or mere association isn't enough to establish a causal connection. Whether the two events constantly accompany one another and whether if one fails to occur, then the other doesn't occur either are just some of the further tests that have to be met.

The Gambler's Fallacy

A brief tale:

> The noise in the casino died to a murmur, but an almost tangible tension took its place. All attention locked on the green baize dice table where David Starr stood. Starr's face was impassive as he gazed at the pile of chips in the center of the table. Only the way in which his fingers tapped the sides of the leather dice cup betrayed the strain he was under.
> "What do you think, Margo?" he asked the lithe girl standing beside him. "Shall I take the pot or let it ride for another toss?"
> She bowed her head for a moment and then looked up. "I think you had better take it, David. You've thrown four sevens in a row, and that means your chance of throwing one on this next round is considerably less than it was."
> Starr nodded, "I suppose you're right." At his signal, the croupier pushed the stacks of chips across the table. A disappointed buzz broke the silence of the watching crowd.
>
> (The End)

Margo's advice to Starr may have been good from a practical point of view—when you have that many stacks of chips it might be best to run *no* risk of losing them. But her argument to the effect that Starr's chances of rolling a seven on the next round are diminished, because he has already rolled four in a row, is a fallacy. Starr's chances of rolling a seven are exactly the same as they were when he picked up the dice. They are always the same, no matter how many times he's rolled a seven (or any other number) in the past. Margo has committed one version of the Gambler's Fallacy.

The Gambler's Fallacy consists in arguing that one or more occurrences of a chance event with a certain probability changes the probability of the event's occurrence in the future.

It doesn't. To see why it doesn't, let's start out by considering the simple case of flipping a coin. If a coin is flipped, there are only two possible outcomes: heads or tails. One way of figuring the probability in this case is to assume that each outcome is equally likely. Thus, the probability of throwing heads is ½ and the probability of throwing tails is ½. This assumption is justified only in cases in which the possible outcomes are distinct and can be specified in advance. It's acceptable, in practice, for cases like dice throwing, coin flipping, roulette, and card drawing. But it's not an acceptable way of dealing with cases like determining the probability of rain tomorrow or the probability that a Zuñi Indian will have an AB blood type.

In cases like the first ones, we begin by determining the total number of possible outcomes an event like tossing a coin can have. We then decide which of those outcomes are of interest to us. The ratio of this second number to the first is the probability of the outcome we're interested in.

Thus, with a two-headed coin there are only two possible outcomes: heads or tails. Suppose heads is the only one of interest to us. The probability of tossing heads, then, is HEADS/(HEADS + TAILS) or $1/(1 + 1)$. So the probability of tossing heads with a fair coin is ½. This way of determining probabilities is called the *mathematical* or *classical* way.

Cases of the second sort mentioned above require that we base probabilities on statistical records of the occurrence of an event in past sequences of events. Suppose we examine medical records and find that out of two hundred cases of known addicts who received methadone, fifty were helped by it. Roughly speaking, the probability that a patient who is an addict will be helped by methadone is 50/200, or ¼. It's necessary to say "roughly speaking" because if we studied the records for another sequence of treatments we might find a slightly different result. The probability is determined with reference to all available sequences. This way of figuring probability is called the *relative frequency* method, for the probability of an event is defined as the relative frequency of its occurrence in the long run.

We would be going too far afield to discuss these two notions at length, but it's worth noticing that the relative frequency method *could* be used to determine probabilities in cases of the coin-tossing, dice-rolling variety. A coin is flipped for several sequences, for example, and the relative frequency of heads and tails is calculated. *In the long run* the frequency of each would be about ½. Of course it might happen that for some sequences there would be many more heads than tails and vice versa, but for a long enough series of flips, heads and tails would average out to about the same number.

Not all cases dealt with by the relative frequency method can be handled by the classical method, however. In our example of the methadone treatment of addicts, the classical method would require us to say that addicts are either helped or not helped by methadone. Hence it would seem that the probability that a person will be helped is ½. But the trouble with this approach is that it just isn't plausible in such sorts of cases for us to make the assumption that the outcomes are equally plausible. The physical characteristics of coins and "fair" dice make it plausible for us to assume that each possible outcome is equally likely to happen. No such assumption is justified when we are dealing with cases like the weather, medical treatment, the probability that an individual will have a certain blood type, and so on. The only guide we can have in such matters as these is not what is possible, but what we have found to be so in the past. Experience and not pure mathematics has to be our guide.

Now, at last, back to the Gambler's Fallacy. No matter how we figure the probability of throwing dice or flipping a coin, either by the mathematical or relative frequency method, each throw or flip is independent. That is, the probability of its occurrence does not depend on what occurred before. Each occurrence is equally probable—always—either because of a justified assumption based on the physical characteristics of the coin or the dice or because of the statistical evidence concerning the way coins and dice behave. If a coin is flipped ten times and comes up heads each time, then the probability that it will come up heads the eleventh time is still ½.

The other version of the Gambler's Fallacy is just the converse of the one discussed. It consists in arguing that because an event *hasn't* occurred in a sequence, it's "due" at any time, that the likelihood of its occurrence is increased by the fact that it hasn't occurred during a sequence. Thus, if Starr had been flipping coins instead of rolling dice, Margo might have said something like "Heads has come up four times now, so there's a better than ever chance that tails will turn up on the next flip." The error is the same as the first version: Each flip is independent, and the probability of tails coming up is the same in every case.

(*Gambler's Note*: The probability of rolling a certain number with dice is more complicated than coin flipping, of course. There are two cubes, six sides, so the possible outcomes number 6 x 6 or 36. A point can be made in more than one way, except for 2 and 12. For example, 7 is a "three-way point": i.e., it can be gotten with 5 and 2, 4 and 3, or 6 and 1. Since each of the numbers could be on either dice in each case [i.e., 1 & 6, 6 & 1; 4 & 3, 3 & 4; 5 & 2, 2 & 5], there are 6 cases which yield 7. Thus the probability of rolling a 7 is 6/36. The probability is the same for each roll!)

Begging the Question
Petitio Principii (Petitioning the Principle)

"Things are seldom what they seem,/ Skim milk masquerades as cream," a Gilbert and Sullivan character laments. So it is with arguments, and question-begging arguments are perhaps the trickiest fallacies in the whole bag. Generally speaking, a question-begging argument is one that *assumes* what it purports to *demonstrate*. The "question" is, of course, the claim that the argument is offered to establish; the question is "begged" because independent grounds for it are not really given. Part of the reason why question-begging arguments are hard to detect is that there are several forms that such an argument can take—the fallacy of Begging the Question can be committed in several ways. It's useful to consider each of them separately before saying more about Begging the Question in general.

a. *When a premise of an argument is (at least roughly) equivalent in meaning to the conclusion, then the argument begs the question.* Consider this brief argument:

> The Attorney General is an odious man for the simple reason that he is hateful in every way.

The reason given for the assertion made in this case is no more than a restatement of the assertion in terms that are different but (roughly) equivalent. To be odious is to be hateful.

The limiting case of this form of begging the question consists in using exactly the same sentence as premise and as conclusion. Thus:

> Snow is white, because snow is white.

People rarely, if ever, say such things with the intent of offering them as arguments. Generally, they merely want to add emphasis to what they say: "I say he's guilty because he is." Nevertheless, if such cases *are* regarded as arguments, then they are question-begging arguments.

b. *When a claim is justified by appealing to a more general version of it and no independent evidence is offered, then the argument begs the question.*

If someone backs up the claim that "The President should support the Wildlife Protection Bill" by saying, "The President should support all bills concerning the environment," he has begged the question. For justification, he has presented only a more general form of the conclusion. For his argument to be legitimate, for his original conclusion to be genuinely supported, he must now give us evidence for the more general claim. In any case, he must support at least one of the two claims by independent evidence.

c. *When the conclusion of an argument is appealed to for the purpose of establishing one of the premises, then the argument begs the question.* This is the form of begging the question that is known as "circular argument," and probably most people have it in mind when they talk of begging the question. Schematically, the form can be represented in this way:

> C is true because A is true.
> A is true because B is true.
> B is true because C is true.

Or the form can be illustrated, appropriately enough, by a circle:

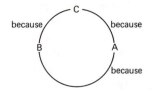

The points which make up the circle may be numerous, of course. Part of what makes a circular argument deceptive is that, if it's long enough, there is a tendency to overlook the fact that the conclusion is used to support a premise which was itself (long ago) presented in support of the conclusion.

It's difficult to give an example of a short argument which is both circular and plausible. In a short argument the circularity is rather obvious, and this makes it difficult to see how anyone could ever regard a circular argument as persuasive. But we do need an example, so we have to keep in mind that the example is quite artificial. Here, first of all, is a clear but somewhat trivial circular argument:

> All claims made in the Bible are true, for they are the words of God himself. We know the Bible represents God's word, for its writers were divinely inspired. The Bible itself makes it clear that the biblical writers wrote "at direction," and the truth of biblical statements is thus beyond doubt.

Circular arguments don't ordinarily come in such precise and obvious circles. Rather, because of vague language and the failure to make connections clear, they are only rough circles. Here is a more realistic example of a circular argument:

> There is no doubt that the policies for the development of new weapons systems formulated by the President's staff ought to be adopted. The President has the responsibility of formulating policies to be recommended to the Congress, and as a delegation of authority, he has appointed a staff to formulate policies which ought to be put into effect. His staff, in response to his charge, has now presented the Congress with the results of their deliberations.

Cutting away the verbiage and eliminating the rambling, this argument boils down to: The recommendation ought to be accepted because it was made by the President's staff, and the staff has the job of making acceptable recommendations. Put this way, the argument is more clearly circular.

The question can be begged in a number of ways; these three ways don't exhaust the alternatives. Yet they are the most common forms, and we really don't have to try to be exhaustive.

Loaded Phrases

"Give a dog a bad name and hang him," folk wisdom tells us is an effective way of dealing with opponents. If you are successful in getting a bad label pinned on them, nobody will worry much about whether they deserve it. Name-calling can undoubtedly influence attitudes, but it can also serve as the basis for a particularly insidious sort of fallacious argument. Phrases like "dangerous radical" and "permissive college administrator" go by the traditional name of "question-begging epithets."

Such phrases are question-begging because no reasons are given for believing that the person tagged with them has the characteristics they imply. Merely to dub someone a "dangerous radical" begs the question of whether he is or not. To use the phrase legitimately, it's necessary to show that the person has certain features (urges the violent overthrow of the government, throws bombs, etc.). That is he is a dangerous radical must come as the conclusion of an argument. Applying the phrase without the argument is an attempt to assume as established what must be shown.

The phrases are "loaded" because they have built into them the assumption that the person labeled with them has the traits associated with the phrase. Thus it's easy to "prove" that the person has one of those traits because he has already been *assumed* to have it. Here's an argument which uses loaded phrases:

> Because government officials are irresponsible, they have shirked their duties and allowed the intelligence agencies to violate the law.

The conclusion of the argument just repeats what is already built into the label "irresponsible." Because of this, the alleged irresponsibility of government officials can hardly be used as legitimate grounds for saying that they have shirked their duties.

Grounds which support either of the claims will support both, but they can't support each other. There must be some independent evidence given.

When loaded phrases are used in arguments the result is no different from question-begging. But again, they aren't typically used in explicit arguments. Rather, their power to suggest is exploited, and they are employed to imply things about people which need to be proved.

Loaded Questions

"Not every question deserves an answer," the Greek sage Publius once opined. Such an opinion makes Publius sound like a haughty fellow, disdainful of those who desire to learn by asking. Perhaps he was, but he was surely right about one kind of question—questions that are loaded don't deserve an answer. A loaded question is one based upon an unstated assumption, so that an answer to the question is also an indirect admission of the truth of the assumption.

A question that used to appear in the advertisements of private power companies is a good example of a loaded question: "Why is the private development of natural resources so much better than public control?" The assumption, of course, is that development by private businesses *is* better, and an attempt to answer the question, as it's put, must start out with a tacit acknowledgement that this is so. Similarly, the question "How can we stop the abuse of marijuana?" rests on the assumption that marijuana is being abused.

Loaded questions are sometimes called "complex questions" because they can be separated into two or more questions. Thus the loaded question "Why do we tolerate professors who teach treason in our universities?" can be divided into:

1. Are there professors who teach treason . . . ?
2. Do we tolerate professors who teach treason . . . ?
3. Why do we tolerate professors who teach treason . . .?

An answer to question (3) takes it for granted that the other hidden questions have been answered in the affirmative. Since a loaded question rests on one or more assumptions that are in fact answers to the unstated questions, the loaded question is just a special form of begging the question. That is, it takes for granted that which it should give reasons and evidence for.

Loaded questions aren't really arguments. Strictly speaking, then, they aren't fallacies, for only arguments can be fallacies. Yet there's reason enough to talk about them in connection with fallacies. They are attempts to get claims accepted (the hidden assumption) without presenting any adequate or legitimate grounds for them. In this respect, loaded questions resemble fallacious arguments. Besides, it doesn't make a lot of difference whether loaded questions are called fallacies or not. The important thing is that they are dangerous and misleading and should be recognized and guarded against.

A particularly tricky sort of loaded question is one that presents alternatives. For example:

Is Linda Koltz guilty of murder or only of being an accessory to murder?

Such questions are more subtle than simple loaded questions, for they give the impression that the questioner is soliciting our own independent opinion. He is, too, but only within the limits he has imposed. We are given a choice of alternatives, but there is the unspoken assumption that these are the only alternatives. We are given the choice of saying Linda Koltz is guilty either of murder or of being an accessory to murder. But this leaves us no room for saying that she is guilty of neither of these crimes but is guilty of some third offense. What's more, it leaves us no room to say she isn't guilty at all, for the question is based on the additional assumption that she is guilty. Loaded questions which offer us a choice of alternatives can thus beg several questions at once.

The obvious and best way to deal with loaded questions is to recall Publius' opinion and not answer them. Rather than giving a direct answer, split the question into its parts, uncover its assumptions, and deal with each part separately. To put this advice into practice, of course, a necessary first step is to *recognize* a question as loaded.

Sophistical Refutations

> Who can refute a sneer?
>
> WILLIAM PALEY
> *Moral Philosophy*

The sophists of ancient Greece were professional teachers who would, for a fee, give private lessons in politics, rhetoric, philosophy, or whatever else a rich student might want to learn. Originally the word "sophist" meant "a learned man" or "an expert in one of the arts." But some of the sophists became notorious for their clever but specious arguments, and the whole group acquired a bad reputation. Plato said of them that they were not *philosophers*, lovers of knowledge, but *philodoxers*, lovers of mere opinion. For money they would teach tricks and deceptions which could be used against opponents in disputes, and they became known as people who could "make the worse seem the better cause." That is, they were identified as men who weren't interested in getting at the truth, but only in winning arguments. They were, in short, the debate coaches of their times.

The way we use "sophist" today reflects the bad reputation of the ancient teachers. A sophist is a person who makes use of arguments which are psychologically persuasive but are flawed and unacceptable. There is a hint also in the way we use the word that a sophist is someone who deliberately uses crafty and misleading arguments.

Sophistical refutations are arguments offered to counter or refute a claim which are such that a sophist might use them. That is, they are misleading and specious counterarguments. To be guilty of using a sophistical refutation is not necessarily to be a sophist, of course. All of us slip at times, and this doesn't mean that we habitually and knowingly practice deceit. What we do by error or ignorance, the sophist does by design.

To people who used to complain to the government about the Army's development of chemical and biological weapons, the Army had a standard reply: Our interest is only in defense, but in order to have an adequate defense we must learn all we can about the properties and use of chemical and biological agents as offensive weapons. Thus, ironically, the same knowledge supposedly adequate for protection is also adequate for attack; one can't be studied without the other.

There is a similar irony in a discussion of sophistical refutations and, in the next section, sophistical defenses. The information that people need to *protect* themselves against these corrupt practices can also be *used* sophistically. The person who can detect sophistries has it in his power to become a sophist. Thus, like most sorts of knowledge, a knowledge of sophistry can be put to good uses or bad, and to acqure such knowledge is also to acquire a moral responsibility for using it properly.

Not all sophistical devices used for refutation are arguments. Nonetheless, as mentioned earlier, it's convenient to talk about them in conection with those that are. The sophistical counterarguments, that is, those devices that are arguments, are all fallacious arguments. They are ones that can be used to argue for a positive position, but because they are typically used as *counterarguments,* they have all been brought together in this one place.

Against the Person
Argumentum ad Hominem (Argument to the Man)

Criminal lawyers have a saying that goes something like this: "When the facts are with you, attack the prosecutor's case, but when the facts are against you, attack the prosecutor." This is, no doubt, good advice about strategy in the adversary system of law, but what it amounts to is a suggestion about when it is useful to argue *ad hominem.* The *ad hominem* is a sophistical counterargument which, in one of its forms, consists in attributing unfavorable charactersitics to the person who has made an assertion and, on this ground, rejecting the assertion.

The *ad hominem* is usually committed in the following way: Ford presents an argument and Hall counters, not by attacking Ford's claims or reasons, but by attacking Ford herself. Hall is guilty, then, of an *ad hominem* sophistical refutation. Schematically, the exchange can be represented in this way:

FORD: For reasons R_1, R_2, and R_3, I conclude S.

HALL: Ford has the unfavorable characteristics C_1, C_2, etc. Therefore I conclude not-S.

Here's the way such a scheme might be filled in:

FORD: Mr. Chairman, there are many people in our country who have recently lost their jobs and have not yet received the unemployment compensation they are entitled to. Though they have applied for it, the snarl of bureaucratic red tape often keeps them waiting for several weeks before they receive their checks. During that time they often must do without food and other necessities or else depend upon the charity of their friends and relatives. We must change our system of registration and payment so that people will receive the money they are entitled to as quickly as possible.

HALL: Mr. Chairman, you have heard my colleague Ms. Ford argue that changes in the systems of registration and payment of unemployment compensation are necessary. But Ms. Ford is very much given to being overly sympathetic to small problems. "Bleeding heart" isn't too strong a term for Ford. Her heart affects her brain, and sympathy clouds her thoughts. The present system of registration and payment is perfectly satisfactory, despite what Ms. Softhearted, Softheaded Ford has said. It requires no change.

It's a fundamental principle of rational argument that a claim must be evaluated on the basis of the reasons and evidence offered for its support and not on the basis of the characteristics of the person who makes it. The characteristics—good or bad, pleasing or revolting—of someone who makes an assertion are irrelevant to the assertion. They count neither for it nor against it. An argument presented by a machine or by the Homeric gods is judged in the same way as an argument presented by a villain or a half-wit. The argument is the thing, and all else counts for nothing.

Strictly speaking, this is an *ad hominem* refutation:

> You have heard Clore tell you that the oil industry is doing all it can to preserve and protect the environment. To put the lie to this statement, I need only tell you something you probably don't know: Clore is an employee of the American Petroleum Institute, an organization supported by the oil companies.

This is sometimes called the "circumstantial *ad hominem*" or the "consider-the-source" fallacy. It involves arguing that a claim shouldn't be accepted, because the person who made it has characteristics which are likely to prejudice him in its favor. This doesn't seem to us such a bad kind of argument because we're quite familiar with the fact that slick public relations men and press secretaries and briefing officers often do their best to put something over on us, to put the best face on the position they have to represent. Consequently, we tend to reject everything they say.

The feeling is understandable and a lot healthier than believing everything they say, but to do so is still to commit the *ad hominem* fallacy. It is to reject a claim on the basis of the personal characteristics of the person who argues for it. An honest evaluation, however, requires that we consider the reasons he presents to support his claim. Personal characteristics can and often should make us *suspicious* about what a person says. They should make us take a careful look at his argument and even raise questions about the evidence and reasons he offers for his conclusion. It's obviously wise to be on guard when dealing with notorious liars, government officials, military spokesmen, industry propagandists, and other such dubious characters. Still, personal traits, including institutional affiliations, are never grounds for rejecting an argument. They are grounds for caution, doubt, requests for more information, and suspicion.

What About You?
Tu Quoque (You also)

The *tu quoque* is a sophistical refutation which involves showing that the person who puts forward an argument has expressed views or acted in a way inconsistent with the argument's conclusion. It consists in saying that the arguer doesn't practice what he preaches or that he holds contradictory opinions so his present claim should be rejected. Here's an example:

> Senator Dawson has accused me of misappropriating campaign funds, of turning them to my private use. The charge is a grievous one, and to answer it I need only say to you that a careful look at Dawson's own practice will make it clear why he makes such an accusation. His own financial dealings are not beyond reproach, and like the cornered snake, he strikes out at me.

Notice that Dawson's charges are not answered. The grounds for them (whatever they might be) are not challenged. Dawson's argument is ignored, but the rejection of his conclusion is demanded on the grounds that he is guilty of the same misdoing. Even if this were true, it's not relevant to an evaluation of his claim. Dawson may be a criminal, but this doesn't mean that his claim is false.

Here is a slightly more subtle case of the *tu quoque:*

> Dr. Boni has called for a repeal of abortion-on-demand legislation. But let me remind you that he was one of the first advocates of such legislation. His current proposal is inconsistent with his earlier views and hence is unacceptable.

This counterargument doesn't consider Boni's reasons for opposing the legislation. It merely points out that his present position is incompatible with his earlier position and, on the covert assumption that an earlier position is preferred, rejects his conclusion. But people change their opinions, and they often do so for definite reasons. Underlying the *tu quoque* is the unacceptable assumption that once a person has taken a position he is committed to it eternally and anything he says inconsistent with it can be dismissed out of hand.

Tu quoque counterarguments are fallacies of relevance. They fail to come to grips with the grounds for a claim stated in the premises of an argument. Instead, they introduce considerations concerning the behavior or principles of the arguer. On this irrelevant basis, they call for the rejection of the argument's conclusion. Because they mention features of the arguer, such counterarguments can be regarded as special cases of the *ad hominem*. But they do have a special character which makes it useful to give them a name and keep them distinct.

Pooh-Pooh

To pooh-pooh an argument or a claim is to brush it aside without consideration, to dismiss it with a cavalier wave of the hand as unworthy of serious attention. A classic case of pooh-poohing is the famous "Strawberry Statement" made by Herbert Deane when he was an administrator of Columbia College. Presented with a list of student grievances, Deane supposedly remarked that being told what students didn't like about the university was of no more importance to him than being told that they didn't like strawberries. That is, he refused to consider the grievances and the reasons underlying them and, in addition, suggested they didn't deserve to be considered.

Pooh-poohing an argument is not refuting the argument but ignoring it. It's a refusal to enter into serious discussion or to attempt to show that an argument ought not be accepted for definite reasons. It's possible, of course, to *argue* that a claim shouldn't be taken seriously or that an argument for it isn't adequate to support it. But pooh-poohing doesn't consist in arguing, but in dismissing without argument.

Another way of pooh-poohing is to appear to accept an argument for a claim but to dismiss the claim as trivial. The small word "mere" is typically used to do the dirty work. (An interesting fact about "mere" is that it's an adjective without a comparative form.) For example:

> Sharing federal revenues with the cities is all right. But revenue sharing is merely a way of redistributing tax dollars and won't solve any real problems. We need to look at other more substantial alternatives.

The implicit assertion here is that the argument and the claim itself are simply not worth bothering about. No effort is made to demonstrate this.

To resort to the tactic of pooh-poohing is to attempt what consumer's are supposed to dream about—to get something for nothing.

The Straw Man

The Straw Man is a weak and insubstantial creature. He is unable to bear the slightest load. He falls with the softest touch, and even a puff of breath will send him tumbling. Strangely enough, it's because of his frailties and failings that the Straw Man is so much in demand. He is often assigned the role of standing in for stronger and better arguments by those who oppose them. He gets the stuffings knocked out of him, and the sophist who set him up to be knocked over can then claim to have refuted the stronger and better arguments. A strange occupation, but the Straw Man never lacks for employment.

There are two ways of using the Straw Man for sophistical refutation. The first way consists in taking a specific argument and presenting a caricature of it. The caricature, of course, is constructed so that it will be easy to destroy by counterargument. When it has been refuted, the pretense can be made that the orginal argument has been refuted. The second way consists in selecting for criticism a weak argument for a position, rather than taking one of the stronger arguments which are available.

The first is a way of *misrepresenting* a particular argument. The second does not misrepresent, but it fails to come to grips with the strongest case that has been made for a claim. The first is a sin of commission; the second a sin of omission. Let's take a more careful look at each of these.

1. The techniques by which arguments and claims are misrepresented are themselves legion. The Straw Man has many wiles. A glance at merely a few of the ways in which a simulacrum of a specific argument or claim is created is enough to illustrate the basic trick.

a. *Exaggeration:* Refutation becomes sophistical when what is argued against isn't the original conclusion of an argument but is an exaggerated version of it.

Suppose Arthur Clarke argued for this claim: "If the United States were willing to spend the money, we could land a man on Mars within the next decade." A sophistical opponent of the space program intent on refuting Clarke might restate the claim in this way: "Arthur Clarke says we can put men on the planets any time we want to." Putting a man on Mars and putting a man on any of the planets are two quite different matters, and our sophist could easily go on to show that Clarke's claim or, rather, the exaggerated version of it, is not convincing. Pluto, he might point out, is about 3,567 million miles from Earth and the technology for going there and coming back simply doesn't exist and couldn't be created in a decade: "What Clarke is saying is absurd and indefensible."

Exaggerating the conclusion of an argument usually makes criticism simple, for an argument's premises are generally tailored to support the conclusion. A similar but stronger conclusion usually can't be supported. The premises are not adequate for it; they were not designed to bear such a load.

b. *"Should" for "Could":* We often argue possibilities. We give reasons for believing that certain things *could* be done if, for other reasons, we decided that they *should* be done. Thus, people argue that it's possible to increase the number of desirable characteristics of the human race by a program of eugenics or "selective breeding." Some argue that the work-week in the United States could be shortened to three days without a substantial loss in production, and so on.

Straw Men are created out of such arguments by a "misunderstanding" that makes it seem that the arguer is recommending a course of action that he is only claiming is *possible*. Thus, the claim "The United States *could* land a man on Mars in the next decade might be misconstrued as "The United States *should*" do this.

It obviously takes two quite different arguments to establish these two quite different conclusions. One is supported by reasons relating to space technology, the other by reasons relating to national goals and priorities. Giving conclusive reasons for why the United States *should not* attempt to land on Mars leaves unscathed the claim that such a landing *would be possible*. Yet the sophist tries to make it seem otherwise.

c. *Ignoring premises:* The conclusions of arguments are supported by reasons and evidence that are stated as premises of the argument. The premises are generally not all of equal importance. That is, several reasons are given to back up a claim, but typically some count for more than others. Such premises are the main props of the conclusion, and the remaining premises are just secondary supports. The secondary supports help bear the load but by themselves aren't adequate to carry it.

An argument can be transformed into a Straw Man by ignoring one or more of the crucial premises and treating the original arguments as consisting merely of the remaining ones. Consider this argument, then see how it can be misrepresented by carefully ignoring the most persuasive premise:

> Sexually explicit novels, films, and paintings should not be outlawed. The freedom of expression is a fundamental guarantee of the Constitution, and this involves the freedom to create, distribute, sell, and buy materials whose content is sexual. Furthermore, past attempts to legislate against so-called pornography have often created a situation in which graft and blackmail were prevalent.

Straw Man version:

> Past attempts to legislate against pronography have often produced a situation in which graft and blackmail were prevalent. Therefore, sexually explicit materials should not be outlawed.

The Straw Man version of this argument is obviously much easier to argue against than the original. That a certain type of law would encourage corruption and widespread lawbreaking is certainly one reason to oppose it. Laws against the use of marijuana, for example, probably cause more harm than good. Yet by itself such a reason is not wholly persuasive. Much more important is the claim that a law against sexual materials violates an acknowledged principle basic to a democratic socie-ty. Someone who accepted the truth of this premise or saw no way to rebut it would have a difficult time finding grounds for a counterargu-ment. The motive to erect a Straw Man and then knock him down would be compelling.

2. The second sophistical way of using a Straw Man, recall, consists in finding one ready-made, rather than creating it to specifications. On virtually every important matter (the existence of God, the legalization of gambling, voting for a President, etc.) a variety of positions exists. And for virtually every position a variety of different arguments is offered to support it. Typically, the arguments vary in persuasiveness or acceptabil-ity. Some are weak and others powerful; some are trivial and others compelling. It is sophistical to take for criticism a weak and trivial argument when there is a strong and compelling one for the same position. With respect to the best argument, a weaker one is a Straw Man.

In a tract called *Six Bridges No Evolutionist Can Cross,* for example, a fundamentalist preacher attempts to refute the theory of evolution. He argues that Darwin could not explain how it happens that there is variation in a trait in organisms of the same species—that some people have blue eyes and others brown, for example. Since this variation is fundamental to Darwin's theory, he concludes that there is no reason to assume evolution took place.

It's true that Darwin could not give an adequate explanation of varia-tion, for Darwin lacked a sound theory of genetics. But modern biology can explain the variation of traits in terms of genetic mutations and developmental processes. The "refutation" of evolution by attacking Darwin is, thus, no refutation at all. More recent and better arguments than Darwin's are available, and the preacher is only beating a Straw Man.

Intellectual honesty demands that if you are opposed to a position and intent on refuting it, then you must choose the best argument for the position that you can find and try to show that even this argument is unacceptable. In fact, if you can see how even the best argument that has been given by someone can be made better, then it's the improved version that should be challenged. If the strongest argument for a posi-tion seems unassailable, there may be nothing to do but accept it and embrace its conclusion, even though the conclusion is unpalatable. To do otherwise is to skirt close to the edge of the abyss, to hold beliefs on grounds you are aware are inadequate.

Refuting a weak or simple-minded argument for a claim proves noth-ing in the long run, if there is a better argument for the same claim that remains untouched. Such a refutation scores debating points, but nothing more.

Trivial Objections

Scenario:

The auditorium is dark except for a single spotlight trained on the lectern at the edge of the stage. John Stapledon steps into the circle of light, and after the applause dies down, he begins his two-minute address on Possible Changes in the Structure of American Government.

Ladies and gentlemen, my time is brief so I shall restrict myself to presenting a single argument. My thesis is this: The American people should vote directly on every bill brought before Congress. My reasons are two. First, participatory democracy is a recognized principle of our country. The representative form of government which we have now is merely a compromise with what were once practical limitations on the direct exercise of the right to vote on issues. Because the business of government had to be carried out with some dispatch and because communication with all or even a large proportion of citizens was slow, if not downright impossible, the writers of the Constitution settled for the second-best form of government—the representational. My proposal, if accepted, would recognize full participation by all citizens.

Secondly, the development of new technology has made it possible to communicate with almost every person in the country at one time. There are almost no people who are not reached by television or radio, and most are reached by both. People can be informed of issues through these media, and communication could easily be made two-way by the use of telephone equipment.

Granted our technology, the following situation is easy to imagine: For three hours on Sunday afternoon people all over the nation gather before their television and radio sets. Bills are read and explained by those who proposed them. Afterwards, every person votes by dialing a code number on his telephone. The code is received by a computer in a network, the votes are tabulated by a central computer, and the results announced.

Direct participation is possible and should be made actual. I have shown you that it ought to be done and that it could be done. Thank you for your kind attention.

Stapledon's argument receives slight applause, and after a short delay, Charlene Metzker steps to the lectern to speak against it:

I urge you to consider these objections to the argument you have just heard. The cost of communication equipment is great. Who shall pay for the use of telephone lines, for the installation of telephones or of television sets for those who lack them, for the computers which are so important to the plan, yet so expensive? The cost of Stapledon's proposal, if enacted, would be tremendous. Moreover, electronic equipment is notoriously unreliable. What will be done if it should break down? Will missing votes merely not be counted? Furthermore, electronic equipment is subject to sophisticated tampering, and the proposal is a clear invitation to criminals to take control of the nation. Finally, what about people who must work during the voting period? Will they be denied their franchise? Stapledon's proposal must be rejected.

Metzker's objections to Stapledon's argument are only pot shots. Metzker snipes away at a few easy targets and lets the big game go by. Her counterargment consists in presenting *trivial* criticisms and, on the grounds of these, demanding the rejection of Stapledon's conclusion. The refutation is sophistical, not because the objections are not relevant, but because they aren't adequate.

Probably no argument is wholly free from objections. But the simple fact that there is some objection to an argument is obviously not sufficient to refute it, even if the objection is well-founded. *Trivial objection* is a sophistical refutation, for it rests on the assumption that a trivial shortcoming is the same as a complete failure. The assumption is obviously false.

Refuting Examples

An example is a case that is mentioned to illustrate a point or a claim (see Chapter 9 for a discussion of examples). To refute an example is to show that it isn't a case, or isn't a good case, of the point it's supposed to illustrate. Refuting examples is a perfectly legitimate occupation, and part of the day's work for the honest arguer. But the criticism of examples can become a sophistical refutation. This happens when the claim is made that the conclusion of an argument must be rejected because the example given isn't a legitimate one.

Suppose, for illustration, Phillips argues that welfare payments are not sufficient to support families that receive them. To support this conclusion he cites the figures given in the government Cost-of-Living Index and shows that welfare payments are substantially below the income level considered to be adequate. To make his point more effective, Phillips mentions the Wallace Hall family as an example of people on welfare who do not have enough money to care for their needs.

Olafson, let's suppose, learns that the Hall family, as a matter of fact, doesn't have too much trouble getting along on the assistance they get. They are, that is, not an example of Phillips's point. If Olafson merely demonstrates to Phillips that his example is no example at all, that it's not what he said it was, everything is in order.

But let's assume Olafson is bolder and argues in this way:

> Phillips has told you that welfare payments aren't sufficient to support a family. This claim is wholly untrue. I have in my possession evidence which conclusively demonstrates that the very people mentioned by Phillips as in dire difficulties—the Hall family—have in fact no particular difficulty in living on the welfare payments they receive.

If Olafson argues this way, he is guilty of a sophistical refutation. He has left unchallenged the grounds which Phillips presented for his conclusion and attacked instead an ill-chosen example. It's true that if there were *no* cases of families on welfare who had difficulties living on the assistance they received, Phillips' conclusion would collapse. But this isn't what Olafson has shown. He's merely shown that the case chosen for illustration is not as it's supposed to be, and on this inadequate premise he calls for the rejection of the argument's conclusion. It is, of course, a bad strategy on Phillips's part to have chosen a bad example.

Sophistical Defenses

Not all tricks and deceptions are on the side of attack. The defense of a position from criticism and counterargument has its own arsenal of deadly weapons available for use. Sophistical defenses are dodges and devices which are employed to protect a claim from objections. Only a few of the more commonly used sophistical defenses will be discussed below, but they are enough to indicate the unpleasant flavor of the rest.

The Red Herring

Back in the days when there were animals in abundance and men could hunt them with an easy (if unexamined) conscience, packs of dogs were used for trailing. Dogs have to be trained to follow certain scents and to ignore others. Otherwise they have a tendency to follow their noses in the direction of a fresher or more interesting smell and so become diverted from the trail they are supposed to be following.

One way of teaching them to stay on the right track is to mislead them deliberately by starting a fresh trail and then whipping them back to the old one. To make a new trail, the smelly carcass of an animal is dragged across the trail the hounds are following. Legend has it that the red herring was once a favorite carcass to drag to mislead the dogs. (Herring must have been considerably cheaper than it is today.)

The Red Herring sophistical defense is practiced in this way. Pratt raises an objection to a claim Kline has made. Rather than answering the objection, Kline diverts attention from it by introducing another matter. He discusses the new topic, perhaps at some length, and never gets back to talking about the objection. Kline may even ask Pratt what she thinks about the new topic and try to engage her in a discussion about it.

Kline's aim, of course, is to throw Pratt off the trail, to get her interested in a tangential matter so she won't press her criticism. No matter how any dispute about the Red Herring is resolved, Kline's original claim is left untouched. As a matter of strategy on Kline's part, of course, the Red Herring he throws out to Pratt must smell enough like the first fish to avoid arousing Pratt's suspicion that she's being played for a sucker. That is, the new topic must be related, but not closely related, to the claim Kline originally made.

To illustrate how the Red Herring is practiced, consider this brief drama:

> Dink Stover is seated before a blazing fire in the living room of his suite of rooms at Yale. It's a crisp fall evening, and Stover is unwinding from a fatiguing afternoon of practicing for the Yale Blue. Seated with him is his friend from Lawrenceville days, Frank Merriwell, who continues to be a classmate. The two young scholars are deeply engaged in a discussion. Let's listen in:

STOVER: You know, Merriwell, I've been thinking. Playing on the Yale Eleven is the best education that can be gotten in college. It teaches a man how to think fast and straight, and it gets him to appreciate the fact that he can't act just for himself, but only for the team. What's more, he gets to be friends with a bunch of wonderful fellows who will be in a position to help him when he gets out into the business world.

MERRIWELL: Oh, I don't know, Dink—if I may call you that—don't you think what's learned in class is more important? After all, college is supposed to be the place to acquire knowledge and to learn how to use it.

STOVER: Don't *you* think, Merriwell, that most good athletes are good scholars also? The two seem to go together. Perhaps it has something to do with the courage and determination required to excel at a sport.

MERRIWELL: I'm not sure that's true. Look at John Randolf Hamilton, III. He's the best wrestler in his class, but old Professor Gertz told me he's not doing well with his German irregular verbs.

STOVER: Oh, Biff will do all right. He just doesn't have the patience to memorize all that bosh. Besides, maybe it's only the footballers who have a talent for study. Anyway, playing on the Eleven teaches a man more than anything I know about in college.

MERRIWELL: Perhaps you're right, Dink.

Stover, in this episode, shows that he has a talent for sophistry that complements his fine reputation as an athlete. He avoids an encounter with Merriwell's counterclaim by tossing Merriwell a Red Herring in the form of a question related to the topic of their discussion. Merriwell takes the bait, and they kick around the Herring for a bit. Somehow Stover never gets around to returning to Merriwell's objection, and he finishes the discussion by repeating his original claim.

Definitional Sulk

In Dickens' *Old Curiosity Shop* the following exchange takes place between two of the characters:

"Did you ever taste beer?"

"I had a sip of it once," said the small servant.

"Here's a state of things!" cried Mr. Swiveller. "She *never* tasted it—it can't be tasted in a sip!"

Mr. Swiveller is apparently one of those people who make up their definitions to suit their purposes. Certainly most of us would think that someone who has had a sip of beer has at least *tasted* beer. But not Mr. Swiveller.

The sophistical defense called the Definitional Sulk consists in responding to a counterexample (a disconfirming case) to a claim by acting the way Mr. Swiveller does. That is, the offending case is ruled out by defining a crucial term in such a way as to exclude it as a counterexample.

Consider as an illustration this press conference dialogue:

SEC. OF DEFENSE: We do not now have any forces in Cambodia.

REPORTER: Mr. Secretary, there are reliable reports from Cambodia that men wearing the uniform of American soldiers have been seen in various parts of that country.

SEC.: There are some members of the American military in Cambodia, technicians and helicopter crews primarily. By "forces" I mean U.S. ground troops, and I repeat, there are no American forces in Cambodia.

There are two sophistical advantages to the Definitional Sulk. The first comes from the fact that the claim is expressed in ordinary English and will generally be interpreted as meaning just what it says. Anyone hearing the Secretary of Defense's assertion above would most naturally assume that he meant there aren't any United States military personnel in Cambodia. It might well be of great political importance to have people believe that this is so. The sophistical advantage, then, is that a claim stronger than the real claim can be made. If no one challenges it, it stands as it would ordinarily be understood.

But if the claim *is* challenged, here lies the second advantage. It's possible to retreat gracefully, though sulkily, from the stronger position. Without appearing to have been lying, it's possible to say that the weaker version resulting from the special definition is what was meant all along: "Why of course by 'forces' I meant 'ground troops'!"

For people who don't know about the special way a word is being used, who didn't hear the challenge and response, if there was one—too bad for them. They simply have to take the statement as wearing the meaning on its face, and they will be wrong. Through no fault of their own, they will be deliberately and calculatedly led into believing something which is not true. The sophist is a cynic, and all too often he is also a politician.

Shifting Ground

Consider another imaginary interview:

REPORTER: Mr. Secretary, in the speech you made in Atlanta last night you said that the U.S. will not become involved in the crisis in the Middle East. Many people have pointed out, though, that we have vital interests in that area. Our need for oil and military bases might force us to give aid to allies or even to take a military role if our interests are threatened. How can you answer such an objection?

SECRETARY OF STATE: Let me first of all make it perfectly clear that I did not claim that the U.S. will not become involved in the Middle East situation. I said that at present we have no *plans* to become involved. However, it's difficult for me to imagine circumstances under which we would be willing to make a commitment of aid or military assistance.

If the reporter has accurately stated the claim the Secretary made in his speech, then the Secretary's response is a case of defense by *Shifting Ground*. This sophistical defense takes place when an arguer refuses to acknowledge the force of an objection, refuses even to deal with it, but instead modifies his position in order to escape it. He gives the appearance of having held this position all along when, as a matter of fact, he has adopted it only as a response to criticism or challenge.

The ethics of honest argument demand that an arguer take a clear and definite position and defend it as stated. If criticism forces a change in the position, then the change should be openly acknowledged. It's no sin against reason to modify a conclusion in reponse to an objection. The sin consists in fashioning a counterfeit conclusion and trying to pass it off as the original.

For the sophist, having the ground-shifting defense available for use is a great advantage. It allows him to sidestep critcism that might shatter the plausibility of his whole claim by adopting a similar but more defensible one. When the heat is off he can easily slip back to his original position, having occupied the altered one only long enough to dodge trouble. In oral presentations, in particular, an arguer may shift from one point to another and back again with all the subtlety of a talker at a carnival jam show.

Hedging

Before Job's troubles began, his life was a pleasant one. And why not, for as Satan asks God, "Hast Thou not built a hedge about him?" People are inclined to protect their claims in the same way that God protected Job—by hedging. To hedge is to refuse to make a clear commitment, to hide behind ambiguous words or vague terms. Hedging makes a conclusion relatively easy to protect. If it's attacked, it's always possible to say,

"Oh, *that's* not what I meant at all," and then provide an interpretation that escapes the objection. Hedging is preneed planning. It's a hiding place to duck into when the shooting gets hot.

A hedged conclusion makes no clear and definite claim, and vagueness or ambiguity is the price it pays for its relative immunity from attack. The hedger doesn't shift ground, because he doesn't take a specific stand. Rather, by vagueness, he marks out a piece of ground so large that when the need arises, he can scurry away from a vulnerable area and say that he never intended to occupy that spot in the first place.

Suppose a hedger presents an argument that has this as a conclusion: "We must alter our educational practices in order to meet the needs of our students." Someone might then ask, "Are you suggesting that we shouldn't give grades any more? If so, I'm very much opposed to what you're saying." The hedger is safe: "Why no, that's not my point. I quite agree with you, grades are important. I had in mind course reforms and matters of that sort."

Then someone else might ask: "Is it your position that students should have a voice in determining courses and their content? If so, I would like to take issue with you." The hedger doesn't have to worry: "I really didn't have that in mind. I suppose it would be possible, but that's not really a part of my position, and I wouldn't want to have to defend it."

And on and on. With enough questions the hedger might eventually be pushed into a corner and there have to make a real defense of a definite claim. But when not under long and unremitting fire, he can hang on to his vague claim and announce a triumph for his argument. The rub, of course, is that if he can twist around so as to dodge all challenges, he really hasn't said much. His conclusion may be kept from harm and his argument described as triumphant, but he has to pay a terrible price. In the final analysis what he claims doesn't really matter, for it's likely to be platitudinous. He hasn't proved anything worth proving.

Shifting the Burden of Proof

Anyone who has ever argued for a claim and defended it against hostile criticism has certainly experienced, to borrow a phrase from Matthew Arnold, "the burden and the heat" of controversy. Everyone longs to escape them, and one of the differences between the honest and the sophistical defender is that the first bears the burden that the other shirks.

Whoever puts forward an assertion, announces a position, or takes a stand must be prepared to support it with reasons and evidence. The person who fathers a claim is the one responsible for its defense, and the "burden of proof" is his and his alone. This means that when his claim (or the grounds for it) is questioned or challenged, it's his job to answer, if he can.

"Shifting the burden of proof" consists in meeting a challenge to a claim by demanding that the challenger disprove the claim. The arguer thus abandons his obligation to support his position and tries to make the challenger assume a responsibility which isn't rightly his. Consider:

CHALLENGER: One of the premises of your argument was that college students don't have the kind of perspective necessary to participate in determining university policy. Why do you believe this is true? It's certainly not obviously true.

ARGUER: Well, I should have thought it was obvious. Will you please tell me what reasons you could possibly have for believing that college students *do* have the necessary perspective?

The arguer doesn't answer the question; instead he responds by tossing one back. What he is counting on is that the challenger won't be able to prove the *opposite* of his conclusion, and it will be accepted as true because it wasn't *disproved*. Shifting the burden of proof may thus be a special case of the *ad ignorantiam* fallacy—asserting that a claim is true because it hasn't been shown to be false.

A challenger may, if he chooses, assume a burden of proof. As we discussed in Chapter 6, he may decide that he wants to do more than merely raise questions about an argument's premises or conclusion. He may, for example, believe that a claim which has been made is wrong and take it upon himself to show that it is wrong. In offering a counterargument, he must then take the responsibility for supporting his own claim in a legitimate way. He is under no obligation to offer such an argument, however. It's up to the arguer to prove his point and to support his premises if need be.

The Exception that Proves the Rule

The story goes that when the Queen of Sheba heard about the fame of Solomon, she came to visit him "to prove him with hard questions." That is, she came to test his knowledge and wisdom. This use of "prove" is rather old-fashioned, but it hasn't completely disappeared: "The proof of the pudding is in the eating," "The President's nominee proved to be unacceptable." This sense of "prove" is still close to its Latin source *probare*, "to try out" or "put on probation."

Most commonly, of course, "prove" is used to mean about the same as "demonstrate" or "show to be true." In this sense, to prove a claim is to offer a proof of it, to provide evidence for accepting it. Thus, we say such things as "Prove to me that LSD causes chromosome damage" and "Can you prove that an all-volunteer army will be successful?"

But in the old saying "That's an exception which proves the rule," the word "proves" has the meaning "tests" and not the meaning "demonstrates." The ambiguity of "proves" opens the way for the aphorism to be used sophistically, and it almost always is. A "rule" or generalization like "All lawyers are corrupt" is *not* supported or shown to be true by a case of an honest lawyer. Rather, such cases show it to be *false*. The case proves the rule only in the sense that it is a *test* of the rule, that it *tries out* the rule.

The sophistical defense that trades on the ambiguity of the "exception that proves the rule" adage is executed in this way:

WILLIAMS: You claimed that no woman has ever been a great poet, but aren't you forgetting about Sappho and Emily Dickinson?

LUKAS: Well, of course, they were great poets, but they are exceptions that prove the rule.

This is sheer sophistry. If Lukas is willing to admit that Emily Dickinson and Sappho were both women and great poets, then he simply must give up his claim. He can't consistently hold that *no* women were great poets and that *two* have been.

Fallacies and sophistries, the Whited Sepulchres of logic, are those illegitimate arguments and illicit practices that tend to deceive. It's important to keep in mind that the types we've discussed here don't constitute a complete catalogue. They are just the major exhibits in what could be a large and varied collection.

The kinds of errors we've examined are important in themselves, for they are often met with in public and private disputes. Yet their importance extends beyond the specific mistakes they typify. They are characteristic examples of bad arguments and dishonorable techniques of defense and refutation. Thus, a study of the kinds we've considered and an appreciation of the sorts of errors or chicanery involved should result in a more sophisticated approach to arguments, criticisms, and defenses in general.

Exercises

Name That Fallacy!

Welcome! Welcome! Welcome!

Once again it's time to play Name That Fallacy! and it's wonderful to have you with us.

The rules of the game are quite simple. You will be presented with a collection of materials that contain arguments, responses to arguments, and defenses of arguments. Some of these will be quite legitimate.

On the other hand, some will not be legitimate. Some will be fallacies and sophistries.

Your job will be to sort out the illegitimate cases from the legitimate ones. When you have found an illegitimate case, you should be prepared to explain *why* it is illegitimate.

When it's possible, you should identify the bad argument or sophistical device by name. Remember, though, that not every violation of rational argument and discussion has a name. For that reason, your explanation of why a case involves such a violation is more important than merely attaching a label.

Here on the Big Board for references purposes is our Official List of fallacies and sophistries. But, again, do not be afraid of straying beyond this list if you have reason to believe that an error of some sort is being committed.

1. Has science encouraged man to feel superior to nature, or is it literature or religion that has done so?

> NATIONAL ENDOWMENT FOR THE HUMANITIES,
> *Report*

2. *GROWER SEES SIGNS OF PLANT INTELLIGENCE*
   Caracas, Venezuela (UPI)

   Orchid grower Alfredo Blaumann contends that plants have intelligence.

   "Man can make a decision in an instant," Blaumann said. "The thought of a plant might take 100 years."

   To back up his point, Blaumann cited the orchid, the most advanced of plant life, which he said has evolved into shapes identical to those of some insects the orchid wants to attract.

   "The German philosopher Emmanuel Kant said things can't be done without will," Blaumann said. "Plants must have enormous willpower to be able to transform their cells. Can something be created by accident?"

3. What are the special qualities welfare mothers possess, to make them the ones chosen to fight the establishment? The basic reason is mothers will fight for their children, to supply their needs, and they will struggle for as long as it takes for their children to grow up. They possess both will and sustained determination to demand long and loud that the political structure allow their children enough to live on decently, and in doing so change the political structure.

> BETSY WARRIOR,
> "Females and Welfare"

4. My motto toward the Congress is communication, conciliation, compromise and cooperation. . . . I do not want a honeymoon with you—I want a good marriage.

> GERALD FORD,
> *Address to Congress,*
> August 1974

5. Why should you take Casavetti's word for it when we tell you that we'll give you the best deal in town on a new or used car?

   That's a good question, and we'll give you an honest answer to it. It's because you can count on us to always deal with you in a fair and forthright way. And, believe me, that's the truth.

   So come by to see us, why don't you.

6. The problems that plague nuclear power plants are serious and worth thinking about before heavy investment is made in them. Quite apart from the question of safety, there is the matter of disposing of nuclear waste produced by the plants.

   The wastes can be trapped and reduced to a solid form so that they do not escape into the atmosphere. But what then? Radioactive solids with a half-life of thousands of years will be an enormous burden on future generations. Unless we solve the problem ourselves, we will be creating a situation in which numerous future generations will have to assume an unfair and undeserved responsibility.

7. I am sorry to have to anounce that an audit of the accounts of the Twentieth Century Club has revealed that a sum of approximately 850 dollars is missing. Efforts were made to disguise this fact by showing that money was paid for certain goods and services by the Club, but the companies shown to have received the money do not exist. Since payments were authorized by Carla Sulakis, I am forced to conclude, however reluctantly, that our Treasurer has been diverting the money from the Club for her own purposes.

   HORACE SMITH,
   President

   I have been accused of diverting funds from the Club accounts for my own personal use, and I would like to say something about that. You will all recall, I am sure, that I give money to the United Fund every year. In my opinion it is a very good charity. You know, they support a wide range of public service organizations that do a tremendous amount to provide assistance to those who need it in this community. For several years I have served on the local Board of Advisors, and I know of no better use to which Club money can be put than this.

   I am offended and saddened that anyone should believe that I would make use of Club funds for my own personal pleasures. Let us hope that no more will be heard of such charges, and that we can all get on with the task of seeing to it that the aims of the Twentieth Century Club are realized in our time. Let us work, together, for a better understanding of our times and of ourselves and try to help one another and our neighbors. We have suffered too much already from divisiveness and controversy.

   CARLA SULAKIS,
   Treasurer

8. Aside from colds, which he had very seldom, [Father's] only foes were sick headaches. He said that headaches only come from eating, however. Hence a man who knew enough to stop eating could always get rid of one that way. It took time to starve it out thoroughly. It might take several hours.

CLARENCE DAY,
The Best of Clarence Day

9. **CAMBER:** I tell you, some M.G.s are so poorly made that they won't even survive the shipment from England. I think they had better start concentrating on quality control if they want to keep their share of the American market.

CUVIER: You say there aren't any good M.G.s, but that's ridiculous. My boyfriend had one for over ten years and ran it for about 150 thousand miles with only minor repairs. I think you'd better pick on some other car, because there are some really top-quality M.G.s.

10. *OATH IS REQUIRED FOR U.S. PASSPORTS*
Washington, Nov. 4, 1971 (AP)
    Secretary of State William P. Rogers has ordered that every person applying for a passport be required to take an oath of allegiance to the United States.

    Department of State officials acknowledged yesterday that Rogers had decided on a mandatory oath even though recent Supreme Court decisions had eased restrictions on passport applications. "There didn't seem to be any real reason why an oath shouldn't be required," one official said.

11. Women are equal to men in all things—*as a matter of fact.* Quite often, all too often, *as a matter of law or custom* this is not at all so. Equal pay for equal work, equal opportunity for all people, these are some of the things denied to women. And these are some of the things that must cease in our society, if the prinicples of American justice are to be more than pious sayings that are ritually uttered when we are in a self-congratulatory mood.

ROBERTA PETERSEN

You have heard Ms. Petersen claim that women are the equals of men in all things. What I would like to ask Ms. Petersen is who is staying at home with her children while she is here making these absurd claims? Who was taking care of her house and her husband? Apparently Ms. Petersen thinks more of making a spectacle of herself in public than she does of fulfilling her obligations. Surely we can't be expected to treat seriously the claim of such a person.

HENRY HALIBURTON

12. Dear Ms. Solomon:

You replied to "Sorry Now" that she shouldn't worry about her slip because "a gentlemen never tells." That's about the most simple-minded thing I've ever heard.

I've worked as a waitress in a club for five years, and the things I've heard gentlemen tell would curl your hair. There's NOTHING they won't tell. You'd better join the 20th century.

HEARD IT ALL

I'm sure you have, but I'll stick with what I said. Those who tell aren't gentlemen in anybody's book.

13. Directive to Agents and Underwriters:

I wish to remind you that it is time to conduct a systematic review of all policyholders who are insured for automobile collison and liability. Our actuarial studies show that the average driver has at least one claimable casualty every seven years. Over the course of the next month, then, I wish you to go through the policies you hold and issue cancellation notices for all those who have not made casualty or liability claims during the last six or more years. If we do not eliminate these people, it is likely that they will all soon be pressing claims against us. They should be issued policy cancellations as soon as is feasible.

Call me direct if you have any customer problems you can't handle.

JERRY SIEGAL,
Vice President, Sales

14. "They tried everything else. Tried shooting me, starving me and breaking me, and they missed. Now they're trying this." It was in this way that Charles Evers, the Mayor of Fayette, Mississippi, responded to the indictment handed down by a grand jury in Jackson. Evers is charged with evading the payment of more than $53,000 in federal income taxes.

August, 1974

15. It is undeniably true that more than $300,000 has been spent in furnishing Postmaster General Ted Klassen's executive suite. Because the Postal Service is in such bad financial trouble, this is indeed a lamentable thing. But what must not be overlooked is that Klassen is not unique among government officials in spending public money to acquire personal comforts. Consider, for example, that when Richard Nixon was President over six million dollars was spent on his homes. Part of it was for security, but a large share of the money went for personal conveniences and comforts. Let's not condemn Klassen, then, for what others have also been guilty of.

HILDA HOFFMEISTER

16. Twinkle twinkle superstar
    To those who said you'd not go far,
    You showed them guts, you showed them nerve
    Now, show them by the Scotch you serve.

    Johnnie Walker Black Label Scotch

17. **MARTINEZ:** Mr. Slote wants you to believe that women are little more than conveniences, in the line of dishwashers, clothes dryers, and vacuum cleaners.

    He said, and I'll quote him, "A woman's place is in the home." Now doesn't that sound as if he believes that women are just so many home appliances that have the remarkable ability of self-repair and automatic operation?

    Well, I want to tell Slote. The same factors that make women such marvelous home appliances also make them marvelous teachers, engineers, test pilots, and executives.

    SLOTE: Actually, Ms. Martinez's criticism is pretty much beside the point. According to her I said, "A woman's place is in the home." Now perhaps I really did use those words, but what I clearly meant was that that's her place *if she wants it to be.* After all, I'm sure even Ms. Martinez would agree that a man's place is also in the home if he wants it to be.

18. There has never been a general or unconditional amnesty in American history. Never. Not once. That's a point that pro-amnesty advocates try to gloss over through vague allusions to "generous" amnesty by past Presidents. But the fact is, either something has always been required of those who received amnesty—an oath to the Union, a return to military units, completion of sentence—or else only a few persons out of many have received pardons because of special circumstances.

    St. Louis *Globe-Democrat*

19. No civilized man would take dinner without wine, Father said, and no man who knew the first thing about it would keep his wine in hot cellars. Mother thought this was a mere whim of Father's. She said he was fussy. How about people who lived in apartments, she asked him, who didn't have cellars? Father replied that civilized persons didn't live in apartments.

    CLARENCE DAY,
The Best of Clarence Day

20. The disgraceful pictures at the news-stands corrupt the morals of boys and girls by presenting to their imaginations the vilest passions, leading to vice, destroying the innocence of youth, and reaping crime and degradation in their later lives.

    THOMAS E. HILL,
Hill's Manual of Social & Business Forms

21. *CRITICIZES TEXT ON EVOLUTION*
    St. Louis, Aug. 23, 1974
    Mrs. Wanda Breckenkamp urged the Ritenour School Board last night to "get back to basic teaching" and eliminate the theory of evolution from the curriculum. She said the board should at least offer creation as an alternative for children.
    "We not only haven't stayed close to the Lord, we are teaching evolution in our schools," she declared. "Isn't that what the Russians teach?"

    St. Louis *Post-Dispatch*

22. Considering the problems of air and water pollution, poverty, clogged highways, overcrowded schools, inadequate courts and jails, urban blight, and so on, it is clear that the United States has more people than it can adequately maintain.

23. Gert Yssel, the leader of the South African campaign against miniskirts was quoted as follows in the *New York Times* (11 January 1970):
    For defying decent dress, God has punished us with the water scarcity, the severe drought in the Cape, the continuous earthquakes in the geologically stable western province, the millions lost on the Stock Exchange, and the decisive setback of South Africa on the gold question.

24. TO: All Sales Representatives
    FROM: T. Laurence Feather
    Many of you are probably aware that last quarter's sales showed a 5% downturn from the preceding period. No doubt this is due in part to recent economic difficulties of a general kind. But we feel that it is also partially a result of a sales staff that is not really doing its best. Some sales personnel apparently do not take seriously the quite reasonable quotas that have been set for them.
    Because of this, starting at the first of next month, those who do not meet their quotas will have this pointed out in a letter sent to their spouse or next of kin. We believe that dependents have a right to know that their breadwinner is not trying hard enough.
    So please try to save yourself from this embarassment. If we all work hard and pull together we will all benefit from it.

25. Dear Professor Greenspan,
    I have to miss class next Wednesday because I have to go out of town. That means that I have to miss the exam. Do you want to give me a take-home exam when I get back or do you just want to base my final grade on the other exams? Either of these would be all right with me.

    Sincerely,
    James Olbringer,
    425-312-987

26. *We burn at those who block the burning of*
    vast amounts of America's coal.
    And would like to claim they don't.

The Environmental Protection Agency by promulgating—or causing to be promulgated—unnecessarily restrictive regulations, will
block the burning of millions of tons of good American coal.

Coal that is critical to America's energy needs.

They have decided that, in implementing the Clean Air Act, the
only way to protect human health from stack gas emissions is to
measure the sulfur-oxides at the top of the stack—instead of at
ground level where people live and breathe.

That's nonsense.

There is a workable, practical, alternate way to meet the ambient
air standards of the Clean Air Act. It is endorsed by the Federal
Power Commission, the Government's own Tennessee Valley Authority and the Federal Energy Administration. But E.P.A. won't
accept it.

Will E.P.A. accept the responsibility for the economic effect their
restrictive decision will have on the country?

Oh no! They'll try to wriggle off the hook by saying you can burn
all the coal in America if you'll just install stack gas scrubbers.

That's more nonsense.

The naked truth is that there does not exist today a reliable non-
polluting stack gas scrubber for electric utility use to eliminate
sulfur-oxide emissions. A conclusion shared by the Federal Power
Commission, T.V.A., and other respected authorities.

At a time when America needs all the coal it can get, it is absolutely senseless for the E.P.A. to stubbornly insist on a particular
method for meeting the ambient air standards of the Clean Air Act. It
is the results that are important—not the method. And we can
deliver the results.

It would be a crime if a significant portion of this vast American
asset went unused because the Environmental Protection Agency
could see only one way . . . their way . . . to meet the mandate of
the Clean Air Act.

We know their way won't work. That's what burns.

American Electric Power Systems

Thinking like a Criminal

According to Chief Inspector Fabian of Scotland Yard, the most important training for catching criminals is learning how to think like a criminal. When you've learned to do this, then you are in a good position to
detect suspicious behavior, ask the right kinds of questions, and anticipate the moves that a suspect might make before he actually makes them.

Committing a fallacy or using a sophistical device is generally not a criminal offense, at least not in the legal sense. It is an offense against rational discussion and persuasion, however, and Chief Inspector Fabian's advice isn't wholly irrelevant to our purposes.

This is an exercise in deception. It is an invitation to use fallacies and sophistical refutations and defenses in a deliberate way.

The aim, of course, is not to warp anybody's character, as Fagin tried to do with Oliver Twist by teaching him how to be an Artful Dodger. The purpose is to prepare you to recognize deceitful devices when used by others and to make them so familiar that you aren't likely to employ one of them by mistake.

(It may be that some characters are already warped so that these pious aims are perverted and the Conscious Deceiver merely improves his skills. This is just another case of "dangerous knowledge," and short of establishing a secret society with special standards for admission, there is no real way to avoid the risk in an open society.)

1. You are attending a public meeting on "Rights in America," and someone presents the following argument:

   > Homosexuals are discriminated against in this country. There are jobs they cannot hold, they are not permitted to serve in the armed forces, and in some states and cities homosexual practices are illegal. It is no business of anybody else what the sexual preferences of an individual are. The "life, liberty, and pursuit of happiness" that each American is supposedly guaranteed is repeatedly denied to homosexuals both by law and by common practice. The laws must be changed, therefore, and discrimination on the basis of sexual preferences must be made as illegal as discrimination on the basis of age, sex, religion, or ethnic affiliation.

   You now rise to make a reply to this argument, but in doing so, you don't employ fair and legitimate means. Rather, you take the following course:

   a. Make a Straw Man out of the conclusion or one or more of the premises
   b. Raise one or more trivial objections
   c. Pooh-pooh a premise
   d. Appeal to popular attitudes in your reply
   e. Use an Against the Person technique

2. You are employed in the business office of a large construction company that sub-contracts a great deal of work. You are also a member of the Rotary Club. Other members include two people who own small businesses that receive sub-contract orders from your company. Because of your position, you have a strong say-so in decisions about sub-contractors.

   You decide that you would like to be president of your Rotary chapter. It would be most helpful to you to have someone willing to nominate you and some people to campaign on your behalf.

To convince the two sub-contractors to be of help to you, use fallacious arguments of the following kind:

a. Appeal to Force
b. Appeal to Pity

3. You have become converted to the beliefs of a group called Psychobionics. You first heard of the group when you listened to TV comedian Lester Lennot describe how his life had improved since he joined. The group believes that within every individual, as a part of his biological inheritance, there is a vital psychological factor of a non-material sort that organizes and directs his behavior. The factor is negatively influenced by a high-sugar diet, inadequate exercise, and exposure to hostility. These produce "bioconfusion" that is expressed in poor personal relationships, inability to concentrate, malaise, and general depression.

Your friends are not persuaded of the acceptability of these claims. To attempt to convince them, you employ fallacious arguments of the following sort:

a. Appeal to Ignorance
b. Begging the Question
c. False Cause
d. Appeal to Authority

4. You are discussing with two friends the question as to whether Indians in American society now have opportunities equal to those of any other group. You present the following argument:

> They have the same opportunities as anyone else *if they want to take advantage of them*. In fact, though, the vast majority of them don't. They prefer to stay on reservations, do little work, and rely on the federal government to take care of their needs. The government educates them, houses them, and gives them food if they need it. If they really wanted to take advantage of the opportunities the society offers, they would get off the reservation, get jobs like everybody else, and work their way up the ladder of success.

Your friends raise the following objections:

a. The vast majority of Indians are not on welfare of any kind.
b. The education provided by the government is often very poor, fails to take into account the real needs of Indians, and does not prepare children to leave the reservations should they want to.
c. Those Indians who leave the reservation often find it difficult to get jobs, for they have had no chance to acquire the skills needed in the society.
d. They also often find it difficult to live in a society that is strange and puzzling to them in many ways.

Rather than meeting these objections head-on in a straightforward honest way, you resort to sophistical tricks of the following sort:

    a. Shifting Ground
    b. Red Herring
    c. Shifting the Burden of Proof

5. You have just published a novel about growing up in the American public school system. The reviews of *Run, Spot, Run* are unmixed—everybody thinks the book is terrible.

    One reviewer, Alice Lefokowitz, writes: "The author's prose brilliantly drives home his theme that time spent in school is mostly wasted, for clearly no one ever succeeded in teaching him the rules of grammar or how to write a coherent sentence."

    Jerome Alexander, a reviewer who is also the author of the novel *Until the Cows Come Home,* says: "A novel like this comes along only once very five years or so. When it does, it makes you wonder what publisher's reader was so spaced-out that he let it slip by."

    You are furious at the reviews of your novel and decide that you will write an article in which you take all reviewers to task and, at the same time, indicate that there were a few discerning reviewers that did appreciate the quality of your book. In carrying out your plan, you make use of the following techniques:

    a. Fallacy of Stress
    b. Appeal to Popular Attitudes
    c. Loaded Phrases
    d. Loaded Questions
    e. Tu Quoque ("You're one too")

Conversations with a Sophist (Part II)

The handpainted red and white sign still hung over the door of the dingy little shop, and a light was burning inside.

    I was slightly surprised to find the Sophist still in business. I don't know what kept him there, because he couldn't have made much money. So far as I knew, I was his only customer. It wouldn't have been a shock to find the shop boarded up like so many others in the neighborhood.

    I was glad that it wasn't, though. I enjoyed putting my intellectual shrewdness to the test and often learning something at the same time.

    "Hello," said the Sophist, "You haven't been here in a long time."

    "I haven't been to London in a long time," I said, "so this must be London."

    "I really don't think you would fool many people with that. Anyone can see that something can be true of many things at once without those things being identical. Still, you're showing some improvement."

"Thanks," I said, not bothering to disguise the sarcasm.

"Are you in the mood for a little contest or would you just like to sit and contemplate your cleverness?"

"I've done that enough. I'll take the opportunity to demonstrate it."

"Very well, then. Today we'll concentrate on fallacies and sophistries. To make things a little more interesting for you, some of the arguments or other formulations that I shall present to you will not be defective in any obviously absurd way."

He looked at me and I nodded.

"You will, of course," he went on, "explain to me just what is wrong with what I say. If you cannot, then I have won the round, and you must pay me."

"Do I have to use Latin names, official terms, and junk like that?"

"Not at all. All you must do is give me a clear and coherent explanation of what is wrong with what I say."

The session went on for a long time that day, and I won't try to tell everything that was said by each of us. Instead, I'll just abstract what I think were some of the most interesting or difficult moves the Sophist made.

(1)

"I passed City Hall the other night," said the Sophist, "and the light was on in one of the offices. There were a number of figures moving around inside that looked just like people. One thing I'm sure of, though, they weren't people. Perhaps they were ghosts or aliens or something."

"How do you know they weren't people?" I asked. "You said they looked like people."

"Because it was after ten o'clock."

"What does that have to do with it?"

"There is a sign outside the building that says 'No person is allowed in this building after 10 P.M.' They were in the building, so it obviously follows that they weren't people."

(2)

"Have you ever heard of W. S. Jevons?" the Sophist asked.

"I don't believe so. Who is he?"

"He was a logician, and he said something very interesting. He said, and I'll quote him, 'The study of logic is not supposed to communicate the knowledge of many useful facts.' "

"So what?"

"Just this. Notice that he says logic is not supposed to convey the *knowledge* of many useful facts. Is it any wonder that people dislike and distrust logic so much? Here is a man who openly asserts that the knowledge of useful facts ought to be kept back by logic."

(3)

"Do you believe the earth was visited centuries ago by beings from another planet?" the Sophist asked.

"I'm not sure about that."

"Well, the claim is that these beings introduced various forms of advanced technology and founded some of the world's religions. A fantastic claim, don't you agree?"

"I guess so."

"Since it's so much different from what we generally accept as being true, the evidence for it must be considerable in order for us to accept it."

"I agree with that."

"Fine, now when you look at the record you can see that the evidence for the claim is supplied only by those who accept the claim. Do you see any trouble with this?"

"No, I don't."

"Well, the trouble is that it's obvious that people who believe in such absurdities are not to be trusted. Consequently, any evidence that they present in favor of the claim is totally untrustworthy."

(4)

"I just read an account of an experiment in behavioral psychology that I think you will find interesting," the Sophist said.

"I'm not sure, I don't know much about science."

"This was not a difficult experiment. A researcher conditioned a rat to jump from one platform to another at the sound of a buzzer. Then he took the rat and tied its legs together. When he sounded the buzzer again, the rat failed to jump."

"So what?"

"I regard it as a rather neat demonstration that a rat with legs tied together can no longer hear. What do you think?"

(5)

"I believe very strongly in astrology, you know," said the Sophist.

"Well I'm not sure you should. I don't think there's much reason to believe it's true."

"On the contrary, I find the evidence quite sufficient."

"What evidence do you have?"

"Well, I'm an Aries, and Arieses are good at perceiving what's true and what's not. I perceive astrology as true."

(6)

"Have you heard it said that many centuries ago a large comet passed by the earth and ended up as the planet Venus?"

"No, I can't say that I have."

"According to that thesis, the comet almost struck the earth. It caused great tidal waves, earthquakes, and so on."

"That certainly sounds fantastic. Do you believe it?"

"Oh, I think so."

"Why on earth do you?" I asked.

"I've looked into the matter quite carefully. I've read astronomers, physicists, and historians on the topic, and so far as I've been able to tell, nobody has been able to show that the claim is wrong. With so many experts working on the matter, it would have been shown to be wrong by now, I should think. In any case, that seems to me a perfectly adequate reason to accept the view."

9/Dangerous Devices:
Analogy, Example, Etc.

For many men that stumble at the threshold
Are well foretold that danger lurks within.

WILLIAM SHAKESPEARE
Henry VI, part III

THERE'S more to rational discussion than presenting and criticizing arguments, detecting fallacies, and asking for definitions. We often make use of various devices to get our point across and to explain and illustrate it. We hope that by making the point vivid we'll also make it persuasive.

There is no more reason to suppose that all these devices have been catalogued than there is to suppose that every blade of grass has been numbered. Yet some are such all-time favorites and loom so large on the horizon of talking and writing that they yell for attention. It's these favored and noisy few that we'll be discussing in this chapter.

Analogies and examples as devices of *illustration* will get lavish attention. Parables and fables as ways of driving home a point will get only short shrift, primarily because most of what can be said about analogies applies also to them. The scenario as a method of exploration and illustration will receive somewhat closer scrutiny, and an examination of the use of analogies in the formulation of *arguments* will wind up the chapter. Because analogical arguments have special features, they have been held out of the chapter on argument in order to discuss them here in a more leisurely fashion.

All the devices discussed here are dangerous in certain ways. Like a set of razor-sharp carving tools, they can be used to do good work, but slips due to carelessness, clumsiness, inattention, or bad intent can cause severe damage. Part of the job of this chapter is to paste on a few warning labels in the appropriate places.

Analogy as Illustration

Drawing an analogy requires no skill in draftsmanship. All it takes is the ability to call attention to some of the ways in which two objects resemble one another. An analogy, crudely put, is no more than a comparison between two things. Both similes and metaphors can be regarded as stating or suggesting analogies. A simile makes the analogy obvious because it comes right out and says that X is like Y—a penguin is *like* a man in a tuxedo. A metaphor only hints at an analogy by, quite paradoxically, seeming to assert that X is the same as Y—that a penguin *is* a man in a tuxedo. Because metaphors do seem to claim that two distinct things are the same, it's usual to say that metaphors are *implied* comparisons. Metaphors and similes both *invoke* analogies; that is, in order for an expression to be a metaphor or simile at all it must involve a direct or implied comparison between two objects. Thus, in discussing analogy we are also discussing certain aspects of similes and metaphors. But our real concern is not with snappy figures of speech that illuminate an object with a brief flash: "Laws are like cobwebs, which may catch small flies, but let wasps and hornets break through" (Swift). The appropriateness and effectiveness of metaphors and similes falls more within the province of literary analysis than that of informal logic. Our concern, rather, is primarily with *extended* comparisons between fundamentally dissimilar objects. That is, we're interested in analogies that have been developed so that several points of similarity between objects are made explicit.

It's possible that someone with nothing better to do might simply draw analogies between two objects for the fun of it. This would be unusual, though, for analogies are normally constructed with some use in mind. Probably the most common and certainly the most welcome way in which analogies are used is for the purpose of illustrating or clarifying a subject that is under discussion. This is the use that we'll be scrutinizing in this section. In a later section, we'll take a look at the other major use of analogy: namely, to formulate arguments.

In the standard run of events an illustrative analogy is presented only after a cold, thorough, and straightforward presentation of a subject has been given. The analogy is then trotted out to make the main points of the exposition more lively and easier to grasp and remember. If claims about the subject are made that require arguments, then these are given separately. The analogy is not used to *prove* anything. It's merely offered as an aid to understanding. But an example will do more to make this function clear than another page of words would.

During the first half of the nineteenth century, controversy about the age of the earth was in full swing. Archbishop James Ussher, at an earlier time, had used Biblical evidence and calculated that the world had been created on Saturday, October 22, 4004 B.C., at eight o'clock in the evening. Quite apart from being doubtful about the amazing details of the Archbishop's estimation, a number of people believed that he was very far off the mark in the matter of thousands or millions of years. Much doubt was cast on Ussher's claim about the earth's age during the eighteenth century, but nonetheless it was the generally held view well into the nineteenth. For many people, belief in the claim was tied up with religious faith. The earth simply *couldn't* be much over six thousand years old, for the Bible would be false if it were. But six thousand years was simply not enough time for such slow-working geological processes as erosion and sedimentation to have produced the world as we know it. Many thousands, even millions of years, would be needed for them to do their work.

Accordingly, the great English geologist Sir Charles Lyell argued that the time scale of the earth had to be pushed back far beyond the estimate of age inferred from Biblical sources. After he gave his reasons for this, he used an analogy to make clear the kind of absurdity that geology would have to accept if the belief that the earth is only a few thousand years old were taken as true.

Imagine what it would be like, Lyell says, if we looked at *two thousand* years of a country's military and civil operations and we were under the impression that they all took place during a *hundred*-year period:

> Such a portion of history would immediately assume the air of a romance; the events would seem devoid of credibility, and inconsistent with the present course of human affairs. A crowd of incidents would follow each other in quick succession. Armies and fleets would appear to be assembled only to be destroyed, and cities built merely to fall into ruins. There would be the most violent transitions from foreign or intestine war to periods of profound peace, and the works effected during the years of disorder or tranquility would appear alike superhuman in magnitude.

The point Lyell wanted to make was that if we rely upon the operation of well-known geological factors to explain why the earth looks the way it does today, then we must assume a vast period of time stretching back from now to the origin of the planet. In order for the changes in the earth to have taken place in a mere six thousand years, we would have to assume incredibly speeded-up processes, ones that take place at a rate much faster than we know they actually do. His analogy illustrates his point vividly and makes it easy to grasp what he is getting at.

Lyell's analogy is between geological history (a sequence of changes in the earth) and human history (a sequence of changes in a country). Just to make discussion easier, let's call a subject under discussion the "primary subject matter" and that which is compared to it the "analogue" or "secondary subject matter." Thus, Lyell's primary subject matter is geological history, and the analogue he offers is human history. With these terms we can now generalize about analogies and say that every analogy consists of two parts: a primary subject matter and an analogue. An analogy, then, is not just the analogue—the analogous subject matter. It is the analogue *plus* the primary subject of discussion. Sometimes, it's true, an analogy is spoken of as the analogue all by itself. When someone says "Let me give an analogy," he ordinarily goes on to state the secondary subject matter. There's nothing *wrong* with using the word "analogy" to refer to the analogue. But since it's impossible to have an analogy without *both* a primary subject and an analogue, there is good reason to say that an analogy *consists* of both. In any case, that's how the word will be used here.

It's worth noticing that the analogue is always the analogue *of* the primary subject matter in an analogy. This, of course, is a way of saying that "analogue" is a word like "brother." Just as no one is a brother without there being someone else with respect to whom he is a brother, so nothing is an analogue without there being a subject matter relative to which it is an analogue. What's more, a person can have several brothers and, similarly, a primary subject matter can have several (or an unlimited number of) analogues. If Lyell had known about movie projectors, for example, he might have compared geological history on a short time scale with a speeded-up film. Or he might have compared it with a 33 r.p.m. record played at 78 r.p.m.

There are no "rules" of analogies in the way that there are rules for living in a boarding house. Nor are there any "instructions" for formulating or evaluating analogies in the way there are instructions for assembling stereo receivers or grading wines. But we can all agree in many cases that a certain analogy is a good one or a bad one. So, without pretending to offer rules or instructions it's possible to generalize about the characteristics of analogies. To do this is simply to try to set down *reasons* for regarding some analogies as excellent and others as faulty.

Sometimes in practice our reasons aren't clear to us, though we aren't in any particular doubt about our opinions. To look for features of analogies that may be ones that make them look good requires an exercise in reflection, and we have to become self-conscious about the praise or damnation we heap on certain kinds of analogies. Success in isolating or identifying the criteria we take for granted or that underlie our actions will put us in the position of being able to act deliberately and critically in future appraisals of analogies. Once we know the features of analogies that we prize, then we can try to make sure that the analogies we draw manifest those characteristics, and we also have a definite basis for evaluating analogies offered by others.

The Analogue Should Be More Familiar than the Primary Subject Matter

This is perhaps the paramount mark of a good analogy, and Lyell's analogy is a fine case of one which meets the mark. From our experience we know about the operations of armies and societies—much more than we know about the operation of geological processes. Accordingly, we can easily imagine what human history would be like if two thousand years of it were treated as jammed into a hundred-year period. This, in turn, enables us to see that the cramming of the events of, say five hundred thousand years into a five-thousand-year period would produce the same kind of insane result. Clearly, the familiar is useful in making the unfamiliar more easily grasped.

If the analogue is as unfamiliar to us as the primary subject matter, the analogy is doomed to failure almost certainly. There is little hope of success in clarifying a subject by relying upon another subject that is as little understood as the first. A chemist would be treading on the thin crust of absurdity if he tried to make clear how carbon forms bonds with other elements by offering as an analogue the way lithium combines with hydrogen. (What is more familiar, of course, is relative to a specific audience. For a group of chemists it would not be peculiar to use an analogue that was generally familiar to chemists, though not familiar to laymen.)

By the same token, it would be ridiculous to offer an analogue that is actually *less* familiar than the subject matter it is supposed to make clear. The action of a man at a shooting gallery is certainly not made easier to grasp by referring to the bombardment of a hydrogen atom by alpha particles. This is an extreme case, of course, but analogies do often fail because the analogue hasn't been carefully chosen. All too often it's as difficult to understand and as unfamiliar as the primary subject itself.

The Analogue Must Be Fitting

An old vaudeville sketch included the following typical bit of wit:

> "Tell me, Mr. Bones, why are false teeth like the stars?"
> "Hmm. I don't know, Mr. Interlocutor. Why are false teeth like the stars?"
> "Why, because they come out at night!" (*Laughter*)

This routine is certainly not offered as an example of humor, but it does embody an interesting and relevant point. It shows that anything can be said to be similar to anything else if you are willing to look hard enough for a resemblance. In a good analogy, though, the analogue ought to be *appropriate* or *fitting*. That is, there ought to be a number of rather obvious points of resemblance between the analogue and the primary subject matter. An analogy is *forced* when there is little similarity between the two subject matters or when elements which are claimed to resemble one another do so only in a remote or tenuous way.

Lyell's analogy between the results of compressing geological history and the results of compressing human history is clearly appropriate. Both sorts of history involve sequences of events in time, so the resemblances between geological changes and changes due to human actions are obvious. The similarities between the subject matters are clear, and the analogy is not strained.

But now consider a case in which the analogue is not appropriate. Suppose someone is attempting to explain the role of the judge in dealing with a criminal matter in our judicial system. To illustrate his point that it is the judge's duty to hear the case, to preside over the court, and to pass sentence, he offers the following: "Just as a wise father must consider the behavior of his children and chastise them if he deems it necessary, so a judge must examine the actions of the defendant and decide whether to punish him or not."

The analogy here hangs together only by the slimmest thread. The relationship between a father and his children is, in almost all respects, quite unlike that between a judge and a criminal defendant. Most importantly, the analogue is not even very similar to the primary subject matter in the one way it is claimed to be—deciding whether to punish after listening to an account of what was done. Unlike the father, the judge must adhere to strict rules of evidence and procedure, even in a case heard without a jury. Moreover, the judge cannot be motivated by considerations of whether or not punishment would be "good" for the defendant. He must decide the question of guilt, again unlike the father, with respect to law and not with respect to his own intuitions, feelings, or unreasoned opinion. He doesn't even have a free hand, should he decide the defendant is guilty, to impose the kind and amount of punishment he desires. The sentence imposed must, like the decision itself, be based on the appropriate laws and legal precedents. In short, the analogue is too unlike the primary subject in too many relevant respects for the analogy to be a good one—the analogue is not *fitting*.

The Analogue Should Be Vivid

An analogy can be a good one even though its analogue is trite. Nevertheless, as a rule a truly effective analogy is one that employs an analogue that has not been worn smooth by a million tongues. Almost every cooperative human activity, ranging from increasing quarterly sales to saving souls, has been compared with playing on a football team. The analogue is generally appropriate and certainly familiar, so judged on this basis the analogy produced is often good. Yet just because of the wide and frequent invocation of the football analogue, such analogies are rarely effective. People have heard so many activities compared to football that when someone launches into a football analogy they simply stop listening. By age and grinding repetition, metaphors like "toe the line" lose their point and become dull. They become, metaphorically, dead. Analogues, too, can die from the same causes, and writing loaded down with dead analogues is almost sure to stink.

Not only does a dead analogue act as a soporific on our wits, but for some unfathomable reason, dead analogues are all too often piled on top of a primary subject matter that is as familiar to us as the analogue itself. When the President tells us that running the government is like running a business he hasn't told us much. Someone else might say with equally good reason that running a business is like running the government. Both activities are about equally familiar to us, so to offer one to illustrate the other is rather pointless, not to mention that each is the dead analogue of the other. What's more, the two subject matters are similar in so *many* respects that to present one as the analogue of the other does very little to illuminate the primary subject. We never have the experience of "I never thought of it like that before, but now I see the point." We are unsurprised by the comparison and undergo no shock of recognition, no sense of suddenly seeing similarities that we hadn't noticed before.

The Analogue Must Not Be Misleading

An analogy is successful when it makes clearer or easier to grasp the features of the primary subject matter that it is intended to illustrate. It's a failure when it doesn't do this. There is, of course, a wide range between brilliant success and dismal failure, and depending upon how well an analogy does its job, we can imagine placing it somewhere along this scale. But there are some analogies that fall below the mere failure mark on the scale. There are some that are worse than worthless. These are the ones that are downright harmful to an understanding of the primary subject matter because their analogues are misleading. That is, the choice of an analogue suggests that there are certain features in the primary subject that it does not really have. The analogue acts as an invitation for us to believe certain things about the primary subject matter because those things are true of the analogue.

Suppose, for example, that the president of Dykeman University wants to stress that the four separate campuses of Dykeman form a single unit under one university-wide administration. To do this he might well say something like the following: "Dykeman University is best thought of as one large family. I, in my role as president of Dykeman, am the head of that family." Ignoring the fact that the president's analogue is as dead as "dead as a doornail" is dead, there is something fundamentally wrong with it. It successfully conveys the idea that the separate campuses of the university are under a central administration, but it suggests more than this. It opens the door for someone to conclude that the president has a completely free hand in governing the campuses of the university, which he probably doesn't have, since there is likely to be a board of trustees that holds the final formal power. It also suggests that the campuses of the university are like the president's children and must unquestionably follow his wise advice and mature directives because they are inexperienced, immature, irresponsible, and incapable of guiding their own actions.

It may be, of course, that this is the way the president likes to think of the university, but it is certainly not a view that would find much support among the faculty and students of most universities. The president's analogue invites us to think about the university in a way that encourages certain other beliefs and attitudes about it. The president of a university is not like the head of a family in any but trivial ways, and the beliefs and attitudes the analogue fosters are mistaken.

The truth is that every analogy is potentially misleading, for the analogue must be different in some ways from the primary subject matter even for there to be an analogy. If they are not different, then the primary and secondary subject matter simply collapse into one subject matter. Because of the need for difference, there is always the possibility that someone will draw an untrue conclusion about the primary subject on the basis of what is true only of the analogue. It would be *possible*, for example, for someone to be misled by Lyell's analogy into thinking that because the history of a nation involves conscious purposes, geological processes also involve conscious purposes—volcanoes that *decide* to erupt, for example. It would be possible, but it would also be unlikely.

There are no general rules to give for avoiding misleading analogues. We simply have to ask ourselves how likely it is that an analogue we are thinking of using will be misinterpreted and then try to avoid employing those that are clear inducements to error. In this, as in so many other matters, we have to be guided by common sense and experience. Just because every analogy is *potentially* misleading doesn't mean that every analogy is *actually* misleading. Anyone who gives directions for getting from Times Square to the Bronx Zoo is saying something potentially misleading. But this is not to say that all directions are equally bad. Obviously some directions are clearer and easier to follow than others, and though we don't have any general rules for giving proper directions, we have a fairly good idea of what kinds of directions are misleading and ought to be avoided. Some people may get lost no matter how good the instructions, and some people may be misled by any analogue. There is risk in both sorts of cases, but the aim in each is to minimize the risk by being careful about what we say.

Another way in which an analogue can be misleading appears in the public prints often enough not to be skipped over. John Randolph of Virginia once said of his political enemy Edward Livingston that "he is a man of splendid abilities, but utterly corrupt. He shines and stinks like rotten mackerel by moonlight." There's no denying that the analogy between the talented and corrupt Livingston and a shining, rotten fish is powerful. It makes just the point Randolph wanted to make, and in this respect it's not misleading. Yet as this case illustrates, an analogue has a powerful potential for influencing attitude. By a sort of "guilt by association" an analogue can mislead. It can modify opinion, not by argument and not by facts, but merely by creating an impression. If the secondary subject matter is one of which we disapprove or one that we find disgusting or reprehensible, then when similarities are pointed out between it and the primary subject matter, we are inclined to view the primary subject in the same way.

Suppose the John Birch Society points out that student Ecoaction groups are organized in a nationwide network in the same way that Communist cells are organized. Certainly this is an illustrative analogy. If we should just happen to know how Communist cells are organized into a national association, the analogue helps make clear and intelligible the way ecology groups are connected with one another. But it would take little wit to guess that something else might be going on here. The point, in fact, would probably not be to help us understand the mode of national organization of Ecoaction. Rather, the aim would likely be to get us to think about Ecoaction in the same way that Communist cells are thought of.

If we fall for such tricks we are being played for suckers. For this reason, if for no other, it pays to be suspicious of all analogies. In the hands of the unscrupulous they can be dangerous. The deliberate use of a misleading analogue is a classic propoganda device and honest people don't employ such tactics. Yet even honest people can err, and just as we have to exercise care to be sure that an analogue doesn't encourage mistaken beliefs about the primary subject matter, so we must take care to see that the analogue isn't so emotionally charged that it will prejudice attitudes towards the subject.

These four characteristics are ones typical of good analogies offered to illustrate or clarify or make vivid a primary subject. As such they provide a basis for raising questions about the effectiveness or suitability of analogies that we find ourselves in the position of having to evaluate. To see how an analogy can be approached critically by relying upon the four marks of good analogies, let's take a quick look at a well-known analogy from Plato's *Republic* and evaluate it.

Socrates, the main speaker in the dialogue, is talking with an old man by the name of Cephalus. He wants Cephalus to tell him what it's like to get old, for he himself may be old someday and he is curious about what to expect. To make it clear to Cephalus why he is asking, Socrates relates his questions to an analogue:

> There is nothing which I like better, Cephalus, than talking with old men. I regard them as travelers who have taken a trip which I too may have to take. So I ought to ask them whether the road is smooth and easy or rugged and difficult. This is a question which I should like to ask you, since you have come to what the poets call "the threshold of old age." Is life harder toward the end or what do you have to say about it?

a. *Is the analogue more familiar than the primary subject matter?*

To most of us it certainly is. Nearly everyone, no matter what his age, has started on a trip at some time and been curious about what the roads will be like or about how hard the traveling will be. On the other hand, a much smaller number of us has reached old age. In short, we know more about taking a trip than we know about growing old. (We are all of course *growing old,* but the question is addressed to a man who is old and near the end of his life.)

b. *Is the analogue fitting?*

Growing old is said to be like taking a journey, and this is supposed to make it clear why Socrates is bothering an old man with questions that he would perhaps rather not think about. We have to ask, then, is growing old like making a trip? Obviously in many ways it is, and though Socrates doesn't spell out the details, several resemblances are suggested by his analogy:

1. Passage through time (living from hour to hour, day to day) is similar to passage across distance (moving from place to place).
2. There are difficult periods in life, just as there are rough stretches of road.
3. A journey eventually comes to an end, and so does life.

Other similarities are easy to imagine, but these are enough to indicate that Socrates' analogy is not strained. Furthermore, the analogy makes its point effectively: It makes it obvious why Socrates is asking Cephalus about his life. After all, if we're planning to take a trip and are curious about the road conditions and about whether it's a hard trip, and we know someone who has gone that way before, it's only natural and sensible that we should ask him what things are like. Similarly, if we want to know what growing old is like and whether things get harder toward the end, then we ought to ask someone who has grown old.

c. *Is the analogue vivid?*

It's difficult to say whether going on a journey as an analogue for growing old was tired and worn in Plato's time. Certainly it is in ours. Plato, in any case, uses it effectively, and that's really all that counts. Great writers can often take time-worn themes, creaky plots, dead metaphors, and trite analogues and do things with them that we lesser mortals can but wonder at. Most of us would be advised to stay away from Plato's analogue because it is trite and it's unlikely that we could present it in such an accomplished way.

d. *Is the analogue misleading?*

We've already noticed that since the primary subject and the analogue are necessarily different in some respects there is always the possibility of the analogue's encouraging a false belief about the primary subject. We have to ask, then, what are some of the ways in which Socrates' analogy might mislead.

1. If growing old is like taking a trip, the analogue might encourage someone to confuse the end of life with the goal of life. That is, when we go on a journey, the goal and the end are the same: namely, to reach wherever it is we are traveling to. The end of life is death, but certainly this is not the goal of life. ("Tell me, Mr. Watson, what has been your goal in life?" "Well, Sir, I've

always tried to die." Unless Watson has been condemned to earthly immortality, which he desires to escape, this would be a peculiar thing for him to say.)

2. The analogue might suggest that just as when we start out on a trip, then change our minds and go back, so when we find ourselves growing old, we might decide to grow younger.

3. Finally, on a trip we sometimes decide to change our destination, and this might lead someone to think that Socrates is suggesting that if we decide not to grow old and die, we might do something else instead.

These are just some of the ways in which the analogue of a journey could possibly mislead. We simply have to decide whether it's likely that these possibilities will be realized, whether they offer a serious threat to the understanding of Socrates' point. Whether they do or not is, to repeat, a matter common sense and experience must decide. In this case, the threats don't seem very real.

Parable and Fable

A *parable* is a simple story that is told to illustrate or explain certain principles or attitudes or certain aspects of a primary subject matter. It is fundamentally no more than an analogy presented in a dramatic or fictional form. One of the differences between the two forms, though, is that a parable doesn't always make explicit the points of resemblance between aspects of the story and aspects of the primary subject matter. Parables must thus be interpreted by the reader in a way that straightforward and explicit analogies don't have to be.

The most famous of all parables, of course, are those given by Jesus in the New Testament. Here is the parable of the "merciful debtor":

There was once a king who decided to settle accounts with the men who served him. At the outset there appeared before him a man whose debt ran into millions. Since he had no means of paying, his master ordered him to be sold to meet the debt, with his wife, his children, and everything he had. The man fell prostrate at his master's feet. "Be patient with me," he said, "and I will pay in full"; and the master was so moved with pity that he let the man go and remitted the debt. But no sooner had the man gone out than he met a fellow-servant who owed him a few pounds; and catching hold of him he gripped him by the throat and said, "Pay me what you owe." The man fell at his fellow-servant's feet, and begged him, "Be patient with me, and I will pay you"; but he refused, and had him jailed until he should pay the debt. The other servants were deeply distressed when they saw what had happened, and they went to their master and told him the whole story. He accordingly sent for the man. "You scoundrel!" he said to him; "I remitted the whole of your debt when you appealed to me; were you not bound to show your fellow servant the same pity as I showed to you?" And so angry was the master that he condemned the man to torture until he should pay the debt in full. And that is how my Heavenly Father will deal with you, unless you each forgive your brother from your hearts.

Like a straightforward illustrative analogy, a parable proves nothing. It's a device for presenting a point interestingly and forcefully. Its use helps a reader grasp the point and remember it, but a parable can accomplish little more than this. Unlike plain analogy, the parable has rather fallen from favor as a literary tool. Perhaps this is because parables have been so closely associated with religion that most people aren't comfortable using them for ordinary everyday purposes. For whatever reason, nowadays we don't rely on parables to do even as much as they are capable of. It's true that parables have little place in general expository writing. It would be quite peculiar to use a parable to drive home a point about long division or to illustrate the way a jet engine behaves on a cold day. Parables simply aren't appropriate for such materials. They seem most appropriate when the primary subject matter is a moral principle or precept. This explains why they have been used so frequently in religious writings, but it doesn't mean, of course, that they are inextricably bound up with religion. Any writing that aims at demonstrating how we ought to behave or the kinds of attitudes we ought to have can make good use of parables. Here, as an example, is a nonreligious parable that might be used to illustrate, among other things, the way a teacher should look upon his work:

> A knight was traveling to London, and as he passed through the town of Ely he came upon three stonemasons busy at their work. "What is it that you are doing?" the knight asked. "Why, Sir," the first answered, "I am smoothing a stone." "I am fashioning the keystone for an arch," the second said. "And you?" asked the knight, turning to the third mason. "I am building a cathedral," he replied.

The secondary subject matter of a parable is the story itself, and the primary subject matter is the principle or feature being illustrated. Almost always, as with an explicit analogy, the point to be made by the parable is stated separately and explicitly. The story of the parable isn't a story *about* the primary subject. Rather, the actions portrayed or the attitudes expressed in the story should have features *like* those of the primary subject. Thus, in the New Testament parable, God is not said to be a merciful creditor, but he is said to be *like* the noble creditor of the story in his dealing with men. Similarly, a teacher isn't either a stonemason or cathedral builder, but the point of the parable is that he should *resemble* the last mason in his attitude toward his work.

A parable should possess the characteristics of a good illustrative analogy that were discussed in the last section. In addition, it should have the structure of a short dramatic narrative. This means that there ought to be at least one character with human characteristics, and some semblance of a plot. A parable shouldn't be rambling and pointless or it will be boring and confusing and do more harm than good.

Fables are probably even less used for illustration today than are parables. Parables at least sometimes appear in after-dinner speeches, but fables hardly ever have even that dubious honor. Yet fables too can be employed to good purpose in the hands of the skillful and inventive. Hopefully, one of the outcomes of this discussion will be to encourage people to try their hands at fable writing.

The most obvious difference between a fable and a parable is that a fable typically uses talking animals as dramatic characters. Sometimes trees and rocks, wind and water, are also personified and made to play a role in the action, but animals generally hold the center of the stage. There are two further and more important ways in which the two forms differ. Fables, first of all, always illustrate a specific point about ethical or prudent conduct. Every fable has a "moral," and ordinarily the moral is illustrated by a case in which a character comes to grief by *not* acting in accordance with some principle of ethics or prudence. Fables characteristically supply *negative* examples of proper behavior. The moral is the fable's primary subject matter, and unlike both analogies and parables, the primary subject is not always stated and discussed apart from its illustration.

Second, fables are satires, something that parables and analogies almost never are. Human vices, follies, and stupidities are held up for ridicule in fables. The use of animals as characters performs two functions that help make satire possible. For one thing, it allows an author to deal with human traits in isolation, something almost impossible to do when writing about human characters. Greed, envy, jealousy, and pride, for example, can be represented in an almost pure form by making them the primary feature of some animal actor. Furthermore, an account of animals behaving like men produces a slight feeling of the ridiculous in us. We're inclined to view their actions in a condescending way, and this attitude distances us from the characters. We can see them without being involved with them, and we are encouraged to be amused by what they do. We are free to laugh at them in a way that we aren't free to laugh at human beings who have their characteristic traits. But in finding them ridiculous, we're also finding ridiculous the things they represent.

Here is a modern fable:

A fat sleek Beagle went out for a walk one day. In his ramblings he happened to pass by a building with a long line of animals in front of it.

"What is this place?" the Beagle asked a Terrier who was standing in the line.

"Why, it's the Animal Welfare Office," the Terrier said.

"Welfare Office!" the Beagle yelped. "Can't you sit up ? Can't you roll over? Can't you play dead? If you weren't so lazy you wouldn't be looking for a handout." The Terrier tucked in his tail, and the Beagle pranced off. Toward evening the Beagle grew hungry. He approached his master and sat up. He rolled over. He played dead, and then for good measure, he extended his paw to shake.

"I have seen all those tricks," the master said. "I'm bored with them all and have no use for them. Go away."

Four days later the Beagle, much thinner now, stood in the line at the Animal Welfare Office. His ears drooped and his tail hung limp.

"Hello there," said the same Terrier. "What are you doing here? Did you forget how to sit up?"

"No," said the Beagle, "I can still sit up."

"Did you forget how to roll over?"

"No, I can still roll over."

"Did you forget how to play dead?"

"I can still play dead."

"Why, then," said the Terrier, "you must have become lazy."

Moral: Industry is no guarantee against misfortune.

The same features that are present in a good parable should be present in a fable. Fundamentally, both must be good analogies, with allowances being made for the difference between the explicit and implicit forms. Furthermore, both must have a dramatic structure. With fables, finally, attention has to be paid to the tone in which they are written. They are basically satirical devices. They don't fit into a context of high seriousness, and they need to be composed with a light hand.

Example

Everyone is bound to bear patiently the
results of his own example.

> PHAEDRUS,
> *Fable 26*

If Gaylord complains that Goudge has short-changed him by giving him a nickel instead of a quarter, he won't be satisfied if Goudge tells him not to worry because nickels and quarters are both coins and Gaylord got coins for change. If Gaylord keeps a cool head, he can point out that, though it's true that nickels and quarters are both coins, there's a difference between them. Similarly, analogies and examples are both called "illustrations," but this doesn't mean that they are the same. Examples and analogies are different in a fundamental way which, to avoid confusion, it's good to keep in mind.

An analogy always involves pointing out features that an analogue and a primary subject matter have in common. Some points of resemblance are necessary for there to be an analogy between the two subject matters. But, on the other hand, there must also be significant differences between them. There must be *two* subject matters. Just because two things resemble one another in a few ways doesn't mean they are identical: the President is not really the captain of a ship.

An example, unlike an analogue, doesn't just resemble the primary subject matter. It is *a part of it* —a case, instance, or sample. A sociologist discussing poverty among Chicanos might describe the Juan Martinez family of Brownsville, Texas, as an example of the way many uneducated migrant workers must live. The Martinez family is a *case* of this way of life. A printer talking about typography might illustrate his lecture by presenting examples of different typefaces: Times Modern, Caledonia, Electra, Baskerville, and so on. The typefaces mentioned or shown are part of the subject matter of the talk. They are cases, not part of some other subject matter. Examples involve only one subject matter, and they constitute a portion of it.

Giving examples is often an easy job to do. Someone who is asked to give examples of biological species that are in danger of extinction needs only to list a few of the many: the ocelot, the Indian tiger, the peregrine falcon, the mountain lion, and so on.

Sometimes to give an example is to do more than just name an instance. When a principle, rule, procedure, or method has been discussed, then to give an example is generally to describe in some detail the way in which the principle, etc., applies to a given case or in a concrete situation. Such examples can be quite complex. Here are some examples of such examples:

(a) In heating egg yolks you must always be careful not to let them curdle. If, for example, you were making a hollandaise sauce in a blender, you would want to add the melted butter to the egg yolks in a thin stream of droplets with the blender going at top speed.

(b) The expression $b^x = N$ is a way of representing the assertion that any number N can be expressed as the power of some base. The number 100, for example, can be represented as the second power of base 10 (10^2); 16 as the second power of base 4 or the fourth power of base 2.

(c) Does the law give you the right to protect your property? Yes it does, but only within certain limits. Life is valued above property in the law, and you cannot take measures of protection which would be likely to cause death or grievous bodily harm to a thief or burglar. For example, if you own a barn that is apart from your house, you are justified in locking the doors, installing alarms, and keeping a watchdog. You are not justified, however, in rigging booby-traps which might cause the death of someone who forces entry, though he does it illegally.

A bit of qualification needs to be added to the assertion that examples are part of a subject matter. Particularly in talking about principles and procedures, actual cases are not always used as examples. Rather, suppositious or hypothetical cases are offered for illustration. The advantage of using such cases is that they can be constructed for the purpose they have to serve. Relevant features can be stressed, and irrelevant and complicating features that typically characterize actual instances can be avoided. In the last example given above, it would be possible to find a real instance which illustrates the principle that the law values life more than the protection of property, and whether a real case is chosen or a case is made up depends in part on the purposes of the writer. Students who study law by the so-called case method learn how legal principles have been applied in past instances and thus come to appreciate the connection between laws and actual situations. For the purpose of law students real examples are no doubt best, but for the ordinary reader a suppositious case might be quite enough. He doesn't need to understand the law the way a law student does.

We evaluate and criticize examples as well as analogies. Some of the features we rely on in making appraisals in both cases are similar, but others are quite different. In any event it's useful to raise the same question about examples that we raised about analogies: What are the characteristic marks of a good example? Again, too, it has to be kept in mind that there are really no "rules" for examples. Any criteria we come up with are only rough generalizations based on the fact that we are already able to point to some examples in praise and to others in disgust. We are, as with analogies, only reflecting on the judgments which we typically make.

The Case Should Be an Example

The most obvious instance of a bad example is one in which what is offered as a case illustrating a point or satisfying a description is not one at all. The person who mentions New York as an example of a state with a unicameral legislature has simply made a factual mistake. The same is true of someone who cites Ernest Hemingway as an instance of a nineteenth-century novelist, Malcolm X as a leader of the Ku Klux Klan, and Betty Friedan as a male chauvinist. To show that examples of this kind are faulty, we only have to prove that an error about a matter of fact has been committed.

The Case Should Be Typical

The phrase "typical example" expresses something about what we ordinarily expect of an example. Unless we are explicitly warned otherwise, we have a right to assume that a case presented to us as an example is a representative sample of whatever is being exemplified. Most Americans like to eat hamburgers. But if someone is discussing this rather uninteresting fact and he presents us with the example of John Stubbs of Cedar Rapids, Iowa, who eats five hamburgers a day and has done so for the last twenty-three years, we have reason to complain. We haven't been offered a typical case, even though it's true that Stubbs is an

American and he likes hamburgers. "Most Americans don't like hamburgers *that* much," we point out. Stubbs is peculiar and not representative. His case makes an *odd* example.

When a case is offered as an example of some general fact or principle, as one that satisfies a certain description, it shouldn't be one marked by some strange feature that clearly sets it apart from cases that illustrate the same thing but lack that feature. The reason this shouldn't be done is simply because an untypical example is an invitation to error. It's easy for someone to be misled into accepting the peculiar feature of the odd example as characteristic of all other cases. We aren't likely to be shoved into error by the Stubbs example because it's such an outlandish case that we recognize it for what it is. But we're often faced with unfamiliar material and sometimes lack the knowledge and experience necessary to know whether or not a case given as an example is a representative one. We have to depend upon the person giving the example to keep our limitations in mind. Conversely, we have to be careful to remember the limitations of others when it's our job to do the explaining.

Someone who mentioned Isaac Aimov as an example of a foreign-born writer who, after coming to this country, wrote a number of books in English would be cheating on the truth if he presented Asimov as a typical case. The fact that Asimov was brought to the United States as an infant makes his case quite different from that of foreign-born writers like Nabokov who immigrated as adults and had to learn to write in English after having grown up speaking and writing another language.

There is nothing wrong with offering an odd, peculiar, or extreme case so long as it is clearly labeled as such. The trouble starts only when such a case is given to us without mention of its strangeness. We are justifiably inclined to take it as typical, and if we're misled, it's through no fault of our own. Giving fair examples is one of the marks of honesty in writing and arguing.

The Case Should Be Clear-Cut

The primary reason for offering an example is to supply someone with an illustration of whatever is being discussed. The aim is to provide him with a definite case in order to get him to see how a rule applies or to recognize some kind of object or activity. Since examples are used as aids to understanding, it's important that they should be clear cases. A *doubtful* case of whatever is being illustrated obviously makes a bad example. So too does a case that is not doubtful but does have *extraneous* or *complicating* features that are irrelevant to the matter being illustrated.

Someone discussing the ways in which the ideas of one thinker influence those of another might take as an example the influence of George Berkeley on David Hume. If he does, he's making a bad choice. Whether Hume read Berkeley or was familiar with his ideas is a matter open to dispute. Much better choices would be the influence of Plato on Aristotle, Bentham on Mill, Bacon on Hobbes, or Darwin on John Fiske, for in these cases there is no doubt that there was influence to some degree. Using a doubtful case as an example sidetracks discussion and argument. Attention centers on the example rather than upon what it is supposed to illustrate.

A tax lawyer explaining to his client the requirement that all capital gains are subject to taxation best does so by describing a simple case in which a person gets money from the sale of property owned by him. There is no need for the lawyer to take a case in which the property was a gift, was twice mortgaged, and was not sold outright but was exchanged for other goods of greater value. The complicated case may be one that falls under the same tax requirement, but the complications add nothing to the illustration. Indeed, they make the example a bad one, for the extraneous features stand in the way of a clear view of how the tax requirement applies.

The Case Should Be Fair

Suppose that Victor Fleischkopf is a member of the Association of Friends of Four-Footed Beasts and has been invited to give a talk on "Animals and their Lovers" to the local Policemen's Benevolent group. "The love of animals is widespread," Victor tells the policemen. "The names of animal lovers are, I'm sure, well known to you all. To mention just a few, there was Adolf Hitler, Heinrich Himmler, John Christy, and Ian Brady. All of these men were inordinately fond of dogs." Much to his surprise, Victor was retained for questioning after his lecture, and an investigation into the Association of Friends of Four-Footed Beasts was begun immediately.

All of this because of Victor's examples. True, all the people he mentioned were animal lovers, but two of them were also Nazis known to be responsible for the deaths of innumerable people, and the other two were convicted mass murderers. It's hardly strange that the Benevolent Policemen should become curious about Victor and his association.

Victor's error is clear. He gave as examples untypical cases, but more than this, he also presented examples untypical in a special way, since the cases he mentioned are of men who possess traits that we detest or regard as immoral. In talking about analogy, we've already seen that it's possible to mislead people by choosing an analogue toward which everyone feels antipathy, disgust, or disapproval. Attitudes are influenced and manipulated without relevant facts or arguments. There is a parallel to this in choosing examples. Taking as an example of some kind of action, or organization, or principle a case that is atypical in a certain way can do much to influence people's beliefs and attitudes.

Influence works both ways, of course, and an example that will incline people toward approval can be selected as well as one that inclines them toward disapproval. Too, it's always possible to bumble along, like poor Victor, and not realize how people will be affected by the cases chosen for illustration. But fairness demands that cases used as examples should be free from incidental features that encourage people to approve or disapprove of whatever is being exemplified merely because some of the cases have such features.

It may, of course, be the nature of what is being discussed that the majority of people find it detestable or reprehensible. If our friend Victor had been discussing mass murderers and had mentioned Ian Brady as an example of one, his choice would have been perfectly fair. We could hardly accuse him of giving all mass murderers a bad name by choosing Brady, because mass murderers have a bad name already. In such a case, it is just the detestable feature that is being illustrated. As such it is fundamental to the example, not incidental to it. It is for this reason that we can say that Victor, perhaps unwittingly, did give animal lovers a bad name by using Brady's name as an example. The feature Brady has that is incidental to the fact that he was an animal lover also happens to be one that we abominate and thus one that can color attitudes toward animal lovers in general.

Scenario: The Song of Atropos

These are the Fates, daughters of Necessity.
Laches is singing of the past, Clotho of the present,
Atropos of the future.

PLATO,
The Republic, Book X

In its original meaning "scenario" refers to an outline or synopsis of the plot of a play or movie. The scenario is supposed to include a description of the characters and settings and to present an account of the action in the order of its development from scene to scene. Over the course of the last couple of decades, however, research corporations and military and social planners have extended the meaning of this theatrical term. A scenario, in the new usage of the word, is a description of a hypothetical sequence of events that might possibly occur in the future.

A scenario is not necessarily bound by what is *likely* to happen but only by what *could* happen, by what is theoretically possible. Thus it can be a device for exploring possibilities and for raising questions about the capacity of armies, social agencies, and so on. It can be a way of considering how we might deal with events or sequences of events which *could* occur.

Attributing to it the most importance that can legitimately be claimed, the scenario is a device for controlled speculation about the future. It can assist in uncovering weaknesses in our present social, military, or organizational structures that might appear under certain circumstances, in providing a possible plan of action under the imagined circumstances, and in locating areas within which decisions need to be made at the present.

One scenario can't be expected to do all these jobs, and there are different ways of writing scenarios, depending upon what the aim of writing it is supposed to be. For the purpose of getting a better understanding of the scenario device, we can distinguish three broad kinds. The distinctions are rather crude, and there's no reason to believe that all scenarios fall into one or other of the types. But, given our limited purpose, these things don't matter much.

One kind of scenario is that which is written to include a variety of possibilities, none of which is particularly likely to occur, or at least no reason has to be given for thinking that any of the events described are at all likely to occur. Such a scenario is just a science fiction sketch, though this isn't to say that it can't be useful. Here's an example of what we can call the *Science Fiction* type:

> The corn and wheat crops in the United States are infested with insects that are resistent to the usual pesticides. Before this is discovered and effective pesticides applied, over 80 percent of the crops have been destroyed. Within a six-month period, existing grain supplies have been used up. There is an immediate bread shortage, followed soon after by a shortage of meat, since grains are no longer available to fatten livestock for the market. The government, against the opinions of its advisors, insists on fulfilling its promises to India and ships out several hundred tons of the strategic stockpiles of wheat and corn. In New York, where the ships are loading, there are riots lasting for two days on the 52nd Street docks in Brooklyn. The riots successfully prevent the grain from being put aboard the ships, but one longshoreman is killed in the process, and injuries are numerous among the rioters and those who oppose them. The government refuses to reverse its decision. The police protest that their forces are not sufficient to deal with the crowd, and on the second day of the riot, the President sends in regular army troops from Fort Dix, New Jersey. The crowd is ordered to disperse, but when they fail to do so, the colonel in charge orders his men to fire into the crowd with automatic rifles. They do so, and forty-three people are killed and 112 wounded. At last, the grain is loaded, and the ships put out for India.

Of what use is a scenario like this? It does depict a situation of a sort which we know to be possible: a domestic crisis, an unpopular presidential decision, riot, violent action by government forces against citizens. Such a scenario can supply a context for raising issues about general policies and practices now accepted as normal. Should definite restraints be placed on military leaders when they are given the job of crowd control? Should the power of making foreign policy now exercised by the President be restricted? Or, more generally, how are we prepared to handle our obligations to foreign countries in the event of a domestic crisis? We have agreed to supply many of them with a certain amount of food, but what will happen when we ourselves require the food we would otherwise send? The scenario is a way of raising hypothetical questions. It's not the only way, of course, and it has limitations. Most important, a scenario must be embedded in discussion which, apart from the scenario, explicitly raises the issues which are illustrated by the story told in the scenario. The scenario is a heuristic or "what if . . ." technique for considering questions, and as such it's not fundamentally different from the kind of suppositious examples that are thought up to illustrate principles or procedures. The main difference is that the stories told in scenarios aren't typical cases or even simplified descriptions of ordinary cases. They are, rather, purely imaginative constructions.

A second sort of scenario is one which we can call the *Battle Plan* variety. It consists in presenting the sequence of steps that, perhaps, *ought* to be taken just in case the circumstances assumed by the scenario ever actually occurred. Such a scenario can't be composed as freely as the Science Fiction sort, and it ordinarily limits itself to assuming that only one major possibility is actually so. Here's an example:

> John Clover, a thirty-five-year-old civilian, is sitting in his dentist's office on the far south side of Chicago. He is listening to syrupy music on an FM station when there is a sudden explosion which throws him out of his chair. The walls tremble and shake but don't fall. A moment later there is a second explosion, not as loud as the first. The radio is still playing. The dentist and three other patients come into the outer office and begin asking themselves what happened. There is much speculation, but in a few minutes the music on the radio is interrupted by a Conelrad alert. The group is told that Chicago's downtown area, over twenty miles away, has been hit by a small ICBM with an atomic warhead. Damage in the immediate area of impact seems total, and the part of the city surrounding the target area is threatened with waves of fire. All members of the National Guard are asked to report, all leaves are canceled for police, firemen, and military personnel. Doctors and nurses are asked to go at once to the hospitals with which they are associated. Other citizens are ordered to stay out of the bombed area and to remain in their houses. Citizens not at home are commanded to return to their homes at once, provided that their houses are close by and they do not have to cross the disaster area to reach them. Clover leaves the dentist's office and drives the mile and a half to his house. Once there, he sits by the radio and awaits further instructions.

Such a scenario as the one above might be written as a way of approaching the question "What should the ordinary citizen, away from home, do when he learns of an atomic attack in a nearby area?" It provides a context for thinking about whether the course of action described is the best one in the circumstances and for becoming aware of factors in such a situation that might easily be overlooked. Not every person away from home, for example, would be close to a radio. Should some other general public information system, such as speakers on street corners and in public buildings, be set up? Or what if the streets are clogged with debris and going home is not practical? Would such an order fill the streets with such a vast amount of traffic that people needed at the disaster area would not be able to travel? Perhaps it would be better if all ordinary citizens stayed exactly where they were when they heard the announcement. Other scenarios starting from the same basic assumption of an atomic disaster could be written. A group of them would present alternatives for action that could then be compared with one another, and in accordance with whatever aims and values were considered most important, the plan, embodied in the scenario, that would best realize them could be chosen from among the possibilities described. Moreover, even those scenarios that present unacceptable plans could still serve the function of supplying a context for raising questions about factors relevant to the general situation they all deal with.

A third kind of scenario is even more rigorous in its restraints than the other two. Though it doesn't consist in making predictions based on specific laws and theories, nor in assessing probability values on a specific body of evidence, it comes closer to these than do scenarios of the first two types. We can call it the *Quasipredictive* scenario. It involves formulating a rough kind of projection or extrapolation from discernable trends or from the likely (in an ordinary nonmathematical sense) occurrence of some event. In making the projection, whatever is judged to be the most likely outcomes of an assumed event are the ones accepted. Thus, the Quasipredictive scenario lies part way between true scientific prediction (as of an eclipse) by means of laws and theories and the imaginative considerations of mere possibilities that are characteristic of the Science Fiction scenario.

For example, at the moment there is no effective, safe, and inexpensive way to determine the sex of a developing fetus and to change it if desired. Yet medical and biological researchers are working on matters related to this possibility, and it seems quite likely that within the next ten to fifteen years "sex choice" will be a reality. What, then, if it were? In what way would the organizations and institutions of our society be affected? What are some of the areas into which such an operation would extend? A scenario might suggest a few answers to these questions:

> Sex-choice procedures have now been available to the public for five years. According to a statistical study by HEW, there has been a marked increase in the number of male babies born compared with the preceding five-year period. Most social scientists believe that this is a result of the desire of many families for their first child to be a boy. For the first time since accurate statistics have been kept, there are more males than females in the population. It is too early to tell whether this trend will continue or level out

as second children are born to families who chose a boy for the firstborn. In Los Angeles a group has been formed to lobby for legislation that will permit polyandry under certain demographic conditions.

The majority of insurance companies have, after a delay, now extended their medical coverage to include complications resulting from sex-choice procedures. The five states in which the procedures continue to be illegal are under great pressure from medical, student, and feminist groups to repeal their laws.

The DAR at its yearly national convention condemned the procedures as "immoral, atheistic, and Communistic." Groups of Catholic laymen continue their opposition, and the Pope, in his recent encyclicle *Dei Voluntas*, restated the Roman Catholic Church's view that the alteration of the sex of a fetus is "contrary to the realization and operation of God's plan and purpose."

The Mothers' Group for Free Choice recently demonstrated in front of HEW offices in Washington. The leader of the group presented the Secretary of HEW with a petition calling for an additional allowance to pay for sex-choice procedures for all expectant mothers on welfare who wish them. The chairman of the National Welfare Rights Organization has repeatedly taken the same stand. The Organization of Militant Women has demanded that the procedures be made available, without cost, to all women, whether on welfare or not.

Clearly, it's possible to ring changes on this sort of approach to a question. A scenario might be developed, for example, that attempts to explore the likely consequences, ramifications, alterations in attitudes and behavior, etc., of the passage of some law or the adoption of some government policy. How would people react and what would be the general social outcomes to a law which restricted, upon penalty of a heavy fine, the number of births in a family to two? Such questions need to be thought about in a serious way, but most often anything like precise prediction is impossible. The scenario is a device that can help fulfill this need. In short, it's a technique for assisting us—compelling us—to think about a problem in concrete terms and with attention to details that might easily be skipped over in a more abstract approach.

There is no necessary limitation on the kind of subject matter of a scenario. Typically, scenarios have been used in thinking about military matters, and because of this they have gotten a bad name. But it's as irrational to reject the scenario technique because of its military applications as it would be to reject English because orders to kill have been written in it. The scenario can be used as a way of approaching questions arising within business, politics, economics, administration, education, and so on and on. It's not the exclusive property of the military and its minions. The amount of rigor introduced into a scenario, the limitations imposed, and the evidence required (if any) for its fundamental assumptions and projections from them can vary enormously. Some can be no more than imaginative "visions" of a possible but not at all likely future, and others can start from assumptions that there are good (though not conclusive) reasons to believe will be true someday. From such assumptions, the next steps taken may be free creations, or they may be conditioned by considerations of what we judge on grounds of present experience to be a likely response by some group to the kind of situation assumed to be actual.

The scenario device is elastic, and it is crude. This is both its weakness and its strength. By itself it can't prove or demonstrate anything about the present or the future, but it is a way to speculate in a controlled manner.

Analogy as Argument

Analogies are used to do more than illustrate, bring to life, or sugar-coat points about some primary subject matter. With a little tinkering, analogies can be turned into engines of argument and used to crank out conclusions. But of all the machinery of informal logic, argument by analogy is the most dangerous. All too often such arguments persuade only because they mislead and confuse. Because this way of arguing has become the most favored way of trying to convince others in social and political disputes, the situation is desperate and appalling.

It's often hard to say just what's wrong with an argument based on an analogy. Even when we aren't persuaded by the argument, the analogy sometimes inclines us to feel that maybe we ought to accept the conclusion. After all, we can't spot any flaws in the argument, so why shouldn't we agree to the conclusion? The best and perhaps the only protection against being misled in this way is to understand the nature of analogical argument, to form a clear idea of the conditions that it ought to satisfy, and—most important —to recognize the limitations of such arguments. Unless we are willing simply to discard *all* arguments by analogy as illegitimate means of persuasion, which is a terribly drastic step, it's very important to gain a good grasp of these matters. Whoever doesn't becomes easy prey for the deceiver and, worse, a prime candidate for self-deception, for we can be led into error by our own analogies as well as by those of others.

It's possible to distinguish more than one kind of argument by analogy, but we can limit our focus to those in which two subject matters are compared with one another and a conclusion is asserted on the basis of the comparison. As with illustrative analogies, such arguments involve a primary and a secondary subject matter. People, organizations, institutions, activities, and virtually anything at all can constitute the primary or the secondary subject matter.

Put quite simply, an argument by analogy consists in asserting a conclusion about the primary subject matter on the basis of its similarities to an analogue. To be more specific, when analogical arguments are looked at carefully, they typically exhibit a three-part structure:

1. The primary subject matter is compared with an analogue, and several characteristics which they have in common are pointed out.
2. The fact that the analogue has a certain additional characteristic C is indicated.
3. Finally, it is asserted as a conclusion that the primary subject matter also has C.

Becoming slightly more abstract, we can represent this structure in a formal scheme like this:

1. PSM has P, Q, R, S . . .
2. A has P, Q, R, S . . .
3. A has C

Therefore, PSM has C

To illustrate these features of structure, consider an argument that a (very bad) biologist might offer:

> How are we to account for the fact that thousands of species of animals and plants have become extinct over the course of millions of years? Perhaps some that lived in a small area met with natural disasters, like floods or forest fires, and were simply wiped out at a blow. But the evidence indicates that this couldn't be true for the majority of cases. Most species died out. Why did this happen?
>
> The reason, I think, is clear. Each species has a definite span of life, and it lives until it reaches the end of the span, then simply dies off. But why should we say a species has a life span? That's easy to answer. Species of animals and plants are like individuals in a number of ways. Both are born or come into existence at a definite time; both change during a period of growth. Both, after a while, reach maturity, and eventually both decline. Now everyone knows that individuals don't live forever. Even if they don't meet with accidents or disease, they eventually die of old age. Human beings, for example, rarely live to be over a hundred, and dogs die around the age of twelve or fifteen. It's reasonable to believe, then, that species are like individuals in this additional respect. That is, they too have a definite span of life, and sooner or later each species dies of old age.

As a second example, consider a famous argument by the English philosopher John Stuart Mill. "How can I know," Mill asked, "that I'm not the only person in the world who experiences pain and pleasures and has a variety of other feelings?" Of course Mill didn't believe it very likely that other people don't have feelings. What he wanted to know was on what grounds we can base our belief that they do. That is, what reason do we have for believing what we believe about other people? Here is his argument, in part:

I conclude that other human beings have feelings like me, because, first, they have bodies like me, which I know, in my own case, to be the antecedent condition of feelings; and because, secondly, they exhibit the acts, and other outward signs, which I know in my own case to be caused by feelings.

The first thing to do in approaching an analogical argument with an eye to understanding and evaluating it is to analyze its structure along the lines indicated above. What is being claimed to be like what? In what ways are they supposed to be alike? What additional characteristic is the analogue said to have that the primary subject matter is, as a conclusion, also asserted to have? In our two examples this analysis is rather simple:

Example 1
1. PSM: Species and their extinction
2. A: Individual organisms
3. Traits that biological species and individual organisms are said to have in common: Both are born at a definite time; both have a growth period; both have a mature period; both have a period of decline.
4. Additional characteristic of A: Individuals have a life span; i.e., they grow old and die.

CONCLUSION: Species also have a life span; they too eventually die of old age.

Example 2
1. PSM: Other people
2. A: Myself
3. Traits that other people and I have in common: I have a body, and so do they; they exhibit "pain behavior" and "pleasure behavior" just like mine.
4. Additional characteristic of A: I know, from my own case that both these features are associated with feelings.

CONCLUSION: Other people have feelings like mine.

It's obvious from these examples that analogical arguments are *arguments*. A conclusion is asserted, and reasons for it are produced. The similarities between the primary subject and the analogue are used as a foundation for making a claim about the primary subject. The premises of the argument (upon analysis) present the similarities and mention another trait the analogue has. The conclusion is that the primary subject also has this trait.

A second's thought will show that the similarities mentioned in the premises will serve as *complete* reasons for accepting the conclusion only if a certain assumption is made. The assumption has to be one something like this: If two subject matters are similar in some ways, then they are similar in any other way as well. This is the principle (or one formulation of it) that often lurks in the background when analogical arguments are offered. People frequently assume it tacitly, though perhaps unconsciously, and make it crucial to their arguments. Also, it is the tacit acceptance of this principle that often makes people feel that they *must* accept the conclusion of an analogical argument, though they think it's wrong. They don't see any way out. Just to have a name, we can call this the "strong analogical principle."

The strong analogical principle is responsible, in a peculiar way, for setting a limit on the value of analogical arguments. An argument can be a *sound* argument only if it is deductively valid and all its premises are true. Here's where the strong principle forces a restriction. *No argument from analogy can be a sound, demonstrative, argument because the strong analogical principle is false.* It is simply not true that if any two things have several traits in common they will always have any other trait in common. No one believes that just because a typewriter and an organ are both run by electricity and have keys, it would be possible to sit down at an organ and type a letter, but in analogical arguments people often proceed as if this were so. The strong principle causes trouble because all too often people who formulate and people who evaluate arguments by analogy fail to recognize that it is false.

If the strong principle were true, an analogical argument would have a form like this:

> If any two subject matters have traits in common, then any additional trait that one has the other will have also.
>
> PSM and A have P, Q, and R in common.
>
> A also has C.
> _____
>
> **CONCLUSION:** PSM also has C.

If the sentences that filled in this form were all true, then the argument would be sound, for the form is that of a valid argument. The strong analogical principle is required to make analogical arguments valid. But the principle is false. Hence analogical arguments cannot be sound.

The strong analogical principle is false as stated, but perhaps it can be modified a bit. In its altered form it may continue to play a role in arguments, although never a role that would turn an analogical argument into a sound argument. Changing the principle is rather easy, for we do recognize that when two things are seen to have a number of common features it frequently (but not always) turns out upon investigation that they also share additional features. With this in mind we can state a weaker and vaguer analogical principle: If two subject matters are similar in a number of ways, then it is likely that they are similar in certain other ways as well. This is *weaker,* for it doesn't claim that two things *always* have another trait in common but only that it is likely that they will. It is *vaguer,* because it's not always clear what is to count as similarity in a "number" of ways. How large must the number be? What's more, it's not always clear just *how* likely it is that the primary subject will have the additional characteristic.

It's weak and it's vague, but it's our own analogical principle. It would be nice to be able to use the stronger and clearer principle. But it would also be nice to be omniscient and not need either one. The stronger principle is false, and we just have to get by without it the best we can. The new principle merely makes open admission of what we all already know to be so and recognize most often in practice. It makes it clear that arguments from analogy are ones that can, at best, only establish their conclusions as likely. The premises of such arguments do provide reasons for accepting their conclusion, but they don't *guarantee* its truth. Even in the best cases, the premises only make the conclusion probable. In short, analogical arguments are a special kind of inductive (nondeductive) argument and are subject to the same restraints and limitations.

The fact that arguments from analogy don't have conclusions that *must* be true, even though the premises are true, seems to leave us on shaky ground. If as sound arguments they are all failures and disappointments, what are we to do? Toss out the whole mess and simply have no truck with analogical arguments? As we've already said, this is tempting, but even if we followed this path others would no doubt continue to insist on using them. We wouldn't be much better off. Besides, we *do* use them, and we neither dismiss them all as worthless nor accept them all as persuasive. We choose among them. Some we brand as acceptable, others as unacceptable. Some we throw aside; others we take to heart. In short, we *evaluate* analogical arguments. The matter we have to face now is one of describing what it is that we look for in evaluation. What marks count toward persuading us to accept an argument from analogy? What traits must it display to incline us in its favor?

The following four traits are ones which are abstracted from our common practices of evaluation. They aren't standards that we set up arbitrarily and then demand that analogical arguments satisfy. Rather, they are based on the ordinary experience that we have in dealing with arguments by analogy. As criteria they are somewhat vague, but this is because they must cover a wide range of cases. They are perhaps best regarded, not as criteria, but merely as suggestions about what makes an analogical argument worthy of acceptance. Even when all the marks are present, all standards satisfied, the conclusion may turn out to be wrong. After all, analogical arguments are nondeductive arguments, and the premises of such arguments, even when true, don't guarantee the truth of their conclusions.

The Premises Must Be True

This requirement is simple and obvious but sometimes neglected. Even to have an analogy, the two subject matters must resemble one another. Just as important is that the sentences of the argument that assert that they resemble one another *in certain specific respects* must be true. The sentences are true, of course, if the primary subject matter and the analogue do have in common the traits they are said to have. If these sentences are false, then the analogy breaks down, and the argument based on it collapses. (It might be possible to establish the same conclusion by means of *another* analogical argument, but not by that one.)

Similarly, the premise which asserts that the analogue has a certain additional trait must be true. If it's *not* true, if the analogue doesn't have the trait claimed, then the argument will not go through. The conclusion, after all, is the assertion that the primary subject has this trait, and if the *analogue* doesn't have it, then it doesn't matter a jot how close the resemblance between the two subject matters is.

The argument that was our first example seems to suffer from the defect that the premises which claim resemblances between species and individuals are false. A close look at the argument shows that it's a peculiar one. The analogy is based on similarities that are really metaphors. Species are not *born,* for example, except in the metaphorical sense that they come into existence during a certain span of time. They obviously cannot *grow,* nor can they become *mature,* at least not in the same sense that individuals can. Taken literally, the premises that assert that individuals and species have in common the traits that were named are simply false. They gain what appearance of truth they have merely because terms like "born" and "mature" can be used straightforwardly with respect to individuals and metaphorically with respect to species of animals and plants. Since the premises asserting that individuals and species have such traits are false, then the analogy breaks down and the entire argument falls into ruins.

This case is tricky because of the metaphors in the premises. It's something of an unusual argument in this respect, though worth paying attention to just because of its peculiarity. Most analogical arguments don't require such imaginative criticism, because their premises are merely straight-out factual claims. It may be hard to learn whether the claims are correct, but this is at least one of the steps that needs to be taken in evaluating analogical arguments (or arguments of any sort, for that matter).

The Degree of Analogy Should Be High

To talk about this second mark of a persuasive analogical argument conveniently we need a few special terms. The traits that an analogue and the primary subject have in common we will say make up the *positive analogy.* Tapes and records, for example, are both inexpensive ways of recording sounds on a plastic material for reproduction by means of a machine designed for the purpose. These features that they share thus belong to the positive analogy that holds between them, no matter which one is treated as the primary subject. The *negative analogy* is the group of traits that belong to one of the subject matters but not to the other. Thus, that records are disc-shaped and have grooves, and that tapes are flat narrow bands with "impressed" magnetic patterns are features that go toward making up the negative analogy between records and tapes. The *degree of analogy* between the two subject matters is relative to the sizes of their positive and negative analogies. The larger the negative analogy or the smaller the positive analogy the less the degree of analogy between them. Or conversely, the larger the positive analogy or the smaller the negative analogy, the more the degree of analogy. Armed with these new terms, we can now discuss our second rough rule of evaluation.

To be effective, the subject matters of an analogical argument should have a high degree of analogy. The larger the number of traits that a primary subject and its analogue have in common and the fewer the dissimilarities between them, then the better grounded is the argument. The reason we are inclined to accept an argument which involves a large positive analogy and/or small negative analogy is based on a common-sense generalization. The more ways in which two things are alike and the fewer ways in which they are different, the more likely it is that they will have one more trait in common. This generalization is not without exception, of course. Even when there is a high degree of analogy between the primary subject and the analogue, it may still happen that the primary subject doesn't have the particular trait that the conclusion of the argument says it does. Degree of analogy is not an infallible guide. But it is a guide.

Consider this case. Garrett Yale is a teacher in a ghetto school, and in his class are two boys, John and James. John and James are about the same age. They have had the same educational background. Both are in good health, like school, and like to read. They both live at home. John wears glasses and James doesn't; John is black and James is white. Yale tests John's reading skill with a standard educational test and finds that he does very well. On the basis of what he knows about the two boys—about the ways in which they are alike and unlike—Yale feels confident in concluding that when he tests James he will find that James too displays a high level of skill.

It's probably obvious—but important enough to be worth saying, anyhow—that the degree of analogy between two subject matters is independent of the premises of an analogical argument. This means that we can fail to be persuaded by an argument and reject it as weak even though we believe there is a high degree of analogy between the primary subject matter and the analogue. It may be simply that the argument doesn't sufficiently stress the extent of the positive analogy. Thus we may criticize or toss out the argument *as formulated.* Another argument that does mention many traits belonging to the positive analogy may still win our approval.

The truth is, though, that we rarely go so far as to reject an analogical argument on the grounds that we believe the degree of analogy is not as high as it could be made. If we can see far enough to see how it can be increased, then this is usually enough reason not to reject the argument. In such a case we aren't so much inclined to accept the argument *as it is* but the argument *as it might be.*

Not to be overlooked with respect to degree of analogy is one more important point. *Analogical arguments are almost always entirely devoted to establishing the positive analogy.* It's close enough to true to say they *never* present the negative analogy. It becomes the job of the reader or listener to work out the traits belonging to the negative analogy and to form some estimate of its size. Since the degree of analogy depends upon a comparison of the positive and negative analogies, this means that he is also made responsible for determining the *degree of analogy.* Is it any wonder that arguments by analogy are the dangerous machines they are! The one who offers the argument has all the advantages on his side. He stresses the similarities between analogue and the primary subject matter, and usually they are clear enough to be undeniable. Then he points out a trait of the analogue and invites us to believe the primary subject also has it. But does it? Well, it certainly seems reasonable that it does. The two cases do seem *very* much alike, just as he said.

So operates the arguer. But what about us, the nonarguers? We must quickly try to think of ways in which the primary subject matter is *unlike* the analogue. If we have to do this in a hurry we are at a great disadvantage. Then we have to try to decide whether the degree of analogy is or is not very high. In an analogical argument, in other words, we must assume a large burden—one that is in some ways larger than the arguer's. Typically, we must do part of his work for him, namely that of determining the degree of analogy.

The Conclusion Must Not Be Stronger than the Premises Can Support

The less the conclusion of an analogical argument claims—the weaker it is—the more we are inclined to accept the argument. On the other hand, the more the conclusion claims—the stronger it is—the more we are inclined to doubt or reject the argument.

A simple case will illustrate the "degrees of strength" that a conclusion of a particular argument by analogy might have.

John Holum is chairman of the St. Louis City-Planning Commission, and he is faced with the task of persuading the mayor's office that St.

Louis can expect to receive government money for the construction of low-income housing. Here are some of the reasons he gives:

The administration has promised to provide money for the building of low-rent residences in places where they are needed.

(a) Money has already been allocated to Boston, and St. Louis and Boston are alike in a number of ways. Both have a large population of families with low incomes; both contain many substandard buildings no longer suitable for habitation. Even with the use of substandard buildings, both cities suffer from overcrowding in poorer neighborhoods. Private businesses in neither city have committed themselves to building more low-rent apartments or houses.

(b) Boston just received $1.5 million for the construction of low-income housing.

Now, Holum can offer one of several conclusions, ranging from very strong to very weak. Each one will be supported by the same premises, but not to the same degree, of course. Here are the conclusions from which he would be most likely to select:

1. St. Louis will receive $1.5 million.
2. St. Louis will *probably* receive $1.5 million.
3. St. Louis will receive some funds for housing.
4. St. Louis will *probably* receive some funds for housing.

The same reasons may be used to support any of these conclusions. Clearly, though, some are better supported than others. The movement is from the strongest claim at the top—that St. Louis will receive exactly the same as Boston—to the weakest at the bottom—that St. Louis will probably get some money. From the standpoint of evaluation, we are more inclined to accept the weakest conclusion than we are any of the others. We are safer in accepting it, for there simply aren't as many ways in which things can go wrong. The strongest conclusion depicts a rather specific state of affairs, and as such it makes a large claim about the world. So many things could happen that there is more risk of our being wrong should be commit ourself to that conclusion.

The general principle that the premises should be strong enough to support the conclusion is hard to apply in practice. It's just a version of the principle that the evidence for a conclusion should be adequate. It's not at all clear when either condition has been met. Some of us are more adventurous than others. We're willing to take more risk, or we're willing to commit ourselves to a conclusion on the basis of reasons that may not be adequate for others to make a commitment. Thus, our criterion for evaluation is a very flexible one. For those of us not given to daredevil stunts, though, the safest course is to accept only those analogical arguments with the weakest conclusions—assuming they are satisfactory to us in other ways.

The Conclusion Should Be Relevant

The more relevant the conclusion is to the positive analogy, then the more likely we are to regard the argument as acceptable. This is a way of saying that we have more confidence in an analogical argument when the characteristic claimed for the primary subject matter in the conclusion is closely connected with other characteristics which the primary subject and the analogue have in common. We are more apt to regard the argument as firmly establishing the conclusion either when we have reason to believe that the traits in the positive analogy are responsible for the additional trait or when they are generally accompanied by or associated with it. As is often the case, an example will make this point clearer than another yard of exposition would, so consider these two arguments.

Here they are in brief form to make comparison easier:

(a) Mrs. Joanne Brass has spoken out firmly and publicly against pornography, and the same is true of Mrs. Hilda Watson. Mrs. Brass owns a car. Thus, Mrs. Watson probably owns one also.

(b) Mrs. Joanne Brass has spoken out firmly and publicly against pornography, and the same is true of Mrs. Hilda Watson. Mrs. Brass is in favor of censorship. Mrs. Watson is probably also in favor of censorship.

The second argument, obviously, is the one that comes closer to satisfying our requirement of relevance. There is virtually no connection between being against pornography and owning a car. The two characteristics are associated in only a haphazard accidental fashion. But the connection between openly condemning pornography and favoring censorship is a very close one indeed. It's close, not because it would be inconsistent or otherwise illogical to speak against pornography and yet be against censorship, but because from a wide range of experience we know that the two accompany one another in our society more often than not.

To be fair to Mrs. Watson, we must remember that it's quite possible she is a woman of taste who believes that pornography is totally bereft of all literary and aesthetic values. She would like to encourage everyone to turn away from it and give his attention to works that are more worthwhile, but at the same time, she abhors censorship based on moral or aesthetic grounds. If we accepted the second argument, we would be wrong about her. Quite possibly. Yet in the absence of more information and knowing what we do about the close association of being against pornography and being for censorship, the argument is persuasive. It is, in any case, a better argument than the first one, for the traits named in the premises are ones relevant to the trait named in the conclusion.

On the matter of relevance between the positive analogy and the conclusion of an argument, the advantage goes to the arguer. Just as it is left to the receiver of the argument to work out the negative analogy and the degree of analogy, so it is left to him to decide about relevance. The arguer may present only the most superficial resemblances between the primary subject and the analogue and, on that basis, try to get us to accept a wholly unrelated conclusion. From our position as evaluators, we must take the analogy in hand, turn it over and over, check the positive analogy and determine for ourselves whether the trait assigned to the primary subject matter in the conclusion is closely connected with those that make up the positive analogy expressed in the premises. It's easy to see from this that another heavy burden is thrust on the shoulders of him who would judge. The way is open for slippery arguers to practice duplicity, for honest people to err, and for recipients of arguments to fool themselves.

Analogical arguments are rickety bridges that span reasons and conclusions, and whoever tries to cross them is taking many risks. The characteristics of good analogical arguments that we have been examining may serve as warnings to the unwary and help those determined to cross to exercise caution. But they aren't guarantees of safety, and possibility of disaster is ever present.

Analogy as Moral Argument

The results of the competition for places in the expedition to explore Rigel-10 were announced a week after the interviews. Being objective about it, I knew that my qualifications were high, and I felt that I had given the right sort of answers at the interview. Nonetheless, I was one of the first of the group that began to gather in front of the tri-d screen to watch the names of those selected roll by.

The tape had run through completely and begun again before I could fully face the fact that my name wasn't on it. With disbelief and anger I saw that Shipton had been given a place and I hadn't. But in spite of my anger, my thoughts were clear. Something was wrong with this setup. Since Shipton was accepted, I should have been accepted also. We were about the same age; both of us were in excellent physical condition and would hold up equally well during the space-time punch that would put us into the Rigel system. My educational background was similar to Shipton's, and I knew that the psychological tests had shown that we were both about equally likely to hold up under stress, fulfill our responsibilities, and get along with other expedition members. What's more, my motivation to join the expedition was at least as great as Shipton's. Considering all of these factors, it became obvious that I ought to have been chosen also. But what could I do about it?

This scenario contains an analogical argument, but it's not like the ones we've been discussing. What sets it apart is that the words "ought" and "should" are used in expressing its conclusion. Analogical arguments which conclude that the primary subject matter "ought to have" a certain characteristic are obviously distinct from those that conclude that the subject matter "has" or "probably has" the characteristic. We'll talk about the differences in more detail below, but for the moment it's enough to notice that arguments of the first sort make claims about what ought to be so and those of the second sort make claims about what is or may be so. The distinction between them is roughly the same as that between sentences like "Hayes ought to be a senator" and "Hayes is a senator." Just for the sake of convenience (and not much more), we'll call arguments by analogy that have words like "ought" and "should" in their conclusion *moral analogical arguments.* The other kind we'll call *factual analogical arguments.*

These names and this way of making the distinction are not particularly happy, and they shouldn't be taken too seriously. For one thing, what we've called factual analogical arguments are often used to establish conclusions of a moral kind. "Ross is guilty of neglect" or "Sloane is a bad father," for example, is a claim that most people would call moral, yet they both might well be offered as conclusions of analogical arguments of a kind we have classed as factual. In short, there can be moral arguments by analogy that don't have "ought" or "should" in their conclusions. It has to be kept in mind, too, that not all moral arguments, not even those that use words like "ought," are arguments by analogy. But so long as these points are admitted and everyone is put on his guard, there's no reason why we can't make the distinction the way we've made it and use the names we've used.

The class of moral analogical arguments is worth special notice. Not only do such arguments have peculiar features that make them unlike the arguments discussed in the last section, but they play an important role in our society. Just as a guess, probably the overwhelming majority of analogical arguments in common use fall into this category. People seem to be more given to invoking analogies to establish what *ought* to be so than to demonstrate what *may* be so. Moral analogical arguments crop up quite often in the area of political disputes, discussion, and decision making, and this fact alone is enough to compel us to take a careful look at them. To ignore them would be to shirk one of the most important jobs of informal logic—providing a critical understanding of those types of arguments that figure significantly in the affairs of ordinary life.

Now to some detailed analysis. Factual analogical arguments, recall, involve pointing out a number of similarities between a primary subject matter and an analogue, observing that the analogue has an additional trait, and concluding that the primary subject has it as well. Something quite different goes on in moral analogical arguments. They are offered in cases in which the primary subject matter does *not* have the additional trait of the analogue. The arguer is well aware of this, and it is, in fact, his starting place. The whole point to his argument is that the primary subject matter does not have the trait but it *ought* to have it, because the analogue has it and the primary subject matter and the analogue are similar in a number of respects. The structure of a moral analogical argument turns out on analysis to be something like this:

1. The primary subject matter does *not* have the characteristic C.
2. The analogue *does* have C.
3. But both the primary subject matter and the analogue have characteristics P, Q, R, and S.

Therefore, the primary subject matter ought to have C.

The argument in the scenario fits the scheme like this:

1. I was not selected for the expedition to Rigel-10.
2. Shipton was selected for the expedition.
3. But Shipton and I have many traits in common: our educational background is similar, our psychological test scores were similar, our physical condition is similar, our motivation is similar.

Therefore, I ought to have been selected for the expedition also.

Here's a more down-to-earth example that also illustrates the structure of the moral analogical argument:

Migrant farm workers receive less pay than the minimum wage prescribed by law. Since they are hired only on a part-time basis, employers are legally exempt from paying the federal minimum wage that must be given to full-time workers employed by companies engaged in interstate commerce. Yet, during the period of their seasonal employment, the migrants are full-time workers like any others. Thus, they ought to receive the federal minimum wage.

In the cases of factual analogical argument discussed in the last section, the principle of argument we saw could be put something like this: When two things have a large number of characteristics in common, if one has an additional characteristic, then the other will probably have it as well. (The criteria for evaluation, of course, were indications of how the principle is best applied in practice. As such, they modified it in certain slight ways.) But when "ought" or "should" is in the conclusion, this clearly can't be the principle. After all, to say that something "ought" to have a certain property (for example, ought to be treated in a certain way) is to presuppose tacitly that it doesn't have the property. As we've already seen, then, moral analogical arguments can hardly be thought of as aiming at establishing the conclusion that the primary subject matter "has" or "probably has" the characteristic at issue. Clearly, then, our analogical principle is not suitable for representing what underlies moral analogical arguments.

But what is the principle of moral analogical arguments? Well, a bit of reflection shows that it has to be something like this: When two things have a number of characteristics in common, if one has a characteristic that the other lacks, then the other *ought* to have it as well. It's generally understood, too, that to say someone ought to have the additional characteristic is to assert that he has been treated wrongly or unfairly. This then lays the groundwork for arguing further that *something* ought to be done to alter the situation and that *certain steps* ought to be taken to do it.

Our principle of moral argument by analogy is fundamentally the same as the dictum "Similar cases ought to be treated in similar ways." Moral and political arguments about rights, duties, and obligations usually start from the assumption that if two people or actions or whatever are like one another, then the ways in which they are dealt with should be alike. If the two cases are not treated alike, then this is considered to be grounds for a grievance. It's in accordance with this principle that we regard it as wrong that minority groups should be discriminated against in education, job promotion, voting, hiring, and so on.

Notice, though, that in actual cases of moral analogical argument our principle of argument can work in one of two ways. That is, on the basis of the same premises two different conclusions can be offered. On one hand, we can argue that John Simpson *ought* to be admitted to Dykeman University, because he is like Thomas Boggs in a number of ways and Boggs was admitted. On the other hand, we can argue that Boggs *ought not* have been admitted to Dykeman, because he is like Simpson in a number of ways, and Simpson was not admitted. Which of these ways of applying the principle we choose will depend on factors that make up the general context of the argument.

The two different sorts of conclusions aren't contradictory. Even though in an actual situation we would choose one way of stating the argument over the other way, the two conclusions amount to the same thing. Primary is the matter of whether *either* Simpson *or* Boggs should be admitted to Dykeman. If the two people resemble each other closely, then if one is admitted, the other should be admitted also; and if one is not admitted, then the other shouldn't be admitted either. Quite simply, the two should be *treated* alike because they *are* alike. But how either (and so both) should be treated is a separate question. Both ways of applying the principle, of formulating the argument, are fundamentally the same, in that each is a demand for similarity of treatment of similar cases.

To summarize: Both ways of arguing rest on the demand for fairness in the application of some rule, standard, or policy, on a demand for the equality of treatment of equal cases. Either way of stating the argument may assume without question that the rules or standards are acceptable so that each is an objection to the *way* in which they have been applied in a given case.

A successful moral analogical argument rests more on the number of *relevant* similarities between two cases than merely on the absolute number of similarities. When two people have the same *relevant* traits, then this is grounds for the argument that they should both be treated alike. Though they may differ in a variety of other ways or be similar in a number of irrelevant ways, the fact that the two cases possess the same *relevant* characteristics is what is of significance in moral analogical arguments. With respect to relevance, there are two important questions that have to be answered in order to evaluate such arguments.

1. What, in the given case, are the features taken to be relevant to deciding whether a rule or policy applies or whether some people should receive a benefit denied to others who also want it? Is the number of children in a family, for example, considered to be relevant to deciding whether a family with an income of under $4,000 a year qualifies for federal food stamps? Are college admission test scores taken to be relevant to determining whether a person is admitted to the University of California or not?

In order to formulate an acceptable moral analogical argument, it has to be known what traits are *regarded as* relevant by some agency, authority, and so on. It's necessary to know this in order to be able to show that two cases similar in the *relevant* respects haven't been treated similarly.

Of course, the decision on the part of some institution or official to treat a particular characteristic as relevant is itself open to criticism. The argument might then become one, not about the unequal treatment of similar cases, but about the standards by which cases in general are judged. When a person acting in an official capacity or a specific social institution is responsible for deciding what traits will be considered relevant for the granting of certain privileges (or for the imposition of certain penalties), the task of learning what traits are considered relevant in policy or practice is reasonably uncomplicated.

The task becomes much more complex when what we are discussing is the treatment of individuals by other individuals. Here we are dealing with matters of ethics, rather than with social values and practices. In our dealings with one another we rarely appeal to explicit policies or spell out in detail what we consider to be relevant in bestowing praise or blame. It's the job of moral philosophy (and fortunately not of informal logic) to investigate and appraise the standards of ordinary moral conduct.

In any case, so far as moral analogical arguments are concerned, in dealing with their formulation and evaluation in such a context we simply must be guided by the reasons that we have for believing that certain traits are relevant and certain ones are irrelevant to treating individuals in a particular way.

2. Of characteristics that are taken to be relevant, are some more important than others? If so, how are they to be ranked? Suppose that in applying to Dykeman University both Simpson and Boggs have to take a series of tests. Simpson makes a high score on the test for general knowledge and aptitude and only an adequate one on motivation; Boggs' scores are just the opposite. Both scores are relevant for admission, but are they equal in importance? If general knowledge and aptitude are taken to be more important than motivation, then there is justification for admitting Simpson and turning away Boggs.

Clearly, then, the *importance* assigned to relevant traits is another factor which must play a role in formulating and evaluating moral analogical arguments. The two cases compared in such an argument must have not only the same relevant traits, but they must have an average of them in the same *degree*. That is, the two cases must be similar in the extent to which they possess an "average" of the relevant features and in the importance assigned to them.

Simpson and Boggs are not comparable cases if a combination of an adequate test score on motivation and a high score on general knowledge produces a higher average than a high test score on motivation and an adequate score on general knowledge. These are grounds for treating the two cases differently, so a moral analogical argument that attempts to establish that they ought to be treated in the same way is not by itself a persuasive one. But, again, it's possible to argue against the ranking of traits in importance, against the way in which "average" of traits is determined. This is another matter that goes beyond an analogical argument that is offered in a context in which the practice is accepted.

Abstracting from the discussion here and borrowing an appropriate criterion from our earlier discussion of factual analogical arguments, we're now in a position to make two definite suggestions about the characteristics that acceptable moral analogical arguments ought to have. As with the earlier "criteria" these features are ones that are based on our practice of evaluating such arguments. They aren't intended to be arbitrary, nor are they imposed from without. They are, moreover, better regarded as suggestions about what to look for when faced with a moral analogical argument than as rigid criteria.

The Premises Must Be True

As with any analogical argument, the two cases claimed to resemble one another in certain respects must indeed resemble one another in those respects. What is asserted to be so of the analogue and of the primary subject matter must indeed be so. The reason these conditions must be met we discussed earlier.

The Degree of Analogy Must Be High

With respect to moral analogical arguments this means that the two cases should be similar to one another in all *relevant* respects *and* that they should possess a combination of the relevant characteristics in the same degree.

By no means have we said all that needs to be said about the problems involved in using and criticizing analogical arguments that are used to establish conclusions to the effect that something ought or ought not be the case. We have, at most, only indicated the kinds of problems that are tied up with the use of moral analogical arguments. Rare indeed is the case in which a moral analogical argument is used alone. Rather, such arguments typically find a place in broader discussions about the relevance and the importance of the traits that are being tacitly or explicitly used as the basis for choice between cases in the distribution of privileges and punishments.

Exercises

Illustrations, Ltd.

Analogy Division

Logic, Inc. has decided to expand. It buys up an independent company called Illustrations, Ltd. and makes it a subsidiary. You are asked to head up the Analogy Division until a suitable permanent person can be found.

Though not terribly excited about the job, you agree to do what's necessary until something more interesting comes along.

Your first day on the job you find everything is a mess. Bundles of illustrative analogies have been sent in for evaluation from contractors but nothing much has been done by way of critical examination. The Division is terribly behind on its work.

Much to your surprise, you find that workers in the division have been operating without any explicit criteria. You quickly change this by setting out the criteria you've found by experience to be most helpful:

1. The analogue should be more familiar than the PSM.
2. The analogue must be fitting.
3. The analogue should be vivid.
4. The analogue must not be misleading.

To help everyone get started working on the backlog of analogies, you pitch in and make a critical evaluation of some of them yourself. In this way, you can make it clear how the standards of evaluation are to be applied in practice.

The analogies that follow are the ones you start with.

(1)

In order for us to see something, light reflected from the object must enter our eyes. Suppose we are looking at objects that are very very far away from us, say the stars or distant planets. If one of these objects is much farther away than another, then we will see two events on each as taking place simultaneously. As a matter of fact, though, the event on the more distant object will have occurred long before that on the closer one.

Or, to invert the illustration, if an observer on Neptune could see all that is taking place on the earth, he might remain for hours quite unconscious of an event important enough to affect the welfare of a whole continent, though that event should happen under his eyes. We can imagine, for example, an observer on Neptune watching the battle of Waterloo from the early dawn until the hour when Napoleon's heart was yet full of hope, and Wellington was watching with ever-growing anxiety as charge after charge threatened to destroy the ranks of soldiers on whose steadfastness depended the fate of a continent.

We can conceive how full of interest the scene would have been to an intelligent Neptunian, and how eagerly he would have watched the maneuvers of either army, and also, what neither army knew, of the approach of Blücher with his Prussians. Yet, while our Neptunian would thus have traced the progress of the battle from his distant world, the conflict would in reality have been long since decided, the final charge of the British army accomplished, the Imperial Guard destroyed, Napoleon fugitive, and the Prussians, who to the Neptunian would seem still struggling through muddy roads toward the field of battle, would have been relentlessly pursuing the scattered army of France.

Adapted with minor modifications from RICHARD A. PROCTOR, *Other Worlds than Ours*

(2)

Every individual in this world must show a concern for his own life and eventual salvation God has specified what he expects of us, and Jesus was given to us as an example of what life in this world ought to be like. The church functions, as it has functioned through history, as the repository of Christian doctrine and learning.

Perhaps an analogy will help make clear what I mean. We are all, let us suppose, pioneers. We were not satisfied with our old home—perhaps the land was too crowded, maybe farming was poor, perhaps it was hard to get a job. For whatever reason, we set off from the East to push toward the great golden land in the West. There we hope to find happiness, peace, and the satisfaction of our desires.

Now, it's going to be a hard trip, and we know that if there's going to be any chance at all of success, we're going to need a crackerjack trail boss. That's what God is. He's a determined, hard-driving boss who keeps us moving when the going gets rough and we get tired and draggy and want to turn back. He's a tough man who has sympathy for us but is still determined to get us through, come what may.

Now the road is hard, and there's no telling what's up ahead. Maybe there's a river too wide to ford, a rockslide blocking a narrow pass, or highwaymen waiting to ambush us. We need a scout, somebody who will go on ahead and prepare the way for us. Somebody who'll tell us what to expect and how to prepare ourselves for it. That's what Jesus, is; he's our scout.

All the time we're traveling we need a place to keep the things we believed precious enough to carry away with us. And we need a place to rest. That place is our covered wagon, of course. It shelters what we hold precious, provides us with protection from the sun, and drawn in a circle, it is a stone in a fortress against intruders. The covered wagon is the church.

There you have it. As we travel the trail that leads into the future, into a newer and brighter land, we experience many hardships. But we have a hard-driving trail boss to keep us on the move, a scout to warn us of the dangers ahead, and a covered wagon to shelter and protect us.

(3)

Suppose that by paying $250.00 you could go into the largest and most exclusive department store in town and pick out and take home anything you could carry away with you. You would have access to the finest silks, precious jewels, handworked bracelets of gold and platinum, fabulous clothes by the best designers in the world.

It would be foolish to the point of imbecility if you paid your money, walked in, and picked out a piece of bubble gum.

Well, that's exactly what many college students do, in effect. They pay a nominal amount of money, and by doing so they gain access to some of the greatest treasures of the intellect in the world. Merely by asking, they can discover things that people labored for years to find out. Just by going to class, they can receive the outcome of years of thought and effort of the most outstanding thinkers and scientists the human race has produced.

Do they take advantage of this? Often they do not. They merely want to know which courses are the easiest ones, which don't have to be taken, and what are the minimum requirements for graduation.

For their money they are offered a fortune, but they choose a piece of mental bubble gum.

(4)

Detecting fallacious reasoning may be compared to a perplexed and entangled mass of accounts, which it requires much sagacity and close attention to clear up, and display in a regular and intelligible form. When this is once accomplished, the matter appears so simple that the unthinking are apt to undervalue the skill and pains which have been employed upon it.

RICHARD WHATELY,
Elements of Logic

(5)

The most important thing a teacher can do is to make a child want to learn. Rather than simply saying, "Here is a book that you have to read," the teacher should make the book so interesting that a child will *want* to read it.

Let me put this in the form of an analogy. As you know, travel agents don't force people to take trips. Rather, they primarily offer their services to those who want to take trips. They give advice, make arrangements, help with the planning, and so on.

Now if a traveler enjoys a trip that he takes, he is obviously going to be more inclined to take another one. He will return to the travel agent again and again and ask for suggestions and help. A travel agent can make a country appear so fascinating and enjoyable that a traveler will want very much to go there.

So it is with books. Like a travel agent, a teacher ought to make a book appear so interesting that a child will want to try it. After the first successful trip, then, the teacher can still serve the very important task of offering advice and suggestions for additional journeys.

The analogy was suggested in a talk by JOHN HOLT,
author of *How Children Learn*.

Example Division

No sooner do you get the Analogy Division straightened out than somebody from the Example Division comes in to ask for help.

"Gosh," she says, "all the people in our division have been watching how you helped out those Analogy guys, and we wondered if you wouldn't be willing to do the same for us."

Even though you sigh at the work involved, you are secretly flattered to be asked. You start out by laying down the standards for Examples:

1. The case should be an example.
2. The case should be typical.
3. The case should be clear-cut.
4. The case should be fair.

You are relieved to see that the Example Division does not have as much work piled up as Analogy did. In fact, there are just a few that you must go through and judge in terms of the criteria. Your fervent hope, of course, is that many of the examples will be perfectly satisfactory so you will not have to explain their shortcomings. You realize that this is too much to expect and, chances are, only a couple will be satisfactory.

1. The only example we have available to us in American history of a President who was impeached by the Congress and removed from office is that of Andrew Johnson.

2. Religious writing will always have a place in our society. It provides the kind of inspiration and feeling of communion with God that no other writing can supply. By religious writing, I have in mind such works as the poetry of Rod McKuen.

3. Walking has always been a favorite exercise for those who are not interested in team sports and like to get out on their own. For example, Ms. Barbara Floegel, who lives in Manhattan, manages to walk twelve miles a day, no matter what the weather is like.

4. Finding the square root of a number means finding a number that, when multiplied by itself, will give the original number. For example, suppose we want to find the square root of 27. We simply ask, what number when squared will produce 27.

5. Philosophers usually have a larger fund of general information than do most other people. Bertrand Russell, for example, wrote about economics, logic, mathematics, science, history, and social reform.

6. There should not be laws against possessing drugs that are not in any way dangerous. The laws against marijuana, for example, ought to be repealed.

7. Modern technology is responsible for the spreading of pollutants over the entire earth. Never before has this been possible. DDT, for example, has been found in fish from all parts of the sea, in birds nesting high in the mountains, and in the fat of Antarctic seals.

8. When you examine the contributions that American society has made to Western culture it is hard not to shudder. Here are just some examples: the electric knife, the mass-produced automobile, the television, the telephone, and plastics.

9. The world has always managed to throw up out of social turmoil a few individuals who promised that they were the ones who were ordained by destiny to save the nation from itself and from threats from without. These are the dictators who, with ruthless determination, pursued their own goals and barely reckoned the cost in human suffering. One can stand for the rest, and such a one was Josef Stalin, the Premier of the U.S.S.R. from 1941 to 1953.

10. More money is spent on pet food in the United States than is spent on social welfare programs. Erwin Plandri, for example, spends eighty-five dollars a week on the horsemeat that it takes to feed the two lions that he keeps on a ranch that he owns near Marysville, California.

Analogy Division: Parable and Fable Section

"Parables and Fables!"

You are shocked to find out that the Analogy Division is also responsible for handling Parables and Fables. For a moment you're tempted to quit the whole business, but on second thought you decide to stay around. At least parables and fables are *stories* and should be more fun to read than a lot of other stuff.

In fact, you think, you might even be able to write a few yourself. Probably better ones than you'll have to sort through.

But to start with, you have to evaluate the ones that you find on your desk. The criteria, you recall, are just about the same as for judging analogies, except you have to remember that they have to have some of the features of fiction. Parables and fables should have something like a plot or, at least they shouldn't be rambling or pointless, and when they are actually used, you have to be sure and make sure that the implicit point is understood.

1. The Oracle at Delphi was known throughout the ancient world as a source of wisdom and good counsel. In addition, it had a reputation for answering every question truthfully.

A man by the name of Therties decided that he could gain fame for himself if he could force the Oracle to give a false answer to a question. Fearing the Oracle's reputation, he decided that the only way he could be sure of getting a false answer was by trickery.

He decided that he would catch a small sparrow and hide it in his hands. He would then ask the Oracle what he was holding. If the Oracle correctly said that he was holding a bird, then he would ask if the bird were alive or dead. If the Oracle said dead, he would show the live bird. But if the Oracle said alive, then he would crush the bird to death and show its body to the Oracle.

Therties caught the bird and went to the Temple of the Oracle. There, in the dim light and with whisps of vapors floating in the still air, he put his first question to the Oracle.

"You are holding a bird," the Oracle answered.

"Quite right," said Therties, "but is it alive or dead?"

Therties' hands tensed around the warm bundle of feathers as he waited for the Oracle's answer.

There was a long pause, longer than before the answer to the first question.

Finally the Oracle spoke: "The answer to that question is in your hands, Therties."

I am reminded of this little story and of the wise answer of the Oracle whenever I think of the fate of the wild creatures that still manage to live in our land. So many have been slaughtered to the point of extinction and so many more are now threatened. There are states that still offer bounties on wolves, and in Wyoming the coyote is still poisoned and trapped. Strip mining has ruined thousands of acres of land where birds, reptiles, and rodents once flourished.

Will any animals ultimately survive this driving and unrelenting onslaught? The answer to that question is truly in our hands.

2. The Grasshopper was worried. He had spent the long summer days at play instead of gathering food for the coming winter. He realized that he would never be able to survive once the cold winds began to blow. He decided, then, he would consult the Ant, who was recognized throughout the Midwest as being a creature of good practical sense.

"You certainly have a problem," the Ant agreed. "I think I have a solution to it, though. The best thing for you to do is to change yourself into a cockroach. After you've done that you won't have any trouble finding a nice warm barn to crawl into, and once inside, the food will be plentiful. You'll pass the winter in real comfort."

"All right," said the Grasshopper, "but how do I change myself into a cockroach?"

"Look," said the Ant, "I've given you the general idea. You'll have to work out the details for yourself."

Government planners are the Ants in our life. We recognize that we have a great many problems in our society, and we go to them for help. What can we do about continued discrimination? we ask. What can we do about deteriorating neighborhoods? What can we do about unemployment?

Well, they tell us, to stop discrimination you've got to get people to treat one another fairly. To stop decay in the cities you've got to get people to stop moving out and build them up again. To stop unemployment you've got to give people jobs.

Notice, though, that that is *all* they say. They set up an agency, give them some money, and let them worry about working out the details.

3. There was a great scholar in the land of Uz who decided that he would compile a great catalogue of all the true sentences in the world.

For ten years he worked, both by day and by night, writing down all sentences that came to him authenticated as true. Some were trivial sentences, some were strange, some were profound, and some were puzzling.

One day, taking a brief rest from his labors, he strolled along a beach. It was a cloudy stormy day, gray and windswept, and there were no people about. Much to his surprise, though, he encountered a small child. The child was sitting on the beach scooping out sand from a hole with a seashell.

As he approached, he noticed that the child had completed his digging and was taking shellfuls of water from the sea and pouring them into the hole.

"What are you doing, my child?" the scholar asked.

"I am emptying the sea into this small hole," the boy said.

"Then that is a task you shall never finish."

"No more than you will finish yours," said the child and vanished into the air.

The scholar abandoned his catalogue and turned his mind to other tasks.

Imaginative Approaches to Real-Life Situations

1. Busted!

You have just walked out of the Fine Arts Theater, where you have been watching Marlon Brando in *The Wild Ones*. A policeman in uniform walks over to you as you start down the street and takes you rather roughly by the arm. "Just keep quiet and come over here with me," he says. He puts you against the fender of a car, searches you, and comes up with a small cellophane bag. You've never seen the bag before! "You're under arrest on suspicion of violation of the narcotics laws," the policeman says.

INSTRUCTION: Write a Battle Plan scenario for dealing with the immediate situation that being arrested for narcotics possession produces.

2. Fire

It's a terribly hot day, and you wish you weren't out on the highway. But you are. You are driving on an Interstate Highway west of Flagstaff, Arizona, and trying to keep cool. You have the windows rolled up and you are drinking 7-Up out of a small cooler in the front seat.

It's hot, but at least the road isn't crowded. In fact, there isn't a car—or anything else—in sight for miles. Things are going smoothly, but suddenly you notice that white clouds of smoke are billowing up from under the hood. In fact, smoke is coming through the air vents. The heat gauge flashes red. At the same times, the white smoke changes to black.

INSTRUCTION: Write a Battle Plan scenario outlining the steps you might take to deal with this situation.

3. Androids

Biological science is rapidly advancing. Genetic engineering is, for the moment, a dream of the future. Perhaps, though, not of the distant future. In fact, you read in the newspaper one day that Rockefeller University, in cooperation with the Harvard Medical School, using funds supplied by the Department of Defense, has succeeded in what used to be described as "creating life."

Less dramatically put, they have been able to assemble a developmental system in the laboratory that produces creatures that are fundamentally indistinguishable from ordinary human beings. These creatures are full-grown in size and did not have to go through any process of maturation. Intellectually, of course, they are still comparable to children. In science fiction terms, the creatures are androids.

INSTRUCTION: Develop a Science Fiction scenario in which you attempt to anticipate the most major social and political problems that the appearance of androids would cause.

4. Marijuana

It seems inevitable that before long marijuana will be legalized—or at least decriminalized—in all states. When that happens, of course, there will be a very high demand for marijuana and marijuana-associated products. This demand will mean big money for those business enterprises that are prepared to take advantage of it.

INSTRUCTION: Write a Quasipredictive scenario in which you outline the new products, promotions, and so on that might be expected in the attempt to exploit marijuana commercially.

Argument Division

Logic, Inc. has decided to make use of its experiences in informal logic and expand its subsidiary Illustrations, Inc. A new division will be added that will deal exclusively with arguments by analogy.

Because of your fine reputation, you are selected to head the new division. The first thing you do, of course, is to list for yourself the criteria that are relevant to evaluating analogical arguments. Also, you note down the special features that moral analogical arguments have, so that you can modify the general criteria in order to deal with them.

After this, you go through a list of analogical arguments and indicate which ones are moral arguments and which are not. Having completed this task, you go back and provide a detailed evaluation of the worth of each argument.

Your classification and evaluation can later serve as a guide for understanding and judging arguments that are sent to Logic, Inc. for an opinion.

(1)

You have listened to the coal companies tell you that after they finish digging out the coal they will restore the land so that it is as good as new.

But I say to you quite simply—it can't be done. If you vote to give them the mining rights, you will be voting to destroy the land forever.

In strip mining the layers of earth are removed one after another to get the seams of coal that lie beneath it. Now most of us are accustomed to thinking of those layers as just plain dirt, as if it were a pile of sand. But that's not the way it is at all. Each of those layers is filled with various kinds of small plants, some of them microscopic, and bacteria. The layers are shot through with beetles, bugs, and worms of a great variety. Now, these plants and these animals play a big role in making the soil what it is. They eat, digest, and excrete substances that affect the alkalinity of the soil, they contribute nutrients to it, they aerate it and keep it loose so that plants can grow in it. The world beneath the soil is a very complicated and extensive ecosystem. Once the dirt is dug up, this system is destroyed, and just putting the dirt back is not going to restore it.

Let me take a comparison. If you took a knife and cut a chunk of flesh out of your leg, ground it up into hamburger, and then stuck it back in the hole you gouged out, you wouldn't expect everything to be the same as before. That's because you know how complicated and tied in with other parts of the body a piece of human flesh is. Well, what I'm saying is that a piece of ground is similarly complicated and tied in with other systems. If you don't want to see this land destroyed, then don't vote for strip mining here.

(2)

According to recent figures, almost seventy percent of the people who are registered will not vote in the next election. Over half who were interviewed did not know who their Congressional representative is. Twenty-five percent couldn't name either of the senators from their state. Yet these are the very same people that we rely upon to make decisions that vitally affect our entire country. They elect the representatives that make the laws, the judges that apply the penalties for their violation, and the executive officers that see to it that these laws are executed. They pass on bonds, and taxes, and school officials.

Let's take a parallel case. Suppose you went to a builder and said, "I want you to build a house for me," and he agreed to do so. "Do you think it needs a poured concrete foundation?" you ask. "I don't know," he says; "I don't know much about foundations." "What size lumber are you going to use for wall studs?" "I don't know," he says; "I haven't given it any thought." "Well," you say, "Are you going to go out and look over the site so you'll know about problems of drainage and soil conditions?" "No," he says, "I don't know enough to tell anything by looking."

I suspect if a builder talked to you in this way, you would change your mind about hiring him to build a house for you. Maybe it's about time we changed our mind about democracy. It seems foolish in the extreme to entrust very important decisions to people who are uninformed and uninterested. There are other ways of seeing to people's needs without allowing them to make the decisions. Now is the time to start considering some of those other means.

(3)

Precisely as a man walking at a great distance from us appears to move much more slowly than one who is walking at the same rate close by, so the apparent rate of a star's motion is diminished in proportion to the star's distance from us. When, therefore, it was found that the star Alpha Centauri is moving more rapidly than other stars, this fact, combined with the great luster of the star, led astronomers to suspect that it must be comparatively near us.

RICHARD A. PROCTOR,
Other Worlds Than Ours

(4)

On Aug. 13, 18-year-olds will have all the rights of adults, except one, purchasing liquor. It seems ridiculous that an 18-year-old can purchase a $4000 car or buy a house, but cannot purchase a $1.60 six-pack of beer.

At a time when equality is such an important issue, this is a very obvious form of discrimination. If our government is going to grant 18-year-olds the rights of an adult, then they should have all of these rights.

St. Louis *Post-Dispatch*

(5)

Photographs that have actually been taken from space reveal in a dramatic way that our planet is very much a spacecraft, turning on its axis while making its endlessly repeated trip around the sun.

This comparison, more than any other, allows us to appreciate the importance of keeping the ship in good repair and functioning properly. We are adrift in the limitless sea of space, and there is no port where we can ever expect to put in. All that we shall ever have is aboard the ship. If we destroy our life-support systems—the atmosphere, the lakes, rivers, and oceans, the forests and swamps—then we will eventually destroy ourselves. If we allow the ship to become more crowded than our necessarily limited supplies can support, then we can expect competition, bloodshed, and almost endless suffering.

What can we do to save ourselves and future generations? We must see to it that an end is put to pollution, that our support system is not strained beyond its capacity. We must see to it that population is limited, that the ship does not become overcrowded. The situation demands that we act now.

(6)

If a national health insurance program should ever become law, people would like it. Right now there are all sorts of complaints about such a program: about how it would cost a lot of money, how it would hurt the private insurance companies, how people with smaller families would be paying a proportionally greater cost of the program than people with larger families, and so on.

The truth is, though, that whenever there has been any new kind of social legislation proposed, people have always initially opposed it and said that it was going to ruin the country. This was particularly so with Social Security. People also said this would ruin the insurance business, that it was unfair to people who paid it but never collected it, that some people would be able to get more money out of it than others, and on and on. After it was passed, though, none of the complaints turned out to be well-founded and none of the terrible predictions was fulfilled.

(7)

The Social Security program has done a great deal to help our society solve the problems of individuals faced with disability and unemployment and old age. There are tens of thousands of widows and orphans whose lives would have been ruined without Social Security. A national health insurance program promises a great deal for even more people. Those who claim that the people say they don't want it may be right. But this may be just because no one has told them the benefits they might expect from it. If a bill establishing such a program were put into law, the complaints would disappear.

(8)

Now, Athenians, I am not going to argue for my own sake, as you may expect me to do. I am going to argue for your sake, so you will not sin against the gods by condemning me. If you kill me you will not find it easy to find a successor for me. I am, to use a ludicrous figure of speech, a sort of gadfly that the gods gave to the state. The state, on the other hand, is a great and noble steed who is slow in his motions because of his large size. He has to be stirred into life. I am the gadfly that the gods attached to the state, and all day long and all places I am always lighting upon you, arousing, persuading, and criticizing you. You will not find it easy to get another like me, and for this reason, I advise you to spare me.

PLATO,
Apology

(9)

The triangular-shaped pieces of flint found by the Leakeys in the Olduvai Gorge in Tanzania are almost certainly tools of some kind. They show no signs of having a place to attach a handle, and very likely they are scrapers or a crude kind of knife. They resemble scrapers that have been found in hundreds of other places throughout the world, including some still-existing cultures. Because of this definite association with manufacture and since the flints show characteristic marks of having been crudely worked with other flints, it seems well-established that they are tools. Who used the tools is another question. Some have suggested that they were made by the extinct anthropoids *Paranthropus*, and this may be so.

(10)

Buyers and users of marijuana are being unjustly penalized by existing laws. Let's assume, for the sake of argument, that marijuana does some sort of damage to the bodies of those who use it—something that has not been clearly established. Well, we also know that ordinary cigarettes cause damage or, as we might put it, "Cigarette Smoking Is Harmful to Your Health." We also know that alcohol is harmful to health, not to mention the social problems that it causes.

Notice, though, that we don't outlaw cigarettes or alcohol. We don't send the police around to arrest people who have been smoking or drinking. We don't search their houses on the suspicion that they might be hiding a carton of cigarettes or a bottle of Scotch.

We simply warn people, then we let them make up their own minds. But those who smoke marijuana get arrested, put on trial, and often sent to jail. This is simply not fair.

10/Writing Logically

You write with ease, to show your breeding,

But easy writing's curst hard reading.

R. B. SHERIDAN
"Clio's Protest"

THIS chapter is devoted to discussing the logic of writing, and exactly what this subject is deserves a word of explanation. The logic we will be concerned with here obviously cannot be the same as the narrow logic of deductive arguments or even the broader logic of inductive ones. Rather, in talking about the logic of composition, the term "logic" must be understood as meaning about the same as it does in the common-phrase "That's logical." Logic, in this sense, concerns *reasonableness.* To tell someone "If you want to get from San Francisco to New York in the shortest time possible, then it's only logical for you to take a plane" is to advise him that, given what he wants to accomplish, going by plane is a resonable thing to do. It's a sensible step to take; it's a good idea.

Now, what about the logic of writing? The phrase is too broad for our subject, for one thing. We won't be concerned with the composition of fiction, poetry, letters, *billets-doux,* proclamations, laws, or press re-leases. Our sole concern will be with expository writing in general and with the essay or paper in particular. Writing is expository when it puts forward facts, provides explanations, and gives arguments. Broadly speaking, such writing aims at communicating information, including the writer's attitude, beliefs, point of view, and so on. More specifically, it aims at presenting a thesis (which may be no more than a certain attitude toward a subject), explaining and supporting it, and getting readers to accept it. The logic of expository writing simply concerns the ways in which these aims can be accomplished. The reasonableness and strategy of organization and presentation, the use of language, and other factors connected with effective communication are thus all matters we can take as belonging to our subject.

The three sections of this chapter give only a brief and general account of the logic of composition. The first section deals with the structure of essays. The second treats logical factors of style, and the last discusses some of the more common snares that catch unwary writers by the heels. By no means all (or even all important) topics get noticed, but there are hints that may be helpful. "Writing maketh an exact man," Bacon said.

Maybe it does and maybe it doesn't, but what is certain is that the person who is careful, thinks about what he is doing, and is self-critical has a better chance of becoming an exact writer. The discussions in the following sections are primarily intended to encourage the development of traits and habits that promote exact and effective writing. Since much of the advice given is presented in the form of "rules of writing," it is important to take a moment to fashion the lens through which such "rules" ought to be viewed.

Bertrand Russell reported that his brother-in-law Logan Pearsall Smith once gave him several simple rules to follow in writing. Russell could remember only two: *Put a comma every four words,* and *Never use "and" except at the beginning of a sentence.* It's not difficult to see that adherence to these precepts would produce a rather bizarre result, and perhaps it's just as well that Russell forgot the rest of the rules.

Not all rules of composition are as peculiar as Smith's, of course. Most are statements of sound practical advice based on thoughtful consideration of what makes a piece of writing effective. To be of value, however, such rules have to be approached with a proper understanding of their character and an appreciation of their limitations. Most important, despite the name "rules," rules of style and organization are *not* rules, at least not in the sense in which there are rules of baseball, quoits, and Monopoly. Writing is not a game, and except metaphorically, it's not possible to win or lose or make an illegitimate move. There is nothing in writing which clearly counts as breaking a rule (except for grammar and spelling, that is), and the rules of writing don't really define the "game" of writing. The rules are merely bits of practical advice that people who believe they have a clear idea of how to write pass on to those who believe they don't. Advice about writing is thus more like suggestions about the *strategy* of playing a game than like the rules of a game. For example, "Try to buy all property cards of the same color" is not a rule of Monopoly, but it's a good suggestion to make to a novice player. Such advice is quite general, of course, and there are special circumstances in which it would be unwise to follow it. Rules of writing, advice about strategy, are subject to the same limitation. All such suggestions mustn't be interpreted strictly and literally, but only loosely and cautiously.

"If you own a hundred thousand francs worth of craftsmanship, spend five sous to buy more," the French painter Degas once advised a student. Writing, like painting, is in part a skill that can be developed; it is a craft that can be improved. Rules may suggest and guide, but in the final analysis everybody is on his own. Writing comes down finally to you and a piece of blank paper, and practice and self-criticism are worth more than any explicit formulas. It is no more possible to write wholly by rules than it is to live wholly by them.

Putting the Bones Together: Logical Articulation

Son of man, can these bones live? And I answered,
O Lord God, thou knowest.

Ezekiel 37:3

Over two thousand years ago Aristotle pointed out that works that move through time need certain traits to give them unity and stability. A building or a painting has a particular sort of stability and unity merely because it doesn't change. But a play or a novel or writing of any kind is dynamic. Something is always happening, and the reader is pulled along by the change. The difference is like that between a still photograph and the perpetual and relentless unreeling of a movie film. To keep the constant change from becoming bewildering and to generate unity and stability from within the flux, the writer must impose a structure on his materials. He must organize what he has to say and make his presentation in a planned and orderly manner.

The organization Aristotle demanded is simplicity itself: Works should have a beginning, a middle, and an end. But the simplicity here is as deceptive as the simplicity of Pilate's "What is truth?" All works that span time have Aristotle's three-part structure in the sense that they make a start, travel along, and then come to a halt. And of course this is not what Aristotle had in mind. He meant that the first part of a work should be of a certain *character*, that it should do certain things, accomplish certain aims. The other two organizational components have to be understood in the same way. Spelling out in any useful detail the character of the components is almost as tough as answering Pilate's question. But it's important to try to do so, if for no other reason than that thinking about such matters helps people become more conscious of their own organizational techniques and more critical of their efforts.

Opening Game: The Introduction

There are a number of purposes to be achieved in the beginning of an essay, but the overarching one is to prepare the way for what is to come. The introduction marks the boundaries, specifies the handicap, and points in the direction of the play. What's more, it has to perform the often subtle and always difficult task of getting the reader interested in the game.

Introductions differ much more than do peas in a pod. A researcher writing about Bantu fertility rites for the *Journal of Cultural Anthropology* probably won't introduce his topic in exactly the same way that Ralph Ginzberg would in *Eros*. Still, more successful introductions do accomplish about the same specific aims, and it's possible to discuss these in a general way.

An Introduction Should Establish a Context

An essay is *about* something, and it's important to indicate the general character of the matter that is going to be discussed in the main body of the work as early as possible. The introduction should supply a context within which issues and problems can be located. No one can write about everything at the same time, and it's helpful to the reader (and to the writer) to see an issue as part of a larger domain. It's not at all necessary to go to great length and to descend into myriad details to point to the general sphere you will be writing about. Often a single sentence will turn the trick:

> A great deal of work has been done recently in psychology and sociology on the causes of criminal behavior in our society.

This simple sentence sets rough boundaries to the discussion. From it, taken alone, a reader can learn that criminal behavior will be talked about and that it will be related to our society, rather than to Russian or Chinese society. He can also discover that two disciplines of the social sciences have been working on criminality, that the work has been recent, and that it has been concerned with causal factors.

It may be, of course, that a single sentence is not enough to draw the boundaries clearly. Other sentences can then follow to restrict the context or to indicate where your main concern will lie. A second sentence after the example above can work many changes. Here are a few possibilities:

> "So far, however, no biologist has concerned himself with this problem."
> "As yet, however, no attention has been paid to the history of criminal behavior."
> "But so far no attention has been given to its economic consequences."
> "No attention has yet been paid to the causes of such behavior in Communist societies."

Any one of these sentences not only restricts the field of discussion, but calls attention to something within the field that has not been done. It opens the possibility that you are going to set about doing what others have failed to do. Thus, the second sentence is well on the way to suggesting that you are onto something important and that what you are saying shouldn't be ignored.

An Introduction Should Announce Intentions

An introduction is the place to present a general sketch of what you intend to accomplish in the body of the essay:

> In this paper I want to examine some of the biological determinants of behavior. I intend to show that in at least one case there is a definite causal link between genetic factors and criminal behavior.

Such a sketch sets up the reader's expectations. Within the general context you have indicated, it shows him where you are headed and prepares him for the job of relating what you say to your overall aim. It gives direction to the essay.

The notice of what you intend to do is usually spoken of as the "thesis" of the work. This term is slightly misleading, for it suggests that all writing has to involve the defense of some claim like "Capital punishment should be abolished" or "The American President should be elected for a term of eight years." By contrast, a topic like "A description of the events that took place during the march on the Pentagon in 1965" doesn't sound like a thesis. But it is. Most generally, a thesis is just a statement of what it is that you are going to do in the essay.

An Introduction Should Relate Your Work to That of Others

An essay that is about a subject on which others have written should take account of that fact. An introduction ought to indicate briefly what positions others have taken or what aspects of the topic they have dealt with:

> Holtzbecker has argued that genetic factors are of no special importance in influencing criminal behavior. Other investigators, such as Black, have accepted this general view.

> Surprisingly enough, no critics have studied the influence of nineteenth-century sociological thinking on the literature of the period.

Such remarks as these not only show your awareness of the work that others have done, but they prepare the way for an account of how your work will supplement or clash with what others have written.

An Introduction Should Indicate the Importance of Your Work

The introduction ought to make it clear to the reader why it is important to do what you are going to do. What is the value of studying the influence of sociological theories on nineteenth-century literature? It's not immediately obvious, but even it were, it is still important to know why *you* think it is worth doing. The reasons you give for the significance of what you intend to do are themselves crucial parts of the essay, for they play a role in determining your approach to the topic. The scholar who believes that a study of sociology and literature in the nineteenth-century is important because it provides evidence of the free flow of ideas in nineteeth-century intellectual circles is likely to deal with his subject in quite a different manner from the person who believes that such a study reveals the unconscious assimilation of scientific ideas in literature.

Along with presenting the reasons why your thesis is important, the introduction should indicate where you believe others have gone wrong or failed. You, of course, intend to right their wrongs or to do the job they have neglected. This ought to be mentioned, at least, though it is perhaps only in the main part of the work that you can make good your claims:

> Holtzbecker's position I hold to be wholly mistaken. Later I shall present evidence that supports my claim that inherited factors do have an effect on certain types of behavior which we classify as criminal.

> In this essay I hope to make a start in overcoming the general neglect of this topic. Though I shall be concerned only with the influence of Herbert Spencer's sociological thinking on Charles Dickens, perhaps this will at least open the way for similar studies of other authors.

The Introduction Should Generate Interest

The introduction should stir up the reader's curiosity. It's not really enough that you should show why your topic is important. The sad truth is that there are many important topics that it's hard to be interested in. What's more, there are incredibly dull essays on perfectly fascinating topics. The introduction should get your reader hooked. It ought to make him curious about how you are going to manage things, how you are going to achieve your aims. One way to do this is to put your claim in a blunt or provocative way:

> The conservation policies of the U.S. Forestry Department have produced great environmental damage.

> Much behavior that we classify as criminal is such only in a trivial technical sense.

Such techniques can be used to involve the reader in the process of substantiating your claim. They provide an element of puzzlement which latches onto his attention. If you're lucky, he will stay with you long enough for you to have a chance to tell him what you want him to hear.

Middle Game: The Body

The body of the essay is where most of the real work gets done. It's where the writer must put up or shut up, where he must make good on his introductory promises. It's where reasons are presented, arguments are offered, and the thesis is developed and elaborated.

Even if you are only describing an event or a bit of behavior and not trying to prove a claim, the body of an essay is still the *argument* of the work. You are, after all, trying to get the reader to share your point of view. You are trying to convince him to look at things in the same way that you do. To this extent, all essays involve persuasion. The persuasive aspect is obvious when explicit claims requiring arguments and the marshaling of evidence are at stake. But even in "descriptions" it is always present.

"Persuasion" is the key to the lock of the successful essay. With this in mind the problem becomes one of strategy: how to persuade the reader. There is no more a single strategy of persuasion than there is a universal solvent. Each writer has to solve the problem for himself. But one way to approach the task is to ask yourself what the reader is likely to accept as "obvious," what he is likely to agree to without persuasion. If you can use the obvious and acceptable in such a way as to show that it adequately supports a definite and unobvious position or point of view, you will have done the best persuading possible. Going from there you may be able to build up support for other points out of a mosaic of the obvious and the established. In short, you must "make a case" for your position, and to do this you may have to make a case for subsidiary positions that contribute to its support.

In presenting reasons and facts to establish a point, you should strive to see that the case you make bears the marks of a good argument. You should make it obvious what *claim* you are making, what *reasons and evidence* support it, why they are *relevant* to it, why they constitute *adequate* support, and why reasons that might be urged against it are inadequate. Make clear also when you have rested your case (made your point), so the reader will understand why it is that later on you regard yourself as free to use your conclusion to support an additional position.

Honest people don't try to persuade by playing on the prejudices and preconceptions of their readers. But it's important to consider what these are likely to be. Chances are you will have to try to overcome some of them, and the dictates of strategy demand that you not ask your reader to assume as obvious a point that he believes to be wrong. Your understanding of (or guesses about) what the reader believes should play a major role in how you approach the problem of persuading him to accept your thesis or point of view.

Every essay should have a discernible principle of organization. That is, materials and arguments should have an order of presentation. The order usually grows out of the general strategy of persuasion that is adopted. Practiced writers get a sense of the steps by which they should make their points, and the order develops as they write. But tyros, novices, and amateurs sometimes do better to think about an order of presentation separately and then consider how they can impose it on their materials. It's for this reason that teachers often force unwilling students to make outlines of their essays before they write them. The value of making outlines is debatable—primarily because most people are not sure what points they want to make until they actually write them down. Once a first draft is written, rewriting can easily take the place of making a detailed outline. What isn't debatable, though, is that an essay should have an order of presentation and that it should be clear to the reader.

The best way to acquire a sense of order, fitness, and rightness in presentation is to do a lot of reading and writing with a critical eye. But for the sake of explicitness and just in case they might be useful, here are a few common types of ordering principles.

a. Most useful, perhaps, is the one already discussed, namely moving from the *obvious to the unobvious.* Essays written in this fashion start from ground that is acceptable to the reader and they aim to pull him up to a plateau of agreement—to a point that he likely wouldn't have accepted initially. From that plateau, the reader can be persuaded to climb the next one, and so to the starry reaches.

b. A second type of sequence is from the *easy to the difficult.* Such an order is obviously most appropriate in works that aim at teaching the reader something. Imagine, for example, the steps you would have to go through to teach someone who knew no arithmetic to multiply and divide fractions. (The words "easy" and "difficult" shouldn't be taken seriously here. The principle is really that of explaining to someone what he needs to know in order to understand something else. "Fundamental to complex" is perhaps a better name.)

c. Moving from the *least interesting* (or least important) to the *most interesting* (or most important) is a frequent ordering strategy. It has the advantage of creating a sense of unfolding drama, which is important in maintaining the reader's interest. What's more, when the reader completes the work, the most significant or impressive point is still ringing in his head.

The sequence in which materials are presented is like the thread that Ariadne strung out to guide Theseus through the labyrinth of the Minataur. The reader depends on the writer to supply him with a thread to follow through the maze of writing. Otherwise, he becomes disoriented, lost, and mistakes side passages for the main way. It's to the writer's advantage to keep the thread of discussion obvious, for if he intends to lead the reader to a conclusion, he can't permit him to wander around aimlessly. Certain principles of organization seem more proper to some topics and materials than others do, and part of the art of writing consists in matching a subject matter with a principle of presentation. In any case, *some* principle should be present, even if it isn't a "natural development" from the material, but has been bodily thrust on it.

End Game: The Conclusion

The conclusion of an essay is a reducing lens that brings to a focus the major elements stressed in the body of the work. It offers the last chance the writer has to persuade the reader, and the most should be made of the opportunity. The evidence and arguments supporting claims you have made should be rehearsed briefly. The main arguments ought to be outlined in the same order as they were presented and their conclusions brought to bear on your major thesis. (In an essay of two or three pages, such repetition is hardly necessary, of course.) Most important, the reader should be left in no doubt about where you stand, what your thesis or point of view is. He may go away fuming and cursing your name, but he should not go away puzzled about what position you have taken.

Constructing a conclusion is a delicate task. In pulling all the threads together and spinning them into a single skein, you must decide what your most important and compelling points are. Writers can be surprised by their own conclusions, for when they look back over what they have written they sometimes see how the materials they have presented can be assembled in a much more forceful way than first appeared. Writers as well as readers will lose full sight of points made early in an essay, and the conclusion brings them all into view at once.

The last impression is often the lasting impression. Thus, conclusions should be carefully worked pieces of prose. All that is done in a conclusion ought to be accomplished *persuasively*. Rhetorical success in writing the conclusion contributes much to the general success of the essay.

Caution: Taking the Above Discussion Too Rigidly May Be Hazardous to Your Writing

The discussion of the three parts of an essay is necessarily extremely general. Perhaps its most important effect, as I said at the beginning, will be to stimulate people to take a greater interest in their own writing and to improve it by self-criticism, experiment, and conscious effort. The guidelines above are painted in strokes broad enough to cover expository writing on any topic. For that reason, anyone who wants to benefit from them must interpret and adjust them to fit his own case. They are like a general recipe for meat stew: take some meat, vegetables, and spices, and cook together in a liquid. But people don't cook "meat stews," they cook *beef* stew, *rabbit* stew, and so on. In making it, they don't use "vegetables" and "spices" but tomatoes, carrots, salt, and pepper. People don't write essays on "any topic" either, so they have to interpret the general recipe given here if they want to produce a tasty essay on a specific topic.

Let me point out another pitfall, lest the unwary stumble into it. The elements that I discussed as making up the introduction, the body, and the conclusion of an essay are elements of analysis. They come from anatomizing essays into separable pieces. But the fact that they are present in essays doesn't at all mean that the elements must be presented separately in writing an essay. In the same paragraph or in the same sentence, for example, a writer may be able both to present his thesis and mention the position taken by others. The two elements can be isolated and talked about, but in actual composition they may merge into a single action. The elements of each of the three parts are not steps in an outline that ought to be followed. A dollar contains a hundred cents, but it can be broken down in many ways.

Through a Glass Clearly: The Logic of Style

Style is the man himself.
GEORGES-LOUIS DE BUFFON,
Discours sur le style

The remark by Buffon quoted above has more to do with the personality of writers than with their moral character. Murderers and other bad men don't necessarily have a bad prose style, but people given to rambling digressions, pointless anecdotes, and hasty conclusions often reveal these traits in their writings. Writing is as much a form of thinking as the running patter that goes on inside the head, and even if first thoughts and first drafts are cloudy and formless, final thoughts and finished essays should be clear and cogent. If "style" is understood to mean something like "the manner of presentation," then the logic of writing clearly must be concerned with style to some extent. The focus of its interest is on features of writing that make for effective exposition. An appreciation of the significance of these features should help anyone who wants to write logically, and if Buffon is right, it should help him or her become a logical person.

Be Brief

Bertrand Russell claimed that the ideal of writing that he derived from mathematics was "to say everything in the smallest number of words in which it could be said clearly." (Fortunately, it was this aim, rather than his brother in-law's rules, that guided him.) Brevity of language is as hard to achieve as the good life, and anyone who has tried knows how hard it is to say in one page what he first said in two. There are, however, a couple of common enemies of brevity that a writer would do well to keep his eye on. By their thievery they can turn a lean strip of prose into a fatty chunk.

Avoid Unnecessary Words

If one word will do the work of two, don't hire the extra one. If a word or phrase can be left out altogether, dismiss it from your employ. Unnecessary words are boring and distracting and if they come in clouds, they blot out your point. There's no need to say, "It is completely unnecessary for me to feel obliged to point out to this audience" when "I don't have to tell you" or "as you know" or "of course" does the same job. The man who says, "We shall be moving pending the completion of certain elements of refurbishment" need only say, "We shall move in when the decorating is finished." Phrases like "with respect to" and "in order to" can generally be replaced by words like "about" and "to," and expressions like "hardly necessary" are hardly ever necessary.

Avoid Padding

"Say the words, take the money, and go home" is an actor's adage that can be modified to fit writing: Say what you have to say and quit. The main aims of expository writing are to tell someone something and to tell it to him in such a way that he will understand and accept it. Thus, each sentence in an essay should have a job to do, and there should be no unnecessary jobs. A sentence should present needed information, advance the argument, or clarify a point. If it does none of these, it should be cut out.

A writer should state his point directly, rather than circling around and buzzing it like a carnival stunt pilot. Consider:

> There is a matter of serious concern I wish to call to your attention. It is a matter of importance to all Americans, whatever their age or economic condition. I am, I hardly need tell you, speaking of national medical insurance.

This passage strives for dramatic effect by making us wonder what the topic is going to be. But it comes closer to generating boredom than drama, and after the first couple of sentences we don't really much care what the topic is going to be. The passage amounts to no more than "I want to talk about the serious matter of national medical insurance," which really has more dramatic power because it is more direct.

A common kind of padding is to present the reader with more information than he needs or wants. The groundwork for making a point must be laid, of course, and this always demands providing some material relevant to it. The reader must be enabled to understand and appreciate the point, but a balance must be struck between inadequate information and superfluous information. Not all material relevant to a matter must be presented, and deciding what to include and what to omit is one of the challenges of writing. Should someone who is concerned in an essay with demonstrating the injustices of our present legal system talk about the history of the system? Probably not. Historical material might help explain how the system came to be unjust, and anyone writing a book on the same topic would certainly have to present such information. A much better strategy for an essay on the injustices of the system, however, would be to concentrate on cases of injustices in the system's present operation and merely allude to its history. (Read the discussion of irrelevancy in the next section.)

Be Simple

Drivers of fat oxen don't have to be fat, and lectures on humor don't have to be funny. Similarly, writing that is about a complex subject doesn't have to be complex. A rough rule to follow, in fact, is that the more difficult and obscure the topic, the simpler and clearer the prose should be. The writer must always keep his reader from falling overboard and being lost, and he has to give this task special attention when the sea is running high and a thick fog threatens to blur familiar objects.

Simplicity and Brevity

Simplicity is often the deadly enemy of brevity. To be simple in giving an explanation or in making a point sometimes requires saying a lot. Unless you are writing for an audience of specialists, a reader must be told much before he can understand what it means to say things like "More work needs to be done on the repressor function of genes" or "The percentile of parity support currently allowed for farm products is unrealistic." It's not necessary to be long-winded and tell a reader all you know about a subject, but you must tell him enough to enable him to understand *what* you are saying and *why* you are saying it. In deciding how much is enough you must decide who your audience is likely to be.

Word Choice

Simplicity in the choice of words is perhaps the most important feature of simplicity in writing. Using words that refer to specific sorts of objects or situations instead of more general abstract words is good policy. Rather than talking about *comestibles,* talk about *food,* or, better, talk about *steak and potatoes.* Abstract words have the great virtue that they allow us to speak about wide ranges of objects without having to name more specific kinds. We can talk about food without having to list each sort of thing we take to be food. The important thing in writing is not to choose words that are more abstract than necessary. If you really want to talk about *modes of transportation* and not just *cars, buses, and airplanes,* then you just must use the more general term. Sticking to common everyday words, when this is possible, makes writing more direct and concrete. Fancy words have jobs to do, but they ought not be made to do jobs that can be done by ordinary words.

Sentence Choice

Hegel is probably the most obscure philosopher who ever wrote in any language, and the fact he wrote in German gave him the opportunity to construct sentences of bewildering complexity. But H. A. Wolfson, in a book that he wrote to explain what Hegel said, sticks to sentences that are short and simple. Though he isn't completely sucessful in overcoming Hegel's obscurity, he at least makes the effort not to mirror it. Short sentences can become boring, and their use is no sure-fire guarantee of simplicity. Yet it is often better to write additional sentences than to try to pack too much information into a single long one. This is particularly so when making qualifications or comments on what is being said. These ordinarily fit best into separate sentences. Consider these sentences and observe that the second way of presenting the same information is clearer:

> Zeno, a Greek philosopher who lived in the fifth century B.C. and was known to later times as Zeno the Eliatic, formulated logical paradoxes that far from being anachronistic puzzles, are of enduring interest to logicians and mathematicians.

> The Greek philosopher Zeno lived in the fifth century B.C. and was known to later times as Zeno the Eliatic. The logical paradoxes that he formulated are not merely anachronistic puzzles, but are of enduring interest to logicians and mathematicians.

Voice Choice

The passive voice contributes not a whit to simplicity, directness, nor brevity. It usually takes more words to say something in the passive voice than in the active, and the passive voice can by itself create a complex and vague sentence. Consider this one:

> An environmental agency *was established* by the President to demonstrate that attention *is being paid* to problems which require immediate attention. *It is expected* that a new head of the agency *will be appointed* within the next few months.

Avoid the passive voice like the plague.

Be Specific

Vividness and clearness of writing often hinge upon how specific the writing is. Descriptions that ascend to the highest levels of abstractness and generality lose in directness. What's more, they often convey less information. Being specific sometimes involves no more than choosing the right word or phrase. Suppose the *New York Times* is holding a competition for the job of battlefield correspondent and four reporters apply for the position. They are shown a short piece of combat footage, and each is asked to describe what happened to the soldier who appears in the film.

Reporter 1: He was shot in the right leg.
Reporter 2: He was shot.
Reporter 3: He was wounded.
Reporter 4: He became a casualty.

Reporter number 1 (who gets the job) provides the most specific description, of course. From 4's account it's impossible to tell whether the man was wounded or killed and by what means either happened. Number 3 does let us know that the man was injured, but not whether it was by a knife, a bomb, or what. Number 2 does a little better, but he still doesn't tell us where the man was shot.

Brand Blanshard, lamenting that philosophers rarely deign to descend to the specific, illustrates their love of the abstract by imagining what several philosophers, compared with other writers, might say about the hanging of Major André, the man who negotiated with Benedict Arnold:

> Swift, Macaulay, and Shaw would say André was hanged. Bradley would say that he was killed. Bosanquet would say that he died. Kant would say that his mortal existence achieved its termination. Hegel would say that a finite determination of infinity had been further determined by its own negation.

Use Examples

Antaeus, in Greek mythology, was a giant wrestler who was invincible so long as he was touching the earth. When it comes to understanding principles, rules, descriptions of procedures, and other abstractions most of us are like Antaeus. We must keep our feet on the ground. We have to keep in touch with concrete cases or we lose our intellectual bearings. Examples are troublesome in many ways. They slow down the pace of exposition, they are distracting, and they can be misleading. (Read the discussion of examples and other kinds of illustrations in the preceding chapter.) For all this they are invaluable and the writer who eschews them totally is likely to leave his reader to wander helplessly in a thicket of abstractions.

Consider how much easier it is to understand the process of converting a decimal number into a binary one once an example has been given. Here's a description of a procedure: Divide the decimal number by 2; the remainder will be 1 or 0. Write the remainder out to the side and then divide the successive dividends by 2, writing the remainder out to the side in each instance, until the dividend is smaller than the divisor. When this occurs, write the dividend as a remainder. Finally, write down the remainders, from the bottom to the top, in sequence. This will be the binary equivalent of the decimal number.

Here's an example of the procedure described:

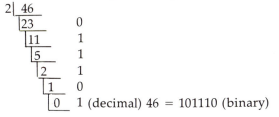

1 (decimal) 46 = 101110 (binary)

Consider another instance in which point and substance is given to a philosphical question by relating the question to an example:

> What is the meaning of a word? This question is abstract and can perhaps best be approached by asking what it is that we do or say when someone asks us what a word means. Suppose that a visitor from Germany approached you and asked, "What does the word 'red' mean?" How would you go about answering his question?

Write for an Audience

Every person of good sense knows that he can't discuss patriotism with a member of the Progressive Labor Party in the same way that he can with a member of the John Birch Society. Even if he wants to make the same points about it, he will try to make them in a way suited to each case. What is true of conversation is equally true of writing. Every writer writes with the aim of being read by someone; no one addresses darkness and the void.

It's of crucial importance that the writer write for a real or imagined audience. Only when he has a definite kind of audience in mind can he shape his material and his thesis into an essay. He must have some notion of what they need to be told, what needs to be explained in detail, and what can merely be mentioned in passing. He must have some idea of what their opinions and prejudices are. These are all factors that play a part in the construction of an essay, and knowledge of them is an aid to answering difficult questions like "Can I take this point for granted, or must I argue for it?" "Is this claim clear, or do I have to say more about it?" "Is it necessary to include this material, or is it so familiar that I need only allude to it?"

To persuade someone to accept a certain conclusion or to share a point of view, you must present reasons and materials that encourage him in that direction. The more you understand your audience, the more likely it is that you will be able to say the right things to carry it along in your direction. There is nothing immoral or reprehensible about this. It is purely a matter of strategy to make a case as strong as you can by relying upon the understanding you have of your readers. It involves, in fact, a recognition of responsibility toward your readers, for it means that you are keeping their needs, strengths, and limitations in mind.

It's not too hard to see the importance of keeping an audience in mind when writing for a real and specific audience—the Annual Convention of Governors, for example. But what about an *imagined* audience? After all, such an audience can have any characteristics you want it to have, and it's not useful advice to tell someone to write for *any* imagined audience. One way to save this advice is say that you should posit a mythical *general reader* or *average person* and write for him. But this is not very helpful either, for it's all but impossible to guess what characteristics such an odd creature has.

The advice to write for an imagined audience (when you don't have a real one) can best be put in two ways. First, the advice means that you should keep in mind that what you write has to be read. It will be read by someone very much like yourself, and it will not be read by posterity (at least not for a while), the Homeric gods, or Mensa the Mind Reader. Instead of an audience like one that fills a theater, imagine that you must explain what you have to say to someone whom you know, that you must make it clear to him and convince him to accept it. "Would I really say this if I were *talking* to someone?" is a good question to ask about what you've written. As writer you must put yourself in the reader's position and try to gauge his reaction to what you have put on paper.

Second, the advice means that you need to decide who you would *like* your audience to be. Suppose you are a psychologist and you decided to write a paper on the inadequacies of classical conditioning as a theory to account for verbal learning. Are you going to write the paper for the *Journal of Behavioral Psychology?* If so, then you will be addressing your professional colleagues, and you can assume that they know just about as much as you do about the topic. If, on the other hand, you are preparing your essay for the New York *Daily News,* you can't make any such assumption about your readers. The whole way in which the essay is constructed and written, the explanations and reasons provided, the very style of presentation, must be different. You must decide what *kind* of audience you want to address.

Writing for people, rather than for the ages or for the gods, helps shape an essay. It gives it order and direction, offers protection against the irrelevant, and keeps the essay intellectually honest. Talking is more basic than writing, and writing by comparision often seems artificial, for it is a private activity. The very privacy of writing drips with danger. It inclines the writer to say things that he would never say if he were looking another person straight in the eye. It invites him to be crude and careless in his arguments and explanations, to be long-winded, and to be obscure. Since the other person is never there in writing, he must always be *imagined* there so the writer can save himself from private vice.

Revise

Charles Darwin was the greatest biologist the nineteenth century produced. But he was far from being the best writer of the time. Writing was very hard for Darwin, and he went through intellectual tortures every time he tried to get something down on paper. In this respect he wasn't so different from the rest of us, and it's easy to sympathize with his reflection on his troubles: "There seems to be a sort of fatality in my mind leading me to put at first my statement and proposition in a wrong or awkward form."

It's a rare person who doesn't suffer from the same fatality that dogged Darwin. Fatality it is, too, for no known way of escaping it exists. Nevertheless, though there is no cure for the disease, there is a remedy for its symptoms. If you write down something you don't want to say or if you put a point awkwardly, the obvious thing to do is to revise. You simply must go back and work over what you have written until you find it satisfactory. The result may never be beautiful, but it should at least be clear and serviceable.

Flaubert, in writing *Madame Bovary*, would sometimes spend hours and even days searching for the proper word to complete a sentence. Most of us lack the time, the patience, and the inclination to go to such lengths. We prefer to write rapidly while the thoughts are flowing freely. There is much in favor of this technique so far as getting ideas down on paper is concerned. Rarely though, does it produce a smooth and coherent piece of prose.

The best of possible techniques is perhaps one composed of spontaneous and rapid writing plus thoughtful and careful revision. What is good of the first draft can be preserved, and what is rough or wrong can be smoothed away and corrected in the second or subsequent drafts. Darwin claimed, by the way, that this procedure did the most to ameliorate the ill effects of his fatality: "For several years I have found that it saves time to scribble . . . whole pages as quickly as I possibly can . . .; and then correct deliberately."

William James, the American philosopher and psychologist, was one of the greatest and most delightful writers of the nineteenth century. He has been described as "the scientist who wrote like a novelist," but interestingly enough his account of the trouble he had writing and of his method of composition is almost the same as Darwin's: "Everything comes out wrong with me at first, but when once objectified in a crude shape, I can torture and poke and scrape and pat it until it offends me no more."

Revision is not likely to turn anyone into a stylist of the caliber of James, but it may at least help him to write the dry but quite clear and adequate prose of Darwin.

Through a Glass Darkly: Incoherence

For now we see through a glass, darkly. . . .
I Corinthians 13:12

A piece of prose or a stretch of speech can be described as "incoherent" when it is disjointed or rambling, when its parts are not logically connected, or when it violates ordinarily accepted standards of grammar or word usage. Kipling wrote that

> There are nine and sixty ways of constructing tribal lays,
> And—every—single—one—of—them—is—right!

There are certainly more than sixty-nine ways to be incoherent, and every single one of them ought to be avoided. "There are as many types of incoherence as human fallibility can commit and human gullibility will tolerate," a recent writer has said. It's not practical to try to present a Dictionary of Incoherence in this brief section, but there's room enough to offer at least an Epitome. A quick look at a few of the most important and most frequent ways in which discourse can lapse into drivel and talk into twaddle is worth the time, for through laziness, inattention, or ignorance we are all prone to become incoherent on occasion. A glimpse of the ugliness of sin does much to keep us virtuous.

Redundancy

Redundancy is no doubt a good thing to have in a spacecraft, because it means there is a back-up system in case anything goes wrong with the primary system. In writing, however, redundancy (or pleonasm, to use a fancy name) is downright undesirable. It's boring, distracting, and a sure-fire way to lose the attention of a reader. No one likes to be told the same joke twice, even if it was funny the first time. Not even an idiot wants to read the same point five times.

Repetition has its place in writing. Putting a point one way and then in another way is a useful technique. Redundancy is, by definition, something which is *more* than enough, repetition that is *needless*. But when does repetition become needless? The answer to this question can be little better than silence: The writer must judge for himself. As a general rule, though, the same point should not be made more than twice. (And if the material is quite difficult or a point very subtle, it should also be made at least twice.) Moreover, the point should not be expressed in the same way both times. Repetition of almost the same words is of no use whatsoever in print, even though in conversation it can be helpful.

Pleonasm is sometimes writ small in phrases. A phrase is redundant when one of its words has the *same* meaning or is *part of* the meaning of another word in the phrase. "Our green and verdant land must be protected from despoilation" contains the redundant phrase "green and verdant." In this context, "green" means the same things as "verdant" so one of these words is totally unnecessary. Here are a couple more examples of sentences containing pleonastic phrases:

"The effects of pollution are visible to the eye of all who will look."
(No one is likely to believe that they will be visible to the ear, so "the eye" can be dropped without tears.)

"The true facts about the origin of the war in Vietnam will never be known."
(There are no false facts any more than there are married bachelors. "True" is unnecessary.)

The use of redundant phrases is harmless so far as *what* is expressed is concerned. Obviously, a pleonastic phrase has the same meaning as a nonpleonastic one, and so nothing is altered or lost by their use. Yet the presence of pleonasms shakes the confidence of readers who recognize them. They are a prima facie indication that the writer doesn't know the meanings of the words that he is tossing around, and a reader who recognizes this is likely to be suspicious about everything the writer has to say. Suspicion and loss of confidence are foes of persuasion.

Inconsistency

I see no objection to stoutness, in moderation.

> W. S. Gilbert,
> *Iolanthe*

"A foolish consistency," said Emerson, "is the hobgoblin of little minds." Presumably what he meant was that people should feel free to change their minds and that statesmen shouldn't hestitate to alter their policies if they decide they are wrong. We can all give a couple of cheers for this attitude, but consistency in writing is far from being foolish. As a characteristic of the main argument of an essay, in fact, it is the most important logical feature.

Inconsistency or contradiction is the assertion and denial of the same statement; it is making two incompatible claims. "The United States has a space program, and the United States doesn't have a space program"is a straightforward contradictory sentence. "George and Muriel are childless, but they have three lovely children" is also a contradiction, through not in such an obvious and direct way. Such inconsistencies as these are so blatant that anyone clever enough to be able to write at all isn't likely to be guilty of them. *Open* contradictions are almost never found in essays and papers, but *hidden* contradictions are often skulking about. All too often they pass unnoticed. What usually happens to grant them admittance is something like this: In arguing for a point, necessary to establish his general thesis, Bigle will make a certain assumption. In arguing for another point, he will make another assumption to help establish it. What Bigle doesn't notice unfortunately, is that the two assumptions are not consistent. They are such that he can't accept *both* of them. If both are necessary to the points he is arguing for, and the points are required to establish his main thesis, Bigle is obviously in bad trouble. If he discovers the contradiction (and is honest) or if it is pointed out to him, he must get rid of at least one of the incompatible assumptions or reconcile himself to failure.

A thesis that is inconsistent or that rests on inconsistent assumptions is worthless. No matter how persuasively and cleverly it has been argued, it must be rejected. It's a cardinal principle of rational discourse that contradictions are not to be tolerated. It may be a truth about human psychology that people can hold inconsistent beliefs, but this doesn't alter the fact that when the inconsistency of an argument or position is revealed, it has been shown to be valueless. It does no good to prove that X is true if in doing so you also prove that X is false. This is incoherence with a vengeance. Inconsistency is the *bête noire* that stalks through the writer's nightmare, and no pains must be spared to avoid it. The prize of critics, of course, is to find a contradiction hiding in a clump of prose. The type of overall inconsistency talked about above is as fatal to a thesis as strychnine is to a rat.

Some inconsistencies, however, are "trivial" in comparison to the first sort and can be regarded as mere slips of the pen or lapses of the tongue. Like bedbugs, they are annoying and unpleasant but not really dangerous. The lonely but boastful long-distance runner who avers that he can run longer and faster than anyone in his heat *seems* to be claiming the impossible accomplishment of running longer and faster than himself. We recognize, of course, that the bragging Mercury is just a careless grammarian. We also realize that when someone says something like "Gibbs was the best dealer of the two" he doesn't mean to suggest that the two were actually three; he means "better," not "best." Such cases as these we can baptize *grammatical inconsistencies.*

There is a second rather common kind of minor inconsistency, ordinarily called *contradiction in terms.* Such inconsistencies occur when the modifier of a word has a meaning that is incompatible with the meaning of the word itself. Asking for the "smaller half" of a candy bar, for example, is a good practice in dieting but not in writing. A "silent scream" just can't be, and no matter how good he is, a pitcher can't throw a "straight curve."

Contradictions in terms also occur when sentences contain incompatible expressions that are used to talk about the same thing. During the war in Vietnam, the American officer who announced that "in order to save the village, we had to destroy it" left doubt in many minds about whether saving villages was such a good policy after all. A "saved" village and a "destroyed" village, many felt, were quite different things.

When the Secretary of Defense, during that same period, described a mission to rescue American prisoners of war that produced no rescues as a "complete success," he puzzled many people. "How can a mission that didn't succeed be a success?" they quite naturally asked themselves. The answer, of course, is that it can't be. As these examples illustrate, there are occasions on which even "minor" inconsistencies can be of crucial importance. If the time comes when every failure is a "complete success," then we'll be in real trouble.

When it comes to the poetic or rhetorical use of language, then of course we don't object to the use of expressions that are apparently inconsistent. Poets who write about "cold fire" and "darkness visible" and sages who advise us that "The child is the father of the man" are obviously using language in a special and uncommon way. When we recognize this we judge (and interpret) their writing by standards different from those we ordinarily use. For us to be able to shift our critical gears the writer has to make it clear that he is deliberately departing from standard practice. If he handles the matter poorly, then he opens himself to the charge of inconsistency when he lapses into rhetoric.

Minor inconsistencies of the sorts discussed *almost* never destroy an essay or argument. Generally, a reader will charitably overlook them and concentrate on the hard kernel of contention. Yet like other faults, even when they are minor they create a bad impression and make the reader wary. They are evidence of carelessness, inattention, or a lack of sophistication in the use of words.

Irrelevancy

Be not careless in deeds, nor confused in words, nor
rambling in thoughts.

MARCUS AURELIUS
Meditations, VIII

Turgenev once commented that if a novelist describes a gun hanging on the wall in the first scene, it should be only because someone is shot with it in a later scene. This advice applies with equal force to essay writing. Each bit of information in an essay, each point or argument, should be directly or indirectly pertinent to the overall thesis. Items which aren't properly connected with the thesis are *irrelevant*.

Turgenev's observation also points up two features of writing that are closely connected with relevance: namely, *coherence* and *economy*. To achieve the maximum of persuasion, the points of an essay should fit together (cohere) as tightly as the parts of a jigsaw puzzle. None of the pieces should have to be forced, and there should be no pieces in the pile that don't have a place in the puzzle. That is, the argument and information in an essay ought to hang together and mutually support the thesis.

Irrelevant items are like extra pieces to a picture puzzle—they can't be used to form the picture, and their presence is distracting and confusing. An essay that presents materials that are not legitimately present violates the economy of good writing. It introduces functionless pieces that weigh down the essay without advancing its cause. Too much extraneous material results in an uneconomical, incoherent, pointless, and rambling work. Far from persuading the reader, it confuses him, annoys him, and in the worst cases, repels him.

An essay needs to be aimed like a rifle at a definite target. Everything said should point in the direction of the target, and nothing should be said that destroys the focus. An essay shouldn't be written with the attitude that, like pellets from a scattergun, a few points will find their mark even without aiming.

Improprieties of Language

"All is flux," said Heraclitus, "and nothing is permanent except change." A man can't step in the same river twice, for the flowing water is forever making it a different river. Language, too, is always undergoing change. Only languages like classical Latin and Greek, Sanskrit, and Coptic have ceased development. They have become frozen, static, preserved, and locked into a final posture like a beetle in ice. Growth has stopped because people no longer use these languages, because there is no need to stretch them to cover new situations or to refine them to make new distinctions. There's no occasion, what's more, for the linguistic play and for the conscious and unconscious departure from accepted standards that play a major role in shaping languages that still have daily jobs to do.

So far as our own language is concerned, it is in flux but not in chaos. It is undergoing change, like all natural and functioning languages, but the change is not so radical that each month or each year or even each decade we find ourselves speaking a different language. If change whirled and whizzed at such a rate, communication would become exceedingly difficult, if not impossible. New words come into the language, old ones acquire new uses, some words drop away totally, others are dusted off only on special occasions, though once they were used daily, and grammar becomes altered. But such processes take place at a relatively slow rate. Underlying the flux of change, there is a foundation of standards governing the grammar of the language and the use of its words. The standards are not rigid and inflexible; they give at least a little when we push against them. The use of "like" where "as" is correct or the use of a double negative doesn't render us unintelligible to other native speakers. Nor are the standards unalterable; they become bent into new shapes by constant and enduring pressure. Finally, they are not imposed upon us from the outside by linguistic gods or elementary-school teachers. The standards are standards *of* the language; they are the rules implicit in the practices of those that speak and write the language. They characterize and define the language, and in a fundamental sense they *are* the language.

Communication is not just facilitated but it is made possible by the fact that the words we use are used *appropriately* only in certain contexts (which may be broad or vague, of course) or with respect to certain objects and by the fact that we all string our words together in the same types of grammatical patterns. We are language users and language makers, and we maintain a balance between remaining static and falling forward. Language is like a ship that is being rebuilt a plank at a time while remaining afloat.

The discussion of grammar, spelling, and the proper use of words in this section is based on the assumption that generally accepted standards are necessary within a language. No one is bound to them with iron shackles, and today's standard may be the next century's archaism. But a writer is probably well advised not to deviate from them too radically, if at all. An essay filled with misspelled words, words inappropriately used, and grammatical lapses is a sturdy barrier to understanding. A reader with good will, sympathy, and patience may simply not be able to figure out what is being said. A reader lacking these saintly virtues is likely to be so disgusted by such a performance that he won't even make the effort to read it through. Communication suffers.

Barbarisms

"Illiterate him, I say, quite from your memory."
Mrs. Malaprop in Sheridan's The Rivals

According to a tradition that may or may not be fanciful, the Greeks called all foreigners "barbarians" because they went "bar-bar" like sheep when trying to speak Greek. Today we reserve the word for people like Attila the Hun, whose shortcomings are more serious than mere linguistic infelicity. Yet, we do continue to employ the related term "barbarism" to refer to particular kinds of cases in which words are involved. When the language is savaged and brutalized in certain ways, we say that barbarisms are being committed. There are at least two varieties of barbarisms common enough to deserve notice.

A barbarism is, first of all, the use of a word that violates the ordinary meaning of the word. Since a word gets its meaning from its use in a language, a barbarism is a violation of the standard use. It is, to be direct, a *misuse* of a word. Public officials who say such things as "The enormity of the task of cleaning up the environment is stupendous" don't mean them at all. Such people are linguistic barbarians, for "enormity" is a noun which means "a great wickedness, an outrageous or monstrous action." Presumably, they want only to say that the job or whatever is enormous, and in trying to do so, they choose the inappropriate word "enormity" instead of the awkward but correct "enormousness."

This sort of barbarism is rife. It flows through the TV set in an unending stream, drenches political speeches and announcements, and gathers in puddles in newspapers, magazines, and textbooks. The person who wants to collect barbarisms for a hobby will discover they are as easy to find as postage stamps. Here are a couple more examples:

1. The President made a statement *inferring* that the defendent was guilty. (The President or his statement *implies;* a person who hears or reads it *infers:* i.e., draws a conclusion.)
2. "The key component in our judiciary system," the Attorney General said, "is the *uninterested* judge." (The first lawyer of the land meant the "disinterested" judge. An uninterested judge is one who is bored by it all and doesn't give a damn about what's happening. A disinterested judge is one who is impartial.)

A squad of words is available to label barbarisms of this first kind. "Catachresis" is the technical term used by linguists for the incorrect use of a word. "Impropriety" and "solecism" also refer to such cases, though "solecism" applies to other sorts of errors as well. A "malapropism" is a misuse of words that produces a ridiculous result. The term is a common noun made out of the name of Mrs. Malaprop, a character in Sheridan's play *The Rivals.* Mrs. Malaprop is given to confusing two words that sound something alike, though they are totally different in meaning. Thus she compliments one man by saying of him that "he is the very pineapple of politeness." Here's a modern and real malapropism:

"It's no secret that my leave from GE runs out in January," Simonds said. He added that his experience with state government would be looked upon as an asset by the company. "It's called cross-pollution and it's becoming more popular," Simonds said.

JOHN O'DONNELL in the Burlington [Vt.] *Free Press*

A barbarism, second of all, is the use of an expression that is not really a word in the language. Most often such an expression is reminiscent of a word, is like a word, or could be a word. It's a barbarism, not because it is intrinsically wrong, but merely because it is not generally recognized, accepted, and used by writers and speakers of the language. In some cases there is recognition and use in some contexts, say in conversation, but in others, such as formal writing, most people prefer to avoid such expressions and to see them avoided by others. Here are some barbarisms of this variety; neither of the underlined expressions is a word in English:

1. The *vagueries* of his position on the economy are difficult to penetrate. (That is, his position is vague.)

2. *Irregardless* of what the president believes, students want a better society, not
a worse one. (This is a nonword which seems to be made of "regardless" and
"irrespective," either of which would be appropriate.)

Grammar

Not even Caesar is above the grammarians.

Sigismund, Emperor of the Holy Roman Empire, attended the Council of
Constance in 1414. At a meeting of the Council, an audacious official of
the Church complained about Sigismund's grammar. "I am king of the
Romans, and I am above grammar," Sigismund is supposed to have
retorted. His reply to the prelate echoes sympathetically in the hearts of
all who have ever come to grips with the million-headed monster that is
English grammar. Is it correct to say "Eat *like* I do" or should we say "Eat
as I do"? Is "Who do you want" correct, or is it "Whom do you want"?
Anyone who writes is forever asking himself questions about grammar,
for English grammar recognizes so many distinctions, special cases, and
exceptions that nobody feels absolute master of them all.

Grammatical demands in English often seem overly rigid or even
irrational. There seems to be little justification for saying that "Whom do
you want?" is correct and the use of "who" in this sentence is wrong or
colloquial. Surely preferring "whom" to "who" in such cases is merely
arbitrary! True enough, considered case by case, grammatical demands
sometimes appear wholly capricious. But grammatical rules are not formulated to cover specific cases and no more. The written rules of grammar aim at being general and consistent. That is, they are framed to cover
broad types of cases and not just special instances. "Whom" is preferred
in the sentence used as an example because of the general rule that
pronouns must belong to the objective case when they are the objects of
verbs or prepositions. "The man to whom I spoke" seems a quite natural
expression which most people appear happy with. They don't feel that
"to who I spoke" would be better or just as good, and yet the phrase is
just another case of the same rule. So too is the use of "them" in the
sentence "I gave them the money."

It obviously matters little that we make occasional lapses and say
"who" in cases in which we should say "whom." But it does matter
whether there are grammatical rules (or practices) that are more or less
consistently followed. When commonly accepted grammatical conventions are radically shattered, communication becomes difficult and understanding becomes problematic. The case against radical departures
from grammatical standards is easy to make, because writing without
reference to the grammar of a language produces expressions that are
nonsense in that language. "President the commission investigate problem to a the appointed" is not a sentence in English, though it contains

nothing but English words and, with an attention to grammar, could be turned into an English sentence.

The grammar of a language must be observed to a certain degree even to be *using* the language. Radical departures from standards produce unacceptable and nonsensical results.

But what about minor departures, small violations? There seems to be no reason to condemn them so long as they don't produce nonsense. Yet, there are at least pragmatic reasons to avoid them. For one thing, it is good to follow general rules in all cases to which they apply because to do so is to acknowledge the rules. Since they make written communication possible, they ought to be supported and not departed from without adequate grounds. Just because the use of a certain word ("as" or "whom") seems arbitrary in some instances is no reason to deny the general rule that demands its use. Furthermore, a writer needs the understanding and confidence of his readers. Violation of grammatical standards can cause puzzlement and misunderstanding, and what's more, it makes the reader doubt the competence and carefulness of the writer. It's not necessary to be a fiend about grammatical correctness so as not to be a cavalier about it. But a concerted effort to write grammatically correct sentences is more likely to produce an effective piece of expository writing than is wanton disregard.

A catalogue of grammatical disasters doesn't have a place here, but there is room for a brief sample of those common enough to be tempting but bad enough to be avoided.

Case Errors. "Just *between you and I,* most poverty programs are failures." Something must be between you and *me*, for English grammar demands that the objective, rather than the nominative case be used when a word is the object of a preposition or verb. "He sold three bags to John and I" involves an error of the same sort.

The "I—me" case error is usually committed by people who know "you and me" is not correct in sentences like "You and me are going to have a lot of fun, sugar." "I" is required because it is part of the subject, and the subject always takes the nominative. John O'Hara liked to use this error in dialogue to show his readers something about the character that spoke it—namely, that he didn't use correct grammar naturally and that his attempts to do so marked him as only partly educated.

Errors of Number. "Everyone must pay *their* taxes or face a penalty." "Everyone" means "each one" so the possessive pronoun must be the singular "his" or "her." "Each of the four children *were* on scholarship" embodies the same error. To use the singular subject and the plural pronoun is to make a mild inconsistency of the sentence.

Dangling Participle. "*Walking into the room,* the flowers immediately struck his eye." The phrase "walking into the room" is a participial phrase which dangles at the front of the sentence. It really modifies nothing, though it appears to refer to "flowers." To correct the error the sentence has to be rewritten so the phrase doesn't dangle and the flowers don't seem so active.

Faulty Reference. "The letter came in an envelope, and *it* was decorated with flowers." It's not clear in this sentence whether the letter or the envelope is supposed to be decorated because it's not clear what the pronoun "it" is intended to refer to. The general rule is that a pronoun refers to the noun that comes closest before it and with which it agrees in number and gender. Neglect of this rule can result in a writer's appearing to talk about something he doesn't intend to be talking about just because he has misplaced a pronoun or used a pronoun when he ought to have repeated a noun.

Lack of Parallel Structure. "We want a man *to mow and feed the sheep.*" To avoid hiring a man who wants to mow sheep, the phrase "to mow and to feed the sheep" ought to replace the ambiguous expression. The italicized phrase is made ambiguous because of a failure to make "feed" parallel to "to mow." It would also help in rewriting to switch around the "to" phrases.

Misplaced Modifier. "*Beautifully wrapped in red cellophane,* he brought a box of candy." Unless we have here a case of a man who dresses in a peculiar fashion, the initial modifying phrase is misplaced. It ought to be put at the end so it can modify "box of candy." Modifiers can be misplaced in several different ways, of course.

Gerund Error. "Do you mind Dunn smoking?" This seems to be a question about whether it's all right with you for Dunn to have a certain mode of existence—Dunn smoking, as distinct from Dunn running, sitting, eating ice cream, and so on. This is not what most people who say such things intend to be asking, though. They want to know if you mind if Dunn smokes. "Smoking," in the example, is a gerund, a verb form used as a noun, and to ask the question intended, the noun or pronoun which precedes the gerund must be possessive. Hence: Do you mind Dunn's smoking?

All the advice given here is worthless unless it's put into practice. The only way to learn to write is to practice writing.

Thus, the most important points made here can be summed up succinctly: Write!

Exercises: Composition Consultants

Composition Consultants is a firm you have just founded. At the moment, you are not only its owner, you are its only employee. You don't expect this state of affairs to last for long, however.

The firm intends to provide advice, analysis, and criticism of expository essays or compositions. The services will be offered to the business and academic community. It is not a term-paper service or a ghost-writing business. Rather, it's something new. It takes papers submitted to it, subjects them to a close reading, identifies their aims, parts, and so on, and provides a report on them. The report is in part an analysis, and it is in part a critical appraisal.

In order to get the business underway, there are three major tasks that you have to perform.

1. You must make an outline or summary of the sorts of things that are involved in writing an effective essay. That is, you must briefly note how such an essay may be put together (the job of an Introduction, etc.) and some of the dangers that an inexperienced or careless writer might run up against.
2. You must provide a sample analysis of an essay. In your analysis, you have to identify the major parts of the essay, evaluate their effectiveness, locate the major thesis of the essay, trace out its arguments, and supply a general appraisal of the quality of the essay, along with recommendations for changes.
3. Finally, to demonstrate that you are a person whose opinion is worth having in such matters, you must write a top-quality essay yourself.

Steps (1) and (2) are fairly easy to carry out, for you just happen to have an old informal logic book around that has a discussion of composition writing which you can abstract advice from. It also contains an essay ("Adam's Navel") that can be used as a subject for your sample analysis and evaluation.

At this point, you take the time to do steps (1) and (2).

Step (3) is harder to take, for it involves actually writing a first class essay that meets all the demands that your summary sets out.

The essay should be around 500 words (approximately two typed pages). But what in the world should it be about? Such sterling topics as "My Summer Vacation" and "The Adventures of a New Penny" don't seem very appealing.

The topic should be generally interesting and not demand any specialized knowledge. After a long time thinking about it, you come up with these topics:

1. Would It Be Possible to Communicate with an Extraterrestrial That Landed on This Planet?
2. Selective Conscientious Objection: Should It Be Allowed?
3. The Wasted Potentials of Television
4. Why Shouldn't We All Vote on Major Issues?
5. The New-Look in Superheroes (Batman Battles the Pushers, Superman Loses Some Superpowers, Spiderman against the Establishment, etc.)

 6. How Come They Don't Make Movies like That Anymore?
 7. It Don't Matter How You Say It
 8. Sometimes It's Good to Be a Quitter
 9. Why I Read Science Fiction
10. Why Not College for Everybody?
11. The One Thing I Would Like Posterity to Remember
12. Too Many People or Not Enough Food?
13. Life-Style in the Year 2976

But which one to choose? Or can you think of a topic better than any of these?

ADAM'S NAVEL

Omphalus is one of the strangest books ever written. It was published in 1857 by the great English biologist Philip Gosse, who wrote it in a desperate effort to reconcile conflicting religious and scientific beliefs. The book, which is almost never read today, presents an interesting philosophical question. Rather than state the question directly, though, let's consider how it is generated by *Omphalus*.

Gosse was an ardent member of an ultrafundamentalist religious sect called the Plymouth Brethren. In addition to espousing a stern moral code, one of the sect's basic tenets was that everything in the Bible is God's word and is thus literally true. Gosse didn't merely pay lip-service to this dogma; he fervently believed it to be correct.

Despite his religious convictions, Gosse was an outstanding biologist and was well acquainted with curent speculations about evolution. Though Darwin didn't publish *The Origin of Species* until 1859, talk of evolution was definitely in the air. Robert Chambers had published a book called *The Vestiges of Natural Creation* in 1844, and in it he had argued that biological species are not fixed but have evolved from earlier ones. Lamarck, the controversial French biologist, had earlier made the same claim. The view had not won more adherents only because no one could imagine what mechanism would allow one species to evolve into another.

The evidence from geology was even more compelling than the speculations of Chambers and Lamarck, and Gosse was equally familiar with it. Geologists had discovered series of fossils that slowly but progressively altered in form from earlier rocks to later ones. Older forms disappeared and newer ones came to resemble species we are familiar with now. Such changes could be accounted for if one were willing to admit that one species could somehow give rise to another species over the course of many thousands or even millions of years. Most geologists were coming to believe that the earth was old enough for such changes to have taken place.

Gosse was aware of such speculations and of the evidence that made them seem likely. But they conflicted with the Bible in two crucial respects. On Biblical evidence the world could not be more than five or six thousand years old—certainly nothing like the millions of years geologists were suggesting. What's more, species had to be unchanging and exactly the same as they were on the day that God created them. Old forms couldn't possibly die out and be replaced by new ones.

A terrible dilemma faced Gosse. As a Christian, he felt forced to believe in the literal truth of the Bible, no matter what the scientific evidence said. But as a scientist, he felt forced to believe what the evidence indicated, no matter what the Bible said.

Faith and reason were in conflict for Gosse, as they were for so many others in the nineteenth century. His beliefs were in strict opposition, and it seemed that he would have to surrender his science or his religion. But which one? He was wholly convinced that *both* were right.

He underwent an agony of intellectual and spirtual strife over his dilemma. He thought about the problem constantly for a long period, and at last he hit upon a truly ingenious way of reconciling the two conflicting positions. Knowing that others faced the same difficulty, to help them Gosse published the results of his deliberations in *Omphalus*.

"Omphalus" is the Greek word for "navel," and Gosse's choice of a title was intended to be a reminder of a minor dispute of the Middle Ages. The dispute was over the question "Did Adam have a navel?" Some theologians argued that Adam did not have a navel, for since he was created from dust it would have served no purpose, and God does nothing without a purpose. Others held that Adam did have a navel, because God created him as the type for all men to come, and he surely must have possessed such a distinctive feature. The same arguments also applied to Eve, of course.

In the ordinary case, a navel would be proof of having had a certain history of development. But since Adam and Eve were created, if they did have navels, they would only apparently, but not really, have had such a history.

In this last point Gosse found the clue that allowed him to solve his problem. Suppose, he reasoned, God created the world and everything in it the exact same way and at the exact same time the Bible claims. Now suppose also He created them in such a way that even on the very day of creation everything *seemed* to have a past. Adam would have had a navel, trees growth rings, mountains would have appeared weathered and eroded, dogs would have had calluses on their footpads, and all animals and plants would have seemed to have developed from others. Likewise, in creating rocks God would have formed them with the fossils we find there already in place.

This must have been what happened, Gosse decided. When we examine fossils we mistakenly regard them as the remains of extinct life, but they are really "the skeletons of animals that never existed." And when we conclude that the earth must be millions of years old because of the way in which mountains have been worn down by erosion, we are equally mistaken. In fact, they have that look just because God created them that way.

The supposition that the world was created with records of an apparent past built into it Gosse called "the principle of prochronic development." The principle is a brilliant intellectual maneuver that allowed Gosse to resolve his dilemma. It was now possible for him both to hold his belief in the literal truth of the Biblical account of creation and to accept all scientific evidence. All contradictions between the Bible and the evidence were reduced to merely apparent ones. Like Adam's navel, geological evidence only apparently, but not really, indicates that the earth and life on it have had a certain history.

Gosse was careful to point out that nothing of science would have to be surrendered if the prochronic principle were accepted. As he wrote, "The character and order of the geological strata . . . the successive floras and faunas . . . would be *facts* still. They would still be, as now, legitimate subjects of examination and inquiry. The principle would demand only that we give up what we regard as actual chronology and realize that the long history we seem to find exists only in the mind of God."

Bitter disppointment was Gosse's only reward in publishing *Omphalus*. To his own mind, he had discovered an acceptable solution to a tremendous difficulty. He had been able to resolve the conflict between the beliefs of religion and the evidence of science, and he was certain others would hail his efforts as brilliant.

Not surprisingly, though, most people treated *Omphalus* as a joke. No one of any intellectual pretentions bothered to take it seriously, and even Gosse's good friend Charles Kingsley had nothing but scorn for the book. "I cannot believe that God has written on the rocks an enormous and superfluous lie," Kingsley wrote.

We are moved in a personal way by the spectacle of Gosse's sincere and desperate effort to keep his world together and, at the same time, be faithful to his religion and his science. The harsh mockery that greeted the principle of prochronic development makes him one of the most pathetic figures in the history of science.

Still, in spite of our sympathies for the man, we are no more disposed to take his principle seriously than were his contemporaries. It seems wild, crazy, no more than an elaborate legpull. Even knowing it was offered in earnest, it's difficult for us to treat it with any kind of respect.

But what's wrong with the principle? It's easy enough to make fun of it, but can we really show Gosse was wrong? Unless we can, maybe the joke is on us.

Notice that Gosse had a definite reason for saying that the world was created at a certain time. His literal reading of the Bible provided at least a rough date for creation—around 4004 B.C. according to one tradition. Also, according to Gosse, the world didn't just come into existence at that time. It was, again according to the Bible, created.

This feature provided Kingsley with a point of criticism. It would be inconsistent with the character of God, he argues, to have created a world in which mankind is deliberately misled about the past. God would be a liar, and no Christian could accept such a view.

But such matters are ones of theology, and Gosse's biblically grounded beliefs about when and how the world came into existence are not essential parts of his principle of prochronology. The principle can be stated in a strictly nonreligious way as a philosophical thesis. And if we can show what is wrong about the thesis, we will also have shown what is wrong with Gosse's principle.

Suppose we put the thesis this way: The world came into existence six thousand years ago with the records of an apparent past already built into it.

The thesis seems to be a claim about the world which, if true, would be an astounding scientific fact. In favor of the thesis we can point out, as Gosse did for his version, that all known evidence about the past is compatible with it. Geological data, fossil studies, and radioactive dating indicating that life on earth began about a billion years ago, and that the planet itself is much older, don't have to surrendered. They are merely data about the apparent past, not the real past, and the thesis places no restriction on present or future research.

This seems very reassuring, but notice though that the same data are also compatible with a vast number of similiar claims that could be formulated. We might say, for example, that the world came into existence a million years ago or three thousand years ago. If we were willing to let the records of the apparent past include books, buildings, and artifacts, we could say it came into existence a thousand or two hundred years ago. And if we were willing to let the records include our memories of the past, we could say it came to be only a minute or a second ago. Memories would be built into our minds in the way Gosse said fossils were built into the rocks.

Such claims are compatible with all evidence about the past, but they aren't compatible with each other. We can't hold, without contradicting ourselves, that the world came into existence six thousand years ago and that it came into existence only a second ago.

This reveals the first definitely suspicious feature of the thesis. Though it is compatible with everything we know about the world, it is not *supported* by any evidence. It is not even capable of being supported by any evidence. No data favor it over other possible claims of the same sort. And since any two such claims will conflict, we have no grounds for choosing it rather than the other.

Contrast this with a situation in which two opposing claims are made about the age of the earth, but neither one asserts that "the records of an apparent past" are built in. In such a case we search for data to show that one of them is favored by the evidence over the other. Geological evidence, for example, supports the claim that the earth is around 4,500 million years old and denies support to the claim that it is six thousand years old. We have plenty of ground for choosing the first over the second.

Another peculiar feature of the thesis that emerges is that there is no way of *disproving* it. It is not only compatible with everything we now know about the world, but it is compatible with all possible evidence. Since it rules out nothing, there is nothing that we could discover, even in principle, to show that it is false.

The phrase "record of an apparent past," which is an essential part of the thesis, effectively begs all questions of evidence. Suppose someone said, "I have found data that show that the earth is more than 5,000 million years old." The question-begging answer in terms of the thesis would be, "It only appears that way because of the built-in records. Actually, it came into existence only six thousand years ago."

The basic characteristic of a scientific claim is its responsiveness to evidence. This responsiveness has two components. It must be possible, at least in principle, to support the claim by appropriate evidence. And it must be possible, at least in principle, for the claim to be false.

Consider a claim like "The core of Mars is composed of nickel." We can neither prove nor disprove this at the moment. Yet we recognize what sort of evidence would count in its favor. Moreover, we also recognize what circumstances would make it false. It is exactly these features that the principle of prochronological development lacks.

The thesis appears to make a startling scientific claim about the world. But when we examine it closely we find that there is no way, even in principle, of supporting the thesis, and there is no way, even in principle, for it to be proved false. *The thesis is in no way controlled by the actual facts of the world.* They neither support it nor count against it.

In spite of its appearance of stating a peculiar fact about the world, it makes no factual claim at all. It is, then, neither true nor false, nor is it capable of being either.

The thesis, in the final analysis, resembles a myth or a poetic vision. It is an interpretation of the world that is imposed on the facts but remains unresponsive to them. There is no point in asking if it is a correct or accurate interpretation, in the way that the question is asked of a scientific claim, for the thesis lacks the very characteristics which would make it a candidate for such a judgment.

Some, like Gosse, may find some version of the principle of prochronic development a satisfying myth, but no one can find it valid.

References

Gosse, Philip Henry. *Omphalos.* London: John van Voorst, 1857.
  This work is quite scarce. A section from it is reprinted in Garret Hardin, ed., *Population, Evolution, and Birth Control* (San Francisco: W. H. Freeman, 1969). The letter giving Charles Kingsley's reaction is also reprinted here.
Gosse, Edmund. *Father and Son.* Baltimore: Penquin Books, 1968.
  Edmund Gosse describes the great intellectual torment his father suffered over evolution and the age of the earth.

11/ The Logic of Puzzles

IMAGINE yourself in this situation. You are faced with two people. One of them always lies and the other always tells the truth. Moreover, one of them speaks English and the other doesn't.

You ask the first, "Are you the one who always tells the truth?" He says something unintelligible in a foreign language. The second one volunteers: "He says that he is, but he is lying." Which is the liar and which is the truth-teller?

This is a logical puzzle. From the information provided and by means of simple reasoning, the correct answer can be found. How to go about finding it, we'll consider later.

One of the more peculiar characteristics of human beings is that they deliberately create obstacles to overcome. The sciences, literature, and the arts owe a great deal to this strange trait of intentionally making the smooth path rough.

But the trait also shows up in ways not tied to matters of high seriousness. Tennis is easier to play with the net down, and there are simpler ways of getting a football from one end of a field to another than sending out eleven men to fight their way past another eleven intent on holding them back.

We don't choose the easier ways of doing things, because the fun of the games — part of what makes them games at all—consists in overcoming the obstacles that we deliberately create.

Logical puzzles are also an expression of the spirit of play and fun that's found in athletics. No one really cares, in one sense, who the liar is in the puzzle above. It makes no difference to our practice or our ideas about the world. Why take puzzles seriously, then?

One reason is that they can be solved by the use of quite ordinary skills and abilities. Unlike many problems in life, they have clear and direct answers. It's possible to enjoy the process of looking for the answers and to experience the feeling of accomplishment that comes with finding them. So logical puzzles offer one sort of intellectual pleasure, a pleasure comparable to that of exercising physical skills and abilities.

But do puzzles have any value beyond providing intellectual pleasure?

Yes they do. Skills of analysis, of drawing inferences, of detecting unobvious connections, and of seeing the same facts from different perspectives are all required in puzzle solving.

They are *skills* and though some people are more talented than others, everybody can improve his level of competence through experience and practice. Anyone with certain basic qualifications can play baseball, and if he works hard at the game, he may get fairly good. He may never be the equal of Babe Ruth, but he can be better than he was when he started.

The same is so with puzzle solving. If the skills required are there, they can be honed to a finer edge. If the abilities are there, the skills can be acquired.

The skills, generally speaking, are skills of reasoning. They are the same as the ones involved in formulating and evaluating arguments and in constructing deductive proofs. (Indeed, as we shall see, some of the very same techniques are required.) Thus, like many other intellectual games, logical puzzles hold out a promise of more than entertainment. They promise an opportunity to exercise and improve reasoning skills.

Because of this, our discussion of puzzles is not so remote from our concern with informal logic as it might first seem. But we don't have to be all that solemn about it. Puzzles are fun. And at this point in the book that's justification enough.

The puzzles we'll be concerned with are ones that are purely logical. Unlike mathematical puzzles, which require that you know (and recognize the need to apply) such esoteric devices as diophantine equations and the formula for the volume of a truncated cone, logical puzzles are solvable by reason alone. Ingenuity, rather than knowledge, is the key that opens the lock. This means, also, that guessing isn't allowed, and any answer must be a *reasoned* answer, one that can be justified.

Unlike riddles and conundrums, logical puzzles don't involve verbal tomfoolery. In a proper puzzle, the sentences stating it are never deliberately misleading. They merely provide information, and the puzzle lies in making use of the information to answer the question that is asked.

Only the information contained in the puzzle's statement is available for use, and it will be adequate to give the answer. There is a slight qualification that needs to be added to this, however. It's not legitimate to import information into the puzzle—to assume what you seem to need. Nevertheless, logical puzzles do require that you make use of "common sense" knowledge and a knowledge of English. For example, it's assumed that everyone recognizes that an object can't be completely red and completely green at the same time, that people with names like "Mrs. Smith" are female, that if two people contradict one another both can't be right, that parents are older than their children, that an uncle is also a brother to someone, that if Smith lives next door to Jones, then Jones lives next door to Smith, and so on.

There are puzzles that are puzzles of inductive logic, but there aren't many of them and they usually involve equipment of some kind. Here we will stick to puzzles that require, besides ingenuity, deductive reasoning. Trying alternatives, following out consequences, drawing conclusions are the sorts of things that must be done in solving the puzzles we'll be discussing.

It needs to be kept in mind, though, that there aren't any automatic or mechanical ways to solve logical puzzles. There are no paper and pencil "machines" that are such that when a puzzle is fed in, the correct solution emerges from the other end. "Logical intuition" and reasoning are required to do logical puzzles, and each person must supply them for himself. Each person has them already, of course, for they are skills we use every day.

We don't use those skills in just the ways required for puzzle solving, though. People who have never worked with logical puzzles before may well feel an initial moment of panic and helplessness. They have, perhaps, never thought *in just this way* or about *this sort of material* before. No one can be taught how to reason, but practical and strategic advice about how to deal with logical puzzles can be given. And that's what this chapter is about.

There are a vast number of logical puzzles, but the types of such puzzles are relatively few. Three of these types are particularly popular and interesting, and each of these we'll discuss separately and make a few suggestions about how to come to grips with them. Other puzzles of the deductive type can be found in the books listed in the notes to this chapter. Exercises at the end of the chapter provide more puzzles of the three types we'll be concerned with.

Smith, Jones, and Robinson

Probably the most common type of logical puzzle is the one often known as the "Smith, Jones, and Robinson" problem. The name comes from the characters in a puzzle by Henry Dudeney, the author of a great number of mathematical and logical puzzles. Dudeney's puzzles have served as models for numerous others of the same sort.

S-J-R puzzles typically involve several individuals about whom a few sentences of apparently pointless information is provided. The problem consists in answering a question about the individuals on the basis of the information. To do this requires drawing conclusions from the data that have been supplied. The data will not yield a direct answer. That is, it's ordinarily impossible merely to "see" the right answer. But the data are always adequate for a solution, and the puzzle aspect lies in this fact. The information must be *made* to yield the correct answer and the only way to get it to do that is by drawing inferences from it.

Here is one formulation of the S-J-R puzzle:

Mr. Smith, Mr. Jones, and Mr. Robinson live in Chicago, Omaha, and Detroit, but not necessarily respectively. They are passengers on a train run by a three-man crew. The men on the crew are named Smith, Jones, and Robinson, and they are engineer, fireman, and brakeman, but not necessarily respectively. The following additional facts are also known about these six men:

1. Mr. Robinson lives in Detroit.
2. Mr. Jones never studied algebra.
3. Smith beat the fireman at billiards.
4. The passenger whose name is the same as the brakeman's lives in Chicago.
5. The brakeman lives in Omaha.
6. The brakeman's nearest neighbor, one of the passengers, is a mathematician.

What positions do Smith, Jones, and Robinson hold on the crew?

The answer to this question is already contained in an implicit or hidden form in the information supplied. It must be squeezed out by a process of logical inference. The sentences that set up the puzzle are, in effect, premises from which conclusions may be deduced. Information that is "concealed" must be uncovered and made explicit.

There are at least two useful devices to use in dealing with S-J-R puzzles, and we will take a look at both of them. Both are ways of keeping track of inferences so that we can keep in mind what we have uncovered and, if necessary, make use of it to draw further conclusions.

The first method is more detailed and systematic than the other. It consists in writing down in one column each conclusion that is reached and stating in an opposite column the information that justifies the conclusion. Conclusions legitimately drawn from the original information may be used as a basis for arriving at additional conclusions. Thus, inferences can be justified by appealing to the original data directly or, by appealing to other inferences, indirectly.

Some inferences, by the way, may turn out to be useless. That is, they may neither answer the original question nor serve as a basis for other inferences that will. This isn't important. Useless steps on the way to an answer don't matter. It's getting a justified answer that counts.

Here, according to the first method, is a way the S-J-R puzzle can be worked out. The numbers in the right column refer to the sentences in the problem above, and the letters refer to inferences drawn from those sentences.

A. Smith is not the fireman.   3
B. Mr. Robinson does not live in Chicago.   1
C. Robinson is not the brakeman.   B, 4

D. Mr. Robinson is not the brakeman's neighbor.	1, 5
E. Mr. Jones is not the brakeman's neighbor.	2, 6
F. Mr. Smith is the brakeman's neighbor.	D, E
G. Mr. Smith does not live in Chicago.	5, F
H. Mr. Jones lives in Chicago.	B, G, 4
I. Jones is the brakeman.	H, 4
J. Smith is not the brakeman.	I
K. Smith is the engineer.	A, J
L. Robinson is the fireman.	I, K

The puzzle is an exercise in deduction. Each of the lettered sentences is a conclusion of an unstated argument that uses as premises the sentences indicated by a number or letter and the general information supplied in the statement of the puzzle. On what grounds do we assert that Smith is not the fireman? The appeal is to sentence 3 of the puzzle, but this is not the whole story, of course. The explicit argument that leads us to make statement A is:

No one can beat himself at billiards.

Smith beat the fireman at billiards.
_____

Therefore, Smith is not the fireman.

Unlike strict problems in deductive logic, in puzzles it is permissible to go beyond the exact sentences of the puzzle and make use of such ordinary information as "No one can beat himself at billiards."

The solution of puzzles of this sort, nevertheless, is no different in principle from the solution of straightforward problems in deductive logic. Behind each of the inferences written down as a conclusion, there is a short and valid argument, such as the one shown above.

As a general strategy in approaching puzzles in this way, it's helpful to write down all the justifiable conclusions you can. They may turn out to be useless, but it may be that out of this "new" information a way of reaching conclusions that answer the puzzle's question may emerge.

The second technique of dealing with S-J-R puzzles involves using a device for keeping track of certain inferences. Inferences aren't made explicit and written down, nor is any justification offered. Rather, both the reasoning and the drawing of many conclusions go on "in the head" and marks are only made to indicate that certain conclusions have been reached.

The usual method is to set up a table or matrix in which all possible combinations of relevant elements are displayed. In our puzzle we want to know what man out of the trio of Smith, Jones, and Robinson holds what position of a crew consisting of an engineer, a fireman, and a brakeman. So here is our table for that:

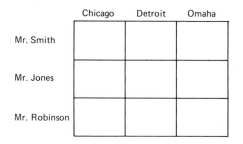

A glance at the puzzle also shows that it's important to be able to place Mr. Smith, Mr. Jones, and Mr. Robinson each in one of the three cities mentioned—Chicago, Detroit, or Omaha. Here is our table for that:

	Chicago	Detroit	Omaha
Mr. Smith			
Mr. Jones			
Mr. Robinson			

If the information expressed in the puzzle justifies our saying that any of these combinations is correct (e.g, "Mr. Robinson—Detroit") then the letter T (for "true") is put in the box corresponding to this. If this combination is legitimate, then the other two ("Mr. Robinson—Omaha" and "Mr. Robinson—Chicago") are not. To indicate this, the letter F (for "false") is put in each of the other two boxes. Line 1 of the problem tells us that Mr. Robinson does live in Detroit, so we can fill in the boxes as described:

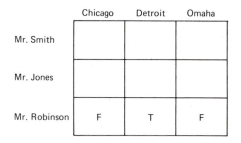

(By the way, some prefer to use 1 and 0 or X and ✔ instead of T and F.)
    The task, once the matrix is laid out, becomes one of correctly filling in the boxes. (Because the problem doesn't ask where each of the passen-

gers lives, we don't really have to complete the second set, unless we find it useful or want to.) We now look back at the information provided and try to see what is there that will allow us to put more Ts and Fs in the appropriate places. This takes no more and no less than just plain thinking. Here's how the process might go.

- A. Sentence 3 tells us that Smith beat the fireman at billiards. Since, as we've mentioned, a man can't beat himself at billiards, this justifies our putting an F in the "Smith—Fireman" box.
- B. Sentence 2 says that Mr. Jones never studied algebra, and sentence 6 says that the brakeman's nearest neighbor is a mathmatician. This means that Mr. Jones isn't the brakeman's nearest neighbor. (We assume, of course, that every mathematician has studied algebra.) According to sentence 5, the brakeman lives in Omaha. This means that Mr. Jones, since he is not the brakeman's nearest neighbor, can't live in Omaha. So we put an F in the "Mr. Jones—Omaha" box.
- C. Since we now know that neither Mr. Jones nor Mr. Robinson lives in Omaha, but one of the passengers does, that means Mr. Smith must. We put a T in the appropriate box.
- D. Knowing now that Mr. Smith lives in Omaha, we can put Fs for the "Mr. Smith—Chicago" and "Mr. Smith—Detroit" combinations.
- E. We now see that we can put a T for the "Mr. Jones—Chicago" combination, for the other two possible combinations under "Chicago" are false. This means now that the "Mr. Jones—Detroit" combination is false, and we can put an F in that box.

We now have determined where each of the three passengers lives, and a glance at our completed table will show this.

	Chicago	Detroit	Omaha
Mr. Smith	F	F	T
Mr. Jones	T	F	F
Mr. Robinson	F	T	F

But we still haven't finished with the train crew.

- F. Mr. Jones is the passenger who lives in Chicago. Sentence 4 tells us that this passenger's name is the same as the brakeman's. Hence, the brakeman is Jones. We can put a T for the "Jones—Brakeman" combination. We can also put Fs for the "Smith—Brakeman" and "Robinson—Brakeman" combinations as well as for the "Jones—Engineer" and "Jones—Fireman" combinations.
- G. We've already learned (in A) that Smith is not the fireman. We now know he is not the brakeman. Hence, he must be the engineer. We put a T to indicate this in the proper box.

H. We've already found out that Jones is not the engineer, because he is the brakeman (see F). Since Smith is the engineer, Robinson isn't, and we put an F for that combination.

I. Robinson must be the fireman. The table shows that he is neither engineer nor brakeman and that neither Smith nor Jones is fireman. Only the fireman's job remains, and only Robinson remains to fill it.

Our puzzle is solved.

	Engineer	Fireman	Brakeman
Smith	T	F	F
Jones	F	F	T
Robinson	F	T	F

Notice that exactly the same kind of process of reasoning went on in solving the puzzle in this way as went on before. The difference in approaches lies mainly in whether or not inferences made, conclusions reached, are recorded and justified. Most who use the matrix approach would not, as we've done here, write down a justification for each of their steps. Rather, they would merely fill in the boxes after "seeing" that they were warranted to do so. We've gone through in a slow and plodding fashion, but someone who has mastered the technique of doing S-J-R puzzles can zip through them in a very few minutes.

Being shown how to do these puzzles and practicing doing them are about the only way to improve the necessary skills. Here, then, is one more worked example of the S-J-R type.

President Zed of Trenton University finds himself faced with a serious problem. In ten minutes he must attend an awards banquet and introduce six distinguished people who have come to Trenton to present awards to the students. Unfortunately, he has lost the list that identified the notables who are to give the awards in their various fields of distinction. He does, at least, remember the names of the visitors and the fields involved.

Present will be Professor Allen, Miss Bowen, Dean Conway, Dr. Dunn, Professor Elrod, and Dr. Fagin. The fields represented are mathematics, English, drama, physics, history, and biology. Fortunately, President Zed also recalls a few scraps of information about the visitors:

1. The biologist is a confirmed bachelor who has sworn never to marry.
2. Professor Elrod is engaged to the daughter of the mathematician.
3. Dean Conway is the ex-wife of the physicist, who divorced her in order to carry on an affair with the person in drama.
4. The person in drama made her stage debut playing Ophelia in *Hamlet*.
5. Dr. Fagin and the mathematician often gossip about the physicist's new romance, but not around Dean Conway or Dr. Dunn.

6. Professor Elrod knows no science, and the only literature he ever reads is French.

7. Only two of the visitors are women.

Using these few facts President Zed, in a burst of unaccustomed rational activity, is able to place each person in his or her proper field. *What is the correct field for each person?*

To solve this puzzle, let's make use of the method of explicit inference and justification. Remember that the sequence of sentences isn't a set one and a different sequence, or even one involving some different sentences, can produce the same result.

A.	Professor Elrod is not the biologist.	1, 2
B.	Professor Elrod is not the mathematician.	2
C.	Dean Conway is not the person in drama.	3
D.	Dean Conway is not the physicist.	3
* E.	Miss Bowen is the person in drama.	C, 7, 4
F.	Dr. Fagin is not the mathematican.	5
G.	Dr. Fagin is not the physicist.	5
H.	Dean Conway is not the mathematician.	5
I.	Dr. Dunn is not the mathematician.	5
J.	Professor Elrod is not the physicist.	6
K.	Professor Elrod is not in English.	6
* L.	Professor Elrod is the historian.	A, B, E, J, K
* M.	Dr. Allen is the mathematician.	B, E, F, H, I
* N.	Dr. Dunn is the physicist.	D, E, G, J, M
O.	Dean Conway is not the biologist.	1, 3
* P.	Dr. Fagin is the biologist.	E, L, M, N, O
* Q.	Dean Conway is in English.	E, L, M, N, O, P

This puzzle involves matching six people with six fields. The process of writing out explicit inferences is a rather slow one, and the table method is clearly the quickest and easiest way of resolving the puzzle. The table needed is one that will plot people against fields.

	Math	English	Drama	Physics	History	Biology
Prof. Allen						
Miss Bowen						
Dean Conway						
Dr. Dunn						
Prof. Elrod						
Dr. Fagin						

It should be quite easy to fill in the matrix now that we have gone through the process of drawing explicit inferences. In truth, it's generally easier to use this method to start with, and most puzzle fanciers prefer it. Its disadvantage, as we've already mentioned, is that it keeps the inferences needed to establish the final conclusion hidden from view. Even when we are told the correct solution or are faced with a completed matrix giving the solution, if we did not ourselves go through the process of reasoning necessary to arrive at the answer, we may continue to be puzzled and dissatisfied. We may not see *why* the correct answer is correct. Keeping a record of explicit inferences helps us to understand what we have done and helps others to follow the same path.

There are a couple more hints about S-J-R puzzles that may be helpful to those who have never done them before.

First it's possible to make use of hypotheses in looking for the general solution to the puzzle. You might, for example, make the hypothesis that Dr. Fagin is the biologist and work out the consequences of this. That is, you "work on the assumption" that the hypothesis is true and see where it leads when taken in conjunction with the information given about the biologist and his or her relations to others.

The method of hypothesis can be useful, but you have to be careful with it. You must be prepared to reject your hypothesis when it leads you into a contradiction. (For example, when you would have to assume that someone is older than himself, or some such.) Also, you must be careful to see that you don't get an answer that's *merely* self-consistent—that doesn't produce a contradiction. To solve a puzzle, you must always be prepared to show that the alternative to your initial hypothesis is *false*, not merely that your hypothesis *could be* true.

Second, it's worth mentioning a purely mechanical detail. The matrices we've developed in our examples play off one set of items against another set. Though it's possible to construct matrices to display the combinations of numerous sets of items, we won't have any use for them in the exercises.

To do the exercises, though, it is necessary to be able to relate the items in several sets to one another so as to be able to join an item in one set with an item from any other set. Here's how this can be done. Start by making a matrix like the ones we've used for two sets. For a third set, write the names of the items in the left-hand column (below those of the first set). *And* write them across the top (after the items of the second set). Repeat the procedure for the next set, and so on. The horizontal and vertical intersection of items in the same set are of no interest to you, and you can ignore them.

This will make it easier to set up the problems in the exercises. But if you don't like the matrix method, then don't use it.

Who's Lying?

A great number of puzzles involve lying and truth-telling, and the task generally is to identify the person who is speaking the truth on the basis of his answer to a question put to him. Liars are understood in such puzzles to be people who always speak falsely and truth-tellers as ones who always speak the truth.

A variant of the liar/truth-teller type of puzzle is one in which a third class of people is introduced. In addition to people who always lie and people who always tell the truth, people who sometimes lie and sometimes tell the truth are given lines to speak. Here, however, we'll stick to puzzles that involve only truth-tellers and liars.

Before saying more about "Who's Lying?" puzzles, let's consider one as an example. We'll then have a case to which we can peg a discussion of general strategies of solution.

> All the inhabitants of a remote village in the Ozarks belong to one of two ancient clans—the Truves or the Falls. The Truves are an upright and highly moral people and speak only the truth. The Falls, on the other hand, are a corrupt and morally degenerate lot. They are the polar opposite of the Truves, and they always lie.
>
> An anthropologist, hearing of this strange village, decided to visit it and study its social structure. No sooner had he arrived than he met three inhabitants of the town sitting outside the feed store.
>
> "Hello," he said, "are you Truves or Falls?"
>
> "We're all Falls," the first man replied.
>
> "No, we're not," said the second. "Only two of us are Falls."
>
> "That's not true, either," the third said.
>
> The anthropologist was wholly perplexed. If these people were going to be of any use as informants, he would have to know what clan each belonged to. *What clan does each belong to?*

The question which the puzzle ends with is, of course, just a way of asking who is lying and who is telling the truth, and we can approach it in just this way. As usual, though, there is no automatic or mechanical way to solve the problem. Its resolution demands thinking and reasoning, pure and simple. Nonetheless, a few pointers about approach are possible, and just the experience of seeing how the puzzle is solved is an important ingredient in learning how to solve others of the same type.

It's useful as a first step merely to write down the sentences that constitute the crux of the problem. Too, stylistic elements can be stripped away and just what the sentences assert put down. It's easier to reason about the sentences when attention can be focused on their content and the distracting elements of the "story" ignored. Here are the three relevant sentences from the puzzle; the numbers stand for the speakers:

1. We are all Falls.
2. Only two of us are Falls.
3. That (i.e., sentence 2) is not true, either.

Next, it's useful to keep in mind just what the logical possibilities with respect to truth and falsity are for any sentence or group of sentences. The Truves always tell the truth, and the Falls always lie. Consequently, for each sentence there are just two possibilities: either it is true or it is false. For any group of sentences taken together there are just three possibilities: all are true; all are false; some are true and some are false. We must, as a matter of strategy, consider each sentence alone and also in company with others in the group. Each sentence must be tested against itself and the other sentences. There must be a reason for saying that a sentence is false or that it is true—that a speaker is a liar or a truthteller—and the reason rests in the sentences and conditions of the puzzle.

It's of no real use in dealing with puzzles like this to construct a matrix the way we did for S-J-R puzzles. The sentences simply must be thought about, separately and in conjunction. We can make a record of what we do, of the possibilities we explore and eliminate, but a record of reasoning is, of course, not reasoning. Everyone must do that for himself. But let's consider how, in accordance with our few hints, our present puzzle can be resolved.

A. We can see at once that all three sentences can't be true, because 2 denies what 1 asserts, and 3 says that 2 is not true. Thus, all three speakers can't belong to the Truve clan.
B. The first speaker says, "We are all Falls." But this can't be true. If it were, speaker 1 would be speaking the truth, and he could not be the Falls he says he is. Speaker 1 has to be lying, and hence speaker 1 is a Falls.
C. Since speaker 1 is lying, then it's false that all three speakers are Falls. This means that either speaker 2 or 3 or both are telling the truth.
D. But *both* cannot be telling the truth. Speaker 2 says, "Two of us are Falls," and speaker 3 denies this. Their claims are contradictory, so only one of them can be speaking the truth. Which one:
E. Speaker 2 must be telling the truth because:
   a. We know from D that either 2 or 3 is lying;
   b. We established in A that speaker 1 is lying;
   c. Speaker 2 says, "Only two of us are Falls," i.e., only two are liars. Speaker 2 is correct and is telling the truth.
So: Speaker 1 is a Falls, 2 is a Truve, and 3 is a Falls.

Lying problems usually can't be solved with ease and with speed, but practice in dealing with them does make solutions come faster and easier. Most important, though, is keeping in mind the relations that the sentences have to one another—one contradicting another, the possibility that both could be true, the necessity that one is false, and so on. Nothing can guarantee a solution, but a constant consideration of what is being asserted makes the task possible.

Here, for practice, is another puzzle that makes use of the same conditions as the one above:

The anthropologist, after much deliberation, finally succeeded in sorting out his informants with respect to their claims. He was about to ask them some questions about their strange practices when suddenly another trio came walking out of the feed store.

"Oh no," he thought, "here we go again! But I suppose I had better take advantage of the situation and interview these people too."

"Pardon me," he said to one of the newcomers. "Can you tell me what clan you belong to?"

"Well, two of us are Truves," said the first.

"Oh no," said the second man. "Only one of us is a Truve."

"That's correct," said the third.

The anthropologist thought hard. *What clan does each belong to?*

This puzzle is of exactly the same sort as the last one and can be dealt with in the same fashion. To start out, we can restate the three claims that are made:

1. Two of us are Truves.
2. Only one of us is a Truve.
3. That is correct. (i.e., only one of us is a Truve.)

Now we can make a record of our reasoning about these sentences. We must give reasons for saying of each sentence that it is true or that it is false.

A. Since speakers 2 and 3 contradict speaker 1, all the sentences can't be true. One or more is false.
B. Is the first sentence true or false? Let's suppose for a moment that it is true. It says, in effect, that two of the three sentences are true. Assuming, as we are, that it is itself true, that means that either the second or third sentence, but not both, must be true. But notice that sentences 2 and 3 say the same thing. Thus, it's impossible for just *one* of them to be true. This means that our assumption that the first sentence is true is incorrect. The first sentence cannot be true. Sentence 1 is false, and speaker 1 is a Falls.
C. Now, is sentence 2 true or false? If it is true, it can be the only one of the three sentences that is, for it says in effect, "Only one of these three sentences is true." But sentence 3, as we've seen, makes exactly the same claim, and just for this reason it's not possible for one of the pair to be false while the other is true. Sentence 2, accordingly, cannot be true. It is false, and speaker 2 is a Falls.
D. For exactly the same reasons, sentence 3 is false, and speaker 3 is a Falls.

So: All members of the trio belong to the Falls clan.

More explicitly in this puzzle than in the last, we considered the logical consequences of assuming that the speakers were telling the truth. In following up the consequences we found that some could not be telling the truth. With this possibility eliminated, only one other remained. We might, of course, also have worked on the assumption that each speaker way lying, but this has a strategic disadvantage. There are various ways of lying in the situation described so that it's quite difficult to follow out the consequences of our assumption.

As a final example of the "Who's Lying?" type of puzzle, let's consider a fictionalized verions of the one which appeared at the opening of this chapter:

> The landing module had no sooner set down on Vega II than Rawlson was met by two of the humanoid inhabitants. He recalled the briefing Feld had given him and knew he would have to be careful. What was it Feld had said? One *glist* or tribe, the Tonarka, was devoted to serving some god of deception and always lied in answer to any question. The Lowto, the only other *glist,* worshipped the god of truth and thus spoke nothing but the truth in answer to a question.
>
> Rawlson knew that he would have to find out what *glist* these two humanoids belonged to if he was going to get the trustworthy information he needed. Without reliable information he would never find the underground city of Klave.
>
> Turning to the first, Rawlson asked, "Are you a Lowto?"
>
> The humanoid said something that sounded like "Jibble-Jibble-Geek" to Rawlson.
>
> Rawlson despaired. They didn't even speak English. But before he could consider what to do, the second humanoid spoke. "He says that he is a Lowto, but he is a Tonarka."
>
> Rawlson was hugely relieved. Now he knew the *glist* of each. What is it?

The solution to this puzzle hinges on the recognition of a point useful in many puzzles of this variety. It is this: In response to the question "Are you telling the truth?" both the liar and the truth-teller must answer yes. So, in this puzzle, the first speaker, since he is either lying or telling the truth, must answer the question in the affirmative. The second speaker correctly acknowledges this, so the second speaker must be the truth-teller —that is, be a Lowto. The first speaker, then, on the basis of what the truth-teller says is a Tonarka.

There are puzzles involving lying different from the breed we've been discussing here. In fact, the last type of puzzle we will discuss can be regarded as merely a different sort of "Who's Lying?"

Who's the Murderer?

Almost as numerous as the lying/truth-telling puzzles are those that involve one or several groups of sentences. A specific number of the sentences is said to be false, and the problem is to identify those sentences. More often than not, the characters in the puzzles are said to be murder suspects, and one of them is said to be a murderer. By discovering which of the sentences in the puzzle have to be false, the murderer is uncovered.

Here is a typical example of the "Who's the Murderer?" type:

> Allison, Baggins, Colt, and Daws are all guests at a house party during which their host, an extortionist by the name of Slate, is murdered. The lone murderer confesses to the other members of the group and decides to give

himself up to the police. In a spirit of fun, one of the quartet suggests that they should make the police work for their catch. They decide that each of them will say only one thing and no more to the police and that *only one of their four statements will be true*. The police, accordingly, will have to exercise their wits in order to determine which of the four is the murderer of Slate. Here is what they say to Chief Inspector East when he asks them for a statement:

ALLISON: I didn't murder Slate.
BAGGINS: Colt did it.
COLT: Allison murdered Slate.
DAWS: I didn't kill Slate.
Who murdered Slate?

Puzzles of this sort are approached in fundamentally the same way as those of the "Who's Lying?" type. It's necessary to consider each sentence alone and in connection with the rest. It's necessary to follow out the consequences of each sentence, assuming it to be true. The advantage in puzzles of this sort, an advantage we don't have in liar/truth-teller type, is that we know exactly how many sentences are false.

The most important step in learning how to solve puzzles of the Murderer sort is, as with the other sorts, practice in doing them and the opportunity of seeing how a few examples are solved. Here, then, is the way the above puzzle can be dealt with. We'll use capital letters to abbreviate the sentences spoken by the four suspects.

1. The first thing to notice is that A and C contradict one another. This means that *both* of them can't be false—since one denies exactly what the other asserts. So either A or C is the true sentence.
2. Suppose that C is true. This means that A is false—that Allison did murder Slate—but it also means that D is false, for only one fo the four sentences can be true. But if D is false, then Daws murdered Slate. Thus, our assumption leads us to say that both Allison and Daws murdered Slate. This is unacceptable, for there is only one murderer. We must abandon our assumption that C is true. But if C can't be true, then C is false.
3. A must then be the true sentence. Will this work? Let's suppose A is true, that Allison did not murder Slate. If so, this means that Colt didn't murder Slate (that B is false), that Allison didn't murder Slate (that C is false), but that Daws did murder Slate (that D is false)! The assumption that A is true works out; it means that all others can be false without producing an inconsistency. *Daws is the murderer.*

Let's take the same puzzle again. But this time let's assume that *only one statement is false*. Who must we say is the murderer under this condition?

1. We can again start with the contradictory sentences A and C. Just because they are contradictory, we know that both cannot be true, nor can both be false. So either A or C is false. Which one?
2. Suppose A is false and Allison did murder Slate. But, since all the other sentences have to be considered true, this means B is true also. But B says that Colt is the murderer. Our assumption that A is false leads to the unacceptable

consequence that Allison is the murderer and that Colt is the murderer. We can't, then, make all the other sentences true and not be led to an inconsistent conclusion if we suppose A is false. A cannot be false, so it must be true.

3. This means that C must be the false sentence of the pair, for as we saw in 1 either A or C has to be false and both cannot be false. Well, how does it work out if we say that C is false? If we assume C is false this gives us a consistent way of satisfying the condition that all sentences but one are true and it shows us who the murderer is. Assuming C to be false, then Allison did not murder Slate (A is true), and Daws did not murder Slate (D is true). Rather, *Colt murdered Slate* (B is true)!

Here is a final puzzle of the "Who's the Murderer?" type. It differs from the ones above in that it consists of several groups of sentences. The puzzle is slightly more complicated than the others, just because a larger number of sentences is involved, but it is approached and solved in exactly the same way. The same strategies of following out consequences and considering whether they are consistent with the conditions of the puzzle are appropriate.

The dead body of Reggie Mortis is found in the library of his house. The medical examiner establishes beyond doubt that Mortis was strangled to death. The case seems quite simple, for Mortis was locked in his library with three men. All of them are capable of murder, and one of them must be the murderer. Statements are taken by the police from each of the three men. Initially Chief Inspector East is confused, but then he discovers that exactly one claim made by each of the suspects is false. Knowing this, East is able to determine who murdered Mortis on the basis of the statements made by the three suspects. Here are the claims that they made:

ALLEN:
(1) I didn't do it.
(2) I don't know who did it.
(3) I've never read *The Lay of the Last Minstrel*.

BRADLEY:
(1) I didn't do it.
(2) Allen didn't do it.
(3) Allen told the truth about not having read *The Lay of the Last Minstrel*.

CASPAR:
(1) I didn't do it.
(2) Allen lied about never having read *The Lay of the Last Minstrel*.
(3) Bradley didn't do it.

On the surface this puzzle looks incredibly difficult, impossible to solve. But it is not. It is really a rather simple puzzle if it is approached in the right fashion. We are given two important conditions in the statement of the puzzle, and these two conditions point in the direction of a solution. We are told:

1. Either Allen, Bradley, or Caspar committed the murder.
2. Exactly one of the claims made by each is false.

(To make it convenient to talk about the claims they make, let's use a capital letter to stand for the person's name and a number to designate one of the three claims that he makes. Thus, "A3" will refer to Allen's third statement.)

Each of the three people denies being the murderer, but condition 1 assures us that one of them is the murder. This means, then, that one of the three sentences A1, B1, or C1 is false. One way of proceeding in solving the puzzle is to try out each of the three possible hypotheses: A1 is false, B1 is false, C1 is false. Condition 2 is that one and only one sentence in each group is false. So each hypothesis requires that we assume that the other two sentences in the group are true. Working in this way we can follow out the consequences of assuming that each is lying about not being the murderer but that the other claims they make are true. All but one of our three hypotheses will lead to inconsistent and hence unacceptable consequences. One of the hypotheses will yield results that are consistent with the two conditions of the puzzle. When we locate this hypothesis we will have identified the murderer. So here we go.

Hypothesis 1: A1 is false. If A1 is false, then Allen is the murderer. But if A1 is false, A2 cannot be true, because if Allen is guilty he does know who killed Mortis. But according to condition 2 only one sentence in each group can be false. Thus, A1 cannot be false without violating a condition of the puzzle. Since A1 cannot be false, it must be true. Allen is not the murderer.

Hypothesis 2: B1 is false. If B1 is false, then Bradley is the murderer. B2 and B3, according to condition 2, we must assume to be true. What are the consequences of this? If B2 is true, then A1 is true, and since there can be only one murderer, C1 is true also. These consequences are consistent and acceptable.

If B3 is true, then A3 is true, and A2 is the false sentence. But if B3 is true, C2 is false. Yet we've already shown that C1, according to our hypothesis, must be the false sentence in the C group. Our hypothesis leads us to say that C1 and C2 are false. But this violates condition 2. Hence, we must give up our hypothesis that B1 is false. B1 must be true, and Bradley is not the murderer.

By elimination of two of three suspects and in accordance with condition 1, that one of the three is the murderer, we can now conclude that Caspar killed Mortis. But just to assure ourselves that this is so, let's examine the consequences of our last possible hypothesis and see if they are consistent with the conditions of the puzzle.

Hypothesis 3: C1 is false. If C1 is false, Caspar is the murderer. C2 and C3, according to condition 2, must be considered true. If C2 is true, then A3 is false, and A1 and A2 are true. Also, if C2 is true, then B3 is false, and

B1 and B2 are the true sentences in that group. If C3 is true, then B1 is true—an outcome consistent with the truth of C2.

The results are satisfying. By assuming C1 to be false, we can give a conditions for solving the puzzle. Thus, the thrid hypothesis is the correct each of the three groups, and the interpretation will satisfy the two conditions for solving the puzzle. Thus the third hypothesis is the correct one: *Caspar murdered Mortis.*

All "Who's the Murderer?" puzzles are fundamentally the same, even though some are complicated by employing several groups of sentences rather than a single group. Following consequences, "testing" hypotheses, will eventually yield a solution that is consistent with the conditions of the puzzle.

The perplexities and bewilderments that we've dealt with in this chapter might be considered intellectually trivial. And in a sense they are. Who cares who the engineer is? Who cares who killed Reggie Mortis? The answer is that nobody does.

In another sense, of course, the puzzles have a value greater than their trivial subject matter. By providing an opportunity to practice reasoning, they hold some promise of an improvement in rational skills. The extent to which these skills can be transferred to practical problem solving is an open question that we can leave to the psychologists to answer. That they are of assistance in solving formal problems, such as those involved in constructing deductive demonstrations or mathematical proofs, is obvious and undebatable.

Perhaps as important as the improvement of skills is the habit of mind that puzzle solving encourages. It encourages you to look for the unobvious connections among things and not to take everything at face value. It encourages analysis, reflection, and the development of a critical attitude.

Anything that promises all of this and is also fun is surely something that ought to be encouraged.

Exercises

Sirius Confusion

The starship *Beagle* has a comand crew of six. They are Altern, Diola, Lampar, Zolan, Smith, and Kline.

An incredibly intense ion storm encountered in the Sirius section has left the crew confused and disoriented. None of them recalls his name or the position he holds on the ship. Among them, however, they still possess a few fragments of knowledge about one another and about the command positions. By pooling the information they have, they hope to be able to discover the proper persons to fill the six command posts.

The posts are these: Captain, First Officer, Information Officer, Navigator, Biomedical Officer, and Engineering Officer.

Here is what their pooled information amounts to:

1. The Biomedical Officer spent ten years as a Professor of Neurobiology at the Space Academy.
2. All starship engineers are trained on Mars.
3. Diola is the only one with a brother in the crew.
4. Smith was born in Moon Colony.
5. Kline never studied navigation.
6. Smith is either the First Officer or the Captain.
7. Earth is the only solar planet ever visited by Zolan.
8. The Captain is the only female in the group.
9. Kline has never seen the Space Academy.
10. No person not born on Earth is permitted to be the Captain of a starship.
11. The First Officer's sister is a member of the crew.
12. Neither Lampar nor Zolan has ever been a teacher.
13. One who has not been to the Space Academy cannot be an Engineering Officer.

Who's the Vampire?

Tolar, Zarnak, and Robeck all have perfectly ordinary jobs and live in an ordinary neighborhood in Grand Rapids, Michigan.

In some order or other, one is a biologist, one a broker, and one a bookie.

These three people also have three hobbies. One is a poet, one a magician, and one a gardener.

Like all people, they also have their little peculiarities. One is an android, one a werewolf, and one a vampire.

After a certain evening, the suspicion of the townspeople fell on these three. The question uppermost in the minds of all was: Who is the vampire?

They had precious little information to go on, but what they had you shall have:

1. The bookie and the android sometimes call up the broker when they want to buy or sell stocks.
2. The magician often entertains the broker and biologist with sleight-of-hand tricks.
3. Tolar never invests his money, but he sometimes gives advice to the biologist.
4. The gardener gives flowers from his garden to the android and the werewolf in the spring and summer.
5. Zarnak refuses to have anything to do with gambling himself, but he never criticizes the broker or the werewolf.

Double Majors

The Double Major Society of the Otherside College of Mortuary Science meets only once a year. The purpose of the meeting is to give the members an opportunity to congratulate one another on their cleverness.

The society has only three members at present. They are the very grave group of Victory, Sting, and Mullins.

Among them, however, they possess six majors: Embalming, Mortuary Management, Necropolis Planning, Cosmetology, Necrology Writing, and Funeral Financing.

The faculty advisor, Ms. Kismit, has trouble keeping straight who is majoring in just what two subjects. She knows that no two students have any major in common, but before the meeting she jots down a few items that will allow her to associate each student with the proper subjects.

1. The Embalming major and the Mortuary Management major are on bad terms.
2. The father of the Embalming major is the uncle of the Cosmetology major.
3. Victory is a close friend of both the Cosmetology major and the Necropolis Planning major.
4. Sting has never studied Mortuary Management.

The Library of Popular Culture

The Library of Popular Culture has not been open for long, but it already has five regular patrons—Ms. Pi, Mrs. Click, Mr. Moon, Miss Whiz, and Mr. Zot.

Each person is especially interested in just one of the five book collections housed in the Library. The collections are: Spy Stories, True Romances, Science Fiction, Gothic Novels, and Detective Stories.

Furthermore, each patron is devoted to just one of the five kinds of music in the Library's collection of popular records. The records are divided into these types: Jazz, Rock, Rhythm and Blues (R&B), Country and Western (C&W), and Folk.

The librarian is a conscientious person who likes to get to know his regular patrons as people. For that reason, he started jotting down notes to himself about these five patrons. The notes include bits of gossip, his own observations, and what the people themselves have told him.

Much to his surprise, he discovers that his notes contain enough information to allow him to tell just what each patron prefers in the way of books and music.

Here are his notes:

1. The ex-spouse of the Science Fiction fan prefers Gothics.
2. The man who has never been married prefers R&B but detests the Spy Stories beloved by his fiancèe.
3. Miss Whiz hates Jazz, and Mrs. Click has no thought of remarriage.
4. Ms. Pi hates True Romances but used to be married to the man who likes Rock.
5. Mrs. Click and Miss Whiz are the only two who know calculus.
6. The divorced man is critical of the preference for Romances shown by one of the two engaged patrons.

7. The Jazz fancier taught calculus to the one who likes Spy Stories.
8. Mr. Moon divorced one of the patrons because he hates the C&W music that she prefers to the Rock he loves.
9. One of those who know calculus is engaged to a patron who has never married.
10. The person who prefers Folk is a business associate of the one who likes C&W and reads Science Fiction.

I Spy a Spy

Joanna's orders from MI-5 were explicit: Find the Falls spy that had penetrated the network.

By a process of elimination she at last narrowed the possibilities to two, Clondist and Alon. It was now a matter of discovering which one it was.

After a week of restless thought she finally hit upon a plan.

She called them both to the radio room and explained to them that she needed them to translate for her. She was going to make a radio call to Vantago, the homeland of the Truves and the Falls, and she didn't know the Vantagoin language. All she really knew about the Vantagoes was that the Truves sect always spoke the truth, while the Falls always lied.

"Calling Vantago, calling Vantago," she said into the mike.

The speaker blared out an acknowledgment in Vantagoin.

"Are you a Falls?" Joanna asked into the mike.

The answer came back in Vantagoin.

"He says that he is not," Clondist said.

"No, no, he says that he is," Alon said.

Now Joanna knew who was the Falls spy.

Who was the Falls spy?

The Perplexity of the Wizard

In the ancient Hypoborean Age, when things were strange and very different from what they are today, there were two groups of people living in the valley of the Eldern River. The first group called itself the Torag, which means "speakers of the truth always." The second was known as the Foldar, or "destroyers of truth."

Now a wizard came from the north to the valley one day, for he had heard of these strange people and wished to see them for himself—for they were strange peoples, even in that day.

Walking into the square of the town, he saw a gathering of five people and went over to them.

"Well met," he said. "I have come to learn your ways and to discover, if I can, how all of you so readily distinguish what is true from what is false. Tell me this, are you all Torags?"

A man spoke first. "No, we are not," he said.

"Just two of us are," a woman added.

"You are lying," said another woman. "Three of us are."

"Come, let us speak the truth," said a second man. "None of us is."

The last person looked thoughtful, then spoke. "The first speaker has spoken truly," he said.

The wizard was hopelessly puzzled and disappointed that his efforts had gotten off to such a bad start. He decided to try to find others he might understand more easily.

Had the wizard been willing to think hard for a moment, he could have learned just exactly how many in the group were Torags and how many Foldars.

Who were the Torags and who were the Foldars?

The Success of the Wizard

Thoroughly confused by his first encounter, the wizard wandered down to the bank of the Eldern, where another group of five were engaged in cleaning fish.

"I don't want to bother you," he said, "but I wish to learn your ways. To do that I must first determine which of you are Torags and which Foldars. Thus, I want to put to you this question: How many of you are Torags?"

Going in a circle, the five answered one after the other.

"I, for one, am a Torag."

"He's just giving you the only possible answer," said the second.

"There are three Foldars in this group," said the third.

"Please don't confuse the man," said the fourth. "The first two are the only Foldars here."

"The first says he's a Torag, but you can't tell from that whether he is or not," said the last person.

This time, instead of moving on, the wizard thought for a few minutes. Then he shook his head and thought for a few minutes more.

"Now I know how many of you are Torags and how many are not," the wizard said.

What did the wizard know?

The Idol of Kur-Wa-Tan

Bokar, the High Priest of Kur-Wa-Tan, was furious. Sometime during the night someone had stolen the great diamond that flashed from the forehead of the idol of Tulek, god of destruction.

Suspicion fell at once on the four American adventurers who had asked for permission to photograph and study the Temple of Tulek. The diamond was missing immediately after their stay in the sacred shrine.

Bokar called the four to his presence.

"One of you has taken the diamond," he said. "If that one confesses, I shall let the others go free. Otherwise, you shall all feel the fang of Sotar, the viper."

The two men and the two women looked at one another, and each answered according to his conscience or character.

"I took it," said Cora Mistople, the youngest of the group.

"I certainly didn't take it," said Carl Hollander.

"Cora didn't take it," said Susan Sullivan. "She's just trying to protect the rest of us."

"Susan's right," said Robert Mizervic. "Cora is trying to protect me. I took the diamond."

Bokar looked annoyed. "You are a very trying group," he said. "The gods assure me that only one of you is telling the truth. On that assumption, I know which one it is. Thus, I know who stole the diamond."

Who stole the diamond from the idol of Tulek?

A Sad Day by the Tumtum Tree

The Jabberwock was dead, and Detective Superintendent Knight was saddened by the the shame of it all. It had been such a fascinating creature. Dangerous, to be sure, but that had been an element of its fascination.

Now it was dead. Sometime during the preceding night someone had sneaked into the grounds of Longleaf Manor and killed the Jabberwock as it slept in its compound. The body lay at the foot of the Tumtum tree, a bloodstained Vorpal blade nearby.

The case was not only sad, it was bizarre. The private watchmen had acted quickly and turned up three trespassers on the grounds. One of them was surely the killer.

The three belonged to some peculiar sect called the Puzzle Club, and they refused to answer direct questions. "We shall each tell you three things," one of them said to the detective, "and one each a lie. If you are clever, you will learn who caused the Jabberwock to die."

There he had it. One of the trio was certainly the slayer, and in an indirect way they were telling him who it was. But Knight wondered if he were clever enough to figure it out from what he had been told.

He had copied down the exact words of each of the three, and now he read their statements through again:

BEAMISH: 1. I didn't kill the Jabberwock.
          2. That's my Vorpal sword.
          3. I've never seen the Bandersnatch.

FRABJOUS: 1. Callay didn't do it.
          2. We all saw the Bandersnatch on the way in.
          3. I've never been to Longleaf before.

CALLAY: 1. The moon was full last night.

2. The Vorpal sword does not belong to Beamish.

3. Frabjous always visits Longleaf on bank holidays.

Superintendent Knight was sure that the names given to him were pseudonyms, but that didn't matter. He had the people. And now, he was sure, he had the killer.

Who killed the Jabberwock?

The Beast of the Sargasso Sea

In the Graveyard of Lost Ships, on the deck of a rotting hulk trapped for over a century in the tangled profusion of the seaweed, a group of six men gathered. One was angry, terribly angry.

"One of you five did it," said Captain John O'Malley. "One of you slipped down to the strongroom last night, opened the lock on the door and let the beast escape. Whoever it was obviously wants us to stay here longer so that he can search for the legendary *Mare Dolorosum* treasure that is supposed to be hidden in one of these ships. Now we have to try to recapture the creature so that we can turn him over to the Brookings Institution for study. That's our job."

The Captain paused for a moment, then went on.

"I'm a going to ask each of you if you know who let the beast loose, and I want an honest answer."

Some of the men looked shamefaced and others defiant as they answered the Captain's question.

"It was Lombardi," said Cervanez. "He did it."

"Latimer did it," said Olafson, staring straight at the man.

"Lombardi didn't do it," said Goodfellow.

"Neither I nor Cervanez did it," said Lombardi.

"Cervanez did it," said Latimer.

"I know all of you very well," said O'Malley. "I'm going to assume, then, that only one of you is telling the truth. On that assumption, I now know who freed the beast."

Who freed the beast of the Sargasso Sea?

Modern Romantic Love

Jill, Clarence, Sarah, and Frank form a romantic rectangle, and when a reporter from *Modern Romantic Love Magazine* approached one of them for an interview about their life-style and personal histories, that person jumped at the chance. They all needed money, and the five-hundred-dollar interview fee was just too much to pass up.

But which of the four was it?

The editors decided to try to hype the circulation of the magazine by running a contest.

"Only one of the four sentences in each group is true," the contest directions stated. "On the basis of the sentences alone and this bit of knowledge, you should be able to determine the identity of our source for the story 'I Was Never Very Good at Competitive Sports.' The first reader to notify us of of the name of our source and provide us with adequate proof of how it was arrived at will win our big Identify-the-Source Prize. The Grand Prize is an all-expense-paid Las Vegas divorce, or a week-long tour of New York's fabulous singles bars, or fifty dollars in cash. Ten second prizes of a full year's subscription to *Modern Romantic Love Magazine* will also be awarded."

Here are the clues *MRL* supplied:

JILL:
1. I used to pose nude.
2. Frank once appeared in a porno flick.
3. Sarah sold her memoirs to *Exposé*.
4. Frank talked to the *MRL* reporter.

CLARENCE:
1. I've never talked to any reporter.
2. Jill has never done any nude posing.
3. Sarah and I eat hamburgers every Friday night.
4. Jill talked to the reporter.

SARAH:
1. Jill didn't talk to the reporter.
2. Clarence works in a bottomless bar.
3. I've never sold my memoirs.
4. I never talked to the *MRL* reporter.

FRANK:
1. I've never been in a porno flick.
2. I saw Clarence talking to the reporter.
3. Sarah used to work in a topless Club.
4. Jill is an undercover agent for the vice squad.

Identify the Source.

Notes and References

In the last few years, I've read at least ten or twelve pounds of books on informal logic. I've learned something from them all, and I'm grateful to their authors. Informal logic is one of the few remaining traditions of unselfishly shared knowledge, and I know the authors will forgive me if I don't name every book I've consulted.

The tradition that I've drawn from, modified, and added to is embodied in Richard Whately's *Elements of Logic* (Boston: James Monroe, 1838) and John Stuart Mill's *A System of Logic*, 8th ed. (New York: Harper and Brothers, 1879). Somewhat more recent embodiments are Irving M. Copi's *Introduction to Logic,* 4th ed. (New York: Macmillan, 1972) and Robert G. Olson's *Meaning and Argument* (New York: Harcourt, Brace, and World, 1969).

I would like to say, though, that I found particularly helpful Nicholas Rescher's brief treatment of informal logic in his *Introduction to Logic* (New York: St. Martin's Press, 1964). Rescher presents the standard criteria and distinctions, and I often relied on his statement and discussion of them to help me make my own beginnings. Where my indebtedness to Rescher or others has been special or substantial, I'll indicate in the notes below.

Also, I hope it's clear to every reader how much I owe the writers of pulp science fiction, fantasy, and detective stories. Though I quoted the work of none of them, they created the kind of style, settings, and characters that I used so freely.

Chapter 1

The method of illustrating the use-mention distinction by using the name of an author was suggested to me by the discussion of that topic in Samuel Gorowitz and Ron Williams's *Introduction to Philosophical Analysis* (New York: Random House, 1965). The book is generally useful for anyone who needs to know about terms and distinctions involved in contemporary philosophy.

Chapter 2

The discussion of the Reference and Idea theories is substantially indebted to William P. Alston's *Philosophy of Language* (Englewood Cliffs, N.J.: Prentice-Hall, 1964). See, in particular, pp. 10-16, but read the whole book. It's very good. See Alston also for a guide to the more sophisticated versions of all three theories.

The now-classic presentation of the Use theory is Ludwig Wittgenstein's *Philosophical Investigations* (Oxford: Basil Blackwell, 1958).

Chapter 3

The standard treatment of ambiguity and vagueness is found in Rescher. I've departed substantially from the standard view on both topics by tying ambiguity to use and vagueness to a certain kind of situation. "Chameleon words" is a label of my own invention, and what I've said about them resembles what most writers say about vague words in general.

I learned about the "red heifer" case and the rabbinical schools of thought from Herbert L. Searles, *Logic and Scientific Method*, 3rd ed. (New York: Ronald Press, 1968), p. 39.

The classical versions of the sophistries of the Sophist in conversations 2, 3, 7, 8, and 9 are given in Ralph L. Woods, *How to Torture Your Mind* (New York: Funk and Wagnalls, 1969), pp. 123, 104, 123, 126, and 126 respectively. (The originals, of course, are from the Cynics, the Stoics, and the Sophists and are scattered through many volumes of the Loeb Classical Library.)

I am indebted to *Time Magazine* (August 26, 1972) for the report on the U.S. Army's list of "incorrect" and "correct" expressions.

Chapter 4

Mill (chap. 8) is particularly good on definition, though his general position differs from the one I presented. Both Copi and Rescher have good discussions, though neither of them adequately connects definition with a theory of meaning. A very informative treatment is found in Chapters 6 and 7 of Olson.

Chapter 5

Rescher distinguishes the uses of language in a brief (too brief) way and so does Copi. Copi leaves out the evaluative class, and Rescher omits the expressive. An informative discussion of confusions connected with the uses of language is in James D. Carney and Richard K. Scheer's *Fundamentals of Logic* (New York: Macmillan, 1964), chap. 4.

Chapter 6

Both Rescher and Copi have a brief discussion of disagreements, though neither includes disagreement about interpretation. I know of no other discussion of challenging arguments.

Chapter 7

A concise and readable introduction to formal logic for those who want to know more about it is Richard C. Jeffrey's *Formal Logic: Its Scope and Limits* (New York: McGraw-Hill, 1967).

Also see Howard Kahane's *Logic and Philosophy* (Belmont, California: Wadsworth, 1969). I found the sections on argument forms (pp. 5-7) and on truth and validity (pp. 8-12) particularly helpful in guiding my own presentation. The treatment of sentential logic in Part One provides a clear and sharp introduction to the topic.

Chapter 8

Every informal logic book deals with more or less the same informal fallacies, though they aren't always classified in the same way. A useful little book devoted almost wholly to various kinds of mistakes in reasoning is Alex C. Michalos's *Improving Your Reasoning* (Englewood Cliffs, N.J.: Prentice-Hall, 1970).

The standard versions of the sophistries of the Sophist in conversations 1 and 4 are presented by Ralph L. Woods in *How to Torture Your Mind* (New York: Funk and Wagnalls, 1969), pp. 130 and 113 respectively.

Chapter 9

Copi, Rescher, and Carney and Scheer all have nice discussions of analogical arguments, though none discusses the use of analogy in moral arguments. Only Carney and Scheer discuss analogies as illustrations. Other than the one in this chapter, I know of no other discussion of criteria for appraising examples or of the use of fables and parables as illustrative devices.

The quotation from Charles Lyell is from his *Principles of Geology* (New York: Appleton, 1854), p. 64.

The New Testament parable is from Matthew 18: 23-35 of the New English Bible.

For a statement and critical discussion of the extinction theory based on the analogy of "racial youth," etc., see George G. Simpson's readable *The Meaning of Evolution* (New Haven, Conn.: Yale University Press, 1952), pp. 187-189.

The Mill analogy is from Mill's *Examination of Sir William Hamilton's Philosophy*, 6th ed. (London: Longmans, 1867), p. 243.

Chapter 10

The way of beginning the first section by discussing the need for structure I borrowed from Sheridan Baker's *The Practical Stylist* (New

York: Crowell, 1962), p. 8. Baker's book is filled with good advice, and anyone interested in improving his writing can learn from it. It's also short.

Russell discusses Smith's rules and his own views about writing in "How I Write," which is reprinted in *Portrait from Memory and Other Essays* (New York: Simon and Schuster, 1951).

The quotation from Brand Blanshard is from his marvelous essay *On Philosophical Style* (Bloomington, Ind.: Indiana University Press, 1967), p. 31.

Darwin describes his writing troubles in his *Autobiography*, ed. by Nora Barlow (New York: Harcourt, Brace, 1959), pp. 137 ff.

The remark by James is quoted by Blanshard, p. 42.

The remark about incoherence is Nicholas Rescher's in his *Introduction to Logic*, p. 100. I am indebted to Rescher for the idea of including a chapter on writing and for guidelines about what might profitably be discussed in it.

Chapter 11

The original S-J-R puzzle is found in Henry E. Dudeney's *536 Puzzles and Curious Problems,* ed. with introduction by Martin Gardner (New York: Scribner's, 1967), p. 214. The version discussed is virtually the same as the one in Rescher's *Introduction to Logic*, p. 11, and it is virtually the same as the one given by Martin Gardner in *Mathematical Puzzles and Diversions* (New York: Simon and Schuster, 1961), p. 120

Gardner's book contains other S-J-R puzzles and also puzzles of the other sorts we discussed. Anyone interested in more should also look at C. R. Wylie, Jr., *101 Puzzles in Thought and Logic* (New York: Dover, 1957). Also see George J. Summers, *New Puzzles in Logical Deduction* (New York: Dover, 1968). My explanations of how to solve the three types of puzzles owe something to the first six pages—unnumbered—of Wylie's book.

Index